HUMAN BEHAVIOR
Improving Performance at Work

HUMAN BEHAVIOR

RESTON PUBLISHING COMPANY, INC.
A Prentice-Hall Company
Reston, Virginia

Improving Performance at Work

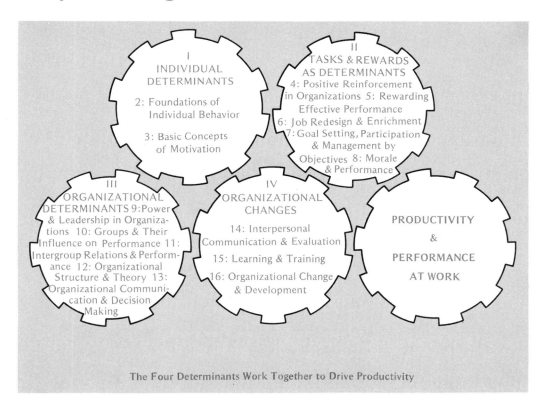

I
INDIVIDUAL
DETERMINANTS

2: Foundations of
Individual Behavior

3: Basic Concepts
of Motivation

II
TASKS & REWARDS
AS DETERMINANTS
4: Positive Reinforcement
in Organizations 5: Rewarding
Effective Performance
6: Job Redesign & Enrichment
7: Goal Setting, Participation
& Management by
Objectives 8: Morale
& Performance

III
ORGANIZATIONAL
DETERMINANTS 9: Power
& Leadership in Organiza-
tions 10: Groups & Their
Influence on Performance 11:
Intergroup Relations & Perform-
ance 12: Organizational
Structure & Theory 13:
Organizational Communi-
cation & Decision
Making

IV
ORGANIZATIONAL
CHANGES

14: Interpersonal
Communication & Evaluation

15: Learning & Training

16: Organizational Change
& Development

PRODUCTIVITY
&
PERFORMANCE
AT WORK

The Four Determinants Work Together to Drive Productivity

Gary Dessler
PROFESSOR OF MANAGEMENT
FLORIDA INTERNATIONAL UNIVERSITY

Library of Congress Cataloging in Publication Data

Dessler, Gary,
  Human behavior.
  Bibliography:
  Includes index.
  1. Employee motivation—Case studies.
2. Performance standards—Case studies. 3. Job
satisfaction—Case studies. I. Title.
HF5549.5.M63D73   658.31'4   79-25234
ISBN 0-8359-2994-9

1 3 5 7 9 10 8 6 4 2

PRINTED IN THE UNITED STATES OF AMERICA

to Claudia and Derek

TABLE OF CONTENTS

PREFACE

Human Behavior provides students in Human Behavior, Human Relations, or Organizational Behavior courses with a practical, contemporary review of essential behavioral science concepts and techniques in a highly readable and understandable form. Its main purpose is to explain to students and managers alike how to improve employee performance and productivity at work through the application of behavioral science methods.

The book has several distinguishing characteristics. A step-by-step method—the "ABCs of Performance"—is used in all chapters to illustrate how each chapter's material can be used to solve performance problems and improve productivity. An integrating model shows how each chapter's material ties in with the rest of the book. Practical applications—such as how to set effective goals, how to appraise performance, and how to enrich a job—are used throughout to enhance readers' managerial skills. Examples for instance, of actual job enrichment and positive reinforcement programs are used extensively to illustrate real-life applications of important techniques. The book taps the latest research findings so that readers get a contemporary view of Behavioral Science in organizations. A case incident and, usually, an experiential exercise are presented at the end of most chapters. The latter give students an opportunity to meet in small groups and apply the concepts and techniques found in each chapter.

While I am solely responsible for the final product, I want to thank several people for their assistance. Reviewers, including Professors Christopher G. DaFlucas, Capital University, Columbus, Ohio; Eugene Gomolka, Virginia Polytechnic and State University, Northern Virginia Center for Graduate Studies; Daniel Harris, Seattle Pacific University, Seattle, Washington; and Milo Pierce, Corpus Christi State University, Corpus Christi, Texas, made extremely useful suggestions, and I appreciate their advice. At Reston Publishing Company, Fred Easter, Executive Editor, and Patricia Rayner, Editor, effectively managed the publication, and design and production of the book.

My son Derek was a source of encouragement and assistance, and my wife Claudia came out of retirement to ably assist me with the preparation of the manuscript and index, as well as with other details of the project.

*   *   *

Acknowledgements: For permitting us to reproduce case or experiential material, I want to acknowledge the following publishers in addition to those mentioned in the text: **Chapter 2:** "A Perception Problem" from Henry Albers and Richard Hodgetts, *Cases and Incidents on the Basic Concepts of Management* (New York: John Wiley, 1972). **Chapter 3:** "Hawkins Nob Hill Plant" is based on "Kiplinger's Question" in Theodore Herbert, *Organizational Behavior: Readings and Cases* (New York: Macmillan, 1976), pp. 360–61; experiential exercise based on George Litwin and Robert Stringer, Jr., *Motivation and Organizational Climate* (Boston: Division of Research, Graduate School of Business Administration, Harvard University, 1968). **Chapter 5:** "The Tarnished Company Image" from Andrew DuBrin, *Human Relations, a Job Oriented Approach* (Reston, Va.: Reston Publishing, 1978); experiential exercise from John Ivancevich, Andrew Szilagyi, Jr., and Marc Wallace, Jr., *Organizational Behavior and Performance* (Santa Monica: Goodyear Publishing, 1977, pp. 470–71). **Chapter 6:** "Memo from the General Manager" from Richard Johnson, R. Joseph Monsen, Henry Knowles, and Borge Saxberg, *Management Systems and Society: An Introduction* (Santa Monica: Goodyear Publishing, 1976) pp. 214–15. **Chapter 7:** "Participation in Milestone Engineering's Planning" from Richard Farmer, Barry Richmond, and William Ryan, *Incidents in Applying Management Theory* (Belmont, Calif.: Wadsworth, 1966). **Chapter 8:** "Allison Auto Parts" from Claude George, *Supervision in Action* (Reston Va., Reston Publishing, 1977) pp. 68–70. **Chapter 9:** "A Foreman's Success at Jackson and Co.", From Albers and Hodgetts, *Cases and Incidents*; "Fiedler, LPC Exercise" based on material presented in Fred E. Fiedler, A *Theory of Leadership Effectiveness* (New York: McGraw-Hill, 1967) pp. 39–41, 267–69. (The use of this exercise is more fully explained in the Instructor's Manual). **Chapter 10:** "The Unstoppable Coffee Klatch" from DuBrin, *Human Relations* pp. 171–73. **Chapter 11:** experiential exercise from Ivancevich, Szilagyi, Wallace, *Organizational Behavior and Performance*, pp. 266–68. **Chapter 12:** "Mad Ludwig" from Bernard Deitzer and Carl Shilliff, *Contemporary Management Incidents* (Columbus, Ohio: Grid, Inc., 1977): "Nationwide Container Company" from George Strauss and Leonard Sayles, *Personnel* (Englewood Cliffs, N.J.: Prentice-Hall, 1972) pp. 346–47. **Chapter 13:** "Locks versus Lives" from,

John Champion and John James, *Critical Incidents in Management* (Homewood, Ill.: Richard D. Irwin, 1975). **Chapter 14:** "Get Off My Back" from Dubrin, *Human Relations*, pp. 211–12. **Chapter 15:** "Charlie, the Railroad Agent," from Arno Knapper, *Cases in Personnel Management* (Columbus, Ohio: Grid, Inc., 1977) pp. 14–15. **Chapter 16:** "What We Need Around Here is Better Human Relations" from DuBrin, *Human Relations.*

GARY DESSLER

HUMAN BEHAVIOR
Improving Performance at Work

1 Human Work Behavior in a Changing World

BY THE TIME YOU FINISH STUDYING THIS CHAPTER,
YOU SHOULD BE ABLE TO:

1. Describe the basic features of three schools of management thought.
2. Compare and contrast three schools of management thought.
3. List some of the "social responsibility" pressures managers have been under during the past twenty years.
4. Give the main purpose of this book and explain its plan.
5. Discuss how you would analyze performance problems with the "ABCs" of performance.

OVERVIEW

The main purpose of this chapter is to explain society's evolving views of behavior at work, and the plan of this book. We first discuss three important "schools" of management—Classical, Behavioral, and Contingency—and explain how each reflects society's evolving values and assumptions about human behavior at work. Today diminishing productivity is a major problem facing managers, and we discuss some of the things—including pressures from government, consumers, and others for "social responsibility," reduced capital investment, and possibly changes in the "work ethic"—that are partly to blame for this. Because improving performance at work is today an important task, the purpose of this book is to explain how managers can improve performance and productivity through the application of behavioral science concepts and techniques; at the end of this chapter we describe how we plan to accomplish this, and the model with which we integrate the topics in this book.

EVOLVING VIEWS OF BEHAVIOR AT WORK: SCHOOLS OF MANAGEMENT THOUGHT

Introduction: Values and Behavior at Work

The tools and techniques a society uses to motivate performance tend to reflect the assumptions and values of the society itself. Thus a society like that of the ancient Greeks, which assumed that hard work was demeaning and to be carried out only by slaves, used discipline, dogma, and fear to ensure performance, instead of "job enrichment," supportive leadership," and "participation." Today, many believe that organizations owe their employees a high "quality of work life." And, as a result, we see an increasing use of techniques like job enrichment, flexible work hours, and participative incentive plans—techniques that are aimed in part at improving life at work for employees.

How did we get where we are today, in terms of our attitudes toward work and the techniques we use to influence employee behavior? To gain the perspective to answer this question we will briefly review three historical schools of management thought—the Classical school, the Behavioral school, and the Contingency school.

The Classical Approach to Management

Until the late 1800s entrepreneur/managers were preoccupied with making their companies as large as possible. This was the period following the industrial revolution, and in America it was a time that saw innovations like the steamboat, the iron plow, the telegraph, the electric motor, and the expansion of a railroad and canal network that opened new markets for producers. In addition, it was an era during which markets were expanding rapidly, and in which entrepreneurs knew that they could partially insulate themselves from the vagaries of the market by making their companies larger. Finally, it was an age in which the protestant ethic of hard work prevailed. It was a "boom" period, a period of growing optimism, and it was one in which the entrepreneur/managers raced to accumulate men, machinery, and money in a quest to make their companies larger than their competitors'.

But by the late 1800s the focus was already beginning to shift from growth to efficiency. As their organizations became large and unwieldly, managers needed new ways to better utilize the resources they had accumulated. Increasingly they sought new concepts and new techniques that would enable them to cut costs and increase efficiency, and it was out of this industrial environment that the Classical school of management emerged.

Frederick Winslow Taylor and Scientific Management. Frederick Taylor was one of the first of the classical management writers. His basic theme was that managers should study work scientifically to identify the "one best way" to get the job done. Taylor was an engineer, a Quaker, and a puritan, and he relentlessly pursued the idea that efficiency at work could be improved through careful, "scientific" analysis. The framework for Taylor's scientific management can be summarized as consisting of four principles:[1]

1. *Finding the "one best way."* First, management—through observation and "the deliberate gathering in . . . of all the great mass of traditional knowledge, which in the past has been in the heads of the workmen . . ."—finds the "one best way" for performing each job.

2. *Scientific selection of personnel.* This next principle requires "the scientific selection and then the progressive development of the workmen." This involves finding each worker's limitations and "possibilities for development" and giving him the required training.

3. *Financial incentives.* Taylor knew that putting the right worker on the right job would not by itself ensure high productivity, and that some plan for motivating workers to do their best was necessary. He therefore proposed that a system of financial incentives be used, in which each worker was paid in direct proportion to how much he or she produced rather than simply according to a basic hourly wage.

4. *Functional foremanship.* Finally, Taylor called for a division of work between manager and worker such that separate managers did all planning, preparing, and inspecting while the workers did the actual work. The worker was to take orders from each of these "functional foremen"—depending upon whether the work concerned planning, machine speed, or inspecting, for example.

Henri Fayol and the Principles of Management. The work of Henri Fayol is also characteristic of the classical management writer's approach to management and behavior at work. Fayol had been a manager for 30 years with a French iron and steel firm before writing his book *General and Industrial Management.* In it he said that managers performed five basic functions, which he called *planning, organizing, commanding, coordinating,* and *controlling.*

He also outlined a list of "principles" of management. He had found these useful during his years as a manager and felt that other managers should use them in carrying out their functions of planning, organizing, commanding, coordinating, and controlling. His principles illustrate his approach to management, some of these are as follows:

The principle of division of work: each employee should be given a separate, specialized activity to perform.

The principle of authority and responsibility: the responsibility an employee has should be commensurate with the authority he is given.

The principle of unity of command: an employee should receive orders from one superior only.

The scaler chain principle: there should be a clear, unbroken chain of authority and communication ranging from the highest to the lowest positions in the organization.

Discussion: Classical Management and Behavior at Work. The classical approach to management was characterized by its almost total emphasis on the technical aspects of efficiency. To these writers an efficiently designed job and organization were of prime importance, and they focused their efforts on developing analytical tools and techniques that would better enable managers to design them. Human work behavior was not unimportant to the classical writers; instead they simply assumed its complexities away by arguing that financial incentives would suffice to ensure motivation. And, while this may seem simplistic today, it made sense at a time when belief in the hard work ethic and in man's desire to maximize his wealth made it easy to assume that man did, indeed, "live by bread alone."

As a result, intentionally or not, the classicists left the impression that workers could be treated as "givens" in the system—as little more than appendages to their machines. "Design the most highly specialized and efficient job you can" said the classicists, "and then plug in the worker who will then do your bidding if the pay is right."

The Behavioral Approach to Management

A series of changes swept across America and the world in the 1920s and 1930s. Increasing numbers of people moved from farms to cities and thus became more dependent on each other. Factories became more mechanized, and the workers' jobs became increasingly specialized and therefore interdependent. The American frontier was no longer the vast, unexplored area that had provided a safety valve for those wishing to start a new life away from the crowded cities.

Slowly, these forces were building toward what William Scott has called the "period of collision," a period resulting from "environmental conditions which draw people into inescapable proximity and dependency on one another."[2] Thus, an era of rapid growth and optimism was slowly giving way in the early 1900s to one in which people felt increasingly closed in and dependent on one another, and Scott believes that if these forces had been left unharnessed, the "collision" effect might have led to brutal competition, then conflict, and finally a degeneration of society.

But this did not happen, because fundamental changes were taking place in society's values. Instead of continuing its "hands-off" policy, government became increasingly involved in economic matters, and a number of law suits were filed to break up huge industrial monopolies. Social movements aimed at giving women the right to vote, electing senators by popular direct vote, establishing a minimum wage, and encouraging trade unions became more popular. Even the literature of the period grew increasingly anti-individualistic as people began to question whether a philosophy based on hard work, individualism, and maximizing profits might not actually have some major drawbacks.

The Hawthorne Studies and Human Relations. In 1927 a series of studies was begun at the Chicago Hawthorne plant of the Western Electric Company that would eventually add an entirely new perspective to the analysis of human behavior at work.

The first of these studies was based on what was then a traditional classical management assumption: that physical working conditions influenced worker output and that, in particular, output improved if the level of illumination at the workplace increased. To test this the researchers, led by Mayo and Roesthlisberger of Harvard, isolated a few workers in a separate room of the plant, where they could watch their reactions to changes in the level of lighting. To the researchers' surprise, however, they found that not only did output not fall as illumination was reduced, it actually increased, at least until it was too dark to see.

Additional studies aimed at explaining this phenomenon were carried out. In the "relay assembly test room studies" for example, a group of workers was again isolated and studied as a series of changes (including changing the length of the work day and of the workers' morning and afternoon rest breaks) were made. Again, however, the workers' performance seemed to depend on factors other than physical conditions or rate of pay.

The researchers eventually explained their unexpected findings as having resulted not from changes in working conditions, but from the changed social situations of the workers. In countless ways, for example, the test room observer had inadvertently made the workers feel they were each "someone special" by showing "his personal interest in the girls and their problems. He had always been sympathetically aware of their hopes and fears. He had granted them more and more privileges."[3] Furthermore:

> No longer were the girls isolated individuals, working together only in the sense of an actual physical proximity. They had become participating members of a working group with all the psychological and social implications peculiar to such a group.

Later studies at Hawthorne, including a massive interviewing program of thousands of workers, only served to confirm and embellish these first conclusions. What emerged was a picture of workers being driven not so much by pay as by needs and wants and desires; workers who felt adrift and degraded by oversimplified jobs and who therefore sought companionship and security in their work groups. And, it became apparent to the researchers that human performance at work depended not only on pay and working conditions, but also on the supervisor's "style" and the employee's belief that the company was treating him or her as a valued, unique individual.

The Hawthorne studies were a turning point in the analysis of human behavior at work and the basis for what became known as the "Human Relations" movement. As the Hawthorne findings became widely known, writers began to recognize that human behavior at work was a complex and powerful force to be dealt with. They began to realize, in other words, that workers were not just "givens" in the system—that, instead, they had needs and desires that the organization and task had to accommodate.

The Hawthorne experiments were ended in 1933 as the country fell deeper into the Great Depression. Between 1929 and 1933 the unemployment rate rose from 3.2 percent to 30 percent. It was a period during which businesses were failing, unemployment was widespread, incomes were dropping, and national morale was low. Individualism and the hard work ethic seemed to have failed, and in their place a new social ethic that emphasized the importance of the group, of getting along with others, of government intervention, and of security arose to take its place.

Other changes were taking place as well. For example, the excess production capacity caused by the depression had stimulated corporate research and development activities and these activities, combined with the technological advances that accompanied World War II, resulted in burgeoning product diversification for the period beginning in the late-1930s. This rapid rate of product diversification in turn meant that workers were increasingly called upon to carry out jobs that were very different from those faced by workers of the classical management era. With the new emphasis on research, development, and product diversification, more and more jobs called for heavy doses of creativity and autonomy on the part of workers. Jobs, in other words, were not as consistently of the routine assembly line–type variety as were the jobs of the classical era, and these new demands for creativity and autonomy combined with the new, evolving social values and the findings of the Hawthorne studies resulted in a new, behavioral approach to management.

Douglas McGregor: Theory X, Theory Y. The work of Douglas McGregor is a good example of this new behavioral approach to performance at work. According to McGregor, the traditional organization, with its highly specialized jobs, centralized decision making, and top down communications was not simply a product of economic necessity but rather a reflection of certain basic assumptions about human nature.[4] These assumptions, which McGregor somewhat arbitrarily classified as *Theory* X, held that most people dislike work and responsibility and prefer to be directed, that people are motivated not by the desire to do a good job, but simply by financial incentives; and that, therefore, most people must be closely supervised, controlled, and coerced into achieving organizational objectives.

McGregor questioned the truth of this view and, in doing so, naturally questioned whether such management practices as specialized division of work are appropriate for the sorts of tasks faced by many organizations today. He felt that management needed new organizations and practices, and that these in turn have to be based on a revised view of the nature of man. What emerged was an alternate set of assumptions, which McGregor called *Theory* Y. Unlike the *Theory* X assumptions, these held that people could enjoy work and that if the conditions were favorable, they would exercise substantial self-control over their performance. Implicit in these *Theory* Y assumptions is the belief that people are motivated by the desire to do a good job and by the opportunity to affiliate with their peers, rather than simply by financial rewards.

Chris Argyris and the Mature Individual. According to Chris Argyris, another writer of the Behavioral school, rigid organizations such as those prescribed by the classical writers hinder workers from utilizing their full potential. He says that as people mature into adults they normally move

From a position of:	*To a position of:*
Dependence	Independence
Narrow interests	Broad interests
Less activity	Increased activity
Subordinate positions	Superordinate positions
Simple behaviors	Variety of behaviors

Argyris says that forcing people to "stick to the rules" and simply take orders from supervisors who closely monitor them inhibits these normal maturation changes by encouraging employees to be passive, dependent, and subordinate. Managers, he says, should encourage employees to take on additional responsibilities and provide employees with the flexibility to grow and mature.[5]

The work of behavioral writers like McGregor and Argyris differs from that of the classical writers in many respects, but perhaps the most important difference is in their views of the interrelationship between a worker and his or her job. The classical writers generally took the worker to be a "given" and assumed that he or she could simply be "plugged into" the job and motivated with money once the most efficient division of work had been laid out. To these people, in other words, efficiency (and in particular highly specialized, efficiently laid out jobs) came first, and the worker came second: little thought was given to whether workers would find these jobs demeaning, to whether work groups would rebel against incentive plans, or to other considerations of this kind. Behavioral writers, on the other hand, started with the worker as their focal point. Whereas the classicist stressed efficient jobs and assumed that workers performed if paid, the behavioralist stressed the importance and complexity of motivating employees and of building an organization and designing jobs for that purpose. Jobs, in other words had to be designed to satisfy employees' needs, since it was only in this way (these writers assumed) that effective employee performance could be ensured in the long run. Thus, where the classicists prescribed highly specialized jobs, behavioralists prescribed enlarged, enriched jobs in which workers had many tasks to perform. Where the classicists prescribed constant and close supervision, the behavioralists prescribed giving workers as much autonomy as possible. Where the classicists prescribed making everyone adhere to a rigid chain of command, the behavioralists prescribed letting employees decide (within reasonable bounds) who they had to talk to in the organization to get their jobs done. The behavioral approach, therefore, resulted in prescriptions very different from those of the classical approach.

The Contingency Approach to Management

Beginning in about 1950 a number of things occurred that led to the emergence of a new approach to management and behavior at work. The decisions managers were called on to make became increasingly complex as their organizations grew larger, as product diversification continued (spurred by the technological advances of the war years), and as computerization and improved communication and travel vastly increased the number of variables managers had to juggle in making their decisions. At about the same time two reports—one commissioned by the Ford Foundation, one by the Carnegie Corporation—alleged that business education in the United States was inadequate and "vocational." The report stressed that future business leaders needed a better grounding in problem solving, management principles, and in a more workable, practical theory of how organizations operate.[6] Then, in the early 1960s a paper entitled "The Management Theory Jungle" by Harold Koontz argued that the variety of management schools, terminology, and assumptions had resulted in confusion and "jungle warfare" between the various groups.[7] Finally, along with these developments, a number of organizational research studies were being carried out in England and America. Their combined effect was to underscore the need for a contingency or situational view of organizations, one in which the appropriateness of the organization and method of management was contingent upon (or dependent upon) the kind of tasks and environments the organization had to cope with. What emerged was an approach to management that held, basically, that both the classical and behavioral approaches to management made sense—but for very different kinds of tasks.

Burns and Stalker: Mechanistic and Organic Management. For example, two British researchers, Tom Burns and G. M. Stalker studied several industrial firms in England, including a textile mill and a number of electronics companies. Their main conclusion was that the appropriateness of either the *mechanistic* (classical) or *organic* (behavioral) approach depended on the kind of task the organization had to accomplish.

The mechanistic approach was appropriate where the task was routine and unchanging. In the textile mill, for example, it was important to have long, stable production runs, and surprises had to be kept to a minimum so that the huge machines did not have to be shut down. Here Burns and Stalker found that management ran the mill with a mechanistic approach, one characterized by an emphasis on efficiency, highly specialized jobs, elaborate rules and procedures for keeping behavior in line, and an insistence that everyone "play it by the rules."

An organic approach, on the other hand, was appropriate where innovative, entrepreneurial activities were important. In electronics firms, for example, the companies and their employees had to constantly make new devices so that they could compete effectively with rival firms. Here Burns and Stalker found that management ran the firms with an organic approach—one characterized by an emphasis on creativity, rather than efficiency. These jobs were not highly specialized since each worker had many tasks to perform—tasks that might change daily. The emphasis was on workers controlling themselves, rather than on being controlled by rules and procedures. These findings are summarized in Exhibit 1.1.[8]

Exhibit 1.1 Summary of the Burns and Stalker "Contingency" Findings

Type of Management	Mechanistic	Organic
Type of Environments	Unchanging	Rapidly Changing
Main Emphasis	Efficiency	Flexibility
How Company is Managed	Emphasis on routine jobs, many rules and procedures	Emphasis on less specialized jobs, fewer rules and procedures
Management Approach That This is Similar to	Classical	Behavioral

As a result of these developments a new school of management emerged, one that has become known as the Contingency school of management. Note that it negates neither the classical nor the behavioral approach, but instead synthesizes them, putting each in its proper perspective.

PRODUCTIVITY: A VITAL ISSUE

A Period of Growing Pressure on Management

The period from about 1960 to the present has also been one in which increasing pressures from diverse interests have been brought to bear on management. It has been a period that has seen the rise of consumerism, increased union activity, government pressure, and affirmative action, to name but a few, and one undesirable effect of these pressures may be the diminishing productivity we are seeing today. In 1978, for example the productivity of workers in U.S. manufacturing industries rose a modest 2.5 percent, which ranked the United States sixth among the world's seven leading industrial nations in productivity gains for that year. We will return to this point in a moment, but first we will look more closely at some of the pressures that are bearing down on management.

Pressure from Groups in the Organization's Environment. You need not look further than your newspaper to appreciate the multitude of groups managers have to cope with, and from whom their organizations must seek support. Daily, there are headlines concerning new government regulations, competitors' price fixing, stockholders' law suits, consumer revolts, community anti-pollution activities, and minority hiring practices, for example. Dealing with these groups is an integral part of all managers' jobs, and it is one that becomes more important the higher one rises in his or her organization.

The consumerism movement is a good example of one of these forces, and has been defined as "the widening range of activities of government, business, and independent organizations that are designed to protect individuals from practices that infringe upon their rights as consumers."[9] Largely as a result of this consumerism movement, managements today are being called upon to back up their products and services as they never have before: for example, one major tire manufacturer recently had to recall hundreds of thousands of its tires; banks now have to fully disclose the actual interest rates consumers will pay; auto manufacturers have to build their cars more safely; and new safeguards have been instituted to insure the privacy of students' records.

Pressures for providing minorities with increased employment opportunities also influence management. Organizations find that virtually all their personnel-related activities are influenced by the mounting legislation in this area. In recruitment, for example one cannot rely on "word of mouth" advertising, usually cannot specify the desired sex in advertising or in any way suggest that applicants 40 to 65 years of age may be discriminated against, and must carefully validate any screening devices (like tests, or interview questions) to ensure that they are not screening out a disproportionate number of minority candidates. Successfully assimilating members of minority groups also has indirect effects on management activities. For example, remedial training programs may have to be established, supervisors may have to be trained to deal with the new employees, and so on.

Society has also recently become more concerned with pollution problems and ecology, and these concerns have added new limitations to what managers can and cannot do. The current concern about environment can probably be traced mainly to the publication of Rachel Carson's *Silent Spring* in 1962. In this book she exposed the dangers of chemical pesticides. She shows, for example, that DDT does not decompose in nature and tends to accumulate on the food chain in increasingly concentrated forms.

Other pollution issues also emerged in the 1960s. For example, smog became a major factor in Los Angeles, Lake Erie was found to be "dying" as a result of waste material being dumped into it, and the disposition of tons of radioactive waste also became a national problem. As a result of these new concerns, managers now face a growing set of laws and regulations, including the 1970 Clean Air Amendments (to the Clean Air Act of 1963), the Federal Water Pollution Act, and the Marine Protection Act of 1972.[10]

In many of these issues (consumerism, minority affairs, ecology), government—local, state, and federal—has played a major role and increasingly limits the activities of managers. In an article entitled "The Grand Scale of Federal Intervention," *Business Week* magazine recently noted, for example, that "hundreds of federal departments, agencies, divisions, and bureaus regulate to one degree or another the nation's commerce." There are agencies whose function is to regulate banking and finance, competition, airlines, communications, and a wide range of other industries. Other agencies regulate employment and discrimination, energy and the environment, nuclear power, and safety and health. And, this listing just covers the major federal agencies. It does not cover state and local agencies, many of which also impact management decision making in one way or another.

Managers often find that these agencies and their regulations affect them most directly in the variety of reports they have to fill out for the federal government. The Food and Drug Administration and the Federal Trade Commission have elaborate reporting requirements for describing the characteristics of products. The Environmental Protection Agency requires information on air pollution. The Securities and Exchange Commission has new disclosure rules that require managers to present detailed information on their operations. The Equal Opportunity Commission requires the submission of data on employment of minority groups. Conforming to the various laws and regulations entails, therefore, not only a substantial *direct* expense (the cost of installing pollution equipment, validating tests, and so on), but also a considerable *indirect* expense because of having to process the myriad of forms to prove that one is, indeed, conforming to the letter of the law.

In the wake of Watergate, managers are also finding themselves under increasing pressures to improve their ethics. Whether it involves disclosing campaign contributions, avoiding price fixing with competitors, rejecting bribes, or some other ethical decision, managers (and employees in general) are under increasing pressure to make the "right choice" rather than just the expedient one.[11]

Pressure for Social Responsibility. In a sense, many of the pressures we have discussed—consumerism, minority affairs, ecology, government, ethics—are but part of a broader pressure for social responsibility that managers find themselves under.

The term *social responsibility* actually has two related meanings. In one sense, social responsibility is an *ethical issue for the individual business person.* This is because management decisions like, "Should I try to maximize owner's profits or spend money to reduce pollution?" are essentially questions of what is right and wrong from the person's own perspective. But the term *social responsibility* also refers to the role the corporation should play in solving social ills. For example, "To what extent should a company become involved in solving social ills like minority unemployment and ghetto conditions?"

There has been a marked increase in society's desire for increased social responsibility by business during the last 30 years, and Hay and Gray say there are several reasons for this. By 1950 the United States had become an affluent society, and scarcity of basic goods and services was no longer a fundamental problem. Ironically, though, other social problems had developed as a direct (and indirect) result of our economic success. There were, for example, "pockets of poverty in a nation of plenty, deteriorating cities, air and water pollution, defacement of the landscape, and a disregard for consumers."[12] Related to this, many believe that employees deserve a better "quality of work life," a quality that reflects the "degree to which members of a work organization are able to satisfy important personal needs through their experiences in the organization."[13] Taken as a whole, therefore, things

seemed "out of balance," and the advocates of change found a fertile climate in the turbulent, antiwar 1960s.

As a result, society has increasingly come to value social responsibilities (like pollution control) as more important than profit maximization. And, as society's values have shifted toward social responsibility, government has begun to legislate things like pollution control, minority rights, and occupational safety and health.

Managers' views of social responsibility are also changing. In one recent study only 28 percent of the managers responding endorsed the traditional notion that "the social responsibility of business is to 'stick to business'." Now 69 percent believe that "profit is really a somewhat ineffective measure of business's social effectiveness." Furthermore, this national sample of managers now ranks "responsibility to customers" ahead of "responsibility to stockholders." Thus, even business executives seem to have incorporated social responsibility into their value systems and into their view of what the role of their company should be.[14]

The Need for Improved Productivity

Many of the current pressures on today's businesses have obviously been enormously beneficial to people in all walks of life—to all who are consumers, or minorities, or workers, for example—but it is possible that they have also contributed in part to the reduced productivity of the American work force. In 1978 (to repeat) the United States ranked sixth among the world's seven leading industrial nations in productivity gains, posting a productivity increase of only 2.5 percent in that year, compared with Japan's 8.3 percent, France's 4.9 percent, Canada's 4.2 percent, West Germany's 3.7 percent, and Italy's 2.9 percent gains. Only Great Britain, with a 1.6 percent increase, registered a productivity gain smaller than that of the United States. A recent government report entitled *Work in America* also notes that worker productivity is low, but cites problems like absenteeism, turnover, wildcat strikes, sabotage, poor quality products, and reluctance by workers to commit themselves to their work tasks as some of the reasons.[15] A recent Gallup poll suggests that 50 percent of all wage earners could accomplish more each day if they tried; 30 percent of the wage earners said those increases could be 20 percent or more.[16] As a share of the gross national product, after tax profits in the 25-year period from 1950 to 1975 declined from almost 9 percent to less than 5 percent.[17] In a 1975 survey of 6,000 business managers, the American Management Association found serious worry over productivity, but two-thirds of the respondents in the survey reported their companies were making no special effort to evaluate executive productivity.[18]

Undoubtedly many factors are contributing to this problem, and the pressures for consumerism, social responsibility, and so on are just one group of them. In addition, many believe the work ethic that once drove people to do their best at work has all but disappeared, and that this may itself be related to the pressures we described above, and to the decrease in craftsmen-like jobs in today's automated society. Capital improvements have also not kept pace with those made by industry in other industrialized nations, and in Japan government expenditures on productivity improvement are over six times the amount spent by the U.S. government, although our federal budget is five times larger than Japan's.[19] Undoubtedly such factors have all contributed to the current productivity crisis in America (and in much of the rest of the industrialized world), but, whatever the causes, many executives today conclude that productivity improvement has become urgent, not just desirable.[20]

A Solution. There are many things we could do to improve this grim productivity picture. For example, we saw that there are many legislated factors that may inhibit productivity, for example pollution control equipment, occupational safety equipment, and validated employment screening. Yet, many believe that reducing or eliminating current legislated controls would actually have a predominantly adverse effect on society. And, in any case, this is not an issue that any individual manager usually has much control over. We could also increase worker productivity by investing more heavily in more modern equipment—whether this involves steel mills or new computerized typewriters for secretaries. While useful, however, this is only part of the solution since, ultimately, virtually all service and manufacturing activities (no matter how automated) rely heavily on human beings. Even in the most highly automated auto assembly plants, for example, poor employee attendance, a resistant attitude on the part of workers, and worker sabotage can drastically curtail productivity. And, in relatively nonautomated industries this is even more the case.

Another way to improve productivity and performance (and the one we focus on in this book) is to improve human behavior at work, by ensuring that employees understand what is expected of them, by removing roadblocks and impediments that may prevent them from doing their jobs, and by ensuring that there are positive consequences for effective performance on the job.

THE PLAN OF THIS BOOK

The main purpose of this book is to explain how to improve employee productivity and performance at work through the application of behavioral science concepts and techniques. There are, in other words, concepts and techniques that are being used today in organizations that have been shown to be effective for improving the productivity and performance of employees, and it is these concepts and techniques—and how to use them—that we explain in this book. We explain, for example, how to use positive reinforcement, how to use job enrichment, how to set clear goals, how to use work groups to improve performance, and how to reduce the sorts of intergroup conflicts that can undermine organizational functioning.

Exhibit 1.2 summarizes the 15 major topics (Chapters) to be covered in this book, as well as how each influences productivity and performance. For example, positive reinforcement (discussed in Chapter 4) can be used to reduce undesirable behaviors (like absenteeism) on the part of employees and to encourage effective behaviors (like selling more accounts). Goal setting (discussed in Chapter 7) is important because unless the employees know clearly and specifically what is expected of them, their performance will suffer. Training (discussed in Chapter 15) is important as well because unless the employee has the skills to do the job he or she will not be able to perform effectively—even if he wants to.

Exhibit 1.2 How the Material in Each Chapter Influences Employee Performance

CHAPTER	INFLUENCE ON EMPLOYEE PERFORMANCE
2: **Foundations of Individual Behavior**	A person's performance—how he or she performs a task and reacts to stimuli like orders from a boss or an offer of a raise—depends in part on that person's *perceptions, personality,* and *abilities,* and understanding what these factors are, and how a manager can work with them to help him improve his employees' performance.
3: **Basic Concepts of Motivation**	To perform a task effectively a person must be motivated to do so, and in this chapter we discuss several theories of what motivation is and how it comes about. We focus on employee *needs* (such as security), since many believe that such needs are the "mainsprings" that drive motivation.
4: **Positive Reinforcement in Organizations**	Many believe that the best way to change behavior—for example, to get someone to work harder—is by giving the person *properly scheduled reinforcement,* in the form of things like rewards or praise. We discuss this, and the subject of how to analyze performance problems in this chapter.

Exhibit 1.2. *Continued*

CHAPTER	INFLUENCE ON EMPLOYEE PERFORMANCE
5: **Rewarding Effective Performance**	Rewards like pay and promotion can be important *positive consequences* of performance, and can therefore lead to improved performance.
6: **Job Redesign and Enrichment**	Rewards that are "built into" to the job itself—rewards like challenge that provide a sense of accomplishment—are also important, and can lead to improved performance when present.
7: **Goal Setting, Participation, and Management by Objectives**	We will see that to perform effectively a person should know clearly *what is expected*, and in this chapter we discuss how to set effective goals.
8: **Morale and Performance**	Morale affects an organization's "bottom line" and productivity, since employees with higher morale have better attendance records and less tendency to join unions.
9: **Power and Leadership in Organizations**	A *leader* can have an important influence on his employees' performance because: (1) it is the leader who should set effective goals, resolve conflicts, reward performance, provide training, and so on, and (2) he or she can directly influence a subordinate's morale, and therefore the organization's "bottom line."
10: **Groups and Their Influence on Performance**	A work group can influence its members' goals, abilities, rewards, and performance, and being able to work with and through groups is, therefore, an important human relations skill.
11: **Intergroup Relations and Performance: Managing Organizational Conflict.**	Because conflict between two groups in an organization—say, sales and production—can lead to hiding of information, "backbiting," and a deterioration of performance, in this chapter we discuss the sources of such conflicts, and their management.
12: **Organization Structure and Theory**	Every organization (a hospital, city, factory, etc.) needs a pattern of approved relationships showing who "reports to" whom, and a division of work showing who is responsible for what tasks. Without such an "organization structure" the multitude of tasks that have to be accomplished —selling the merchandise, producing it, hiring workers, etc.—would not get done, or done as well.

Exhibit 1.2. *Continued*

CHAPTER	INFLUENCE ON EMPLOYEE PERFORMANCE
13: **Organizational Communication and Decision Making**	In many cases, how well a manager performs—at building the new plant, hiring subordinates, or organizing his or her company—depends on how good his *decisions* are, and good decisions, in turn, depend on good communications.
14: **Interpersonal Communication and Evaluation: Developing Supervisory Skills.**	Almost everything a manager does—setting goals, appraising performance, resolving conflicts, etc.—involves interpersonal, "face to face" communicating. Being able to communicate effectively, therefore, contributes to a manager's performance (and that of his or her subordinates) and we discuss how to do so in this chapter.
15: **Learning and Training**	To perform a job effectively an employee has to have the necessary *skills*, and the purpose of this chapter is to explain how to train employees and thereby improve their skills.
16: **Organizational Change and Development**	Frequently, performance deficiencies are identified, and it becomes necessary to *change* some aspect of the organization—its structure or reward system, for example. In this chapter we explain how to accomplish such changes more effectively. We also discuss organizational development, which is aimed at increasing the level of trust and cooperativeness in an organization so as to improve its ability to react to problems.

We will use the model presented in Exhibit 1.3 to tie together the topics we discuss and to emphasize that they all influence each other and performance and productivity. As you can see, we assume that there are four important determinants of behavior—*individual, task and rewards, organizational,* and *organizational changes* and that these all "drive" performance. Part I of this book discusses *individual* determinants of behavior and includes Chapter 2, Foundations of Individual Behavior, and Chapter 3, Basic Concepts of Motivation. Part II explains how the nature of a person's *task* and the way he or she is *rewarded* affects his or her performance. This section includes chapters 4–8: Positive Reinforcement in Organizations, Rewarding Effective Performance, Job Redesign and Enrichment, Goal Setting, Participation, and Management by Objectives, and Morale and Performance. Part

Exhibit 1.3 Determinants of Productivity and Performance at Work

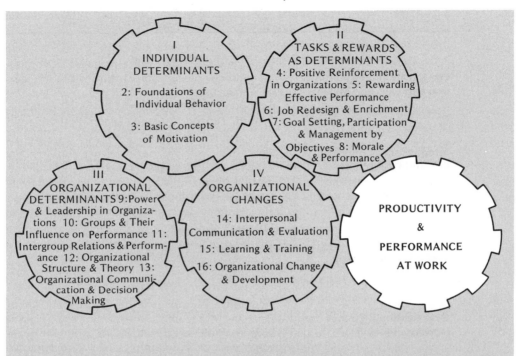

The Four Determinants Work Together to Drive Productivity

III turns to *organizational* determinants of performance, in Chapters 9–13: Leadership and Power in Organizations, Groups and Their Influence on Performance, Intergroup Relations and Performance: Managing Organizational Conflict, Organization Structure and Theory, and Organizational Communication and Decision Making. Finally, Part IV explains how *organizational changes* influence performance and includes Chapters 14–16: Interpersonal Communication and Evaluation: Developing Supervisory Skills, Learning and Training, and Organizational Change and Development.

Analyzing Performance Problems: the "ABCs" of Performance

Managers need an organized method for analyzing performance problems and determining which (if any) of the concepts and techniques we discuss in this book can solve the problem. For example, is performance low because the person hasn't the skills to do the job? Is it because his or her work group is preventing the person from performing well? Is it because rewards are inadequate?

In this book we are going to use the "ABCs" of performance to help us analyze performance problems and develop solutions. While we will develop this theme more fully in later chapters, we basically assume that performance can be analyzed in terms of its *antecedents, behavior,* and *consequences.* *Antecedents* are all those things that come before the actual behavior (like company policies, orders from the boss, and assigned production standards) that together determine whether or not the person knows what is expected of him. (Thus, if a person does not know what you expect in terms of "good performance" it is unlikely that the targets he or she will shoot for will be the same—or as high— as yours.) *Behavior* refers to whether the person has the ability to do the job—whether or not he could do the job *if he wanted to.* For example, does the person have the necessary training and abilities to do the job? Are there roadblocks or impediments (like a resistant work group) that are preventing the person from doing his job? Finally, *consequences* refers to all those things that happen *as a result of* performing the task. For example, is the person praised and rewarded for effective performance? Are employees who do not perform well rewarded anyway? Are some employees traditionally rewarded for performing poorly?

Let's look at an example. Suppose our performance problem is that our company's salesmen are very lax in filling out the necessary sales reports. The sales reports are important because they help us keep track of where the salesmen have been and what the disposition of each customer is, and they also provide us with essential information on which to build our production schedules. The sales manager insists that it is a "training" program and asks the training director to develop a training program that will show the salesmen how important the reports are and how to fill the reports out. Before setting up the program, however, the training director decides to analyze the "ABCs" of performance as follows:

> *Antecedents.* Do the salesmen know what is expected of them? After speaking with the salesmen it is apparent to the training director that they do indeed understand the importance of the sales reports and also how to fill them out. In this case, therefore, the antecedents are okay.

> *Behavior.* Could the salesmen fill out the reports in a timely manner if they wanted to? Do they have the ability to do so? Are there any roadblocks or impediments preventing them from filling them out in a timely manner? Here the training manager finds that while the salesmen themselves have the ability to fill out the forms there are in fact some organizational impediments to doing so. Salesmen complain, for example that they often have difficulty getting blank copies of the forms. The training director decides to solve this aspect of the problem by having the sales manager issue the salesmen a large supply of the forms at the beginning of each year, even though this means some wasted printing expenses.

Consequences. What are the consequences of performing? Are salesmen rewarded the same whether they fill in the forms or not? Are there negative consequences to processing them? The training director interviews the salesmen and finds the following. The forms are quite long and difficult to fill out. Some salesmen tried spending all day Saturday just getting their paperwork out of the way, but they quickly found that they were better off spending that time out in the field, meeting with customers, since they were rewarded on sales volume—not on submitting forms. In fact, no salesman can remember having been praised or in any way recognized for getting the forms in on time. The other element of the problem therefore seems to be in the "consequences," the training director decides. The solution here involves having the forms revised so that they are shorter and easier to fill out and holding a monthly "lottery" in which all salesmen who submitted a complete set of sales reports for the preceding four weeks are eligible for a $50 bonus. After six months, the sales manager calls in the training director to congratulate him on the success of the changes and to let him know that he sees now why the training director wanted to analyze the problem before assuming it was a training problem.

This same basic approach to analyzing problems via the ABCs of performance can be applied to a wide array of problems. For example, as we will see in ensuing chapters, it can be used to analyze why: an employee's performance is not up to par; a work group is resisting efforts to institute a new incentive plan; two departments are constantly in conflict; and, attendance in the organization is poor.

CHAPTER SUMMARY

1.   The classical management approach grew out of managers' needs for improving the efficiency of the organizations and resources they had accumulated by the late 1800s. Characterized by the work of Taylor and Fayol, the classical approach placed an almost total emphasis on the technical aspects of efficiency and left the impression that workers could be treated as "givens" in the system.

2.   The behavioral approach grew out of changes that were occurring in society— changes that reflected increasingly anti-individualistic values. This school of thought had its beginnings in the Hawthorne studies in which management experts first addressed the fact that workers were driven not so much by "pay" as by needs and wants and desires. As a result of the Hawthorne findings, the recognition grew that human behavior at work was a complex and powerful force, and that workers had needs and desires that the organization and task had to accommodate. McGregor (with his Theory X and Theory Y), and Argyris (who explained how organizations can inhibit normal growth processes) are two more recent representatives of the Behavioral school of management.

3.   The contingency approach to management emerged at a time when management experts saw they needed a theory that would help synthesize the Classical

and Behavioral schools. Its main impetus, however, was a series of studies carried out in England and America (such as those by Burns and Stalker) that showed how the appropriateness of either the "mechanistic" (classical) or "organic" (behavioral) approach depended on the kind of task the organization had to accomplish.

4. The period from about 1960 to the present has been one in which increasing pressures from diverse interests have been brought to bear on management. Pressure groups include consumers, unions, governments, and minorities, for example, and one result of these pressures has been that managers have had to recognize that it has "social responsibilities" that go beyond maximizing profits. Partly as a result of these pressures, but as a result of decreased capital investment and changed work values as well, low productivity has become a major problem in America.

5. The main purpose of this book is to explain how behavioral science concepts and techniques can be used to improve productivity at work. As indicated in our model (Exhibit 1.3), we assume there are four major determinants of performance at work—individual, task and rewards, organizational, and organizational changes—and that these, working in unison, can bolster performance. We explained how each chapter will address the question of improving productivity and performance. And we emphasized, that in analyzing performance problems it is useful to focus on the antecedents, behavior, and consequences of the activity in question—the "ABCs" of performance.

DISCUSSION QUESTIONS AND PROJECTS

1. Compare and contrast the Classical, Behavioral, and Contingency schools of management. How were each appropriate to the attitudes and values that prevailed when they were popular?

2. Do you think that pressures like consumerism and equal employment opportunity have influenced productivity? Why? Why not?

3. What are the four important determinants of behavior we stress in this book? What are some other factors that influence employee performance that we have not mentioned?

4. Analyze the following incident using our "ABCs" of performance; in other words, indicate what questions you would ask in analyzing the "ABCs" and in determining the source of the problem:

> Glenda Farrell has been editor at Crippen Publishing for a year now, but she finds that no matter how much she badgers her authors they are continually late in meeting deadlines. Whenever a story or a book is due on March 15th, for example, she rarely gets it before the middle of April, and so on. The delays are causing havoc with her production schedules and she is trying to figure out how to get her authors to submit their manuscripts on time. How would you go about solving this problem using our "ABCs"?

CASE EXERCISE

The Dean's Problem

When Joe Miller took over as Dean of the School of Business at Kendall University, he had high expectations. He wanted to make his school "the best in the South," and he defined "best" in terms of excellence in teaching and publishing. He felt that faculty publishing was important because university faculty are usually rated by their peers in terms of their publication records, and he felt that if he could get his faculty to publish more and better papers, he could thereby improve his school's "image." However, because he also felt that faculty owe it to their students to prepare for class and to do a good job of "turning their students on" to the subject matter, he rated teaching excellence very high as well. His approach to leadership was to assume that he was dealing with highly professional, self-motivated individuals who would do their jobs as long as they knew what was expected of them. He therefore told each faculty member that he wanted him or her to do "their best" in the classroom and in publishing journal articles. By the end of his second year at Kendall U., however, his expectations had not been met, and most faculty members were still teaching and publishing at about the same level they were when he first took the job.

During lunch with the Dean of Education last week, Joe Miller described his disappointment, and the former suggested that what the business faculty needed was some "faculty training." Specifically, he suggested that the business faculty needed: (1) a training program aimed at showing its members how to develop lesson plans, use video aids, and generally do a better job of teaching; and (2) a separate training program (preferably given by a "distinguished scholar") that aimed at showing them how to get ideas for research papers, where to go for research money, how to determine which journals to try to get published, and how to write better research reports. The education dean underscored the importance of this kind of training by explaining that "it is a fringe benefit that is especially important at our university." After all, he said, the deans at Kendall U. had traditionally followed a policy of allocating raises more or less across the board; "Remember," he said, "we've never had much money to allocate for raises anyway, and the last thing we want to do is start demoralizing some of our older faculty members. Therefore, fringe benefits like special training programs are very important."

Questions
1. Do you think that Joe Miller should proceed with the training program? Why? Why not?

2. Analyze the "ABCs" of performance in this case. Do you think faculty members know what is expected of them? Do you think they probably have the ability to do better if they want to? What are the consequences of their behaving as the dean wants them to? Are they rewarded for their performance?

3. What, if anything, does this case tell you about the relationship between rewards and performance? About the functions of a leader?

4. What would you do now if you were in Joe Miller's place?

NOTES FOR CHAPTER 1

1. D. S. Pugh, *Organization Theory* (Baltimore: Penguin, 1971), pp. 126–27. See also Daniel Wren, *The Evolution of Management Thought* (New York: Ronald, 1972).

2. William Scott, *Organization Theory* (Homewood, Ill.: Irwin, 1976).

3. F. L. Roethlisberger and William Dickson, *Management and the Worker* (Boston: Graduate School of Business, Harvard University, 1947), p. 21.

4. Douglas McGregor, "The Human Side of Enterprise," in Edward Deci, B. von Haller Gilmer, and Harry Karn. *Readings in Industrial and Organizational Psychology* (New York: McGraw-Hill, 1972), p. 123.

5. Chris Argyris, *Integrating the Individual and the Organization* (New York: John Wiley, 1964).

6. See Daniel Wren, *The Evolution of Management Thought*, ch. 19.

7. See Harold Koontz, ed., *Toward a Unified Theory of Management* (New York: McGraw-Hill, 1964).

8. Tom Burns and and G. M. Stalker, *The Management of Innovation* (London: Tavistock Publications Ltd., 1961).

9. David Aaker and George Day, "A Guide to Consumerism," *Journal of Marketing* (July 1970), pp. 13–14.

10. Robert Hay and Edward Gray, "Social Responsibility of Business Managers," *Academy of Management Journal* (March 1974).

11. See Steven Brenner and Earl Molander, "Is the Ethics of Business Changing?" *Harvard Business Review* (January–February 1977), pp. 57–71.

12. Robert Hay and Edward Gray, "Social Responsibility of Business Managers," pp. 135–143.

13. J. Richard Hackman and J. Lloyd Suttle, *Improving Life at Work* (Santa Monica, Calif.: Goodyear, 1977), p. 4.

14. Brenner and Molander, "Ethics of Business," p. 69.

15. *Work in America: A Report of the Special Task Force of the Secretary of Health, Education, and Welfare* (Cambridge: M.I.T. Press).

16. Quoted in Thomas Connelan, *How to Improve Human Performance* (New York: Harper & Row, 1978), p. 4.

17. Connellan, *Human Performance*, p. 7.

18. Mildred Katezell, *Productivity: The Measure and the Myth* (New York: Amacom, 1975), quoted in Joel E. Ross, *Managing Productivity* (Reston, Va.: Reston Publishing Co., 1977), p. 3.

19. Ross, *Managing Productivity*, p. 3.

20. See "How to Promote Productivity," *Business Week*, July 24, 1978.

I: *INDIVIDUAL DETERMINANTS OF PERFORMANCE*

The main purpose of this part of the book is to describe some important individual determinants of performance including perception, personality, abilities, and needs. We consider these to be "individual" determinants because they come from "inside" each person and because every person is unique with respect to his or her perceptions, personality, abilities, and needs.

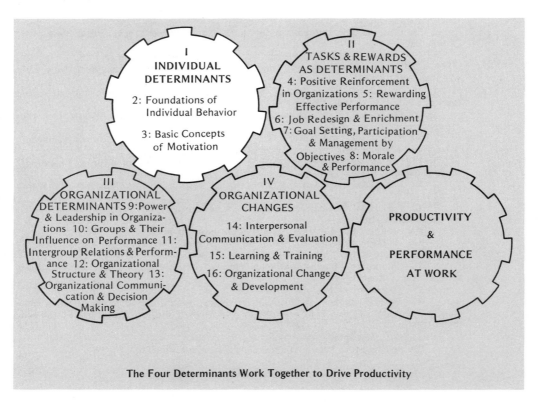

The Four Determinants Work Together to Drive Productivity

Individual determinants are important factors in employee behavior and perform-ance. This is because even on the same job, with the same reward system, and in the same organization no two employees are ever going to react in exactly the same way to some stimulus (like an order from the foreman), nor are they going to perform in exactly the same way. Everyone *perceives* or defines stimuli based on his or her own education and background; everyone's *ability* to perform a particular task is different; and everyone's *needs*—for security, for friendly relationships, for money, etc.—are unique. Therefore, if we are to improve performance in an organization, we have to start by understanding these individual determinants of performance and how a manager can influence these determinants in his or her organization. In Chapter 2, Foundations of Individual Behavior, we discuss perception, personality, and ability; and in Chapter 3, Basic Concepts of Motivation, we explain what motivation is and how a person's needs affect his or her motivation.

How exactly do individual differences like perception, personality, abilities, and needs affect productivity and performance? A detailed answer will be presented in the next two chapters, but to gain an initial perspective, consider how these factors might affect the "ABCs" of performance. For example, assume an employee's production is inadequate, and that you want to analyze the problem using the "ABCs" approach. Ask for example,

> *Antecedents.* Does the person understand what is expected of him? Is the person's work group, position, or stress causing him to *misperceive* your instructions, or to "read into them" something you hadn't intended?

> *Behavior.* Could the person do the job if he or she wanted to? Has he the *ability* and/or *personality* to do the job?

> *Consequences.* From the employee's point of view, are the consequences for performing positive ones or are they negative? Is the person's work group causing him to *perceive* the consequences of performing to be negative instead of positive? Are the rewards valuable to the employee? Do they satisfy his or her important *needs*?

2 *Foundations of Individual Behavior*

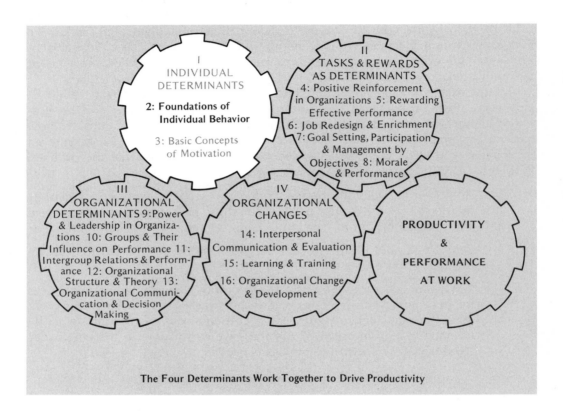

The Four Determinants Work Together to Drive Productivity

BY THE TIME YOU FINISH STUDYING THIS CHAPTER, YOU SHOULD BE ABLE TO:

1. *Explain the mechanism of perception.*
2. *Present some examples of how perception affects employee performance.*
3. *Compare and contrast two theories of personality.*
4. *List several examples of personality traits.*
5. *Explain how to influence personality and abilities at work.*
6. *Explain how you would use personnel tests to improve employee performance.*

OVERVIEW

The main purpose of this chapter is to discuss three important individual determinants of behavior—perception, personality, and abilities. We first discuss perception and explain how the way we see or perceive a stimulus is influenced by our needs, organizational positions, and work groups, and how a person's perceptions influence his or her behavior. Personality is the second important individual determinant of behavior, and we discuss two important theories of personality: Freudian theory, and the theory of personality traits. Human abilities are a third important individual determinant of behavior, and one that is related to personality. We therefore discuss different types of abilities, and the subject of personnel research and testing, through which an organization can assess a job applicant's personality and abilities and decide if he or she is appropriate for the task.

INTRODUCTION: THE IMPORTANCE OF INDIVIDUAL DETERMINANTS OF BEHAVIOR

In Chapter 1 we distinguished between individual, reward and task, organizational, and change determinants of behavior. The main purpose of the present chapter is to focus on the first of these, on three basic *individual* determinants of behavior: perception, personality, and ability. These are determinants that are inside the person and that influence how that person perceives the world and responds to orders and other outside stimuli.

Everyone knows that a stimulus—an order from a boss, an offer of a raise, a training program—can have different effects on different people. For example, one employee might leap at the chance for a $10 raise, while another might shun it. One person might emerge from a training program with excellent skills, while another may apparently learn nothing. One worker might "jump" whenever the boss gives orders, while another may laughingly ignore them.

To a large extent, the reason for these anomalies is that people differ in their perceptions, personalities, abilities, and needs. As illustrated in Exhibit 2.1, these factors act much like filters, adding to, detracting from, and often distorting the effects of the stimulus. In terms of *perception*, for example, a person's biases often influence how he evaluates a job candidate; thus women, or members of minority groups are sometimes perceived as less qualified for jobs, quite aside from their actual qualifications. *Personality* is important, too. For example, some employees are more confident and dominant than others, and this influences how they react to challenges or to being "chewed out" by the boss. People also differ in their *abilities*. For

Exhibit 2.1 Individual Determinants of Behavior Act as Filters

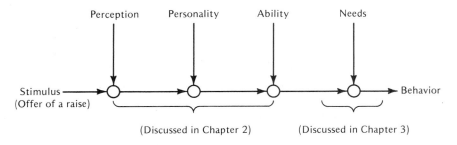

example, some have a great deal of dexterity and so are able to perform intricate, detailed manipulations on an assembly line that others might find impossible. People also differ in their *needs*—for challenging tasks, for security, and so on, but we will delay our discussion of this until the following chapter. In summary, individual determinants of behavior like perception, personality, and abilities (as well as needs) are important to us because they influence how the person sees the world and reacts to its stimuli and, therefore, how the person performs at work.

THE ROLE OF PERCEPTION IN INDIVIDUAL BEHAVIOR

What Is Perception?

We all react to, and behave on the basis of, stimuli that reach us via our sense organs, but how we *define* these stimuli depends on what we bring along with us from past experiences, and what our present needs and values are.[1] In other words, our behavior is not motivated just by the actual stimuli "out there," but by our *perceptions* of those stimuli, and our perceptions are distorted by our experience, situation, and needs.

The phenomenon of perceptional distortion is probably most familiar when it involves inanimate objects. For example, when a door swings open toward us, its rectangular shape actually goes through a series of distortions[2] because of the changing distance between us and the parts of the door. The door first becomes a trapezoid, with its nearest edge looking wider than the hinged edge, and the trapezoid then grows thinner until all we can see is a vertical line the thickness of the door. Yet, while these changes are all distinguishable, what we actually "see" or perceive is an unchanging door swinging on its hinges. What has occurred is that our knowledge of what we think the shape should be has caused us to compensate in our minds for any apparent changes in the shape of the door, and we thus perceive the shape of the door as unchanging or constant. A similar phenomenon occurs when we try to match the sizes of near objects with those of far ones. When we look down a row of arches, for example, the farthest one usually looks smaller than the closest one, and its perspective size is in fact smaller (because it is farthest away). Based on our experience, however, we know that the arches are actually equal in sizes, so what we perceive is a compromise between the perspective size of arch and its actual size. For example, the nearest arch in Exhibit 2.2 seems about twice that of the farthest arch. But, if you measure the arches, you will see that the size of the nearest arch is actually more than four times that of the farthest arch. What happens is that *our desire to see objects as we expect them to be—as stable and permanent— causes us to perceive the difference in height of the arches as less than it actually is.* In summary, we tend to assume that features of objects like size, color, shape, and location are constant, and this assumption distorts our perception of what we actually see.

Exhibit 2.2 Effect of Size Constancy on Perception

Here there is no difficulty in perceiving that the arches on the right receding in perspective are all of the same size, and that they are the same as the three arches in the background. The conditions are thus good for size constancy. Now measure on this page the reproduced height (perspective size) of the nearest arch and compare it with the reproduced height of the distant arches. You will find that the near arch is more than four times as high (in perspective size) as the distant arch.

Source: Ernest R. Hilgard, *Introduction to Psychology*
(New York: Harcourt, Brace, Javanovich, 1962), p. 452.

Exhibit 2.3 Effects of Patterning on Perceptual Structuring

The proximity of the lines that appear to be in pairs
leads us to see three pairs and an extra line at the right.

The same lines as above, but with extensions, lead to
the opposite pairing: three broken squares and an extra
line at the left.

Source: Ernest R. Hilgard, *Introduction to Psychology*
(New York: Harcourt, Brace, Javanovich, 1962), p. 194.

This desire to see objects as stable and constant only accounts for
part of our perceptual distortion; in addition, the proximity, similarity, or
continuity of objects also leads us to "organize" the objects so they seem
more stable. In Exhibit 2.3 for example, the *proximity* of the lines leads us
to see three pairs of lines and an extra line at the right. But if, as in the
bottom of the exhibit, we bend the tops of the lines, our perception of the
lines change, so that we now see an extra line at the left and three pairs of
lines to the right. The *similarity* of objects also influences the way that we
perceive them. In Exhibit 2.4, for example, all the dots and circles are equally
spaced, but we tend to see them as horizontal rows because of the similarity

Exhibit 2.4 Effects of Similarity and Structuring on Perception

o   o   o   o   o   o   o   o

•   •   •   •   •   •   •   •

o   o   o   o   o   o   o   o

•   •   •   •   •   •   •   •

o   o   o   o   o   o   o   o

Note: Because the circles, and the dots, appear to
"belong" together, we perceive rows instead of columns.

Source: Ernest R. Hilgard, *Introduction to Psychology*
(New York: Harcourt, Brace, Javanovich, 1962), p. 195.

of the alternating circles and dots. As another example of how we organize objects, we tend to *close in* missing gaps in what we see; we thus perceive the pairs of lines in Exhibit 2.5 as boxes rather than as just pairs of angled lines. In summary, how we perceive things is influenced by how we want to see them, and we always want to see things as constant, or in such a way that they are organized into patterns that "make sense."

Exhibit 2.5 Effect of Closure on Perception

Note: We tend to "fill in" the missing gaps and see boxes, rather than just sets of curved lines.
Source: Ernest R. Hilgard, *Introduction to Psychology* (New York: Harcourt, Brace, Javanovich, 1962), p. 194.

The resulting perceptual distortions are probably most familiar when they involve inanimate objects, but the same distortions occur when viewing people and people-related stimuli, subjects to which we now turn.

Constancy: the Question of What Is Expected

Just as we impute stable, predictable characteristics to objects, we also impute consistent and repeatable characteristics to people and events. For example, we tend to associate characteristics like industriousness and honesty with certain socioeconomic classes, but not with others. We tend to assume (or once tended to assume) that women were fit only for certain jobs, not for others. Similarly, we tend to *stereotype* people according to age, sex, race, or national origin and to attribute the characteristics of this stereotype to everyone we meet who is of that age, sex, race, or country. In other words, with people, as with objects, we develop (through experience) certain meanings; meanings which are not necessarily inherent in the "stimulus" itself. This process helps us to quickly deduce (with varying degrees of accuracy) the important characteristics of the stimulus and helps us to avoid having to make fresh guesses every time.[3] In practice, this tendency to stereotype people can affect the accuracy of managers' decisions as the following two examples illustrate.

Example One. "Don't like old people." Researchers have found, for example, that the generally negative stereotypes that many people have about older workers (such as "they don't perform as well as younger workers," "they aren't flexible," or "they don't take risks") affects how older people—*regardless of their actual performance*—are treated and appraised.[4]

In one recent laboratory study the subjects were 142 undergraduate business students who were told they were "Division Managers." Their task in the study was to make decisions based on a series of incidents presented to them in memo form. For example, the first incident concerned "resistance to change" and was a memo from a foreman about a shipping room employee who was unresponsive to customer calls for service. Other memos reflected instances of "lack of creativity," "cautiousness and slowness of judgment," "lower physical capacity," "distinterest in technological change," and "untrainability." In each memo, the age of the errant employee was indicated by the researchers who hypothesized that the decision each subject made (such as "here's how I'd handle this overly cautious employee") would depend on whether he thought the employee in the incident was young or old.

The results of this study showed a consistent bias against older employees. In every case where the subjects thought an *older* employee was involved they viewed the problem described in the memo as more acute. Similarly, the corrective actions they recommended were also different when they thought an older employee was involved. With the first incident, for example, the subjects said they would have more difficulty getting the shipping employee to change behavior when they thought he was old, than when they thought he was young. And, when they thought the employee was young, most subjects suggested simply talking with him to encourage him to change his behavior. When they thought he was old, most suggested finding someone else to handle the employee's job. Similar results occurred with the incidents that focused on creativity, cautiousness, and so on. In summary, subjects perceived a particular problem as more acute and suggested more drastic solutions when they thought the problem employee was older rather than younger.

Example Two. "Don't trust the union (or the management)." Another study focused on how stereotypes affect labor-management relations.[5] The subjects in this experiment were 76 members of a central labor council and 108 industrial relations or personnel officers, all of whom lived and worked in the San Francisco Bay area. The question the study sought to answer was, "Will a member of labor or management perceive a particular person differently depending upon whether that person is identified as belonging to labor or management?"

Each subject was shown pictures of two "ordinary looking, middle-aged, moderately well dressed men." According to accompanying descriptions, the two men were similar in terms of age, health, marital status, job history, and outside interests. In one case, however, the man was described as a "local manager of a small plant," and in the other as the "secretary treasurer of his union." The subjects were told to look at the pictures and then describe each man by indicating which of a list of 290 adjectives like "honest," "mature," and "dependable" best described each man.

The most striking finding of this study was that when a subject described a man, the description varied depending on whether the man in the picture was described as from labor or management. Thus, when the men in the pictures were described as union men, one group of union subjects described them as being honest, conscientious, dependable, and so on. And yet, when these same men were described as *managers* to a *second* group of union subjects, the same men were viewed as much less honest and dependable. Similarly, when the men were described to half the *managers* as being managers, the two were rated much more favorably than when they were rated by managers who thought the two were union leaders.

In Sum: Perception and Performance at Work

Our perceptions of people and events are strongly influenced by what we expect these people and events to be. The two examples we discussed concerned perceptions of older workers and union/management leaders, but the same idea applys to a wide range of work-related situations. For example, whether we *perceive* a leader as having high or low influence with his or her boss will temper how we react to the leader—quite aside from his or her *actual* influence. Similarly, whether or not we perceive management as fair and supportive affects how we view its attempts to raise our standards and its offers of rewards.[6] Such perceptions, in turn, affect how we perform. With this in mind, we should look more closely at some of the factors that mold (or influence) perceptions.

SOME FACTORS THAT MOLD OUR PERCEPTION

A multitude of things influence how we "see" the world. For example, a partial list of these would include the following:

> *Needs.* A person's *needs* effect his or her perceptions. For example, when shown "fuzzy," ambiguous pictures of objects, hungry people tend to "see" them as food, while others do not. Similarily, tell an insecure employee that you want to see him in your office later in the day, and he might spend the day worrying about being fired, although you only wanted to discuss some small matter. Or, tell a person who has been out of work for a year that you can only offer her a job at half her previous pay, and she might jump for it although she turned it down ten months ago.

Stress. People who work under stress tend to perceive things less objectively than do those who are not. In an experiment, for example, a group of employment interviewers were told they were under pressure to hire more employees: they subsequently perceived candidates' qualifications as being much higher than did a group of interviewers who were not under pressure.[7]

Education, Background and Values. Our perceptions are also influenced by our education, background, and values. Based on our experiences, for example, we learn to associate certain groups with certain behaviors (i.e. "stereotype" them), and we then tend to expect everyone from that group to behave in the same fashion. Thus, we might expect policemen to be autocratic, or Southerners lazy, for example.

A person's *position* in his or her organization—whether he is in "sales" or "production," for example—and the person's *work group* also affect how he or she "sees" things, and we turn to these two factors next.

How a Person's Position Influences His or Her Perceptions

A person's position or role in the organization is another important factor that molds his or her perceptions.

Example One. "How I see the problem." The classic study of this was carried out by Dearborn and Simon.[8] In this study a group of 23 executives, all employed by a large manufacturing firm was asked to read a case that was widely used in policy courses in business schools. The case described the organization and activities of a moderate-sized company that specialized in the manufacture of seamless steel tubes. The executives were told to read the case and to individually write a brief statement on what they considered to be the most important problem facing the company—the problem "a new company president should deal with first." The executives differed in terms of their functional backgrounds: six were sales managers, five were production managers, four were accounting managers, and eight were classified as "miscellaneous" and included members of the legal, research and development, public relations, industrial relations, medical, and purchasing departments. The researchers hypothesized that the executives would tend to perceive and define the problem in terms of their own departments' activities and goals—in other words, in terms of their positions in the organization.

The researchers found that a manager's position did in fact influence how he perceived the "most important problem" facing the company. For example, out of six sales executives, five thought the most important problem was a sales problem. "Organization problems" were mentioned by four out of five production executives, but by only one sales executive and no accounting executives.

Example Two. "If I'm a manager, management is great." A similar study was carried out in a medium-sized midwestern firm that produced home appliances and was aimed at determining how becoming a foreman or union steward influenced the perceptions and attitudes of workers.[9] As a first step in the study, virtually all factory personnel at the company—2,354 workers, 145 union stewards, and 151 foremen—filled out questionnaires that dealt with employees' attitudes and perceptions about the company, the union, and various aspects of their jobs. During the next year and a half 23 of the workers were made foremen and 35 workers were elected stewards.

How did becoming foremen or stewards influence how these workers perceived the company? The researchers hypothesized that workers placed in a job would tend to take on or develop attitudes that were in keeping with the expectations associated with that job. In other words:

> Since the foreman role entails being a representative of management, it might be expected that workers who are chosen as foremen will tend to become more favorable toward management. Similarly, since the steward role entails being a representative of the union, it might be expected that workers who are elected as stewards will tend to become more favorable toward the union.[10]

And that was in fact what the researchers found. New foremen came to see the company as a better place to work compared with other companies, developed more positive perceptions of top managers, and became more favorably disposed toward the company's incentive systems. New stewards came to look upon labor unions in general in a more favorable light, developed more positive perceptions of the top union officers at the company, and came to prefer seniority to ability as a criterion for moving workers to better jobs.

Sometime later, the researchers were able to show what happened to an employee's attitudes and perceptions when he was forced to leave the job as foreman or steward and return to being a worker. This opportunity arose when the company was forced to cut its work force during an economic recession. Because of the recession many rank and file workers had to be laid off, and 8 of the 23 workers who had been promoted to foremen had to return to the worker role; only 12 were still foremen (the rest had left the company). Over the same period, 14 of the 35 new union stewards had returned to the worker role and only 6 were still stewards (the rest also had left the company). Here, as you probably expected, when they returned to being workers the new foremen and stewards again began to perceive the company from the point of view of workers. For example, most of the "gains" that were observed when workers became foremen were "lost" when they became workers again: they no longer had particularly positive perceptions of top managers, they became less favorably disposed toward the incentive systems, and so on.

Findings like these can be generalized to other, similar situations in organizations. We know, for example, that the members of a department tend to adopt the attitudes, values, and goals of their own department and thus develop somewhat narrow viewpoints: production does not appreciate sale's problems, sales does not appreciate purchasing's problems, and so on: In other words, their *roles* in the organization influence how people perceive their own, and others' problems. In Chapter 11 we will see that the resulting interdepartmental misunderstandings are a main cause of interunit conflict.

How Group Pressure Effects Perception

Most people recognize that groups can influence the behavior of their members: college students work hard to be accepted by their fraternity brothers, workers "slack-off" so as not to incur the wrath of others in their work group, and the Smiths go into debt to keep up with the Joneses.

While few would deny that groups can influence the *behavior* of their members, it may not be so obvious that groups can also influence how their members *perceive* things. Several examples could be cited, but the most famous study of this was carried out by Asch and his associates. In this study the subjects were asked to compare and match lines of various lengths, and Asch arranged for all but one of the subjects (who was thus "naive") to give erroneous answers so he could study the responses of the naive subject.

Of the 59 naive subjects, about one-fourth reported the true lengths of the lines, even though this meant contradicting the erroneous length reported by the rest of the group. Asch reports that the remaining naive subjects "yielded" and agreed with the group for one (or more) of three reasons:

> *Distortion of perception.* A small minority of the naive subjects reported that they were unaware that their estimates had been distorted by the majority and that they actually came to perceive the majority estimates as correct.
>
> *Distortion of judgment.* Most of the subjects who yielded belonged to this category. These subjects lacked the confidence in their own perceptions and came to believe that their perceptions were inaccurate while those of the majority were accurate.
>
> *Distortion of action.* These subjects did not come to view their perceptions as inaccurate nor did the group distort their true perceptions. Instead, these subjects yielded because of what they felt was an overwhelming need to go along with the group. They were afraid to appear different or as outsiders and therefore willingly parroted the majority position, although they knew it was incorrect.[11]

In summary, a person's work group influences his or her perception, judgment, and performance at work. Employees tend to take on the values and points of view of their work group, and as a result come to define situations not just as individuals but also as members of the group. To the person on the assembly line who covets the friendship of his peers, management's offer of a better raise may fall on deaf ears if the person believes it may cost him his friends. Similarly, if his group has come to view the foreman as ineffective, or the company as unfair, the individual members of the group will tend to see things similarly through the eyes of the group.

Summary and Implications

Perhaps the main point of this section is that a manager can never assume that his employees perceive things as he does—or as they "really" are. To the manager, the new incentive system, or the new machine may look like excellent ideas, ones that no "rational" employees could possibly resist, for example. But to the employee, these innovations may look not so much like a way to earn more, but rather like a threat to his or her job security, or to the friendship of his or her peers. Similarly, management may set antecedents or goals that it views as fair, but these will not be useful targets if they are seen by employees as unreasonable. Management may believe the employees could do their jobs if they wanted to, but if employees have doubts, their performance will likely suffer. And, to management the offered rewards may seem highly attractive, but if the employees come to distrust management's motives, such rewards may have little or no impact on performance. Everyone perceives things differently, in other words, and how a person perceives things may be quite at odds with reality.

We saw that perceptions reflect, first, our desire for constancy—our desire, in other words, to see things as we expect them to be and to read into people and situations interpretations that make sense to us, based on our previous experiences with similar people and situations. And our perceptions are also influenced by stress, by needs and values, by organizational roles, and by group pressure. This list is not exhaustive, but does help to illustrate the sorts of things that influence and distort our perceptions of the "real" world.

Add to this the fact that we usually react not just to one stimulus, but to a complex of stimuli: we are, in fact constantly bombarded by stimuli from superiors, subordinates, friends, enemies, family, and so on. No wonder, then that decisions made by those in organizations are not always "rational," or, rather, are rational only when viewed from the unique point of view of the decision maker.

Some Implications. These findings on perceptual distortion suggest some implications for management practice. For example:

PERCEPTUAL FINDINGS	SOME MANAGERIAL IMPLICATIONS
1. CONSTANCY: We form stereotypes and assume that what has happened in the past will again happen in the future.	1. When interviewing applicants for a job, do not look at the person's resume before interviewing him. Make an independent judgment in the interview, and then compare this to his background as described in the resume.
	2. In a selection interview, interviewers tend to form snap judgments during the first few minutes of the interview, and the rest of the interview usually won't change the interviewer's mind; therefore, consciously postpone your decision until the end of the interview. Then review your notes and make a decision.
2. NEEDS AND VALUES: Our needs and values influence how we perceive people and events.	1. When developing product plans, don't assume that others share your values. For example, when the Edsel car was designed by Ford some years ago, Ford executives thought its distinctive vertical grill would remind buyers of exotic Italian sports cars. Most potential Edsel buyers were not familiar with the sports car though, and to them the grill just looked strange.
	2. Use several raters when evaluating an employee's performance: each will tend to see the employee's performance from a slightly different point of view, and perceptual biases due to values will more likely be cancelled out. In universities, for example, professors are often evaluated by their peers, by the department chairmen, and by students.
3. ORGANIZATIONAL POSITION: A person's position in the organization affects how he perceives things.	1. When defining an organizational problem, use a group composed of representatives from several departments.

PERCEPTUAL FINDINGS	SOME MANAGERIAL IMPLICATIONS
	2. Remember, when dealing with representatives of other departments, that their points of view are probably quite different from yours, since they are colored by their experiences with, and loyalties to, their own departments.
4. GROUP PRESSURE: An employee's group influences not just how he behaves, but how he perceives things.	1. In implementing any organizational change, it is advisable to get at least the tacit approval of the work group involved, perhaps by first "selling" the change to the group's informal leader.
	2. If an employee is not working up to his potential, it is useful to ask "how, if at all, is his work group influencing his view of things"?

PERSONALITY AND BEHAVIOR

Personality Defined

Many people believe that a person's personality is a fundamental determinant of his or her behavior. In fact, to many people *personality* is probably the first thing that comes to mind when they think of the individual determinants of behavior. We tend to categorize people as "introverted," "dominant," "mature," or "paranoid," for example, and, by and large, these labels tend to conjure up visions of particular kinds of behavior.

Such familiar labeling notwithstanding, the subject of personality is actually quite complex and even today psychologists cannot agree on how to define it: in one study, for example, psychologist Gordon Allport discussed almost 50 definitions of personality.[12] For our purpose, we will define personality as the characteristic and distinctive traits of an individual, the stable and shifting patterns of relationships between these traits, and the ways the traits interact to help or hinder the adjustment of a person to other people and situations.[13]

While psychologists may disagree on how to define it, they don't disagree on the fact that *personality* is a very inclusive term. A person's "personality," in other words, reflects many things, and some of these are presented in Exhibit 2.6. The person's *physiology* and *abilities* are reflected, since things like body size and intelligence become aspects of our personalities and

Exhibit 2.6 Kinds of Traits Representing Different Aspects of Personality

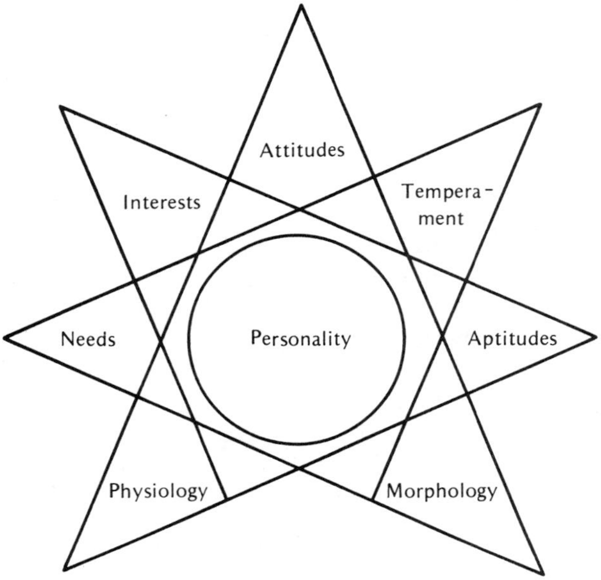

Note: In this diagram, personality is shown as an integrated whole, which can be viewed from different directions: from one direction we see one kind of trait, from another we see another kind of trait.

Source: Ernest R. Hilgard, *Introduction to Psychology* (New York: Harcourt, Brace, Javanovich, 1962), p. 452.

influence how other people see us. Related to this, a person's temperament—his or her characteristic mood—is influenced by certain inherited physiological patterns.[14] Someone's personality also reflects his or her *interests* and *values*. And, *social attitudes* (toward labor unions, communism, and so on) reveal aspects of personality such as dogmatism and authoritarianism. *Needs* and motivational dispositions, stylistic *traits* like politeness and sociability, and *pathological* trends like schizophrenia are some other important facets of someone's personality.

Personality Theories

Psychologists do not agree on what personality is, or even on how to define it. As a result, at least two major types of theories have emerged. One is more abstract, and emphasizes unmeasurable concepts like *id* and *ego*; this theory is based on the work of Sigmund Freud. The second broad class of personality theory focuses more on measurable traits like *dominance* and on the person's actual behavior. We will discuss them both briefly.[15]

Freud's Theory of Personality.[16] The work of Sigmund Freud has had an enormous impact on the history of civilization, and the terms that he used to explain the structure and dynamics of personality have become household words.

Freud's personality theory assumes that there are three basic structures that comprise the personality and influence individual behavior: the id, the ego, and the superego.[17] The id corresponds closely to what most people think of as the "unconscious." To Freud, the id is a storehouse for all instincts and contains in its "dark depths" all of those instincts, wishes, and desires that unconsciously direct and determine our behavior. All of our drives and desires reside in the id, and it is therefore the reservoir of a sort of "psychic energy," which Freud called *libido.* According to Freud, the id—this storehouse of our drives and desires—is totally oriented toward increasing pleasure and avoiding pain, and it strives for immediate satisfaction of its needs: psychologist Duane Schultz, in interpreting Freud's theory, says that "the id drives people to want what they want when they want it, without regard to what anyone else may want or need. It is a purely selfish, pleasure-seeking structure—primitive, immoral, insistent and rash."[18] Like a newborn infant, the id has no perception of reality.

This primitive and blind component of the personality requires some type of rational master, and this role is filled by what Freud called the *ego.* The function of the ego is to delay or redirect the drives of the id so that the person's actions are rational given the demands of the situation he finds himself in: It is, for example, the ego that keeps a person working at a job he or she dislikes. The ego may be thought of as "reason" or "rationality," and in Freud's theory a continuing battle rages between the ego and the blind and demanding desires of the id.

The third structure of personality, according to Freud, is the *superego.* The superego, in Freud's scheme, is the same as what we often call conscience, and reflects our conception of what is right and wrong, a conception that consists (at least intially) of the rules of conduct set down by parents. The superego is in some ways the antithesis of the id, since in its relentless and blind intensity it strives solely for moral perfection, and, in so doing, it seeks to inhibit the id, particularly with respect to sex and aggression. In summary, "the id is pressing for satisfaction, the ego is trying to delay it, and the superego urges morality above all."[19] As a result, Freud's human being has been described as:

> Basically a battle field. He is a dark cellar in which a well-bred spinster lady (the superego) and a sex-crazed monkey (the id) are forever engaged in mortal combat, the struggle being refereed by a rather nervous bank clerk (the ego).[20]

In Freud's personality theory, the unconscious, instinctual drives of the id and superego are constantly battling each other and seeking to break out from the bonds of reason—the ego. The friction that develops as the person becomes torn between the conflicting demands of these forces is *anxiety*, an ominous feeling that all is not well. Such anxiety creates an internal tension that must be reduced, and, if serious enough, it signals the person that his ego is in danger of being overwhelmed by the drives of the id. There are many ways to deal with this threat to the ego, such as leaving the threatening situation, or trying to follow the dictates of the conscience. But if these more rational techniques fail, a person may evoke one or more defense mechanisms like *repression* (an unconscious denial of the existence of the thing that brings us pain), *rejection* (attributing the disturbing impulses to someone else), or *rationalization* (convincing ourselves that there was in fact a rational explanation for our thought or act). In Freud's theory the specific defenses that are used, how the person deals with anxiety, and the character and strength of the ego, id, and superego are assumed to be biologically based, but influenced strongly by the experiences a person has as an infant, child, and youth.

Personality Traits Theory. Another way of looking at and understanding the structure of personality is by focusing on the underlying traits that comprise it. The trait approach "proposes that an individual can be described in terms of a constellation of traits, such as affiliation, achievement, anxiety, aggression, and dependency. The traits and the amounts of each trait that each person has is assumed to be fairly stable, and the differences in personality and behavior between two individuals is assumed to be a result of differences in the amount of each trait that each person has."[21]

The question of what these traits are and how they should be measured has been the focus of heated debate (and considerable research) for at least 50 years. Hundreds of traits have been proposed, and it would be useful to look at one illustrative set of them.

As shown in Exhibit 2.7, one psychologist has taken more than 20 individual personality traits and has combined them into five general, or basic, traits. The individual personality traits are listed on the left of the exhibit and include behaviors like "cheerful versus depressed," "talkative versus silent," "unshakable versus easily upset," "trustful versus suspicious," "broad interest versus narrow interest," and "assertive versus permissive." After analyzing the statistical relationships between these various traits, the researcher came to the conclusion that they represented five categories of general, basic traits, which he calls social adaptability, emotional control, conformity, inquiring intellect, and confident self-expression.

Exhibit 2.7 Five General Personality Traits

Individual traits	General traits
Cheerful vs. depressed; talkative vs. silent, introspective; adventurous vs. cautious; adaptable vs. rigid; placid vs. worrying, anxious	Social adaptability
Unshakable vs. easily upset; self-sufficient vs. dependent; placid vs. worrying, anxious; limited overt emotional expression vs. marked overt emotional expression	Emotional control
Readiness to cooperate vs. obstructiveness; serious vs. frivolous; trustful vs. suspicious; good-natured, easygoing vs. self-centered, selfish; conscientious vs. not conscientious	Conformity
Broad interests vs. narrow interests; independent-minded vs. dependent-minded; imaginative vs. unimaginative	Inquiring intellect
Assertive vs. submissive; talkative vs. silent, introspective; marked overt interest in opposite sex vs. slight overt interest in opposite sex; frank, expressive vs. secretive, reserved	Confident self-expression

Source: Modified from D. W. Fiske, "Consistency of Factorial Structures of Personality Ratings from Different Sources," *Journal of Abnormal and Social Psychology*, Vol. 44, 1949, pp. 329–344. Reprinted in Clifford Morgan and Richard King, *Introduction to Psychology* (New York: McGraw-Hill, 1966), in Fred Luthans, *Contemporary Readings in Organizational Behavior* (New York: McGraw-Hill, 1977), p. 206.

Note: More than twenty individual traits, shown on the left, were used in getting ratings of 128 men. A factor analysis of the ratings yielded the five general, or more basic, traits listed on the right.

Human Abilities and Behavior[22]

Abilities like intelligence and dexterity are often viewed as integral components of personality, and for good reason. When most people think of someone's personality, it is often (at least in part) in terms of the person's abilities, so that they may describe the person as "smart," or "agile," or "artistic."

Abilities play a crucial role in performance at work, and some have summarized this role as:

Performance $= f$ (ability $\times$ motivation)

What this means is that a person's performance is seen as a function of his or her abilities *and* motivation; one without the other won't suffice. In other words, even the most highly motivated person will not perform well —as a golfer, a company president, or a machinist—unless he or she also has the *ability* to do the job. (Conversely, even the most able employee will not perform satisfactorily if not motivated.)

Types of Abilities. There are many types of abilities. *Mental abilities* include "intelligence" and its building blocks like memory, inductive reasoning, and verbal comprehension. *Mechanical ability* deals essentially with the comprehending aspects of mechanical jobs and would be important, for example, for mechanical engineers or machinists, who must be able to visualize how a particular piece of machinery works. *Psychomotor abilities* include such things as dexterity, manipulative ability, eye-hand coordination, and motor ability. Such abilities might be important for employees who have to put together delicate electronic components, or who work as card dealers in Las Vegas, for example. People also differ in their *visual skills*, for example in their ability to discriminate between colors and between black and white detail (visual acuity).

In addition to these general abilities that we all have, there are also *job specific* abilities—abilities that are learned through training, experience, or education. We test for these abilities when we are interested in determining the candidate's proficiency on some job, such as punch press operator, typist, or forklift operator.

PERSONALITY, ABILITIES, AND PERFORMANCE AT WORK

Influencing Personality and Abilities at Work

There are two basic ways an organization can influence the personalities and abilities of its members. First, particularly with respect to abilities (since personalities are rather difficult to change), various organizational training, development, and orientation programs can be used to change or modify the existing abilities and values of employees. Second, the organization can influence the personalities and abilities of its members by judiciously screening and selecting employees whose personalities and abilities are appropriate given the nature of the organization and the job involved. In some of the following chapters we focus on the first of these methods and on the processes of training and development. While the second of the approaches—careful screening and selection—is more properly in the domain of personnel management, it is still useful for us to briefly discuss personnel testing, since it is largely through such testing that the organization can identify individual differences among job candidates and select those whose personalities and abilities are most appropriate for the organization and for the jobs that have to be staffed.

Personnel Research and Testing

Everyone is familiar with the fact that some people are simply better at some tasks than are others. Most people could practice for years, for example, and never play golf like Jack Nicklaus, manage like Harold Geneen, or sing like Barbra Streisand. In other words, a person's performance on some task is strongly influenced by that person's personality and abilities and this is generally true whether the job involves being president of ITT, or running a punch press for a factory that builds Fords.

Matching the needs of the job with the abilities of the employee is the basic task of personnel research. By carefully analyzing a job's requirements—for manual dexterity, visual acuity, and so on—psychologists have been able to successfully deduce what human traits and skills are required to successfully perform the job and then screen and assign employees on this basis.

An example of this is presented in Exhibit 2.8. This exhibit presents an Expectancy Chart which shows the relation between scores made on a particular psychological test, the Minnesota Paper Form Board, and the success (as measured by their performance ratings) of junior draftsmen in a steel company. The Minnesota Paper Form Board is a test of mechanical comprehension, and, as you can see on the chart, applicants for the job of junior draftsman who scored high on the test were much more likely to perform their job well than those who did not score high. For example, applicants with test scores between 57 and 64 had a 97 percent chance of

Exhibit 2.8 Expectancy Chart

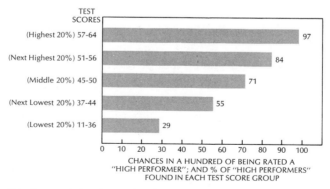

TEST SCORES

(Highest 20%) 57-64	97
(Next Highest 20%) 51-56	84
(Middle 20%) 45-50	71
(Next Lowest 20%) 37-44	55
(Lowest 20%) 11-36	29

0 10 20 30 40 50 60 70 80 90 100

CHANCES IN A HUNDRED OF BEING RATED A "HIGH PERFORMER"; AND % OF "HIGH PERFORMERS" FOUND IN EACH TEST SCORE GROUP

Note: Expectancy chart showing the relation between scores made on the Minnesota Paper Form Board and rated success of junior draftsmen in a steel company. Example: persons who score between 37 and 44 have a 55% chance of being rated above average; those scoring between 57 and 64 have a 97% chance. Therefore, the higher the score, (probably) the higher the person's performance rating on the job. This is because, previously, 55% of those with scores between 37 and 44 were high performers; while 97% of those with scores between 57 and 64 were high performers.

Source: Ernest J. McCormick and Joseph Tiffin, *Industrial Psychology*, 6th ed. (Englewood Cliffs, N.J.: Prentice-Hall, Inc., 1974), p. 105. Reprinted by permission.

being rated above average once they became junior draftsmen. On the other hand, those with scores between 37 and 44 had only a 55 percent chance of being rated above average. While this particular example focused on mechanical comprehension and the job of draftsman the same approach is applicable to almost any job. The basic idea is always to analyze the human requirements of the job, and from this draw some conclusions as to what personality traits and human abilities can be expected to predict effective performance. Then, applicants are tested for these traits and abilities.

Using Formal Tests as Selection Tools

For many companies, formal tests are an important component in the selection process. There are thousands of standardized tests available, ranging from performance tests to interest inventories. Most of these have been checked for *validity* (will it accurately measure what it is supposed to measure?) and *reliability* (will the same person be rated about the same in several different trials with the same test?). Most tests also have established *norms*, or standards, for different groups like college graduates, minorities, and different age brackets.

Tests are not infallible, and you should not rely solely on their results when evaluating a candidate. Not only are tests far from "perfect"—in terms of predicting who will or will not be successful on the job—they are also viewed by some candidates as an invasion of privacy. Furthermore, recent equal employment opportunity legislation has laid down severe penalties for companies who make discriminatory use of tests. The Equal Employment Opportunity Commission (EEOC) specifies strict guidelines for proving how valid and reliable a test is and for ensuring that it is properly administered.

There are four basic types of tests.

Achievement and Performance Tests. These tests measure the applicant's abilities. The simplest example is the one in which the applicant is asked to demonstrate his or her ability to do some job—secretaries are usually asked to take typing tests, for example. Classroom examinations in statistics, finance, or management, are also examples of achievement tests.

Aptitude Tests. These measure an applicant's aptitude or potential to do some job. Some, like the General Aptitude Test Battery (used by the U.S. Department of Labor) measure a broad range of aptitudes such as verbal ability, numerical ability, and motor coordination. Others focus on specific aptitudes, such as doing creative work, or understanding the workings of machinery. Intelligence (or IQ) tests are one kind of aptitude test.

Personality Tests. These are really not tests at all but are devices for measuring different facets of an applicant's personality. They include "tests" like the Rorschach (or "ink blot") Test and the Edwards Personal Preference Schedule. These are used to measure such aspects of the applicant's personality as self-confidence or to determine which basic motives are the most important.

Interests Tests. These "interest inventories" usually compare the applicant's interests with those of people working in various occupations who have previously taken the test. The Strong-Campbell Interest Inventory and the Kuder Preference Record are two widely used interest inventories.

As you might imagine, interest inventories such as these can be very useful for career counseling, but they are also useful for evaluating an applicant's potential for the job. If you can hire an applicant whose interests are about the same as those of successful incumbents in the job for which you are recruiting, your candidate obviously has an increased chance of success on the job.

Developing a Test. What makes a test like the Graduate Record Exam useful for college admissions directors? What makes a mechanical comprehension test useful for a manager trying to hire a machinist?

The answer to both questions, of course, is that people's scores on these tests have been shown to be *predictive* of how they perform. Thus, other things equal, students who score high on the graduate admissions test usually do well in graduate school. Applicants who score high on the mechanical comprehension test perform better as machinists.

In order for any selection test to be useful, you have to be fairly sure that scores on the test are related in a predictable way to performance on your job. In other words, it is imperative that you "validate" the test before using it: you have to be sure that test scores are a good *predictor* of some *criterion*, like job performance. This *validation process* is a complex procedure usually administered by an industrial psychologist. The bare skeleton of the procedure for validating a test would be as follows:

1. First, from job descriptions and job specifications determine the human traits and abilities you think are necessary for doing the job well,

2. Then, have an industrial psychologist develop test items that will enable you to test job applicants for these abilities and traits,

3. Next, administer the test and have the psychologist determine if test performance "predicts" (is significantly related to) performance on the job.

4. If the test scores and job performance *are* significantly related, you can begin using the test as a selection device to screen applicants for your job. Some time later, you might want to *revalidate* the test to ensure that it is still predicting performance.

Summary. To perform satisfactorily, a person must have the ability (and often the personality) to do the job, and testing provides one way to assess an applicant's personality and abilities. The basic idea is always to determine what abilities (or, for that matter, what personality traits like "dominance") are predictive of success on the job and then to screen candidates on this basis.

In Sum: Tying Personality and Ability to Performance at Work

Why do people behave as they do? In this last section we've discussed two important "individual" determinants of behavior, determinants that come from within the person and determine whether—and how well—he or she can perform a task. *Personality* is important, because how a person acts is partly determined by his or her personality, such as whether the person is confident, or submissive, for example.

Particularly for executive jobs (but for other jobs as well), assessing a candidate's personality and determining whether that personality "fits" the requirements of the job is often the difference between successful and unsuccessful performance. Thus, effective leaders are often assertive and dominant. But airmen who staff missile silos have to be calm under pressure and like effective policemen are not obsessively aggressive, and Apollo astronauts are not hard to get along with. *Abilities* are also important, because having the "right" abilities is a necessary prerequisite for efficiently performing a wide range of tasks.

Perception, personality, abilities (and the needs we discuss in the next chapter) are important *individual* determinants of behavior. Together with the *reward system and task*, and *organizational* factors like the leader and work group, they help to determine how productive the employee will be.

Perception, Personality, Abilities, and the "ABC s" of Performance. We can gain another perspective on how these individual factors influence performance by considering them in the context of our "ABC s" of performance. For example, assume an employee's performance is inadequate, and that you want to analyze the problem using the "ABC" approach. Notice how in analyzing the person's behavior, you have to take into account "individual" factors like perception, personality, and abilities:

Antecedents: Does the person understand what is expected of him? Is the person's work group, position, or stress causing him to misperceive your instructions, or to "read into them" something you hadn't intended?

Behavior. Could the person do the job if he or she wanted to? Has he or she the abilities and/or personality to do the job?

Consequences. Are the consequences for performing positive or negative? Is the person's work group causing him to perceive the consequences of performing to be negative, rather than positive? Has the person's experience with your organization caused him to perceive that the proposed consequences of performing will be negative or not forthcoming, regardless of what you have told him?

CHAPTER SUMMARY

1.   Individual differences in perception, personality, and abilities are important determinants of one's performance. These sorts of individual differences help explain why employees—even those on the very same job—perform differently and react differently to some stimulus—like the offer of a raise.

2.   The mechanism of *perception* is important because it distorts and screens how a person sees the world. For example, people tend to see objects and persons as they *expect* them to be and, furthermore, *proximity*, *similarity*, and *closure* also influence the way we see things. Similarly, *stereotypes* that people build up through their experiences influence their perceptions.

3.   Some of the things that influence our perceptions include: stress, needs and values, organizational role, and group pressure.

4.   A manager can never assume that his or her employees perceive things as he does—or as they "really" are. Because people have different needs, roles, work groups and experiences, everyone's perception of things tends to differ. As a result, for example, a manager may think she has set clear goals for a subordinate. However, since the subordinate's perceptions are influenced by many things, including group pressure, her subordinate may actually perceive the goal somewhat differently—he may not think she is serious, for example. Similarly, perceptions influence whether a person thinks he or she has the ability to do a job and how the person assesses the attractiveness of the promised rewards.

5.   We defined "personality" in terms of the "characteristic and distinctive traits of an individual," but there are actually several theories of what personality is. For example, Freud's personality theory assumes that there are three basic structures that comprise the personality and influence individual behavior: the id, the ego, and the superego. As another example, *personality trait* theory assumes that a person's personality reflects a constellation of traits including personal adaptability, emotional control, conformity, inquiring intellect, and confident self-expression.

6.   Abilities (like intelligence, and dexterity) are often viewed as integral components of personality because when we think of someone's personality it is often partly in terms of a person's abilities like "he is smart, agile, and artistic." In any case, abilities play a major role in performance because even the most highly motivated person will not perform well—as a golfer, for instance—unless he or she also has the ability to do the job. Types of abilities include mental abilities, mechanical abilities, psychomotor abilities, and visual skills, as well as *job specific* abilities one learns through training.

7.   Many jobs require people with specific personalities and abilities and there are two ways an organization can influence these two individual determinants of behavior. One is through training, development, and orientation, and the second is through judiciously screening and selecting employees whose personalities and abilities are appropriate, given the nature of the organization and the job involved.

8.   Available selection tests include achievement and performance tests, aptitude tests, personality tests, and interest tests. The basic idea is always to determine what abilities (or, for that matter, what personality traits like "dominance") are predictive of success on the job, and then to screen candidates on this basis. In the next chapter we turn to another important individual determinant of behavior—needs.

DISCUSSION QUESTIONS AND PROJECTS

1.   Give several examples (based on our discussions in this chapter) of how our desire to see objects as we expect them to be—as stable and permanent—causes us to perceive things as different than what they actually are.

2.   Give some *actual* examples of how your perception has caused you to see things as different from what they really are. For example, have you ever found yourself "stereotyping" a person and coming to conclusions about that person based on perceptions that later proved inaccurate?

3.   Compare and contrast the two main theories of personality that we discussed. How, if at all, do you think Freud's theory can be applied in improving employee performance? Give some examples.

4.   To what extent do you think you tend to describe a person's personality in terms of that person's traits? As an exercise, the class can choose one person with whom they are all familiar (say, some politician). Then, each student should try to describe that person's personality in terms of the traits listed in Exhibit 2.7. Was there much agreement among the students in the class? What do you think caused the differences?

5.   Assume that you are manager and that you have a problem because employees are producing poor-quality merchandise. Explain how you would use formal tests to help you analyze the "ABCs" of performance.

CASE EXERCISE

A Perception Problem

Brownson & Associates had been called to the Webster Company when it became evident that there were some serious production problems. "I've been president of this company only three months," said Mr. Peterson, "but it doesn't take long to realize that we have a problem. I don't know what's bugging the work force, but whatever it is, find it and help us do something about it." With this introduction, Hal Brownson and his team of consultants began their work at Webster. It was six weeks before the team felt ready to make its first report to management. Mr. Brownson served as spokesman.

"Gentlemen, my associates and I have been spending quite a bit of time in your firm, trying to determine how efficiency can be improved. Naturally there are two sides to the problem—the mechanical and the human. We believe your problem is definitely the latter. Although we have not yet had time to uncover all of the problem areas, we would like to show you the results of our early investigation. George, would you take over?"

George Ritter walked up to the podium. In his hand he carried several overhead transparencies.

"Gentlemen, I have worked out some tables that I would like to show you. The data should prove quite interesting in pinpointing one of your problem areas."

Mr. Ritter then proceeded to put two transparencies on the overhead. The two were as follows:

Case Exhibit 1 Do You Tell Your Subordinates about Changes Which Will Affect Them in Advance of Their Happening?

Responses	Always (100%)	Almost Always (90-99%)	Very Often (70-89%)	Often (60-69%)	Usually (50-59%)	Sometimes (21-49%)	Seldom (1-20%)
Top managers said of themselves	60	40					
Middle manager's rating of top management	30	30	40				
Middle managers said of themselves	71	29					
Lower level manager's rating of middle management	17	27	29	12	10	5	
Lower level managers said of themselves	85	1.5					
Worker's rating of lower level managers	12	18	22	24	18	5	1

Case Exhibit 2 Do you Encourage Your Subordinates to Speak Freely with You Regarding any Problems They Might Have?

Responses	Always (100%)	Almost Always (90-99%)	Very Often (70-89%)	Often (60-69%)	Usually (50-59%)	Sometimes (21-49%)	Seldom (1-20%)
Top managers said of themselves	70	30					
Middle manager's rating of top management	55	25	14	6			
Middle managers said of themselves	85	14	1				
Lower level manager's rating of middle management	45	32	12	6	5		
Lower level managers said of themselves	93	7					
Worker's rating of lower level managers	31	22	18	10	8	7	4

Questions
  1. What are the implications of Case Exhibit 1? Explain.
  2. What are the implications of Case Exhibit 2? Explain.
  3. What, taken together, do the two exhibits tell you about perception?
  4. In light of the two exhibits, what recommendations would you expect Brownson & Associates to make?

NOTES FOR CHAPTER 2

1. Ernest R. Hilgard, *Introduction to Psychology* (New York: Harcourt, Brace & World, 1962), p. 186.

2. Hilgard, *Psychology*, p. 190.

3. Timothy Costello and Sheldon Zalkind, *Psychology in Administration* (Englewood Cliffs, N.J.: Prentice-Hall, 1963), pp. 315–16.

4. Benson Rosen and Thomas Jerdee, "The Influence of Age Stereotypes on Managerial Decisions," *Journal of Applied Psychology*, 61, no. 4 (August 1976), pp. 428–32.

5. Mason Haire, "Role Perception in Labor-Management Relations: An Experimental Approach," *Industrial and Labor Relations Review*, 8, no. 2 (March 1955), pp. 204–216.

6. See, for example, Gary Latham and Lise Saari, "Importance of Supportive Relationships in Goal Setting," *Journal of Applied Psychology*, 24, no. 2 (April 1979), pp. 151–56.

7. R. E. Carlson, "Selective Interview Decisions: The Effects of Interviewers' Experience, Relative Quota Situations, and Applicant Sample on Interview Decisions," *Personnel Psychology*, vol. 20 (1967), pp. 259–280.

8. DeWitt C. Dearborn and Herbert A. Simon, "Selective Perception: A Note on the Departmental Identifications of Executives, *Sociometry*, 21 (April 1958), pp. 140–44.

9. Seymour Lieberman, "The Effect of Changes in Role on the Attitude of Role Occupants," *Human Relations*, 9 (1956), pp. 385–402, reprinted in Henry Tosi and W. Clay Hamner, *Organizational Behavior and Management*, A Contingency Approach, rev. ed. (Chicago: St. Clair Press, 1977), pp. 169–177.

10. Tosi and Hamner, *Organizational Behavior and Management*, p. 171.

11. Sidney W. Asch, "Effects of Group Pressure upon the Modification and Distortion of Judgments," in Guy Swanson, Theodore Newcombe, and Eugene Hartley, *Readings in Social Psychology* (New York: Henry Holt, 1952), pp. 6–7.

12. Gordon Allport, *Personality, A Psychological Interpretation* (New York: Henry Holt, 1937).

13. The definition is by Clifford T. Morgan and Richard A. King, *Introduction to Psychology* (New York: McGraw-Hill, 1966), p. 460.

14. Hilgard, *Psychology*, pp. 452–53.

15. There are actually many other types of theories and ways of categorizing them. One type, *situationism*, regards the situation(or the stimuli in a situation) as the basic determinant of individual behavior. Another, *interactionism*, emphasizes the importance of person-situation interactions in the development of personality. See Norman Endler and David Magnusson, "Toward an Interactional Psychology of Personality," *Psychological Bulletin*, 83, no. 5 (1976), pp. 956–74.

16. See Duane Schultz, *Theories of Personality* (Monterey, Calif.: Brooks/Cole, 1976), pp. 16–45.

17. This section is based on Schultz, *Theories*, pp. 16–45.

18. Schultz, *Theories*, p. 24.

19. Schultz, *Theories*, p. 26.

20. D. Bannister, "Psychology as an Exercise in Paradox," *Bulletin of the British Psychological Society*, 19 (1966), pp. 21–26, quoted in Schultz, *Theories*, p. 26.

21. Endler and Magnusson, "Toward an Interactional Psychology," pp. 956–74.

22. This section is based on Ernest J. McCormick and Joseph Tiffin, *Industrial Psychology* (Englewood Cliffs, N.J.: Prentice-Hall, 1974), pp. 136–74.

3 *Basic Concepts of Motivation*

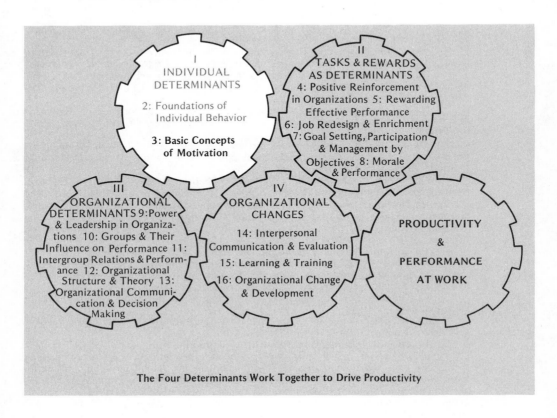

I
INDIVIDUAL
DETERMINANTS

2: Foundations of
Individual Behavior

**3: Basic Concepts
of Motivation**

II
TASKS & REWARDS
AS DETERMINANTS
4: Positive Reinforcement
in Organizations 5: Rewarding
Effective Performance
6: Job Redesign & Enrichment
7: Goal Setting, Participation
& Management by
Objectives 8: Morale
& Performance

III
ORGANIZATIONAL
DETERMINANTS 9:Power
& Leadership in Organiza-
tions 10: Groups & Their
Influence on Performance 11:
Intergroup Relations & Perform-
ance 12: Organizational
Structure & Theory 13:
Organizational Communi-
cation & Decision
Making

IV
ORGANIZATIONAL
CHANGES

14: Interpersonal
Communication & Evaluation

15: Learning & Training

16: Organizational Change
& Development

PRODUCTIVITY
&
PERFORMANCE
AT WORK

The Four Determinants Work Together to Drive Productivity

*BY THE TIME YOU FINISH STUDYING THIS CHAPTER,
YOU SHOULD BE ABLE TO:*

1. *Explain why human needs are the "mainsprings of motivation."*
2. *Discuss three "needs" theories of motivation.*
3. *Give examples of how perceived equity (or inequity) affects performance.*
4. *Explain the expectancy theory of motivation.*
5. *Present several implications of these motivation theories.*

Exhibit 3.1 How Motivation, Incentives, and Frustration Are Related

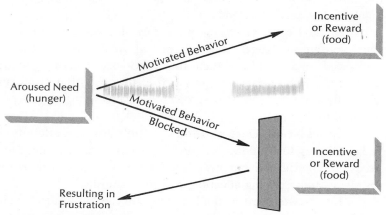

Note: Motivation takes place when you see an incentive or reward that can satisfy an *AROUSED* need. Frustration occurs when a barrier is placed between you and that incentive or reward.

Abraham Maslow and the Needs Hierarchy

Maslow says that man has five basic categories of needs: physiological, safety, social, ego, and self-actualization needs.[3] He says these needs form a hierarchy or ladder (as in Exhibit 3.2) and that each need becomes active or aroused only when the next lower level need is reasonably satisfied.

Exhibit 3.2 Maslow's Needs Hierarchy

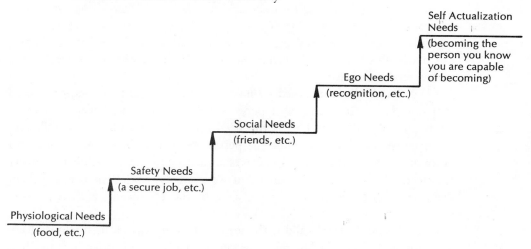

Note: Each higher order needs become active only when succeedingly lower level needs are fairly well satisfied.

Physiological Needs. The lowest level in Maslow's hierarchy contains the physiological needs. These are the most basic needs we all have, for example, the needs for food, drink, shelter, and rest.

Safety Needs. When the physiological needs are reasonably satisfied—when you are no longer thirsty, have had enough to eat, have a roof over your head, and so forth—then the safety needs become activated. They become the needs which the person tries to satisfy, the needs that motivate him. These are the needs for protection against danger or depravation and the need for security.

Social Needs. Once a person's physiological and safety needs are satisfied, according to Maslow, they no longer motivate behavior. Now the social needs become the active motivators of behavior—needs such as for affiliation, for giving and receiving affection, and for friendship.

Ego Needs. Next in the hierarchy are the ego needs, which McGregor has interpreted as:

1. Those needs that relate to one's self-esteem—needs for self-confidence, for independence, for achievement, for confidence, for knowledge, and
2. Those needs that relate to one's reputation—needs for status, for recognition, for appreciation, for the deserved respect of one's fellows.

One of the big differences between these ego needs and the physiological, safety, and social needs is that the ego needs (and the self-actualization needs we discuss next) are rarely satisfied. Thus, according to Maslow, people have a constant, infinite craving for more achievement, more knowledge, and more recognition. On the other hand, the physiological, safety, and social needs are finite: they can be and often are fairly well satisfied. As with all needs, ego needs only motivate behavior, says Maslow, once the lower level needs are reasonably satisfied.

Self-actualization Needs. Finally, there is an ultimate need; a need that only begins to dominate a person's behavior once all lower level needs are reasonably satisfied. This is the need for self-actualization or fulfillment, the need we all have to become the person we feel we have the potential for becoming. This is the need that drives an artist to express herself on canvas, the need that motivates a student to work all day and then take a college degree in night school. This need, as with the ego needs, is rarely if ever satisfied.

Discussion. How valid is the idea that needs form a hierarchy as Maslow proposed? The Maslow theory is very difficult to test, since technically it would be best to test it at different points in time as the subjects satisfy their lower and then higher level needs. Researchers who have attempted to test the theory in this way have generally not found much support for it.[4] Maslow himself, by the way, never carried out any experiments to test his theory and, in fact, developed it based on the observations he made as a clinical psychologist. Other experts, noting the unlikelihood of finding that needs form a neat five-step hierarchy have attempted to reformulate Maslow's theory in various ways. Alderfer, for example, classifies needs as either *existence* (food and shelter), *relatedness* (affiliation), or *growth* (achievement, self-actualization) needs and reports that such a three-step hierarchy seems to make sense.[5] Based on studies of the Maslow theory, the following conclusions appear to be warranted:

> In practice, the needs probably form a two-, not a five-, level hierarchy. Based on a variety of studies, psychologists today believe that needs are arranged in a two-level hierarchy. At the lower level are physiological and security needs. At the higher level are social, esteem, achievement, and self-actualization needs. These include needs to feel important and to be treated as a capable individual. Needs apparently do not fall into a neat five-step hierarchy the way Maslow proposed. It is more useful to assume a two-level hierarchy, in which the higher level needs become aroused only when the lower level needs for food, security, and so on are reasonably satisfied. Thus a person won't start craving achievement, recognition, or a more interesting job until (from his or her point of view) the lower level needs for existence and security are fairly well fulfilled.[6]

> Blue collar workers (and many white collar workers) still seem to value "existence" needs like security more highly than needs for achievement or self-actualization. Particularly in more developed countries, one might assume that because of unions, welfare, and so on, existence needs like those for shelter, food, security, and so on are already well satisfied and that as a result it is the higher level needs—such as for achievement—that workers most value. The findings suggest, however that workers still seem to value "bread and butter" issues like security and pay much more highly than noneconomic factors like how much variety the job provides.[7] In one study the researcher found that "type of work" had in fact become an important consideration in determining what made a job good or bad from the point of view of employees, but that job security still was by far the most important factor. In other studies researchers have similarly found that issues like pay, security, and good working conditions are all valued more highly by workers than are "high level needs satisfiers" like challenging work.[8]

Frederick Herzberg and the Motivator-Hygiene Theory

Frederick Herzberg argues that man has two different sets of needs.[9] One, "lower level" set derives from man's desire to avoid pain and satisfy his basic needs. These include the needs for such things as food, clothing, and shelter, as well as the need for money to pay for these things. The "lower level" set is similar to Maslow's physiological and safety needs.

Herzberg states that people also have a "higher level" set of needs. This other set of needs "relates to that unique human characteristic: the ability to achieve, and to experience psychological growth." Included here are the needs to achieve a difficult task, to obtain prestige, and to receive recognition. This set is similar to Maslow's social, ego, and self-actualization needs.

Herzberg has carried out studies to more precisely determine what people want and what motivates them. In one study he asked several hundred engineers and accountants to explain things about their jobs that they found "exceptionally good" (and therefore motivating) or "exceptionally bad."

His findings are summarized in Exhibit 3.3. According to Herzberg, these findings mean that the work factors that lead to job satisfaction and motivation (the *motivators*) are different from those (the *hygienes*) that lead to job dissatisfaction. Specifically, if these hygiene factors (like better working conditions, salary, supervision) that appear on the left of Exhibit 3.3 are absent, employees become dissatisfied. But—and this is extremely important—adding more and more of these hygiene factors (like salary) to the job will not motivate employees once the factor (like salary) is adequate: these hygienes can only keep them from becoming dissatisfied.

On the other hand, the "job content" or motivator factors on the right of Exhibit 3.3 (achievement, recognition, etc.) *can* motivate employees. Thus, according to Herzberg, if you continue to build more opportunities for achievement and recognition into the job, then your employees should become more motivated. (This is the basis for the job enrichment approach we will discuss in Chapter 6.) But, says Herzberg, if motivators like opportunities for achievement are missing from the job, workers won't necessarily be dissatisfied; they just will not be highly motivated.

Discussion. Herzberg uses a very unique method for testing his theory, and, as a result, his theory has elicited a great deal of criticism and is very controversial. Basically, to repeat, his method involved asking workers to explain what job-related incidents made them feel exceptionally good or exceptionally bad about their jobs. Based on these self-reported incidents, Herzberg and his associates then concluded that the presence of motivator factors like achievement and recognition makes the workers feel good and the absence of hygiene factors like adequate salary and security makes them feel exceptionally bad.

Many writers feel that asking workers to explain what makes them feel exceptionally good or bad about their jobs almost invariably results in

Exhibit 3.3 Summary of Herzberg's Motivation-Hygiene Findings

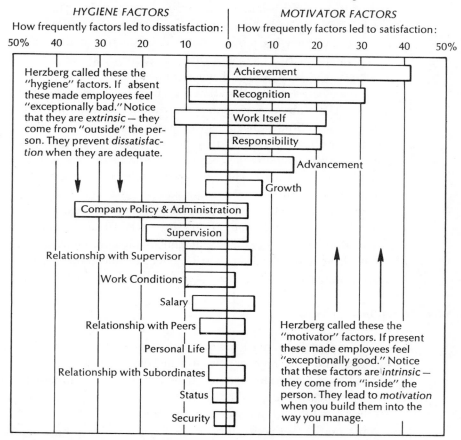

HYGIENE FACTORS

How frequently factors led to dissatisfaction:

MOTIVATOR FACTORS

How frequently factors led to satisfaction:

50%   40   30   20   10   0   10   20   30   40   50%

Herzberg called these the "hygiene" factors. If absent these made employees feel "exceptionally bad." Notice that they are *extrinsic* — they come from "outside" the person. They prevent *dissatisfaction* when they are adequate.

Achievement
Recognition
Work Itself
Responsibility
Advancement
Growth
Company Policy & Administration
Supervision
Relationship with Supervisor
Work Conditions
Salary
Relationship with Peers
Personal Life
Relationship with Subordinates
Status
Security

Herzberg called these the "motivator" factors. If present these made employees feel "exceptionally good." Notice that these factors are *intrinsic* — they come from "inside" the person. They lead to *motivation* when you build them into the way you manage.

Source: Adapted from Frederick Herzberg, "One More Time: How Do You Motivate Employees," *Harvard Business Review* (January-February 1968).

biased responses. Victor Vroom, for example, says that employees are naturally defensive and tend to blame other, extrinsic factors like pay, supervision, and working conditions (hygienes) for their dissatisfaction, but tend to take the credit themselves (achievement on the job, and so on) for their satisfaction.[10]

Perhaps as a result of this, in most cases where Herzberg's original research method is used, the findings support his predictions.[11] In one extensive literature review, for example, a writer analyzed the findings of 20 studies) that used Herzberg's technique and found that only 3 failed to support the theory.[12]

On the other hand, in those instances where Herzberg's method is *not* used, his theory is usually not supported. Probably the main problem that has cropped up is that motivator and hygiene factors are found to be associated with *both* satisfying and dissatisfying situations. In other words, hygienes like pay and work conditions do *not* just prevent dissatisfaction, and motivators like a challenging job *can* cause dissatisfaction if they are absent.[13]

In summary, Herzberg's theory is probably a useful but oversimplified explanation of how needs influence motivation in organizations. On the one hand, Herzberg's contention that (1) hygienes only prevent dissatisfaction while (2) the absence of motivators cannot cause dissatisfaction is clearly indefensible.[14] Studies have shown that hygienes like pay *can* satisfy needs and increase motivation and that the absence of motivators like recognition *does* mean that important needs will be unsatisfied, and the person dissatisfied. On the other hand, Herzberg's work helps to emphasize that lower level needs (the ones satisfied by hygienes like pay and security) are relatively finite and quickly satisfied. However, higher level needs (those satisfied by recognition, challenging work, and so on) are rarely satisfied. As a result, building "motivators" into the work by making it more interesting and challenging should have a powerful and lasting effect on motivation, especially for employees whose lower level needs are fairly well satisfied.[15]

Need Achievement Theory

In its simplest form, need achievement theory aims at predicting the behavior of those who rank high or low in achievement motivation, which has been defined as a "predisposition to strive for success."[16] Basing his ideas on a projective personality test known as the Thematic Apperception Test (TAT), psychologist John Atkinson formulated the concept of the "need to achieve," arguing that it is a personality trait.[17] People who are high in need achievement are highly motivated to strive for the satisfaction that is derived from accomplishing (or achieving) some challenging task or goal. They prefer tasks for which there is a reasonable chance for success and avoid those that are either too easy or too difficult. Relatedly, such people prefer obtaining specific, timely criticism and feedback about their performance.

Most of the studies in this area have been carried out by Atkinson and his colleagues and suggest that there is a strong relationship between achievement motivation (a high need to achieve) and both economic and entrepreneurial success. They have found, for example, that societies high in achievement motivation had relatively high economic growth rates and those low in achievement motivation had lower rates. They have also found that the proportion of students entering entrepreneurial occupations was greater among those with high needs to achieve, and that achievement motivation training produced significant increases in entrepreneurial activity.[18] Others have found that achievement motivation can be learned, and that trainees who do increase in this trait perform better than those who do not.[19] Taken as a whole, the research findings suggest three conclusions:

1. People have different degrees of achievement motivation.
2. Through training, a person's achievement motivation can be increased.
3. Achievement motivation is directly related to performance at work.

Is There an "Ultimate Need"?

Management expert Saul Gellerman agrees that we all have needs for things like money, status, achievement, and recognition. And he agrees that if one of these needs is not satisfied, then a person will be motivated to satisfy it. But he also says that we do not only seek money, or status, or achievement for its own sake. Instead these are only vehicles that the person uses in his constant quest to be himself, or to be the kind of person he thinks he should be.[20]

> The ultimate motivation is to make the self-concept real: to live in a manner that is appropriate to one's preferred role, to be treated in a manner that corresponds to one's preferred rank, and to be rewarded in a manner that reflects one's estimate of his own abilities. Thus we are all in perpetual pursuit of whatever we regard as our deserved role, trying to make our subjective ideas about ourselves into objective truths.

> Gellerman argues that, above all, most people have a need to be treated as valuable individuals and to become, in Maslow's terms, the person they are capable of becoming. Each has his or her own concepts of who he is, and what he deserves, and each wants to be treated in a manner that supports this self-concept. Each person is strongly motivated to behave in a way that satisfies that need.

> This is also, in large part, what Maslow and the other psychologists we discussed are saying. Whether we call it the need for self-actualization, or for achievement, or for recognition, each is saying that over and above the lower-level physiological or safety needs, most people have this need to be treated as valuable individuals.

Summary: Human Needs and Motivation

People have many different needs. These include a number of existence or physiological needs, (including those for food, shelter, warmth, and so on) and needs for security, affiliation, esteem and recognition, self-control and

independence, competence, achievement, and self-actualization. The needs
fall into a rough two-level hierarchy, with existence and security needs on
the bottom and needs for affiliation, achievement, and so on on the top. The
lower level needs are finite and are relatively easy to satisfy. The higher level
needs, such as for achievement, are never completely satisfied. The lower level
needs can be satisfied only by outcomes that are concrete and *external* to the
person. These external (or hygiene) outcomes include things such as food,
money, and praise. On the other hand, "the need for self-actualization and
competence seems to be satisfied only by outcomes given *intrinsically* by
persons to themselves."[21] Thus, many believe that to appeal to a person's
higher order needs, the "rewards" you provide will have to be such that the
person himself derives a sense of accomplishment from performing a difficult
task: here, in other words, complexity and challenge will have to be built into
the job as "rewards."

EQUITABLE REWARDS AND HUMAN MOTIVATION

Equity Theory

The equity theory of motivation assumes that individuals are strongly motivated to maintain a balance between what they perceive as their inputs, or
contributions, and their rewards. The theory focuses on the exchanges that
take place between the organization and the individual, in terms of the inputs
made by the latter (such as effort), and the outcomes he or she receives for
these in terms of pay, recognition, or promotion. In equity theory, the net
"value" of the exchange (to the person) may then be expressed as a ratio of
inputs to outputs or rewards. A perceived equity or inequity then results when
the person compares his input/reward ratio with those of others in the
organization (or what he believes are the ratios of others in the organization). Basically, if a person perceives an inequity, the theory states a tension
or drive will develop in the person's mind, and the person will be motivated
to reduce or eliminate the tension and perceived inequity.

Implications

According to equity theory exactly *how* the person goes about reducing what
he perceives as an inequity depends on whether he is paid on a piece-rate
basis or on a straight salary basis (see Exhibit 3.4). Equity theory could
supposedly explain a variety of input/reward inequities, but most studies have
focused on the relationship between a person's performance and his financial
rewards—especially under- or overpayment. Thus:

Exhibit 3.4 The Effects of a Perceived Inequity on Performance

	Employee thinks he is underpaid	Employee thinks he is overpaid
Piece-rate Basis	Quality down Quantity the same or up	Quantity the same or down Quality up
Salary Basis	Quantity or quality should go down	Quantity or quality should go up

1. If a person is paid on a *piece-rate* basis and thinks he is *overpaid*, the quantity the person produces should stay the same or may decrease, since producing *more* would simply increase the financial rewards to the person and therefore increase his perceived inequity even more. However, quality should increase since this should allow an increase in the inputs a person sees himself as providing, thus reducing his perceived inequity.
2. On the other hand, if the person is paid per piece and views himself as *underpaid*, the quality of his work should go down, and the quantity he produces will probably increase, depending upon how much the person is paid per unit he produces.
3. If the person is paid a *salary*, regardless of his output, and he views himself as *overpaid*, then either the quantity or quality of his work should increase since this will reduce the perceived inequity.
4. However, if the person who is paid a salary and believes he is underpaid, then his quantity and quality should both decrease. This is summarized in exhibit 3.4.

Research Findings

The prevailing evidence supports most of the predictions of the equity theory of motivation.[22] In one study, subjects being paid on an hourly basis believed they were being overpaid; they significantly outperformed those who saw their pay as equitable. In a follow-up study, subjects who were paid a piece-rate basis and who believed they were being overpaid reacted by producing less than did those who viewed their pay as equitable, therefore effectively lowering their pay. The "equity" effects are usually most dramatic when the person believes he or she is being *underpaid*. A person who is being paid on an hourly basis can be expected to drastically curtail both the quantity and quality of his work if he perceives himself as being underpaid. If an underpaid person is being paid on an incentive, piece-rate basis, then quality can be expected to go down; quantity will generally increase, assuming that producing more units will reduce the inequity from the point of view of the employee.

EXPECTANCIES AND HUMAN MOTIVATION

Many psychologists today believe that to motivate people, it is not enough to offer them something to satisfy their important needs. The reason for this is that (even if the reward is perceived as important and equitable) for the person to be motivated, he will also have to believe he has the *ability* to obtain the reward. For example, telling a person you will appoint her salesmanager if she increases sales in her district will probably not motivate her if she knows the task is virtually impossible.

Expectancy Theory

The *expectancy theory of motivation* assumes that a person's motivation to exert effort is based on his or her expectations for success.[23] Probably the most popular version of expectancy theory was formulated by Vroom and is based on three concepts: valence, instrumentality, and expectancy.[24] Other valence-instrumentality-expectancy (VIE) theories of motivation have been proposed, but they are all similar to Vroom's theory in their concepts and implications.

Valence represents the value or importance that a particular outcome has for a person. It reflects the strength of a person's desire for, or attraction toward, the outcomes of particular courses of action. Perhaps the simplest way to interpret valence is to assume that outcomes represent rewards such as pay, promotion, and recognition. The valence of each outcome or reward then represents the positive or negative value ascribed by the individual to each outcome or reward.

Instrumentality reflects the person's perception of the relation between a "first level outcome" (such as high performance) and a "second level outcome" (such as a promotion). For example, it might reflect the extent to which a person believes that performance on his part will be instrumental in getting him a promotion. *Expectancy* refers to the perceived relationship between a given level of effort and a given level of performance. In other words, it refers to the extent to which the person feels that his efforts will, in fact, lead to the first level outcome, in this case, performance. The Vroom model attempts to predict (a) what task a person will choose and (b) what level of effort he will put forth on that task, based upon a knowledge of the valences, instrumentalities, and expectancies involved.

In sum, Vroom argues that motivation involves a three-step process:

1. Does the person feel that the second level outcome, such as promotion, is important to him, or high in valence?
2. Does he feel that high performance—the first level outcome in this case—will be *instrumental* in getting him his promotion?
3. Does he feel that exerting *effort* will in fact result in increased performance?

In summary, the strength of a person's motivation to perform effectively depends on two things: (1) the person's belief that effort can be converted into performance and (2) the net attractiveness of the outcomes (rewards) that are perceived to stem from good performance.[25]

Research Findings

Most of the research findings support expectancy theory. Vroom, for example, studied a group of students and found that about three-fourths of them chose to work for employers whom they ranked as being the most instrumental in fulfilling their goals.[26] In another study researchers surveyed over 600 production workers in a unionized appliance factory, all of whom were paid on an incentive basis. The researchers had the workers fill out questionnaires aimed at measuring the instrumentality of high and low performance for three specific outcomes: making more money in the long run, getting along well with the work group, and promotion to a higher salary rate. The results of this study indicated that workers that reported high instrumentalities tended to be higher producers.[27] A variety of other studies have been published recently which also support one or more components of the expectancy theory of motivation.[28]

Conclusions and Implications

Actually, not all the findings support the expectancy theory of motivation,[29] but there are still some fairly solid conclusions we can come to concerning it. These are:

1. Employees who believe that high performance is instrumental in obtaining rewards perform better than do those who do not.
2. The same holds true for the "expectancies" link between effort and performance. Where employees believe that effort on their part will lead to effective performance they generally exert more effort than where such a link is not evident.

A main drawback to expectancy theory is that it seems to assume that people employ a rational decision process. It assumes, for example, that individuals thoroughly explore all their available alternatives, weighing the possible consequences of each and then rank the consequences or outcomes of each alternative. In practice, however, we know that people usually do not make decisions in such a rational manner. For example, the results of several studies indicate that individuals basically cease their search for alternatives once a satisfactory one has been obtained.[30]

In any case, there are some useful implications we can draw from expectancy theory. Of these, perhaps the most obvious is that pay and other rewards should be made contingent on performance.[31] The expectancy theory research findings indicate that high-performing employees are those that see a strong relationship between performing their jobs well and receiving rewards they value.[32] Therefore, according to many experts, organizations should put more emphasis on rewarding people (through pay, promotion, better job opportunities, etc.) *contingent on their performances.* And, these experts argue, that if an organization *does* decide to reward employees on the basis of their performance, it would be self-defeating to keep such rewards a secret; instead *rewards should be publicized* so that all employees can develop a clearer understanding of the relationship (instrumentality) between performance and reward.

MOTIVATION THEORIES: MODEL AND IMPLICATIONS

A Model of Motivation

It would be useful for us to summarize and integrate these motivation theories, and to do so we can use the model illustrated in Exhibit 3.5. As you can see, we can think of motivation within an expectancy theory framework. Expectancy theory, you will recall, states that motivation will occur if the incentive is of value to the person and if the person is reasonably sure that effort on his or her part will result in accomplishing the task and obtaining the incentive.

Therefore, as you can see from our model, for motivation to take place, several things must occur. First, the incentive must be important to the person. Here, theorists like Maslow, Herzberg, and Atkinson would suggest that certain needs—such as for recognition, esteem, and achievement—are the most important in our society. Related to this, we also know that the incentive cannot just be important, but must also be viewed as

Exhibit 3.5 A Model of Motivation

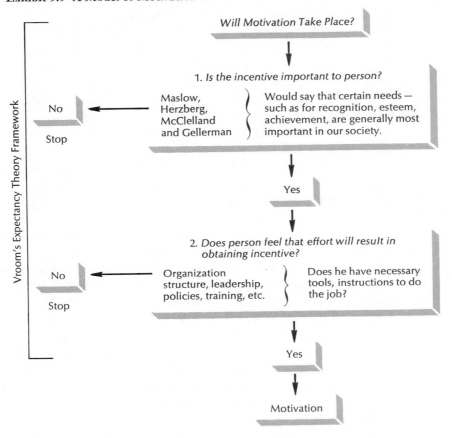

equitable if it is to elicit the desired motivation. (An *in*equitable reward can also elicit motivation if, for example, a person paid a salary believes that she is overpaid.) Furthermore, the person must feel that effort *will in fact lead* to rewards. Here, as you can see, other, "nonmotivational" matters must be addressed, including individual factors like skills, organizational factors like organization structure, and "change" factors like adequate training.

Implications of Motivation Theories

Rewards Should Be Tied to Performance. Expectancy theory assumes that motivation is greatest when obtaining rewards is contingent on performance. For those tasks and people for whom pay is the most obvious reward this would argue for an emphasis on incentive bonuses and piece-rate pay plans. For *all* jobs it would argue for tying *non*financial rewards (like advancement, recognition, and praise) to performance.

Outcomes or Rewards Should Be Equitable. Evidence from studies of equity theory suggests very clearly that whether or not the reward is perceived as equitable has important implications for one's motivation. For example, employees who are paid on a straight salary basis but who feel they are underpaid will reduce the quality or quantity of their performance, while those who believe they are being overpaid will improve their performance.

A Person Should Have the Ability to Accomplish the Task to Be Motivated to Do So. Evidence from studies of expectancy theory and need achievement theory suggest that if a person believes there is little or no chance of successfully completing a task (and therefore obtaining the reward), that person will probably not be motivated to accomplish it. Thus, always ask, *"Could the employee do the job if he or she wanted to?"*

It is Useful to Distinguish Between Lower Level "Existence" Needs and Higher Level "Psychological" Needs. Existence needs are those people have for food, clothing, shelter, and security. Existence needs are most often satisfied by extrinsic rewards such as money. Psychological needs are the needs people have for recognition, achievement, and self-actualization. These can be satisfied only somewhat by extrinsic rewards such as recognition from superiors and peers. In general, psychological needs satisfaction must come from within the person and be derived from an interaction between the person and the task: scientists developing a new vaccine, craftsmen producing a product, and the weekend hobbiest building a stereo set are all examples of those who are driven to satisfy psychological needs. It is useful to think of the existence and psychological needs as forming a two-level hierarchy, so that psychological needs only become activated as the existence needs become fairly well satisfied. This suggests that trying to tap employees' psychological needs (say, be giving them enriched, more challenging jobs) may be ineffective as long as basic needs like those for adequate salary and security are not satisfied.

Motivation Theories and the "ABCs" of Performance. A knowledge of these motivation theories can help you to better analyze the "ABCs" of performance. Assume an employee's performance is inadequate, and you want to analyze the problem using the "ABC" approach. Ask:

> *Antecedent:* Does the person know what is expected of him?
>
> *Behavior.* Could the person perform if he or she wanted to? Is it clear (to the person) that effort on his part will in fact lead to performance? Does he or she have the necessary skills?
>
> *Consequences.* Are the consequences positive for performing? Are the rewards valuable to the person? Are they equitable? Does he or she understand that performance will result in rewards?

A Final Word. The theories we discussed in this chapter explain motivation on the basis of intangible concepts like needs, equity, and expectancies. They assume, for example, that to motivate a person one must satisfy his or her needs, provide equitable rewards, and ensure that the person expects to obtain the rewards.

Not all experts agree that motivation can or should be explained on the basis of cognitive abstractions like needs. Instead, they prefer to focus on a person's actual behavior, and they explain all behavior by its consequences. We turn to such a "behavioristic" theory in the following chapter.

CHAPTER SUMMARY

1. Basically, people are motivated or driven to behave in a way that they feel leads to rewards. Thus, there are two basic requirements for motivating someone: (1) the incentive or reward must be important to the person and (2) he or she must feel that effort will probably lead to obtaining the reward. This is the essence of Vroom's expectancy theory of motivation.

2. Maslow says that people's needs can be envisioned in a hierarchy. Each succeedingly higher level need does not become aroused until the next lower level need is fairly well satisfied. Working up the hierarchy, the five Maslow needs are: physiological, safety, social, ego, and self-actualization.

3. Herzberg says that the work factors involved in producing job satisfaction and motivation are separate and distinct from those that lead to job *dis*satisfaction. Those leading to job dissatisfaction (if they are absent) are the hygiene factors. These include extrinsic factors such as supervision, working conditions, and salary. The factors leading to satisfaction and motivation (if they are present) include intrinsic job factors such as achievement and recognition.

4. In its simplest form, need achievement theory aims at predicting the behavior of those who rank high or low in achievement motivation. People who are high in need to achieve are highly motivated to strive for the satisfaction that is derived from accomplishing (or achieving) some challenging task or goal.

5. Researchers today believe needs form a rough two-level hierarchy, with existence and security needs on the bottom, and needs for affiliation, achievement, and self-actualization on the top. The lower level needs are finite and are relatively easy to satisfy. The higher level needs are never completely satisfied.

6. The equity theory of motivation assumes that people are motivated to maintain a balance between what they perceive as their input (or contributions), and their rewards. The theory has received a good deal of support and we know, for example, that people paid on an hourly basis who believe they are underpaid generally reduce both the quantity and quality of that which they are producing.

7. According to Vroom, the strength of a person's motivation to perform depends on two things: the person's belief that effort can be converted into performance, and the net attractiveness of the outcomes (rewards) that are perceived to stem from good performance.

DISCUSSION QUESTIONS AND PROJECTS

1. Why are human needs the "mainsprings of motivation"?

2. Explain Maslow's hierarchy of needs theory. Describe a practical example that seems to support his theory. (The class might want to break into groups of four or five students and develop examples within the groups.)

3. Compare and contrast the Maslow and Herzberg motivation theories.

4. What is "need achievement theory"? How does it compare with the Maslow and Herzberg theories?

5. Explain equity theory—what it is and its implications. Do you think that people are really motivated by perceived inequities? Give some examples to support your position.

6. Compare and contrast (1) the expectancy theory of motivation with (2) the idea of analyzing performance problems in terms of the "ABCs" of performance. Do you see any similarity between the two?

7. "I don't need to know about any fancy motivation theories," your boss tells you, "What they all come down to is that you should practice the golden rule— do unto others as you would have others do unto you." Explain why you agree or disagree with this statement and why.

7. Working individually, think of some jobs that you were especially motivated to carry out. What was it about the job, your manager (if any), and the way you felt that so motivated you? Discuss your answers in class.

8. Explain why an understanding of the needs theories of motivation are important when analyzing the "ABCs" of performance.

CASE EXERCISE

Hawkins' Nob Hill Plant

Mr. Kiplinger is plant manager of the Nob City division of the Hawkins Company. He was originally transferred to Nob City in 1960, ·from the home office in Altoona (Pennsylvania). He, his wife, and their four children reside in Nob City. Reporting directly to Mr. Kiplinger are his key staff officers, the office manager, the personnel and safety manager, and the production manager. Other supervisors include foremen who report directly to the production manager.

The workers have a certain set of expectations concerning their own rights and privileges. Some of these "privileges" are obvious, while others are rather subtle. One of the more widely held values on the part of the workers is what they call "leniency." The workers know they have a job to do and expect that, in the process of doing it, management will leave them alone. The main obligation they feel to the company is that of producing. Obedience to supervisors is displayed so long as it is directly related to a job to be done. Hostility is directed toward management when discipline or forced obedience is exerted as a means of asserting the will of management. Conversely, the workers commend management when given certain privileges or when flexibility is shown in discipline.

"Job-shifting" provides another route for circumventing formal supervisory authority and is a type of vertical and horizontal mobility in the plant. Job-shifting is done by "bidding" for a vacancy in the plant, prompted either by desire for a job with higher status or as a means to escape an unpleasant foreman. The foremen resent this practice, since they feel that they should have the prerogative of choosing their own subordinates—and not the other way around.

A third right includes the use of company material for home repairs. The workers expect ¨that they should have access to the company's finished product, either without charge or at a very large discount, and that company equipment should be made available for use in repairing broken down machinery or household furnishings.

One day Skip Kiplinger received a call from the home office notifying him that he could expect about two million dollars' worth of new equipment to be added to his plant's equipment, in conjunction with the addition of a new brake-lining product line. Along with the equipment addition, the home office notified Skip that they were transferring Louis Hirtmann from the plastics division in Pottstown to replace the retiring Ed Patterson as production manager. Hirtmann was a former Army officer and had an outstanding industrial record too. It was hoped by the board of directors that the change of leadership and the addition of equipment would add considerably to Hawkins' profit margin.

One of Hirtmann's first moves was to stop the practice of allowing workers to have access to company equipment and to reduce the discount given on the purchase of company-made equipment. He was able to do this after showing Kiplinger that several thousands of dollars in sales had been lost from abuse of this particular privilege, in the last year alone; some workers had resold company equipment at considerable profits. Another move was to eliminate the job-shifting policy and to replace it with a new seniority system. The new system was roundly applauded by foremen and other supervisory personnel, but workers became noticeably irritable and frustrated. Hirtmann believed that once an order was given, it was to be followed without question. Generally he paid attention to employee grievances only when they reached critical proportions.

Hirtmann made rounds every hour to check on the progress of the work flow. In the course of six months he instituted many technical changes designed to speed up production and reduce labor costs. These improvements were reflected in the profit margin: but during this six-month period, dissension had been building up, almost unnoticed tensions in the plant ran high, and employees were becoming very defensive. Dissatisfaction over the installment of new machinery became a focal point of the disruption. If the company could afford two million dollars for machinery, workers grumbled, it could afford higher wages.

About the eighth month Hirtmann was notified by the home office that he would attend a month-long managerial seminar in Chicago. Mr. Kiplinger decided to leave Hirtmann's post vacant in his absence, and to have each shift foreman be responsible for his particular shift with no further supervision.

Kiplinger learned through the foremen that the women on the first shift wanted their rest room painted and, because the room was exposed to the afternoon sun, they also asked for some shades and a fan. Without hesitation Kiplinger told the maintenance crew to go to work on the job. In addition he told the foremen to feel free to handle such minor grievances and requests on their own authority until Hirtmann returned.

Within the next week another request was presented. This time the workers complained about working a six-day week. Kiplinger considered the point and proposed that if production reached 20,000 pounds per day (a 5,000 pound increase), he could then institute a short shift on Saturday running from 7:30 A.M. to noon. Within a few days production reached the level indicated. Unfortunately, now Kiplinger was in a difficult position because the Altoona office demanded even more production to meet their orders. Kiplinger then had to go back to the workers and ask them to continue on the six-day schedule for another few days until the orders were filled. Although there was some grumbling, most of the workers continued to operate willingly. Within a week the press for more production was reduced so that it was possible to institute the promised short day on the following Saturday.

It had been the practice to blow a steam whistle in the plant at the beginning and end of the shift, as well as at five-minute rest periods and at lunch. One of the workers suggested that the company use the public address system instead. At first, employees ridiculed the new system but in a few days they took announcements as a matter of course; in one instance when the announcement was not made, the employees returned from lunch just the same. Later on in the month the announcements were dropped, yet the employees started and stopped work promptly.

Between the first and the last of the month the daily output of the plant had increased steadily from 25,000 pounds to about 33,000 pounds.

Kiplinger was puzzled. He could not understand why production was up 32 percent with no production manager present.

Questions

1. Why do you think production was up by 32 percent with no production manager present?

2. How specifically do you think Hirtmann's actions influenced plant workers' "higher order needs"? The plant's hygienes?

3. Do you think Hirtmann's leadership style was appropriate for this situation?

4. Do you think that giving employees more "freedom," as Kiplinger did, was viewed as an important "consequence" of good performance? Why? Why not?

5. What would you do now if you were Kiplinger?

EXPERIENTIAL EXERCISE

Purpose: The purposes of this exercise are:

1. To provide you with information on what your needs are.

2. To give you information on what behaviors characterize people with different needs.

Required Understanding: This exercise can be used either prior to or after reading this chapter.

How to Set Up the Exercise: Readers should work on this exercise individually.

Instructions: First, fill in the following questionnaire:

	Yes	No
1. When you start a task, do you stick with it?		
2. Do you try to find out how you are doing, and do you try to get as much feedback as possible?		
3. Do you respond to difficult, challenging situations? Do you work better when there is a deadline or some other challenge involved?		
4. Are you eager to accept responsibility? Do you set (and meet) measurable standards of high performance?		
5. Do you seem to enjoy a good argument?		
6. Do you seek positions of authority where you can give orders rather than take them? Do you try to take over?		
7. Are status symbols especially important to you, and do you use them to gain influence over others?		

	Yes	No

8. Are you especially eager to be your own boss, even when you need assistance, or when joint effort is required?
9. Do you seem to be uncomfortable when you are forced to work alone?
10. Do you interact with other workers, and go out of your way to make friends with new workers?
11. Are you always getting involved in group projects, and are you sensitive to other people (especially when they are "mad" at you)?
12. Are you an "apple polisher," and do you try hard to get personally involved with your superiors?

Second, score your answers. According to Litwin and Stringer, "Yes" answers to questions 1–4 mean that you have a high need to achieve. You prefer situations which have moderate risks, in which you can identify your own contribution, and in which you receive concrete feedback concerning your performance.

"Yes" answers to questions 5–8 mean that you have a high need for power. You prefer situations in which you can get and maintain control of the means for influencing others.

Finally, "Yes" answers to questions 9–12 mean that you have a high need for affiliation. You have a strong desire to maintain close friendships and positive emotional relationships with others. (Keep in mind that a quick test like this can give you only the roughest guidelines about what your needs are.)

Next, if time permits, each student can write down on a sheet of paper the number of questions he or she answered "Yes" to for each of the three needs (achievement, power, affiliation). It is not necessary to sign your names. Pass these sheets on to your instructor.

Your instructor can then list respondents vertically on the board (No. 1, No. 2, etc.) and the number of "Yes" answers (for each respondent) in each of three columns headed achievement, power, and affiliation. (Student 1, for example, might show 2, 2, and 4 in the respective columns.) Did the test appear to distinguish between students on the basis of their needs? Do you think you could identify people in your class who have high needs to achieve? For power? For affiliation? What does this exercise tell you about the factors that characterize people who are high (or low) on each of these three needs? How do you think this information could help you as a supervisor?

NOTES FOR CHAPTER 3

1. Edward Lawler III and John Grant Rhode, *Information and Control in Organizations* (Pacific Palisades: Goodyear, 1976).

2. See, for example, Joel Leidecker and James Hall, "Motivation: Good Theory-Poor Application," *Training Development Journal* (June 1974), pp. 3–7.

3. This section is based on Douglas McGregor, "The Human Side of Enterprise," *The Management Review* (November 1957), pp. 22–28, 88–92, reprinted in Max Richards and William Nielander, *Readings in Management* (Cincinnati: Southwestern, 1974), pp. 433–41.

4. See, for example, Mahmoud Wahba and Lawrence Bridwell, "Maslow Reconsidered: A Review of Research on the Needs Hierarchy Theory," *Organizational Behavior and Human Performance*, Vol. 15, No. 2 (April 1966), pp. 212–40.

5. Clay Alderfer, *Existence, Relatedness, and Growth: Human Needs in Organizational Settings* (New York: The Free Press, 1972).

6. For some examples of studies in this area see: Mahmoud Wahba and Lawrence Bridwell, "Maslow Reconsidered: A Review of Research on the Needs Hierarchy Theory," *Organizational Behavior and Human Performance*, 15, No. 2 (April 1976), pp. 212–40; Vance Mitchell and Pravin Moudgill, "Measurement of Maslow's Needs Hierarchy," *Organizational Behavior and Human Performance*, 16, No. 2 (August 1976), pp. 334–49; John P. Wanous, "A Cross-Sectional Text of Need Hierarchy Theory," *Organizational Behavior and Human Performance*, 18, No. 1 (February 1977), pp. 78–97.

7. Chester Schriesheim, "Job Satisfaction, Attitudes Toward Unions, and Voting in a Union Representation Election," *Journal of Applied Psychology*, 63, No. 5 (October 1978), pp. 548–52.

8. See, for example, M. Schwartz, E. Jenusaitis, and H. Stork, "A Comparison of the Perception of Job Related Needs in Two Industry Groups," *Personal Psychology* (Summer 1966).

9. See, for example, Frederick Herzberg, "One More Time: How Do You Motivate Employees?" *Harvard Business Review* (January–February 1968).

10. Victor Vroom, *Work and Motivation* (New York: John Wiley & Sons, 1964); a group of psychologists recently found that Vroom seems to be correct. See Ann Harlan, Jeffrey Kerr, and Steven Kerr, "Preference for Motivator and Hygiene Factors in a Hypothetical Situation: Further Findings and Some Implications for Employment," *Personnel Psychology*, 30, No. 4 (Winter 1977).

11. See, for example, M. Scott Myers, "Who Are Your Motivated Workers?" *Harvard Business Review*, 42 (January–February 1969), pp. 73–88.

12. H. H. Soliman, "Motivator-Hygiene Theory of Job Attitudes," *Journal of Applied Psychology*, 54 (1970), pp. 452–56.

13. See, for example, Marvin Dunnette, John Campbell, and Milton Hakel, "Factorial Contributions to Job Satisfaction in Six Occupational Groups," *Organizational Behavior and Human Performance*, 2 (1967), pp. 143–74.

14. Edwin Locke, "Nature and Causes of Job Satisfaction," in Marvin Dunnette's *Handbook of Industrial and Organizational Psychology* (Rand McNally, 1976), p. 1315.

15. For findings that do not support Herzberg's theory see, for example, Locke, "Nature and Causes," p. 1318. For a paper that supports Herzberg's theory, see, for example, Steven Kerr, Ann Harlan, and Ralph Stogdill, "Preference for Motivator and Hygiene Factors in a Hypothetical Interview Situation," *Personnel Psychology*, 27 (1974), pp. 109–124; Harlan et. al. have found that employees do tend to favor motivators when discussing jobs: see Anne Harlan, Jeffrey Kerr, and Steven Kerr, "Preference for Motivator and Hygiene Factors in a Hypothetical Interview Situation: Further Findings and Some Implications for the Employment Interviews," *Personnel Psychology*, Vol. 30, No. 4 (Winter 1977).

16. John Campbell and Robert Pritchard, "Motivation Theory in Industrial and Organizational Psychology," in Dunnette, *Handbook*, pp. 63–130.

17. See John W. Atkinson, "Motivational Determinants of Risk-Taking Behavior," *Psychological Review*, 64 (1957), pp. 359–72.

18. David McClelland, *The Achieving Society* (New York: Van Nostrand Rinehold Co., 1961).

19. Douglas Durand, "Effects of Achievement Motivation and Training on the Entrepreneurial Behavior of Black Businessmen," *Organizational Behavior and Human Performance*, 14 (August 1975), pp. 76–90.

20. Saul Gallerman, *Motivation and Productivity* (New York: American Management Association, 1963), p. 290.

21. Edward Lawler III and John Grant Rhode, *Information and Control in Organizations* (Pacific Palisades: Goodyear, 1976), p. 14.

22. See, for example, J. Stacey and Adams and William Rosenbaum, "The Relationship of Worker Productivity to Cognitive Dissonance About Wage and Equity," *Journal of Applied Psychology*, 46 (1962), 161–64; Laurie Larwood, Michael Kavanagh, and Richard Levine, "Perceptions of Fairness with Three Alternative Economic Exchanges," *Academy of Management Journal*, Vol. 21, No. 1 (March 1978), pp. 69–83; Michael Carrell, "A Longitudinal Field Assessment of Employee Perceptions of Equitable Treatment," *Organizational Behavior and Human Performance*, Vol. 21, No. 1 (February 1978).

23. David Nadler and Edward Lawler III, "Motivation: A Diagnostic Approach," in J. Richard Hackman, Edward Lawler III, and Lyman Porter, *Perspectives on Behavior in Organizations* (New York: McGraw-Hill, 1977), pp. 26–38.

24. Vroom, *Work and Motivation*. For other versions see, for example, G. Graen, "Instrumentalities Theory of Work Motivation: Some Experimental Results and Suggested Modifications," *Journal of Applied Psychology Monograph*, 53 (1969), pp. 1–25; Lyman Porter and Edward Lawler III, *Managerial Attitudes and Performance* (Homewood, Ill.: Dorsey Press, 1968); Campbell and Pritchard, "Motivation Theory," pp. 79–84.

25. David Nadler and Edward Lawler, "Motivation," p. 35.

26. Victor Vroom, "Organizational Choice: A Study of Pre-imposed Decision Processes," *Organization Behavior and Human Performance*, 1 (1966), pp. 212–25.

27. B. S. Georgopoulus, G. M. Mahony, and N. W. Jones, "A Path Goal Approach to Productivity," *Journal of Applied Psychology*, 41 (1957), pp. 345–53; described by Campbell and Pritchard, "Motivation Theory," p. 87.

28. See, for example, John Sheridan, John Slocum, Jr., and Byung Min, "Motivational Determinants of Job Performance," *Journal of Applied Psychology*, 60, No. 1 (February 1975); Robert Pritchard, Phillip de Leo, and Clarence Von Bergen, Jr., "A Field Experimental Test of Expectancy-Valence Incentive Motivation Techniques," *Organization Behavior and Human Performance*, 15, No. 2 (April 1976); William Liddell and Robert Solomon, "A Critical Reanalysis of a Test of Two Postulates Underlying Expectancy Theory," *Academy of Management Journal*, 20, No. 3 (1977), pp. 460–64; Lawrence Peters, "Cognitive Models of Motivation Expectancy Theory and Effort: An Analysis and Empirical Test," *Organization Behavior and Human Performance*, 20 (1977), pp. 129–48. Expectancy theory has also been supported in a cross-cultural study of Japanese workers: see, for example, Tamao Matsui and Toshitake Terai, "A Cross-Cultural Study of the Validity of the Expectancy Theory of Work Motivation," *Journal of Applied Psychology*, 60, No. 2 (April 1975); for some of the debate concerning why expectancy theory may not be valid, see, for example, William Liddell and Robert Solomon, "A Critical Reanalysis of a Test of Two Postulates Underlying Expectancy Theory," *Academy of Management Journal*, Vol. 20, No. 3 (1977), pp. 460–64.

29. See, for example, J. Richard Hackman and Lyman Porter, "Expectancy Theory Prediction of Work Effectiveness, *Organizational Behavior and Human Performance*, 3 (1968), pp. 417–26; D. O. Jorgenson, M. D. Dunnette, and R. D. Pritchard, "Effects of the Manipulation of a Performance Reward Contingency on Behavior in a Simulated Work Setting," *Journal of Applied Psychology*, 57 (1973), pp. 271–80; Frederick Starke and Orlando Behling, "A Test of Two Postulates Underlying Expectancy Theory," *Organizational Behavior and Human Performance*, 19 (1977), pp. 311–24; Liddell and Solomon, "Critical Reanalysis," pp. 460–64.

30. See, for example, Peer Soelberg, "Unprogrammed Decision Making," *Papers and Proceedings*, 26th Annual Meeting, The Academy of Management, December 27–29, 1966, pp. 3–16.

31. Based on Nadler and Lawler, "Motivation, p. 35.

32. Nadler and Lawler, "Motivation," pp. 29, 32.

II: *TASK AND REWARDS AS DETERMINANTS OF PERFORMANCE*

The main purposes of this part of the book are to explain how to use positive reinforcement, and to explain how an employee's task, rewards, and morale affect his or her performance. We will proceed as follows:

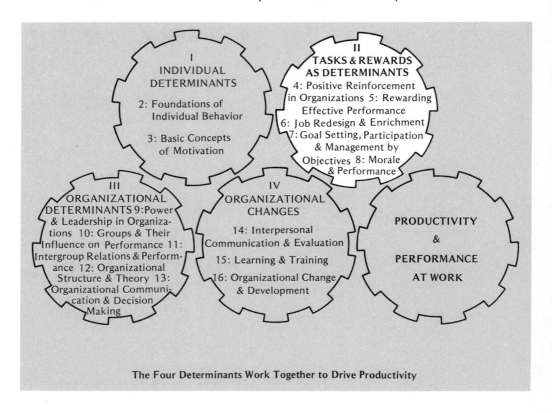

I
INDIVIDUAL DETERMINANTS

2: Foundations of Individual Behavior

3: Basic Concepts of Motivation

II
TASKS & REWARDS AS DETERMINANTS
4: Positive Reinforcement in Organizations 5: Rewarding Effective Performance 6: Job Redesign & Enrichment 7: Goal Setting, Participation & Management by Objectives 8: Morale & Performance

III
ORGANIZATIONAL DETERMINANTS 9: Power & Leadership in Organizations 10: Groups & Their Influence on Performance 11: Intergroup Relations & Performance 12: Organizational Structure & Theory 13: Organizational Communication & Decision Making

IV
ORGANIZATIONAL CHANGES

14: Interpersonal Communication & Evaluation

15: Learning & Training

16: Organizational Change & Development

PRODUCTIVITY & PERFORMANCE AT WORK

The Four Determinants Work Together to Drive Productivity

In Chapter 4, Positive Reinforcement in Organizations, we explain how to use positive reinforcement to improve performance. In this chapter we also discuss the "ABCs" approach in more detail, and briefly introduce the topic of how to set effective goals. In Chapters 5 and 6 we turn to important rewards, and their effects on performance. In Chapter 5, Rewarding Effective Performance, we discuss "extrinsic" rewards like pay and promotion and how these can be used as important positive consequences to improve performance. In Chapter 6, Job Redesign and Enrichment, we turn to *intrinsic* rewards, and how "enriching" a job or task can increase its challenge and thus its intrinsic or "built-in" rewards. In Chapter 7,

Goal Setting, Participation, and Management by Objectives, we return to the topic of goal setting, and we explain how to set clearer, more effective goals, goals that help ensure that employees do in fact know what is expected of them. Finally, in Chapter 8, we turn to another "reward", one whose relation to performance is much harder to pin down than is that of pay, or a challenging job. Here, we discuss Morale and Performance, and we will see that while morale's direct effect on performance may be unclear, it *can* have a major indirect effect, through its influence on attendance and other factors.

An employee's task and rewards both have an important influence on his or her performance. For example, assume the employee's attendance record is very poor, and that you want to analyze the problem using the "ABCs" approach. Ask, for example,

> *Antecedents.* Does the employee know what is expected in terms of "good attendance"? Is the *standard* for good attendance clear? Does he or she think the standard is equitable?

> *Behavior.* Could the person attend more regularly if he or she wanted to? Are there any impediments to better attendance—like the absence of a day care center for employees children?

> *Consequences.* What are the consequences of good attendance? Are people *paid* or *promoted* the same, regardless of their attendance? Is the *job* so challenging that the person wants to come to work? What is the consequence of coming to work—For example, is the person so *dissatisfied* that coming to work actually has negative consequences?

4 *Positive Reinforcement in Organizations*

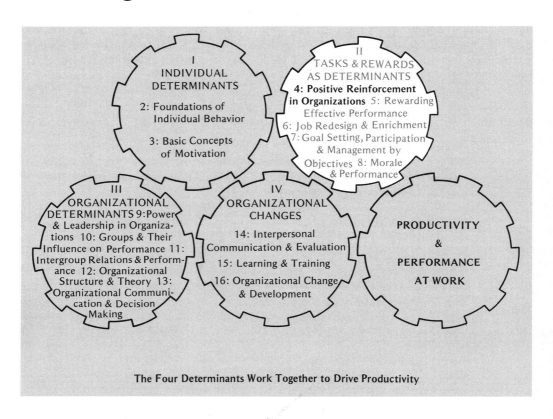

I INDIVIDUAL DETERMINANTS

2: Foundations of Individual Behavior

3: Basic Concepts of Motivation

II TASKS & REWARDS AS DETERMINANTS
4: Positive Reinforcement in Organizations 5: Rewarding Effective Performance
6: Job Redesign & Enrichment
7: Goal Setting, Participation & Management by Objectives 8: Morale & Performance

III ORGANIZATIONAL DETERMINANTS 9: Power & Leadership in Organizations 10: Groups & Their Influence on Performance 11: Intergroup Relations & Performance 12: Organizational Structure & Theory 13: Organizational Communication & Decision Making

IV ORGANIZATIONAL CHANGES

14: Interpersonal Communication & Evaluation

15: Learning & Training

16: Organizational Change & Development

PRODUCTIVITY & PERFORMANCE AT WORK

The Four Determinants Work Together to Drive Productivity

BY THE TIME YOU FINISH STUDYING THIS CHAPTER, YOU SHOULD BE ABLE TO:

1. *Apply positive reinforcement.*
2. *Explain the theory underlying behavior modification including schedules of reinforcement.*
3. *List the questions you would ask in analyzing the "ABCs" of performance.*
4. *Cite the characteristics of useful goals.*
5. *Explain the main steps in analyzing performance problems.*
6. *Describe some actual applications of positive reinforcement.*

OVERVIEW

The main purpose of this chapter is to explain how to modify behavior in organizations through the use of positive reinforcement. We first discuss the theory underlying behavior modification (sometimes called "operant conditioning") and then explain how to implement a positive reinforcement program. Such a program, we will see, involves identifying performance deficiencies and then determining the causes of the deficiencies by analyzing the behavior as well as its antecedents and consequences. The positive reinforcement program then involves eliminating any impediments to behavior and setting clear goals and providing feedback in the form of positive reinforcers like praise and rewards. Finally, we discuss some examples of positive reinforcement programs. As you read this chapter, keep in mind that positive reinforcement *is used to* modify behavior *by giving properly scheduled* rewards. *In organizations, however, the use of positive reinforcement is usually combined with setting clear goals, and with analyzing the employees actual* behavior *to make sure they could do their jobs if they wanted to.*

BEHAVIOR MODIFICATION THEORY

Some Basics

The use of behavior modification (a term that is often used synonymously with *operant conditioning*) is a powerful tool for changing employee behavior. It is based on the work of B. F. Skinner and is built on two principles: (1) that behavior which appears to lead to a positive consequence ("reward") tends to be repeated, while behavior that appears to lead to a negative consequence tends not to be repeated;[1] and (2) therefore, by providing the properly scheduled rewards, it is possible to influence people's behavior.

Operant conditioning is similar in some respects to the *classical conditioning* made famous by Pavlov. Pavlov had carried out experiments on the digestive systems of dogs in the early 1900s. During one of these experiments he noticed that the dog salivated not only when food was placed in its mouth but also when other, associated stimuli were presented. For example, Pavlov found that if he presented a "neutral" stimulus (ringing a bell) every time food was presented to the dog, the dog eventually salivated in response to the bell alone.

In classical conditioning the sequence of events (ringing bell leads to salivation) is *independent* of the subject's behavior. The response is simply a reflex action and the subject (in this case the dog) is "at the mercy" of his environment and past conditioning history.[2]

Operant conditioning is different. Here the consequences (rewards or punishments) are made to occur *as the consequence of the subject's response* (or lack of response). Thus, whether or not rewards (or punishment) are forthcoming is *dependent* on the subject's *voluntary* behavior. His or her behavior is thus said to "operate" on the environment (in such a way as to elicit the reward or punishment); with Pavlov's classical conditioning the subject's behavior is simply "respondent" to the stimuli. Both classical and operant conditioning are basically learning theories. They both explain how learning takes place and habits are formed as a result of repeated reinforcement over time.

Behavior Modification Emphasizes Behavior and Consequences

Behavior modification is distinguished by its emphasis on behavior and consequences. It assumes, first, that behavior is more important than its psychological "causes," so the behaviorist always focuses on specific behaviors rather than on intangibles like "morale," "personality," or "needs." For example, if you tell a behaviorist that one of your salesmen has too aggressive a personality, he or she would probably respond by asking *what specific behavior* led you to believe that this is so. You respond by saying that the salesman calls prospective clients four or five times a day, often bothers them at home, and puts his feet on his desk when a client is in his office. To the behaviorist these specific behaviors (calling clients at home, and so on) are the sorts of things that can and should be changed or "modified," and there is a rather well-developed technology, or approach, that he or she can use to modify these behaviors. In contrast, Freudian psychologists (with their emphasis on the id, ego, and superego), human relations advocates, and psychologists like Maslow might try to deal, instead, with the salesman's *personality*, on the assumption that making him "less aggressive" would result in acceptable behavior. Similarly, if you tell a behaviorist that you want to improve the "morale" of your employees, his or her first response would probably be "tell me what specific behaviors (such as too many absences, or poor quality output) you have observed that lead you to believe you have a morale problem?" The behaviorist would then focus his or her technology on changing those behaviors rather than on "boosting morale."

Related to this, behavior modification is distinguished by its focus on the *consequences* of behavior. For example, suppose that all your new employees are given a two-hour lecture describing the importance of wearing safety goggles in the factory, and yet you notice that after the first day few continue to wear them. Your first reaction might be that the training program was inadequate, and you therefore have your training expert rewrite the program, perhaps adding some vivid examples of the problems caused by not wearing the goggles.

The behaviorist would probably approach this problem differently. After satisfying himself that the employees understand the need for wearing the goggles, he would probably focus on the *consequences* incurred by those who wear them. For example, he or she might find out that employees that wear them are often ridiculed by their coworkers (who call them "sissies") and that, in fact no one who has *not* worn the glasses has been hurt by flying specks in over two years. He further determines that employees who faithfully wear the glasses are never rewarded by getting praised by their supervisors, or with time off, or a better job. Thus, what the behaviorist discovers is that there are actually negative consequences attached to the acceptable behavior, while at the same time there are no immediately apparent positive consequences or rewards. If the employee does wear the glasses he is ridiculed by his friends and not reward by his supervisor; on the other hand, if he does not wear them there are apparently no negative consequences. To the behaviorist, manipulating the negative and positive consequences of behavior by supplying properly scheduled reinforcements (like praise, time off, or a raise) is the cornerstone of behavior modification.

Types of Reinforcement

Let us suppose that you are a manager and that your employees are chronically late for work. You want to use operant conditioning to train them to come in on time. There are four types of reinforcement you could use: positive reinforcement, negative reinforcement, extinction, and punishment.

First, you could focus on reinforcing the *desired* behavior (which in this case is coming to work on time). Here, you could use either positive or negative reinforcement. *Positive* reinforcement would include rewards like praise or raises. *Negative* reinforcement also focuses on reinforcing the *desired* behavior. But instead of providing a positive reward, the "reward" is that the employee avoids some negative consequence. For example, the employee is not harassed or is not reprimanded for coming in late: thus the reward is a "negative" one—employees come in on time to avoid some negative consequence like harassment, a reprimand, or a pay cut.

Alternatively, you might focus (as many managers seem to) on reducing the *un*desired behavior (coming in late) rather than on rewarding the desired behavior. With operant conditioning there are two types of reinforce-

Exhibit 4.1 Types of Reinforcement

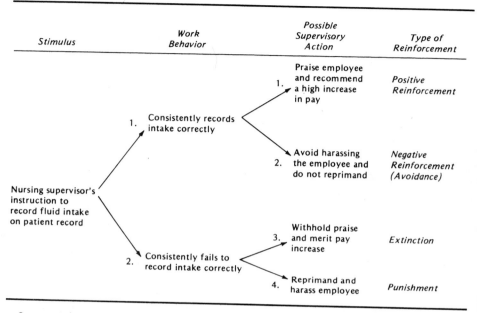

Source: John Ivancevich, Andrew Szilagyi, Jr., and Marc Wallace, Jr., *Organizational Behavior and Performance* (Santa Monica: Goodyear, 1977), p. 84.

ment you can use to reduce *un*desired behavior: extinction and punishment. (These are all summarized in Exhibit 4.1.) People tend to repeat behavior that they've learned leads to positive consequences. With *extinction*, positive reinforcement is withheld so that over time the undesired behavior (coming in late) disappears. For example, suppose your employees learned from experience that lateness seemed to be unrelated to their merit raises—that despite being late, employees still received such raises. Extinction would involve withholding merit raises from chronically late employees to make them unlearn their "bad habits." *Punishment* is a second method of reducing the frequency of undesired behavior. Here, for example, you might reprimand or harass late employees. Punishment is the most controversial method of modifying behavior, and this is one reason why Skinner recommends extinction (rather than punishment) for decreasing the frequency of undesired behaviors.[3]

   Summary. We have discussed four types of reinforcement: positive reinforcement, negative reinforcement (avoidance), extinction, and punishment. Positive and negative reinforcement are conceptually quite different from extinction and punishment since the first two focus on getting employees to learn the *desired* behavior. Extinction and punishment, on the other hand, focus on unlearning the *un*desired behavior and cannot be of much use in teaching persons the correct, desired behavior.

Schedules of Positive Reinforcement[4]

The schedule with which you apply positive reinforcement is as important as the type of reinforcement you decide to use. Basically (as you can see in Exhibit 4.2) there are two basic schedules you could adhere to. First, there is continuous (or "mass") reinforcement. Here (to use our example) you might praise or otherwise reward an employee *each and every time* that person arrives for work on time. Second, you could follow a "partial" reinforcement schedule and provide positive reinforcement only *part* of the time, according to some schedule. If you opt for such a schedule, there are four specific schedules you could follow: fixed interval, variable interval, fixed ratio, and variable ratio.

Exhibit 4.2 Schedules of Reinforcement

Type of Reinforcement:	*Explanation*
I. Continuous (or "mass")	Reward each and every time desired performance occurs
II. Partial	Reward part of the time
1. Fixed interval	According to fixed *time* periods
2. Variable interval	According to variable *time* periods
3. Fixed ratio	After fixed numbers of desired responses
4. Variable ratio	After varying number of responses

Fixed Interval Schedule. A fixed interval schedule is based on time. Here a reinforcer (reward) is administered only when the desired response occurs *and only after the passage of a specified fixed period of time* (since the previous reinforcement). For example, at the end of each week you might go around and praise each employee who came to work on time every day of that week.

Variable Interval Schedules. Variable interval schedules are also based on time. However, reinforcement is administered at some *variable* interval around some average. For example suppose you want to provide reinforcement on the average of once a day for all employees who come to work on time. You could visit them on an *average* of once a day: once on Tuesday, skip Wednesday, three times on Thursday, etc., in such a way that the praise averages out to about once a day.

Fixed Ratio Schedule. A fixed ratio schedule is based on units of *output* rather than on time. With a fixed ratio schedule, rewards are delivered only when a fixed number of desired responses occurs. Most piecework incentive pay plans are on a fixed ratio schedule. The worker is "rewarded" every time he produces a *fixed number* of pieces.

Variable Ratio Schedule. Variable ratio schedules are also based on units of output, but the number of desired outcomes necessary to elicit a reward changes from time to time, around some average. The Las Vegas-type slot machines are probably the best examples of rewards administered according to variable ratio schedules. The number of times you can expect to "hit a jackpot" with such machines *on the average* over the long term is predictable. Yet the jackpots come randomly, on a variable interval schedule. Thus you might get no jackpots for 5 tries and then hit two jackpots in a row; you might go 50 turns without a jackpot and then get one.

Summary. Examples of various schedules of reinforcement are presented below:

Schedules of Reinforcement	Examples of Rewards
Fixed interval	Weekly paycheck
Variable interval	Praising employee once on Monday, twice on Tuesday, skipping Wednesday, etc.
Fixed ratio	Piece-rate pay based on units produced
Variable ratio	Modified piece-rate bonus plan for salesmen, with commission sometimes given after two big sales, sometimes after one big sale, sometimes not at all, etc., averaging out to one bonus per two big sales

Which Ratio Schedule Is Most Effective? Several conclusions can be drawn from research into the effectiveness of different reinforcement schedules:

1. Continuous (or "mass") reinforcement schedules usually result in the *fastest* learning. In other words, the way to get someone to learn quickly is to reinforce desired outcomes continuously, each and

every time they occur. The drawback is that the desired behavior also diminishes very rapidly once you stop reinforcing them.

2. Partial reinforcement schedules (any of the four we discussed) lead to slower learning but stronger retention. In other words "learning is more permanent when you reward correct behavior only part of the time."[5]

3. The two reinforcement schedules based on output (fixed ratio and variable ratio) are both more effective than are those schedules based on time (fixed interval and variable interval).[6]

4. Of the four partial reinforcement schedules we discussed (fixed and variable interval, and fixed and variable ratio) variable ratio reinforcement is the most powerful at *sustaining* behavior.[7]

Criticisms of Behavior Modification

Behavior modification has some powerful detractors who have criticized it on ethical, theoretical, and practical grounds.

Ethical Criticisms. Behavior modification is criticized, first, on moral and ethical grounds. Detractors say that it is inhumane, restricts freedom of choice, and constitutes a threat to the concept of personal autonomy.[8] Critics also say that the idea of rewarding or reinforcing performance is tantamount to bribery[9] and that behavior modification is used to manipulate and mold participants into another person's concept of the ideal person.[10] Similarly, Argyris argues that behavior modification is the antithesis of the kind of healthy learning that should be going on in organizations, learning in which people are taught to grow and to keep "open" the question of what impact they are having on others and how they may modify their impact if they want.[11] One writer claims that behavior modification "insults the intelligence" of most workers.[12] Others argue that behavior modification emphasizes *extrinsic* rewards like pay when in fact people can and should derive most of their satisfactions at work from *intrinsic* rewards like the challenge of their jobs. On the whole, opponents of behavior modification see it as a process that strips employees of their free will and makes them little more than appendages to their machines; proponents, on the other hand, argue that they are not interested in shaping personalities but instead in eliciting specific job performances, and that in any case we are all constantly being manipulated or conditioned in other ways—for example, through religion, education, or politics. Other proponents point out that while behavior modification may not be perfect, the use of positive reinforcement like praise and promotion is still superior to the use of punishment and threats which now prevail in organizations.[13]

Theoretical Criticisms. The basic theory underlying behavior modification has also been criticized. Proponents argue that behavior modification (outside of carefully controlled laboratory experiments) is a vastly over-simplified approach and that it disregards employee's perceptions, beliefs, and expectations.[14] Others argue that the theory is unsound because the emphasis on extrinsic rewards may actually detract from employee intrinsic motivation.[15] (These critics argue that extrinsic and intrinsic rewards are not additive and that, for example, an engineer who derives satisfaction from the intrinsic challenge of his or her work may actually get less, not more, satisfaction when performance is tied to extrinsic rewards like incentive pay.) Locke argues that behavior modification in industry is actually not behavior modification at all—that it "is neither new nor behavioristic."[16] He argues that Skinner's theory assumes that people do not think, but that, instead, their behavior is controlled and molded by its repeated consequences, and that by regulating these consequences one can modify behavior. Locke says that far from assuming this sort of mechanical learning on the part of employees most industrial applications of behavior modification are actually based on the assumption that people do think[17]—about their rewards, the opinions of their peers, and so on.

Practical Criticisms. Others argue that practical applications of behavior modification in industrial settings will always be limited, at best. Argyris points out that successful behavior modification programs so far have been implemented mostly with groups such as younger students in school and patients with varying behavioral disorders, all of whom tend to be more dependent and submissive than the average employee.[18] Another expert argues that behavior modification will never be very useful in work organizations for four reasons: (1) it is too difficult to define and measure the complex behaviors most employees engage in, and therefore rewards cannot be tied directly to them; (2) a worker's behavior can simultaneously produce rewards from one group (like management) and punishment from another (like peers); (3) it is difficult to tie rewards to performance because of necessary time lags (for example, people generally only get paid at most once a week); and (4) the reinforcement that one worker gets influences not only his or her own behavior, but that of others as well.[19]

It is helpful to keep these criticisms in mind when applying behavior modification in organizations. They help illuminate the sorts of problems that can be encountered and they help stress that it is no panacea. On the other hand, behavior modification has apparently been quite successful in many industrial applications, and it provides a relatively concrete approach for analyzing performance problems at work and for modifying employee behavior.

IMPLEMENTING A POSITIVE REINFORCEMENT PROGRAM[20]

In addition to understanding the basics of behavior modification (such as what schedule of reinforcement is best) there are three additional things we need to explain before we are ready to apply "behavior modification in practice." First, most industrial applications of this technique only make use of *positive reinforcement* (and are therefore usually called "positive reinforcement" programs). Punishment, in particular, is generally not used because of ethical considerations. Second, because we always want to direct (or modify) behavior toward some specific standard (like "produce 20% fewer rejects"), *goal setting* is usually an important component of industrial positive reinforcement programs. Finally, since implementing a program like this involves considerable planning, *analyzing the performance problem* and determining where the problem lies becomes crucial. (For example, it would be foolish to try and use positive reinforcement to improve product quality if the problem is not motivation, but inadequate skills.) In the previous section we discussed the basics of reinforcement. Now, in this section we turn to: (1) a more detailed explanation of how to analyze the "ABCs" of performance; (2) basic aspects of goal setting; and, (3) how to analyze performance problems (a process in which finding the cause through the "ABCs" is but one part).

The "ABCs" of Behavior

Management expert Thomas Connelan has developed a simple but effective technique for analyzing performance problems, a technique that is based on what he calls the "ABCs" of performance. He argues that any behavior—such as moving a drill bit, writing a report, or wearing a hard hat—can be analyzed in terms of its *antecedents*, the *behavior* itself, and its *consequences*. For example, suppose you are interested in determining why, even after training, employees still produce a large number of rejected parts. Connellan would argue that to solve this problem we have to focus on *antecedents* (like our instructions to the employees), the *behavior* itself (for example, do the employees really have the skills to do the job right?), and on the *consequences* (for example, are there positive consequences for reducing the number of rejects?).

The *antecedent* is what happens before the behavior, and what stimulates the behavior in the first place. Antecedents include things like directions from the boss, company policies, notices on the bulletin board, and job routing cards, which "cue" the employee to the fact that he or she is to behave in a certain way. For example, if we tell an employee that he is producing too many rejects, that notice is an antecedent. The *behavior* in this case is the overt action the employee engages in on his job, in this case the activities he goes through producing acceptable or unacceptable items. *Consequences* are what happens after the employee behaves in a certain manner on the job, and may include overtime pay, reprimand for excessive scrap, rejection from coworkers, bonuses, and promotion. According to Connelan, determining why so many rejects are being produced involves analyzing the antecedents, behavior, and consequences (rather than searching for psychological causes like low morale, unsatisfied needs, or low motivation).

Specifically, we have to determine where the problem lies (whether in the antecedent, behavior, or consequences) by asking the questions like those listed in Exhibit 4.3. For example, we can determine if the problem lies in the antecedent by asking questions like: "Does the employee know what is expected?" "Are the standards clear?" "Have they been communicated?" and "Are they realistic?" Very often, in other words, performance is not up to par not because employees don't *want* to do a good job, but rather because they haven't been told clearly what a good job is—what their performance standards are. Similarly, we can analyze the *behavior* itself, by asking questions like: "Can the behavior be performed?" "Could the employee do it if he or she wanted to?" and "Does something prevent its occurrence?" Finally, we can analyze the *consequences* of the person's behavior, for example, by asking questions like: "Are the consequences weighted in favor of performance?" and "Are improvements being reinforced?"

With these questions (see Exhibit 4.3) in mind, let us assume you were just appointed training director of your company and that the president has come to you with the following problem. Six of your company's plant foremen recently went through an intensive two-day occupational safety training program, to sensitize them to the need for improved plant safety and to ensure that they more closely monitor and enforce the company's safety rules. For the first few days top management noticed a marked increase in rules enforcement as well as in the early morning safety meetings between the foremen and their workers, but after two weeks safety enforcement had fallen to pretraining levels. The president feels that the training program was inadequate and that a new, improved training program using a "programmed textbook" might be worthwhile.

Before jumping to conclusions, however, you ask him for some time to analyze the problem; by studying the "ABCs" you determine the following:

Antecedent: Does the individual know what is expected? You determine that the answer to this question is "yes." The foremen know that they are supposed to be enforcing

Exhibit 4.3 Performance Analysis Questions

Antecedent

1. Does the employee know what is expected?
   Are the standards clear?
   Have they been communicated?
   Are they realistic?

Behavior

2. Can the behavior be performed?
   Could the employee do it if his or her life depended upon it?
   Does something prevent its occurrence?

Consequence

3. Are the consequences weighted in favor of performance?

4. , Are improvements being reinforced?
   Do we note improvements even though the improvement may still leave the employee
   below company standards?
   Is reinforcement specific?

Source: Thomas K. Connellan, *How to Improve Human Performance: Behaviorism is Business*
(New York: Harper and Row, 1978), p. 51.

the rules. They also know to what extent accidents are to be reduced, and they generally agree that such a reduction is feasible and realistic.

Behavior: Can the behavior be performed? In this case you determine that the behavior is in fact "doable." The foremen know what is expected of them, and from their training program they received a detailed list of specific actions they can and should take in order to reduce accidents at work.

Consequences: Are the consequences positive for performing correctly? Is there good feedback? Are improvements being noticed and reinforced? Here you determine that the answers to most of the questions are "no." The foremen whose departmental safety improved for the first week received no positive recognition from the plant manager. What they did encounter, however, was considerable "static" from their workers, most of whom felt the new safety-related activities were eating into what would otherwise have been their free time. You also discover that, ironically, it is the foremen who do *not* take the time to emphasize safety who are rewarded, since the productivity of their departments remain relatively high while those of the departments that engage in the safety activities encountered a small drop in productivity. In this case, then, it appears that it is the *consequences* of the behavior that have to be modified (although in other situations it might have been the antecedents, the behavior itself, or all three).

As we explained in Chapter One, the "ABCs" of performance can be used to determine the cause of a multitude of behavioral problems. For example, it can help you explain why: an employee's performance is not up to par; a work group is resisting your efforts to institute a new incentive plan; and, attendance in the organization is unsatisfactory.

Four Types of Consequences. In analyzing any situation remember that there are four types of consequences that can be used to modify behavior. First, you can add a *positive consequence for the right behavior* (positive reinforcement), for example by praising an employee for wearing his safety helmet. Second, you can *remove negative consequences for the right behavior* (avoidance), for example, by lowering the temperature in the plant so that employees who wear their hard hats no longer perspire because of them. Third, you can *remove positive consequences for the wrong behavior* (extinction), for example, by no longer allowing employees who do not wear the hard hat to be eligible for incentive raises. Finally, you can add *negative consequences for the wrong behavior* (punishment), for example, by having supervisors chastise employees for not wearing their safety hats. Finally, remember that the *schedule of reinforcement* has an important influence on how quickly the employees learn the desired behavior and on how long and how tenaciously they adhere to the desired behavior.

Setting Goals and Providing Feedback

Introduction. *Goal setting* and *feedback* are integral parts of most industrial applications of behavior modification. Clear goals are important because behavior modification is usually aimed at bringing about a desired change in employee behavior, and this generally means bringing employee behavior up to some specific standard or goal—production of 20 units per hour, four sales reports submitted per week, less than 3 rejected units per day, or zero absences per month, for example. Related to this, feedback is important since it is through feedback in the form of "positive reinforcement" (like praise and rewards) that employees find out how they are doing relative to their standards and what the consequences of their performances are (in terms of, say, praise, and rewards).

Characteristics of Useful Goals. Useful standards or goals have several characteristics:

1. They are always output rather than process oriented. Thus, if the job involves installing door handles, standards should be stated in terms of "handles installed," rather than in terms of "installing handles."

2. Standards are generally set for quantity, quality, timeliness, cost, or some combination of these (such as "sell five new accounts per month").

3. Effective standards are also specific and state specific, attainable levels of performance, rather than generalities like "do your best."

4. Effective standards or goals also *fit the requirements* of the job in that they are standards over which the employee has some control. For example, it would be useless to evaluate assembly line workers in terms of how many units they produce per hour if they are working on a machine-paced assembly line. Similarly, it would generally be a waste of time to evaluate a plant manager in terms of company sales; instead, production-related standards like "reduce production costs by 10 per cent each year" would better fit the requirements of this job.

5. Effective standards are *realistic*, in that while high enough to be challenging, they are not so high as to be unattainable.

6. Finally, goals or standards should be *observable* rather than stated in general terms like "better morale," "improved manager development," or "improved company image." Observable indicators that can be turned into specific, measurable, observable standards or goals include return on investment, units produced per hour, number of program errors, and dollar volume sold.

Setting effective standards or goals and articulating these standards to employees is usually not an easy task, but it is a crucial one. There is often a wide gap between what you want and what your employees *think* you want, and unless they are provided with specific, attainable standards, performance often suffers, not because they do not want to produce up to par, but simply because they do not know what par is.

Feedback and Reinforcement. In behavior modification the terms *feedback* and *reinforcement* are used more or less interchangeably, since it is through reinforcement like praise that an employee gets feedback on how he has performed relative to his goals.

Ideally, any feedback should be tied specifically to the *goal* ("you were under by two units"), be as *immediate* as possible, be *self-administered*, and be *positive*, not negative. For example, let us suppose you want to increase sales by instituting an improved incentive plan. You might start by giving

each salesman a specific, attainable sales quota as well as a book in which
to report, immediately following each sale, the amount of his or her monetary commission.[21] As sales manager you tell each salesman that the record
book will be examined first on a continuous (perhaps daily) basis and later
intermittently. The reinforcement that your examination provides will cause
each salesman to make entries immediately after each sale, rather than at
a later date. And recording the commission in the book will directly reinforce each sale as it is made (provide self-administered feedback), and each
sale will in turn serve as a stimulus for each subsequent selling situation.
In theory (and probably in practice) the salesman's recognition that sales
are increasing will motivate him or her to continue making entries and will
become a self-generating reward.

In Summary: How to Analyze Performance Problems

The main steps in analyzing performance problems and modifying behavior
may be summarized as follows. First, identify a performance improvement
area (such as quality control, sales, or inventory control), and then specify
the desired performance levels in this area. (Desired performance levels might
be specified in terms of scrap rates per year, sales volume per month, or inventory as a percent of sales, for example.) Next, determine the *present performance* for the areas you chose in step one. Here, experts have found that
it is usually not advisable to depend solely on historical reports (concerning
scrap rates, for example) but instead to dig deeper, perhaps by looking for
unrecorded scrap, or untagged inventory. In other words, employees sometimes intentionally or unintentionally underestimate or pad their reports, and,
because of this, their reports should be supplemented by your own direct
"hands on" observations of current performance levels.

Step three is to analyze the causes of the performance deficiency by
analyzing the *behavior* as well as its *antecedents* and *consequences*. We check
the antecedents, for example, by asking, "Does the employee know what is
expected?" as well as the other questions listed in Exhibit 4.3. We analyze
the behavior itself by asking, "Can the behavior be performed?" Here, for
example, we are interested in determining if the employee can do the job if
he or she wanted to, or if, instead the person is hampered by something that
is out of his or her control. (For example, perhaps the person has had inadequate training or does not receive timely shipments of raw materials.)
Finally, analyze the consequences of behavior. Here, for example we ask:
"Are the consequences positive for performing correctly?" "Are they negative
for performing correctly?" "Are they positive for performing incorrectly?"
"Are they negative for performing incorrectly?" "Is there good feedback?"
and "Are improvements being noticed and reinforced?"

The next step is to develop a plan to change the behavior and to implement this plan as a pilot project in one area. The plan may involve changing the antecedents to behavior (perhaps by setting more specific, concrete goals), removing roadblocks to effective performance (perhaps by providing training), or changing the consequences of behavior (for example by providing feedback in the form of properly scheduled positive reinforcement for effective behavior).

Finally, once the pilot project has been declared successful, the program can be implemented in all defective areas. The behavior change and performance improvement is then monitored and measured and the program is continued, or modified, as needed.[22]

APPLICATIONS: POSITIVE REINFORCEMENT PROGRAMS IN PRACTICE

Introduction

While positive reinforcement may still be a controversial technique in many circles, there is no doubt that it is being used successfully to improve employee performance in actual work situations. At 3-M Company, for example, "a conservative estimate of our cost savings in 1977 alone is $3.5 million, and that is not including employee morale which is difficult to quantify."[23] At Emory Airfreight savings reportedly amount to over $2 million per year.[24] Many other examples could be cited, and to round out our discussion of positive reinforcement it would be useful to describe some actual applications of this technique.

Modifying behavior through positive reinforcement can be used to improve performance in a wide array of areas.[25] For example, programmed instruction techniques that are based on providing immediate, positive feedback have long been used successfully in work organizations for the purpose of training employees.[26] Positive reinforcement has also proved successful in training the hard core unemployed.[27] Other successful applications include quality control,[28] coping with executive drug and alcohol problems at work,[29] controlling absenteeism,[30] and cost savings.[31] Some examples of these applications follow.

Programmed Instruction Techniques

Programmed instruction is one of the oldest and most widespread examples of the use of positive reinforcement in work organizations. Whether the programmed instruction device is a book, machine, or manual, programmed learning always consists of three functions:

1. Presenting questions, facts, or problems to the learner
2. Allowing the person to respond
3. Providing feedback on the accuracy of his or her answers

Thus, the person receives immediate feedback regarding the correctness of responses, and, if correct, the person can continue to the next question; incorrect responses require a rerouting to an earlier step so that the material can be relearned. Programmed instruction has a multitude of applications including, for example:

Computer programming
Statistics
Sales procedures
Office procedures
Industrial safety
Bank teller operations
Blueprint reading[32]

and many organizations are using programmed instruction to some extent. For example it is being used in:

IBM—to train computer programmers
Maytag—to teach electronics
Zenith Corp—to teach features of their color TV to wholesale representatives and to teach electronics to quality control personnel
Humble Oil—to teach service station attendants basic job skills

Positive Reinforcement at Emory Airfreight

Probably the best known application of behavior modification in industry was implemented at Emory Airfreight Company under the direction of Edward Feeney, a company executive. His basic approach was to design methods that (1) let employees know how well they were meeting specific goals and then (2) rewarded improvement with praise and recognition.

Feeney looked into dozens of airfreight operations and found wide discrepancies between (1) what *should* be done (and what employees *thought* they were doing) and (2) what *actually* was being done. For example, in the airfreight business small shipments intended for the same destination fly at lower rates when shipped together in containers (rather than separately).[33] Thus, by encouraging employees to increase their use of containers, management knew it could get better prices from the airlines and thereby incur substantial cost savings.

A "performance audit" aimed at determining how often such containers were actually used showed that workers only used them about 45 percent of the time, although they *thought* they were using them about 90 percent of the time. Management felt that actual usage could be boosted to 90 to 95 percent. A reinforcement program was established complete with elaborate instruction workbooks for managers, detailing how to give recognition, rewards, and feedback. These workbooks went so far as to enumerate no less than 150 kinds of rewards ranging from a smile to detailed praise like "you're running consistently at 98 percent of standard, and after watching you I can understand why." A basic element in Feeney's approach was to make it clear to the employees what their standards were and to tell them how close they were coming to meeting those standards.

In addition to the employees' getting positive reinforcement from their supervisors, Feeney and his team built additional feedback mechanisms into the workers' jobs. For example, Feeney set up a checklist for a dock worker to mark each time he used a container. Then, at the end of each shift a worker totalled his own result, and he and his supervisor could see immediately how close he had come to the 90 percent goal. Only *positive* reinforce- from the supervisor was stressed, however. For example, if the worker had not met the goal, he wasn't criticized: instead, he was reinforced for keeping an honest record of his use of containers.

The results of this "container usage" program were impressive. In 80 percent of the offices where it was tried, container usage rose from 45 percent to 95 percent in a single day. Savings just from container usage amount to over $500,000 a year, and Feeney has also successfully implemented positive reinforcement programs in the company's sales and operation areas.

Setting up a positive reinforcement program at Emory usually involves a four-step process.[34] The first stage involves the *performance audit*. Here a specific performance improvement area is chosen, and actual performance is compared with desired performance. In the second stage, specific, concrete goals are set for each worker. Here, as is often the case, Emory found that it was helpful to get supervisors and workers involved in the goal-setting process since this kind of participation not only enhanced acceptance of the goals but also stimulated the employees to generate their own goals and ways of attacking the performance deficiencies. (In other words, "participation" or a form of "management by objectives" is often used in conjunction with the overall positive reinforcement program.) In the third stage some form of "self-feedback" is developed to enable the worker to monitor his or her performance. This may be a checklist showing the number of containers used, or a graph showing the number of items rejected per hour, for example. In any case, "this process of self-feedback maintains a continuous schedule of reinforcement for the worker and helps him obtain intrinsic reinforcement from the task itself."[35] Finally, it is the fourth stage of the behavior modification program—providing positive reinforcement—that is the distinguishing characteristic of most such programs and the one that separates them from most other motivation plans. At Emory, for example, the supervisor reviews the worker's self-feedback report (concerning container usage, for example) and praises the positive aspects of the person's performance.

Sales Improvement in the Bell System

Positive reinforcement has also been used to improve sales in a unit of the Bell System.[36] In January 1974 this operating unit ranked 16th out of 20 in terms of "total items sold as a percentage of opportunities to sell," an important indicator of sales in the Bell System. Specifically, whereas many of the other Bell System Companies were maintaining a sales average of more than 100 percent, representatives in this company had a sales average of about 80 percent. The manager of this division brought in a consultant, and together they developed a behavior modification program that relied on goal setting, feedback, and reinforcement.

The overall program contained several elements. First, key managers and supervisors attended skill-building workshops that focused on goal setting, feedback, and techniques of positive reinforcement. Next, goal setting (especially for the service representative salespersons) was improved several ways. For these employees goals had previously been set haphazardly, for a period of six months to a year. With the new system, the goal setting cycle ranged from one day to one month. In this way, the representatives had specific targets for, say, a day, a week, or a month. At the same time, the feedback cycle was shortened. Representatives previously got feedback on a monthly basis when computer printouts were made available. As part of the new program, most offices shortened the feedback cycle so that employees got feedback on their performance on a daily or weekly basis. This shorter cycle was especially important for the salespersons who were least effective. For these people to improve their "batting average" from, say, 60 percent to 100 percent (as they might have had to if they had only monthly, or semiannual goals) would have seemed an insurmountable task, but with daily or weekly goals and frequent feedback the employee's behavior could be "shaped" by having them shoot for daily goals of 65 percent, then 67 percent, and so on.

Finally, the use of shorter term goals and more immediate feedback was combined with an increased use of positive reinforcement. Employees who were already performing well were reinforced with praise and recognition on an intermittent basis, and their performance subsequently improved. The results were especially striking with the "low performance" personnel, however. With these people, whether their actual performance improved, decreased, or exactly met their daily or weekly targets the supervisor always looked for (and usually found) something to reinforce. For example, if a person did not attain his or her goal, but still showed an improvement over the previous day, the supervisor might have said, "Mary, I see you have gone from 60 to 67 percent. Not only is that improvement, but even greater than the improvement of 65 percent yesterday. What do you think we ought to shoot for tomorrow?"[37] Occasionally, an employee maintained or did not match his or her previous performance level. Here the feedback cycle was sometimes shortened to even less than a day so that improvements from, for example, 60 percent to 61 percent could be obtained and reinforced.

Controlling Absenteeism in an Electronics Firm

Positive reinforcement has been used effectively to control employee absenteeism.[38] An electronics manufacturer found that it had an acute absenteeism problem and that tardiness was a problem as well. Management concluded that a program should be initiated to reward the desired behavior (prompt and regular attendance) and a program was initiated. Under this program the employees could qualify for a monthly drawing of a prize only if they had perfect attendance and punctuality records for the period. This eligibility for the monthly drawing was contingent upon the desired behavior—good attendance. All absences of any kind precluded employee eligibility; the program was described in a company bulletin. A drawing was held on the last work day of each month in which a winner was selected *at random* from a basket containing the names of all employees who had maintained perfect attendance and punctuality records for that month. A $10 cash prize was awarded to the winner of each monthly lottery. In addition, the names of all employees who qualified were listed on the plant bulletin board. (Note that this was an example of variable ratio scheduling since the "jackpot"—the $10 prize—was awarded by randomly drawing names out of a basket.) The results of this program were fairly impressive: the average monthly savings amounted to about $282. The total yearly savings was over $3,000.

Summary: Behavior Modification Applications

Research on the effectiveness of reinforcement in organizational settings has been very limited, but several conclusions seemed warranted. First, it *can* be effective, and positive reinforcement in particular has been used successfully for years (for example, as part of the programmed learning devices often used for training). Second, it is important that your employee clearly understand that rewards are contingent on good performance: therefore, emphasizing the relationship between performance and rewards is always imperative. Third, it is clear that when people are continually *not* rewarded for good performance, decreased motivation and performance (extinction) may result. Fourth, if you must "punish" an employee for doing something wrong, at least take the opportunity to carefully explain what was done wrong, what the desired results were, and how positive rewards will result from those desired outcomes. Fifth, keep in mind that effective goal setting is usually used in conjunction with positive reinforcement to modify behavior.

Finally, remember that variable ratio schedules of reinforcement are the most powerful for sustaining motivated behavior. While the schedule may not be practical for salary (since people expect to be paid regularly), it can certainly be used for praise, and, very often, for the financial incentives we discuss in the following chapter.

CHAPTER SUMMARY

1.   Behavior modification is based on two principles: (1) behavior which appears to lead to a positive consequence (a "reward") tends to be repeated, while behavior that appears to lead to a negative consequence tends not to be repeated; (this is also known as the "Law of Effect") and (2) therefore, by providing the properly scheduled rewards, it is possible to influence people's behavior.

2.   We discussed four types of reinforcement. Positive reinforcement includes rewards like praise. Negative reinforcement involves allowing the employee to avoid some negative consequences: both these types of reinforcement focus on reinforcing the desired behavior. You might also focus on reducing the *un*desired behavior. Here you could use extinction (by withholding all rewards) or punishment. In this book we will focus primarily on positive reinforcement.

3.   There are basically two schedules of positive reinforcement you can use: continuous or partial. With the former you reward an employee immediately, *each and every time* that person performs the desired behavior. With the latter you provide reinforcement immediately, *but only part of the time*, following one of four specific schedules: fixed interval, variable interval, fixed ratio, and variable ratio. Variable ratio is the most effective at sustaining the desired behavior, although continuous reinforcement results in the quickest learning.

4.   In organizations, modifying behavior by means of a positive reinforcement program involves: identifying a performance improvement area (like quality control) and specifying the desired performance level (goal) in that area; determining the present performance in the area; analyzing the causes of the performance deficiency by analyzing the antecedents, behavior, and consequences; and then developing a plan to change behavior (perhaps by setting clearer goals, providing training, or changing the consequences of behavior by providing feedback in the form of praise and rewards). We recommended testing the program in one pilot area, and then implementing it in all defective areas. Note that the positive re-

inforcement program involves more than just providing properly scheduled rewards (or "consequences"); in addition, you have to ensure that there are no impediments to effective *behavior*, that the *antecedents* of behavior (in terms of goals, standards, policies, and so forth) are clear, and that the employee knows what is expected of him or her.

5. Characteristics of useful goals include: they are output rather than process oriented; they are set for quantity, quality, timeliness, or cost (or some combination of these); they are specific; they fit the requirements of the job; they are realistic; and they are observable.

6. We discussed several applications of positive reinforcement programs including: programmed instruction techniques; and positive reinforcement at Emory Airfreight, the Bell System, and in an electronics firm.

7. In the remainder of this part of the book we will proceed as follows. In the next two chapters—Rewarding Effective Performance, and Job Redesign—we focus primarily on important *consequences* of behavior, such as pay, promotion, and challenging jobs. Then, in Chapter 7 (Goal Setting) we return to the topic of goal setting, and to an explanation of how to ensure that employees do, in fact, know what is expected of them. Finally, in Chapter 8 (Morale and Performance), we turn to another important consequence of behavior—a more satisfying job—and here we explain how improving morale can improve an organization's "bottom line."

DISCUSSION QUESTIONS AND PROJECTS

1. Discuss what is meant by "schedules of positive reinforcement." Give some examples of different types of schedules.

2. Develop at least two examples of how you would use positive reinforcement. Your answer could include relationships with family, teachers, other students, subordinates at work, etc.

3. Compare "operant conditioning" with "classical conditioning."

4. Discuss the criticisms of behavior modification.

5. The dean of the business school has a problem: the faculty members are negligent about posting office hours and do not want to counsel students. List the specific questions you would ask in analyzing the "ABCs" of performance in this case. (The class might break up into groups of four or five students to work out this project.)

6. In what way are goal setting and feedback integral parts of most industrial applications of behavior modification?

7. What are the characteristics of useful goals? Give an example of a situation in which you were given exceptionally useful (or unuseful) goals—by a boss, or an instructor, for example.

8. Discuss how you would go about analyzing performance problems if you were called into an organization as a consultant.

9. As a project, find an example of an organization that is now using behavior modification and write up an explanation of how it is doing so.

CASE EXERCISE

Feed Them Peanuts

Don Franklin, President of Flagler Electronics Corporation, knew that something was radically wrong in his company's engineering department, but he couldn't figure out exactly what the problem was, or what he should do about it. All he knew for sure was that for the past six months the attendance of the engineers that comprised this department was 40 percent worse than average (they were all calling in sick) and their former willingness to "pitch-in" and work overtime on rush jobs had completely evaporated. In fact, when he told them last month that Flagler had a chance to get a large new customer if they'd all pitch in over the weekend to develop a sales proposal, their response shocked him. Based on past experience he had expected them to go along with his request rather willingly and just arrange to take off a few days at a later date. In this case, however, those that were willing to work at all (only 3 out of 10 were willing) demanded to be paid time and a half for Saturday and double time for Sunday and, in addition, to be given an extra paid vacation the following Friday. Don wasn't happy with these conditions, but he knew that Flagler would lose an important new customer if he refused, so he went along with the engineers' requests.

About a month later he was trying to figure out what was going sour in this formerly committed and enthusiastic department.

As near as he could figure out, the only significant change in the department had been his appointment of a new engineering director, Mark Lawrence . Mark had been an engineer in the department for five years and was generally acknowledged to be a highly motivated (some said driven) person, and one whose educational and practical experience had been outstanding. He replaced Lou Waters, who was stepping down as director. Don felt that Lou had been too much of "laissez-faire" leader. In other words, he tended to take a "hands-off" attitude towards the engineers in the department and to let them do their jobs pretty much as they pleased, as long as they got their jobs done. The engineers viewed him as supportive, in that he was always willing to "go to bat for them" with Don and the people in the other departments; however, the engineers did feel that he had a tendency for "sweeping problems under the rug" instead of confronting them. His aim seemed to be to keep all the engineers happy, and though he did not come across as a strong, decisive leader, he was successful in maintaining the morale of the engineers. As one of the engineers put it when Lou stepped down, "Lou made this place a good one in which to work. He always made me feel important, there was never any tension, and everything went fairly smoothly. Sure, we had our problems, but what department doesn't?"

Mark, on the other hand, turned out to be a very different type of manager. Don had been looking for a more energetic, "take-charge" kind of leader, and in this he was not disappointed. Mark jumped into his new assignment with tremendous energy and seemed to be everywhere at once. He would rise at 4:00 A.M., get to work at 6:00 A.M. and spend an hour setting specific assignments for the engineers in the department. By the time they began straggling in at 9:00 or 9:30 A.M., he had already gotten "a whole day's work done" as he put it, and he would then spend the rest of the day speeding from place to place, constantly checking on each engineer's progress, holding meetings with Don and the other managers, working out in the community talking with customers, and recruiting at the university for new engineers, for example. He made it clear to the engineers that he thought Lou Waters had been too much of a "softy" and that henceforth all engineers were expected to be in their offices from 9 to 5 and to take no more than a half hour for lunch. He also moved quickly to consolidate his power and obtained an agreement from Don that no engineers were to discuss substantive matters with him without Mark's approval. Mark thereby maneuvered himself into a position whereby he was clearly the one who controlled the department's resources, as well as the engineers' raises and promotions. At the same time, Mark began using a "carrot and stick" approach to motivating the engineers: by word and deed he made it clear to the engineers that those who did what they were told would get large raises, while those who did not would receive no raises at all. Similarly, Mark tied other rewards and punishments directly to performance: engineers who performed well (in Mark's eyes) were rewarded, while those who did not or who disagreed with Mark were punished or, at least, not rewarded.

While none of the engineers had quit yet (there was an oversupply of engineers in the area), it was still clear to Don that the department was having its problems. In addition to the problems mentioned above, the company physician reported that many of the engineers were complaining of stress-related ills like "knotted stomachs." Another of Don's managers mentioned to him over coffee one day that "the grapevine" had it that Mark was a highly ambitious individual.

Don didn't know what to do. He had been maneuvered into the position of promising not to discuss substantive matters with the engineers themselves, without Mark's permission. On the other hand, he felt that if he did not get to the bottom of the matter immediately, he might find himself without a viable engineering department. He suspected that Mark might be part of the problem, but on the other hand, he couldn't see how Mark's energy and enthusiasm and his habit of clearly linking rewards and punishments to performance could be dysfunctional. (In fact, he had just read an article in the *Harvard Business Review* explaining why rewards *should* be tied directly to performance.) Last week he had asked Mark if he really thought his "carrot and stick" approach was the best way to proceed, and Mark had replied, "Well, you know how those psychologists motivate monkeys, don't you? They feed them peanuts."

Questions

1. How would you go about defining and analyzing the problem at Flagler Electronic?

2. Do you think that tying "extrinsic" rewards like pay and promotion to performance was a good idea in this case? Why? Why not?

3. What effect (if any) do you think Mark's actions had on the degree to which the engineers' higher level needs were satisfied?

4. To what extent (if at all) was Mark applying the principles of operant conditioning that we discussed in the beginning of this chapter? What, if anything, does the experience in the engineering department tell you about the use of "operant" conditioning in industry? What are some of its potential pitfalls? What can be done to avoid these problems?

5. If you were advising Don Franklin, what would you tell him to do at this point?

EXPERIENTIAL EXERCISE

Purpose: The purpose of this exercise is to give you an opportunity to apply reinforcement to an actual problem.

Required Understanding: You should be thoroughly familiar with our discussion of reinforcement.

How to Set Up the Exercise: Break the class into groups of four or five students. All students should read the following statement:

You are the instructor in this class and, having just attended a seminar on "operant conditioning," you think you'd like to try applying this method in class.

Instructions

1. Each group should develop at least two good examples of how they could use "operant conditioning" as instructors in this class. Make sure to indicate the type of reinforcement, and the schedules.

2. If time permits, a spokesman from each group should provide the class with a synopsis of his or her group's recommendations. Which recommendations seem most likely to get results? What drawbacks do you see to these recommendations? Do you think using "operant conditioning" would result in a "dehumanizing" experience for students? Can you think of any instructors who seem to use "operant conditioning" in the classroom?

NOTES FOR CHAPTER 4

1. W. Clay Hamner, "Reinforcement Theory and Management in Organizational Settings," in Henry Tosi and W. Clay Hamner, *Organizational Behavior and Management: A Contingency Approach* (Chicago: St. Claire, 1974), pp. 86–112. This principle is also known as the *law of effect.*

2. Hamner, *Organizational Behavior*, p. 89.

3. Hamner, *Organizational Behavior*, p. 95.

4. Hamner, *Organizational Behavior*, pp. 99–103.

5. Hamner, *Organizational Behavior*, p. 100.

6. Gary Latham and Gary Yukl, "Assigned Versus Participative Goal Setting with Educated and Uneducated Woodsworkers," *Journal of Applied Psychology*, Vol 60, (1975), pp. 299–302; also "The Effectiveness of Performance Incentives under Continuous and Variable Ratio Schedules of Reinforcement," *Personnel Psychology*, Vol. 20 (Summer 1976), pp. 233–242. Robert Pritchard, Dale Leonard, Clarence Von Bergen, Jr., and Raymond Kirk, "The Effects of Varying Schedules of Reinforcement on Human Task Performance," *Organizational Behavior and Human Performance*, Vol. 16, No. 2 (August 1976), pp. 205–230.

7. Joblonski and DeVaines, Quoted in "Operant Conditioning Principles Extended to the Theory of Management" in Hamner, "Reinforcement Theory," p. 100.

8. For a review of some of these criticisms, see Harold Babb and Daniel Kopp, "Applications of Behavior Modification and Organizations: A Review and Critique," *Academy of Management Review* (April 1978), p. 287.

9. H. Waird, "Why Manage Behavior? A Case for Positive Reinforcement," *Human Resource Management*, 11, No. 2 (1976), pp. 15–20.

10. Fred Luthans and Donald White, Jr., "Behavior Modification: Application to Manpower Management," *Personnel Administration*, 34, No. 4 (1971), pp. 41–47..

11. Chris Argyris, "Beyond Freedom and Dignity, by B. F. Skinner: A Review Essay," *Harvard Educational Review*, 41, No. 3 (1971), pp. 550–67.

12. Fred Fry, "Operant Conditioning in Organizational Settings: of Mice or Men?" *Personnel* (July–August 1974), pp. 17–24.

13. For a review of this see Craig Schneier, "Behavior Modification in Management: Review and Critique," *Academy of Management Journal* (September 1974), p. 542.

14. See William Mikulas, *Behavior Modification: An Overview* (New York: Harper & Row 1972).

15. See, for example, W. Clay Hamner and L. W. Foster, "Are Intrinsic and Extrinsic Rewards Additive: A Test of Deci's Cognitive Evaluation Theory of Task Motivation," *Organizational Behavior and Human Performance*, 14 (December 1975).

16. Edwin Locke, "The Myths of Behavior Modification in Organization," *Academy of Management Review* (October 1977), p. 550.

17. See also, Jerry Gray, "The Myths of the Myths about Behavior Modifications in Organization: A Reply to Locke's Criticism of Behavior Modification," *Academy of Management Review* (January 1979), pp. 121–31.

18. See Argyris, "Beyond Freedom."

19. W. F. Whyte, "Skinnerian Theory and Organization," *Psychology Today*, 5, No. 11 (1972).

20. This section is based largely on Thomas Connellan, *How to Improve Human Performance: Behaviorism in Business and Industry* (New York: Harper & Row, 1978), pp. 48–75.

21. This example is from Luthans and White, "Behavior Modification," pp. 41–47, reprinted in J. Richard Hackman, Edward Lawler III, and Lyman Porter, *Perspectives on Behavior and Organization* (New York: McGraw-Hill, 1977), pp. 307–14.

22. For a discussion of performance analysis, see Connellan, Human Performance, pp. 51–57; Thomas Rotundi, Jr., "Behavior Modification on the Job," *Supervisory Management* (February 1976), pp. 23–28; Robert Laxer, "Behavior Modification as a Managerial Technique," *The Conference Board Record* (January 1975), pp. 22–25.

23. "Productivity Gains from a Pat on the Back," *Business Week*, January 23, 1978, p. 56.

24. "Gains," p. 56.

25. See R. T. Ulrich, T. Tachnik, and J. Mowbry, eds., *Control of Human Behavior,* Vol. 1 and 2 (Glencoe: Scott Foresman, 1970); Schneier, "Behavior Modification."

26. See, for example, C. R. Rummler, et. al., eds., *Managing the Instructional Programming Effort* (Ann Arbor: University of Michigan, 1967).

27. J. D. Hodgson and M. H. Brenner, "Successful Experience: Training the Hard Core Unemployed," *Harvard Business Review,* 46, No. 5 (1968), pp. 148–56; R. D. O'Connor and J. Rappaport, "Application of Social Learning Principle to the Training of Ghetto Blacks," *American Psychologist,* 25, No. 7 (1970), pp. 659–61.

28. E. E. Adam and W. E. Scott, "The Application of Behavioral Conditioning to the Problems of Quality Control," *Academy of Management Journal,* 14, No. 2 (1971), pp. 175–93; T. E. Nathan and W. H. Wallace, "An Operant Behavioral Measure of TV Commercial Effectiveness," *Journal of Advertising Research,* ·5, No. 4 (1965), pp. 13–20.

29. D. M. Bretower, *Behavioral Analysis in Business and Industry: A Total Performance System* (Kalamazoo, Mich.: Behavior data, 1972).

30. Jerry Wallin and Ronald Johnson, "The Positive Reinforcement Approach to Controlling Employee Absenteeism, *Personnel Journal* (August 1976), pp. 390–92.

31. See, for example, "At Emory Airfreight: Positive Reinforcement Boosts," *Organizational Dynamics* (Winter 1973).

32. Babb and Kopp, "Applications of Behavior Modification."

33. "At Emory Airfreight: Positive Reinforcement Boosts."

34. This is based on W. Clay Hamner and Ellen P. Hamner, "Behavior Modification on the Bottom Line," *Organizational Dynamics* (Spring 1976).

35. Hamner and Hamner, "Behavior Modification," reprinted in W. Clay Hamner and Frank Schmidt, *Contemporary Problems in Personnel* (Chicago: St. Claire, 1977), pp. 284–98.

36. This is based on Connellan *How to Improve Human Performance,* pp. 170–74.

37. Connellan, *How to Improve Human Performance,* p. 172.

38. Wallin and Johnson, "The Positive Reinforcement Approach."

39. John Ivancevich, Andrew Szilagyi, and Marc Wallace, *Organizational Behavior and Pérformance* (Santa Monica, Calif.: Goodyear, 1977), p. 124.

5

Rewarding Effective Performance

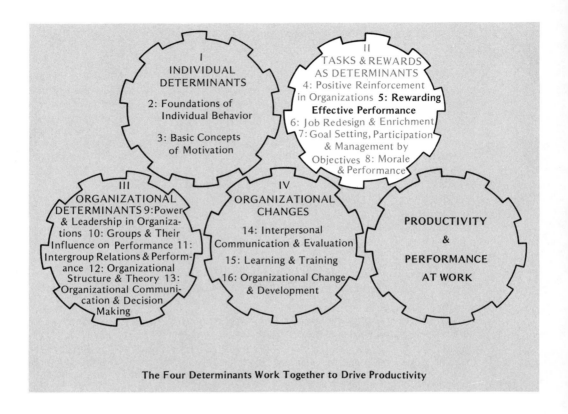

The Four Determinants Work Together to Drive Productivity

*BY THE TIME YOU FINISH STUDYING THIS CHAPTER,
YOU SHOULD BE ABLE TO:*

1. *Explain how pay based on time (like salary) can be used to improve performance.*
2. *Describe several types of financial incentive plans.*
3. *Compare and contrast incentive pay and positive reinforcement.*
4. *Explain why incentive plans fail.*
5. *Explain how to make promotions a more useful reward.*
6. *Compare and contrast four-day workweeks and flexitime.*
7. *Answer the question: Do extrinsic rewards detract from intrinsic ones?*

OVERVIEW

The main purpose of this chapter is to explain how three important "extrinsic" rewards—pay, promotion, and benefits—influence performance in organizations. These are rewards that organizations distribute to their members, and they can be contrasted with "intrinsic" rewards that employees "give themselves," (rewards like the sense of achievement that comes from accomplishing a difficult task). We first discuss the relationship between pay and performance, including the bases for determining pay, and the differences between (1) pay based on time and (2) performance-based (incentive) pay. We next explain how promotions—another important extrinsic reward—can be more closely tied to performance, and, finally, discuss financially based benefits and nonfinancial ones (like flexible working hours). A main point we stress in this chapter is that to motivate performance the rewards have to be linked as closely as possible to performance—rewards must be seen as a consequence *of performance.*

INTRODUCTION: THE IMPORTANCE OF EXTRINSIC REWARDS

Organizations distribute many kinds of rewards to their members. These range from obvious, tangible, extrinsic rewards like pay, promotion, and benefits to intrinsic, intangible rewards like opportunities for achievement, challenge, and self-actualization. In this chapter we will focus primarily on extrinsic rewards including pay, promotion, and benefits. Then, in the next chapter we will focus on motivation plans like job enrichment that are aimed primarily at eliciting productivity through the use of intrinsic rewards.

Extrinsic rewards such as pay and promotion are among the most obvious and important consequences of behavior, and, as a result, their relationship to human behavior at work is undeniable. Ironically, however, complete discussions of this topic have begun to appear in behavior-at-work textbooks only recently, because of the emphasis (or overemphasis) theorists placed on intrinsic rewards during the immediate past. Turn-of-the-century scientific managers viewed motivation and productivity as largely a result of extrinsic factors, and their prescriptions emphasized improved working conditions and financial incentive plans as the primary modes of productivity improvement. Beginning with the Hawthorne theorists, however, there began, as discussed in Chapter 1, a gradual de-emphasis of the importance of extrinsic rewards. Instead, these theorists, and the behavioral scientists that followed them, laid the primary blame for low productivity on factors like low morale, lack of leader supportiveness, and highly specialized, unchallenging jobs. Some, like Herzberg went so far as to say that extrinsic rewards like money were not even motivators, but instead only served to ensure that employees did not grow dissatisfied.

Today, for many reasons, theorists are again beginning to recognize the importance of extrinsic rewards. First, from a practical point of view, it is becoming obvious to managers and researchers alike that extrinsic rewards are among the most important, obvious, and flexible consequences of behavior and that, as a result, they play a powerful role as positive reinforcers. Relatedly, as discussed in Chapter 1, America today is facing a crisis in productivity, with productivity increases lagging well behind those of the other major industrialized nations. Some experts also believe that the values of American workers are changing and that they are no longer driven as much by the desire for craftsman-like jobs. Finally, as pointed out in the last chapter, modifying behavior directly by modifying its *consequences* (like pay, and promotion) is often a much more manageable, and possibly more effective, way to attack performance problems than is attacking them indirectly through psychological causes like needs and morale. As McClelland has somewhat sarcastically pointed out, "Psychologists long ago proved to their own satisfaction that money doesn't motivate, yet employers continue to do fairly well on the assumption that it does."[1]

PAY AND PERFORMANCE

Basic Aspects of Pay

Of all the rewards organizations have at their disposal, none is as important, visible, or flexible as pay.[2] While rewards like praise, promotion, and more interesting jobs are certainly important, most people work, first for money and, as a result, "pay is the most important single motivator in our organized society."[3]

Bases For Determining Pay. There are essentially two bases on which to pay employees: increments of time and volume of production.

Most employees are paid on the basis of the time they put in on the job. For example, blue collar workers are usually paid hourly or daily *wages*: this is often called *day work*. Some employees—managerial, professional, and usually secretarial and clerical—are *salaried*. They are compensated on the basis of a set period of time (like a week, month, or a year) rather than hourly or daily.

The second basis on which employees are paid is called *piecework*. Piecework ties compensation directly to the amount of production (or number of "pieces") the worker produces. It is therefore most popular as an incentive pay system. In one simple version, for example, a worker's hourly wage is divided by the standard number of units he or she is expected to produce in one hour. Then for each unit he produces over and above this standard he is paid an incentive rate (per piece). Salesmen's commissions are another example of compensation tied to production (in this case, sales).

Job Evaluation. No matter which basis is used for paying employees, management has to have some method for determining specifically how much (or at what rate) to pay them. For example, should management pay $4.00 per hour? or $5.00? or $6.00? Should it pay $2.00 per widget produced? or $4.00? or more? Determining specifically what rate to pay for each job is the purpose of *job evaluation,* which entails essentially four steps:

> *Evaluate the job.* Actually find the "value" of the job in relation to other jobs.
> *Develop wage grades.* Classify the jobs into various wage grades, such as Secretary II, Secretary III, and Secretary IV. This permits management to slot jobs with similar requirements into grades for pay purposes.
> *Use wage curves.* Develop and use wage curves to relate jobs and grades to wages.
> *Price the jobs.* "Fine-tune" the prices to be paid for each of the jobs in the organization. This typically involves making wage surveys to find out what competitors are paying, establishing compensation policies, and reviewing a number of other factors.

The overall purpose of job evaluation is to determine the relative worth of each job. Basically, job evaluation involves comparing jobs to one another based on their content, which is usually defined in terms of "compensable factors" like skills, effort, responsibility, and working conditions.

Pay Based On Time

Pay based on time—for instance, by the hour, week or year—occupies a unique if somewhat confusing position as a motivation tool. On the one hand, most employees are paid wholly or in part on the basis of time, and most surveys indicate that they prefer to be.[4] Yet, on the other hand, most experts would agree that rewards that are not performance based do not motivate performance.[5]

No one would argue, of course, that people would come to work if they were *not* paid, since most people obviously work to earn a living. The experts simply argue that pay based on time merely ensures that workers will show up for work, but that only performance-based pay can motivate a more than average performance.

Time-Based Pay and Performance. There are, however, at least two popular explanations for why time-based pay *can* motivate performance. The first of these is based on the Herzberg Motivator-Hygiene theory of motivation. Herzberg and his associates argue that, like working conditions, money is usually just a hygiene that prevents dissatisfaction. They say that if the amount of pay a person receives is not sufficient, the person will become dissatisfied, but that adding additional pay beyond this "adequacy" level will not motivate additional performance—for this, motivators like more challenging work are required. Assuming Herzberg is correct (and we pointed out in Chapter 3 that his theory has many critics) money could still motivate performance in two ways. First, if the pay a person is receiving is not viewed as adequate, then one would assume that even minimally acceptable performance might not occur, at least until the pay was raised to acceptable levels. In other words, says Herzberg, the person whose pay is not adequate will not even produce a "fair day's work."

> The existence of a standard of a "fair day's work" has been well documented in systematic studies by industrial psychologists and sociologists as well as industrial engineers. It is likely that poor hygiene (like low pay) will depress performance below the level of the "fair day's work." Correction of this poor hygiene, or the application of monetary incentives not related to motivators, may return performance to the norm.[6]

Second, Herzberg's theory also assumes that until the hygienes in the work environment (pay, working conditions, and so on) are adequate, employees will remain dissatisfied, and attempts to motivate them by appealing to their higher level needs for achievement and self-actualization (for example, by enriching their jobs) will probably be fruitless. If this is true, then money may not be a "motivator" directly, but unless the person's pay is at least adequate, it might prove impossible to motivate that person through "motivators" like more challenging jobs.[7] Thus, Herzberg's theory provides one set of explanations for why even time-based pay plays an important role in motivation and performance.

The equity theory of motivation provides a second explanation of why time-based pay can be motivating. As we discussed in Chapter 3, the equity theory of motivation assumes that individuals are strongly motivated to maintain a balance between what they perceive as their input, or contributions, and their rewards. The research findings we discussed indicated that if a person is paid based on time—a straight salary—*and believes he is overpaid*, then the quantity or quality of his work will probably increase, because this will reduce the perceived inequity. (On the other hand, if the person feels that he is underpaid, then the quantity or quality of his work will decrease).[8]

In summary, there are at least two viable explanations for why a time-based pay plan can motivate performance. First, unless the person's pay is at least adequate, it seems unlikely that techniques (like job enrichment) that are aimed at tapping a person's higher level needs will be ineffective. Second, there is considerable evidence that the way the person perceives his or her *relative* pay has important implications for that person's performance; thus, when a person is paid on a straight salary basis, a perception that he is being overpaid can, and probably will, improve his performance.

Pay Based on Performance

Some Background. The use of financial incentives—financial rewards paid to workers whose production exceeds some predetermined standard—was popularized by Frederick Taylor in the late 1800s. As a supervisory employee of the Midvale Steel Co., he had become increasingly concerned with what he called "systematic soldiering." (This was the tendency of employees to work at the slowest pace possible and produce at the minimum acceptable level.) What especially intrigued him was that some of these workers still had the energy to run home and work on their cabins, even after a hard 12-hour day. Taylor knew that if he could find some way to harness this energy during the workday, huge productivity gains would be possible.[9]

At this time, primitive "piecework" systems were already in use. Workers were paid a piece rate (based on informal performance standards) for each piece they produced. However, they knew that if their earnings became excessive, the piece rate would be cut. As a result, most workers produced just enough to earn a decent wage, but little enough so that their rate per piece would not be cut. One of Taylor's great insights was seeing the need for a standardized, acceptable view of a *fair day's work*. As he saw it, this fair day's work should depend not on the vague estimates of foremen, but on a careful, formal, scientific process of inspection and observation. It was this need to *scientifically* evaluate each job that led to what became known as the scientific management movement.

Today, whether they are called piece-rate plans, incentives, management bonuses, or sales commissions, performance-based plans that tie employees' pay to performance are widely used. It is estimated that about 60 percent of manufacturing firms surveyed use wage incentives, that from two-thirds to three-quarters of all the sales forces in the United States use incentives, and that almost 80 percent of manufacturing firms have executive bonus plans.[10]

The widespread use of financial incentives reflects the fact that, under the right conditions, they can substantially improve productivity. In a recent study for the National Science Foundation, researchers listed "six critical ingredients of systems that effectively raised job satisfaction and worker motivation," and heading the list was "financial compensation of workers which must be linked to their performance and to productivity gains." The study team found that when workers' pay is linked to their performance, the motivation to work is raised, productivity is higher, and they are likely to be more satisfied with their work.[11] Many other researchers have come to similar conclusions.[12]

This is not to say, of course, that financial incentives are a panacea, since for several reasons they may fail. In some cases, for example, what starts out as a financial incentive plan becomes a tug-of-war between management and labor, each of whom is determined not to be outsmarted by the other: the result in such cases is often group restriction of output.[13] In other situations—such as where there is a machine-paced assembly line, and the workers have virtually no control over their own output—incentive plans are simply inappropriate.

Incentive Pay and Positive Reinforcement. A financial incentive can be viewed as a specific kind of positive reinforcement, and in many quarters the terms are used interchangeably. As a result, it is useful to keep in mind that much of our discussion of positive reinforcement in the last chapter applies also to financial incentives. For example, the incentive itself should usually be only part of the overall behavior modification program. In addition to providing these positive *consequences,* management also has to ensure that employees know what is expected of them (antecedents) and that the required *behavior* is not being blocked because of insufficient training, inadequate supplies, the person's abilities, or some other reason. Providing *properly scheduled* rewards is important as well.[14]

Types of Incentive Plans. There are many effective plans in use, and a number of ways to categorize them. It is typical, for example, to distinguish between *individual* and *group* incentive plans, and between plans appropriate for *plant* personnel and *white collar* employees like sales persons and managers.

Piecework is the oldest type of individual incentive plan and the most commonly used. Earnings are tied directly to what the worker produces by paying him or her a "piece rate" for each unit produced. Thus, if Smith gets 20¢ a piece for stamping out doorjambs, he would make $20 for stamping out 100 a day and $40 for stamping out 200 a day.

On the other hand, some organizations use group incentive plans, particularly for their plant personnel. Here, each member of the group receives a bonus based on the output of the group as a whole. This can be advantageous when several jobs are interrelated and a worker's performance therefore reflects not only his or her own effort, but that of the person's co-workers as well. The disadvantage is that the "link" between the person's performance and pay is not as clear as it is with an individual plan, and therefore the latter is generally more effective.[15]

Another well-known plan—this one aimed at involving all of the organization's members—was developed in 1937 by union representative Joseph Scanlon. The Scanlon Plan has two basic features. First, financial incentives aimed at cutting costs, and thereby increasing efficiency, are installed. Second, a network of departmental and plant screening committees is established to evaluate employee and management cost-cutting suggestions. The plan is essentially a suggestion system and assumes that efficiency requires company-wide, or plant-wide, cooperation. Usually, all, or virtually all, employees in the plant participate in the plan. Workers, supervisors, and managers make cost-cutting suggestions, which are screened and evaluated by the various screening committees. If a suggestion is implemented and successful, all employees typically share in 75 percent of the savings.

The Scanlon Plan has been fairly successful. Employees make many suggestions, and they accept the need for technological changes and a work climate "hostile to loafing" results. The plan tends to encourage a sense of partnership and sharing among workers, less overtime, and employee insistence on efficient management.[16] In one recent study, labor costs were cut by about 10 percent and grievances were cut by half after implementation of the Scanlon Plan.[17] However, the plan is generally more successful where there is strong management commitment to it and where the firm is small (under 1,000 participants).[18]

Why Incentive Plans Fail.[19] There are a number of reasons why incentive plans fail. A perception on the part of employees that their production standards are unfair is one prevalent problem that contributes to the demise of many incentive plans. As we discussed in the last chapter, a person's standards must be realistic, fair, and attainable, and to the extent they are not, motivation will not take place. In addition, one of the most persistent problems undermining incentive plans is the employees' belief that standards will be raised if they are met or exceeded.

Peer pressure and group restrictions are also contributing factors. On the one hand, if the group views the plan as fair, it can keep "loafers" in line and maintain high production, but the opposite is also true. If for any reason the group views the plan as not in its best interest, it will—through education, ostracism, or punishment—see that the production levels of group members are held to a minimum.[20]

A number of other problems, some obvious and some not so obvious, can result in the failure of incentive plans. Some plans, for example, fail because employees do not understand them. Perhaps details of the plans are not communicated to the employees, or the communications are simply not understandable. In any case, employees generally have to understand how their effort and performance will lead to rewards, or the incentive plan will motivate them. Similarly, for the plan to succeed, the employees should believe they have the ability to successfully perform their tasks; this implies that the necessary structure, tools, training and so forth must be available. In other words, it is not sufficient to simply provide the positive consequences; the employee must have the ability to engage in the necessary behaviors. Other incentive plans have failed because they created inequitable wage structures within the organization. In one such failure, for example, production workers were placed on an incentive system under which (it turned out) they earned more than higher skilled workers who were not under the plan. Still other plans have resulted in intergroup conflicts over who has "tight" standards and who has "loose" ones.[21] And, some have been unsuccessful because of inadequate or inequitable performance appraisal systems.

When to Use Incentive Plans. There are a number of practical considerations that will help determine whether an organization can pay its employees based on time or performance. For example, paying employees based on *time* is usually indicated when units of output are difficult to distinguish and measure, when employees are unable to control quantity of output, and when there is not a clear relationship between effort and output. Similarly, when delays in the work are frequent and beyond the employees' control, when quality considerations are especially important, and where the investment in industrial engineering and methods analysis, which installing an incentive plan requires, is not feasible, pay based on time is more appropriate. Conversely, a *performance*-based pay plan is more appropriate where units of output can be measured, where there is a clear relationship between effort and output, where delays are few or consistent, where quality is less important than quantity (or at least easily measured), and where competitive conditions require that unit labor costs be definitely known and fixed in advance. This is summarized in Exhibit 5.1.

Exhibit 5.1 When to Base Pay on Incentives (Instead of Time)

	Base Pay on Incentives	*Base Pay on Time*
Units of output	Easy to measure	Hard to measure
Employee's control of output	They can control it	They can't
Effort/Reward relationship	Clear	Not clear
Work delays	Under employee's control	Beyond employee's control
Quality	Not too important	Paramount
Good supervision and agreement on what is a "fair day's work"	No	Yes
Must know precise labor costs to stay competitive	Yes	No

PROMOTION AND PERFORMANCE

A promotion is an important organizational reward—one that is similar, in two respects, to pay. A promotion, first of all, is usually associated with a *raise* in pay, although most experts would consider *any* advantageous transfer—for example, from the night shift to the day shift—as a promotion, although it involves no increased responsibility or pay.[23] Promotion also parallels pay in that both can be either time-based or performance-based. In the case of promotion, a time-based plan would be based on seniority, while a performance-based plan would be based on ability and performance.

As a result of these parallels, much of what we said about time-based versus performance-based pay plans applies to promotions as well. The most important thing, of course, is that, generally speaking, promotion (or pay) best motivates performance when it is seen as a consequence of performance. As a result, seniority plans that simply reward attendance will obviously reduce the motivating potential of promotions.

How Promotion Decisions Are Made

There are at least three main areas in which promotion-related decisions must be made, and any of the resulting decisions has an impact on motivation and performance.

Decision One: Seniority or Competence? Probably the most important decision concerns whether promotion will be based on seniority or competence—or some combination of the two. From the point of view of motivation, promotion based on competence is the more attractive alternative. However, an organization's ability to use competence as a sole criterion obviously depends on several things, most notably whether or not the firm is unionized or governed by civil service requirements. Union agreements often contain a clause, such as the following, that emphasizes seniority in promotions: "In the advancement of employees to higher paid jobs when ability, merit, and capacity are equal, employees with the highest seniority will be given preference."[24] While this might seem to leave the door open for giving a person with less seniority (but slightly better abilities) the inside track for a job, labor arbitrators have generally held that where clauses like these are binding only *substantial* differences in abilities can be taken into account. In one case, for example, the arbitrator ruled that seniority should be disregarded only where an employee with less seniority stood "head and shoulders" above the employees with greater seniority.[25] Similarly, many organizations in the public sector are governed by civil service regulations that emphasize seniority rather than competence as the basis for promotions.[26]

Decision Two: Formal or Informal? Next (particularly if the decision is made to promote based on competence) a decision must be made as to whether the promotion process will be a formal or informal one. Many organizations still depend on an informal system. Here, the availability and requirements of open positions are kept secret, and the promotion decisions are made by key managers from among employees they know personally, or from among those who, for one reason or another, have impressed them with their activities or presence.[27] Needless to say, however, when employees are not made aware of what jobs are available, what the criteria for promotion are, or how promotion decisions are made, the link between promotion and performance is largely broken, and the effectiveness of promotion as a positive reinforcer is diminished.[28]

Other organizations go to the opposite extreme and establish formal, published promotion policies and procedures. Here, employees are generally provided with a formal promotion policy statement that describes the criteria by which promotions are awarded. Formal systems often include a policy of open posting of jobs, which states that open positions and their requirements will be posted and circulated to all employees. Many organizations compile detailed information on the qualifications of employees (particularly those in management). For example, many organizations use manpower replacement charts as illustrated in Exhibit 5.2. These show the present performance of each position holder and the promotion potential of possible replacements. Many organizations have installed computerized information systems for maintaining qualifications inventories on hundreds and possibly thousands of employees. The net effect of these various actions is twofold: (1) first, an organization can ensure that all qualified employees are considered for openings; and (2) promotion becomes more closely linked with performance in the minds of employees, and, as a result, its effectiveness as a reward increases.

Decision Three: How to Measure Competence? Finally, where promotion is to be based on competence, a decision has to be made concerning how competence is to be measured.

The problem here is usually compounded by the fact that *potential* as well as prior performance has to be considered. As we will see in later chapters, there are many ways to evaluate an employee's past performance. Some organizations use "graphic rating scales," others have supervisors periodically report "critical incidents" of especially good and poor behavior on the part of employees, and others use a management by objectives program in which supervisor and subordinate jointly set goals for the latter, who is then evaluated based on his or her attainment of these goals. While the subject of performance appraisal will have to wait for our later discussions, the important point now is that the means used to evaluate performance have an

Exhibit 5.2 Management Manpower Replacement Chart

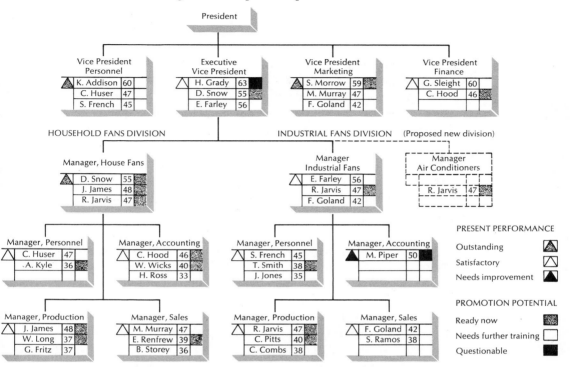

Source: National Industrial Conference Board, *Developing Managerial Competence: Changing Concepts, Emerging Practices,* 1964.

important impact on motivation and performance. For example, if the rating scale is viewed by employees as too ambiguous, if those doing the rating are considered biased, or if the goals that are set are viewed as unfair and unattainable, performance will suffer and the promotion plan will be crippled. (This applies to performance-based salary raise decisions as well.)

Evaluating a candidate's *potential* for a job is an even more difficult matter. Here, the organization has to find some valid procedure for predicting a candidate's future performance. Many organizations simply use prior performance as a guide, and extrapolate or assume that (based on the person's prior performance) he or she will perform well in the new job. On the other hand, many organizations use the sorts of psychological tests discussed in Chapter 2. For example, one survey found that about 21 percent of the responding firms used personnel tests in considering hourly workers for promotion.[29] Another study found that almost 50 percent of the responding companies used tests in identifying employees with executive potential.[30] (As we discussed, the use of such tests—and, in fact, virtually every step in the promotion decision procedure—is subject to equal employment guidelines that are aimed at ensuring that employees are not discriminated against on the basis of age, sex, national origin, religion, or race.)

For assessing management potential, many organizations have gone beyond testing and are now using *assessment centers*. In a typical assessment center the applicant is exposed to a series of "real life" exercises. His or her performance is observed and assessed by experts, who then check on their assessment by watching the participant once he is back at his old job. The centers have proven effective in many organizations, most notably the Bell System. Others, however, feel that a thorough evaluation of a participant's personnel file and an interview will provide information comparable to the results of the assessment center, at considerably less expense.[37]

Discussion. An important point to remember is that the decisions made at each step of the promotion process have a major influence on employee performance in general, as well as specifically on whether promotions are viewed as positive rewards. To the extent that the promotions *are* based on competence, procedures and criteria *are* formal and public, and the evaluations *are* viewed as fair and valid, the promotion can be used as a positive force for performance. To the extent that promotion is based on seniority, and to the extent that the procedures and criteria used are secret and informal, and the evaluations are viewed as unfair, promotions will not be seen as a consequence of performance and their influence as a reward will diminish. Behavior, remember, is largely a result of its consequences. To the extent that a promotion is clearly a consequence of performance, performance should improve. On the other hand, to the extent that promotion is a consequence not of performance, but of some other behavior like patronizing the boss, then it is that other behavior that will be encouraged.

OTHER BENEFITS AS REWARDS

Financially Based Benefits

Virtually all organizations provide their employees with financially based rewards such as vacation time, insurance benefits, and retirement benefits. Most also provide secondary services like partial college tuition and cafeteria services. Unlike incentive pay, promotions, or even salary, benefits like these are distinguished by the fact that they are usually available to *all* employees based on their membership in the organization, although the amount of the benefit may be in proportion to the importance of the job. Since these benefits are specifically *not* tied to performance their influence as rewards is obviously limited. The closest comparison would be to time-based pay plans. As with these plans, benefits probably only encourage performance above what the job requires if employees view themselves as "overpaid" in benefits (relative to other films), or if the benefits are so bad to begin with that increasing them brings performance up to the level it should have been.

There are many types of financially based benefits. For example, most organizations provide pay for time not worked, in the form of unemployment insurance, paid vacations and holidays, sick leave, severance pay, and, in certain industries (for example, auto making) supplemental unemployment benefits. The latter provide, in effect, for a "guaranteed annual income" and supplement the employees usual unemployment benefits, thus enabling the workers to better maintain their standards of living during periodic shutdowns.

Most organizations also provide various insurance benefits. These include workmen's compensation (for injuries at work), life insurance, and, usually, hospital, accident, and disability insurance. Finally, most organizations also provide various retirement benefits in the form of social security and pension plans.

Financially Based Benefits and Employee Performance. Some experts have argued that benefits can be made more useful as rewards by letting each employee choose his or her own "mix" of benefits. One example of this is the so-called cafeteria benefit plan. This enables employees to pick and choose from available options and literally develop their own benefit plans. As of now, these cafeteria plans are used mostly for management employees, but it is likely that their use will spread to nonmanagers as well.

The idea of individualizing benefits so that they become more valuable to each individual employee makes some sense. For a reward to have any chance of motivating performance, it has to be viewed by the employee as valuable, and the basic idea behind cafeteria plans is to let each employee choose those benefits that are of most value to him or her.

Individualizing benefits does seem to be necessary. In one study, for example, 400 employees were asked their preferences for seven benefits. The younger employees were significantly more in favor of the family dental plan than were older employees. Younger employees also showed a greater preference for a compressed workweek. As might be expected, preference for the pension option increased significantly with employee age. Married workers showed more preference for the pension increase, and for the family dental plan, than did single workers.[32]

The Four-Day Workweek and Performance

A number of organizations in America and Europe have switched to a four-day workweek. Here employees work four 10-hour days instead of the more usual five 8-hour days.[33]

Advantages. Four-day workweek plans have been fairly successful in terms of boosting productivity. Productivity appears to increase in response to reduced startup and shutdown times. Workers are more often willing to work some evenings and Saturdays as part of these plans. According to a study by the American Management Association, 80 percent of the firms on such plans reported that the plan "improves business results"; three-fifths said that production was up, and almost two-fifths said that costs were down. Half the firms also report higher profits. Even the "four-day firms" *not* reporting positive results reported that cost and profit factors at least remained the same. A study by the Bureau of Labor Statistics suggests that the four-day workweek *is* generally effective (in terms of reducing paid overtime, reducing absenteeism, and improving efficiency). Furthermore, workers also gain. There is a 20 percent reduction in commuter trips and an additional "free day" per week, factors that are of growing importance with the current shortages of gasoline. Additional savings (for example, in child care expenses) may also occur.

Keep in mind, though, that we do not have a lot of experience with shortened workweeks, and it is possible that the improvements are short-lived. In one study, for example, four-day (40-hour) weeks resulted in greater employee satisfaction and productivity and less absenteeism when evaluated after 13 months, but these improvements were not found after 25 months.[34]

Disadvantages. There are also some disadvantages, some of them potentially quite severe. Tardiness, for example, may become a problem. Of more concern is the fact that *fatigue* was cited by a number of firms as a principal disadvantage of the four-day workweek (excessive fatigue was the major reason for adopting eight-hour days in the first place). Furthermore, the implications of the extended workday and its impact on family life are at this point unknown.

Partly as a result of these disadvantages (and partly as a result of the fact that some researchers have found the effect of the four-day workweek on employee performance to be negative rather than positive), some experts have argued against implementation of this plan. For example, one argues that the four-day workweek will diminish in popularity because "too many employees do not like this approach," "it can reduce productivity because of employee fatigue," and "productivity could drop if unions use the four/40 as a beginning bargaining point to go to a four/36 and then a four/32 hour week."[35]

In summary, particularly with the increasing cost of transportation, the four-day workweek does have the potential for increasing productivity. However, because of its potential disadvantages it has to be used prudently and it would probably be advisable for management to attempt it in one or

two departments as a pilot project before implementing it on an organization-wide basis.

Flexible Hours and Performance

Many organizations have experimented with "flexitime" in an effort to improve employees' morale and productivity by giving them more discretion over their hours of work. Here management lets employees build a flexible workday around a central core of midday hours, such as 11 to 2. It is called "flexitime" because the workers themselves determine their own starting and stopping hours. For example, they may opt to work from 7 to 3, or 11 to 7, and so on.

Many flexitime programs have been quite successful.[35] Because less time is lost due to tardiness, the ratio of man-hours worked to man-hours paid (a measure of productivity) increases. Flexitime programs have also been shown to reduce absenteeism and to cut down on "sick leave" being used for personal matters. The hours actually worked seem to be more productive, and there is less slowing down toward the end of the workday. Workers tend to leave early when work is slack and work later when it is heavy. The use of flexitime also seems to be related to increased employee receptiveness to other changes.

Flexitime is also advantageous from the worker's point of view. It may reduce the tedium associated with the timing of their work and democratize their work. It also tends to reduce the distinction between managers and professional workers and requires more delegation of authority by supervisors.

There are also a number of disadvantages. Flexitime is complicated to administer and may be impossible to implement where large groups of workers must work interdependently.[37] It also requires the use of timecards or other time records, and this can be disadvantageous from the point of view of the worker. In total, however, the effects of flexitime on performance, morale, absenteeism, and turnover seem to be overwhelmingly positive, and flexitime therefore seems to be one "benefit" that can clearly and directly improve productivity.

DO EXTRINSIC REWARDS DETRACT FROM INTRINSIC ONES?

In Chapter 3 we distinguished between extrinsic and intrinsic rewards. We said that extrinsic rewards were those that come from "outside" the person; and which the organization uses to reward employees. These extrinsic rewards, discussed in this chapter, include pay, promotion, and benefits. Intrinsic rewards are different. According to Maslow, Herzberg, and others, intrinsic rewards come from "within" the person and derive from that person's ability to satisfy higher order needs for competence, self-determination, and self-actualization.[38] In the next few chapters we are going to discuss techniques like job enrichment, which is aimed at building more challenge into jobs so that workers find them intrinsically rewarding.

Until recently, most experts assumed that the effects of intrinsic and extrinsic rewards were additive and that a worker would be more motivated to complete a task that combined both kinds of rewards than a task where only one kind of reward was available.[39] Recently, however, some experts have raised the question of whether "highly challenging and intrinsically rewarding" jobs are amenable to incentives: "Are incentives in this situation the cause of mercenary feelings which *detract* from the main source of satisfaction—the job itself—and ultimately lower job effectiveness? Or do they spur the employees on to greater heights?"[40] In other words, do extrinsic rewards (and particularly incentives) detract from the "built-in" rewards of, for example, a very challenging job? Or are extrinsic and intrinsic rewards additive? Since 1966, a good deal of research has gone into studying this question.

Much of the work in this area has been done by psychologist Edward Deci and his associates. They have carried out numerous studies and believe they have found that a person's intrinsic motivation to perform a challenging task decreases when he or she is put on a piecework type plan. Deci says that financial rewards made contingent on task performance *can reduce the intrinsic motivation* to do that task and that contingent payment plans are therefore not compatible with techniques like job enrichment.

On the whole, the findings suggest that extrinsic rewards often do seem to detract from intrinsic motivation. Therefore, considerable caution should be used before installing incentive pay plans on jobs that are inherently challenging and intrinsically motivating.[41]

REWARDS AND THE "ABC s" OF PERFORMANCE

Rewards like the ones we discussed in this chapter can clearly have a direct effect on performance and productivity. For example, assume that your employees' performance is inadequate, or that a new reward system has been implemented but does not seem to have resulted in any appreciable change in performance. You want to analyze the problem using our "ABCs" of performance. Based on our discussions in this chapter, rewards might enter into your analysis as follows:

Antecedents. Do employees know what is expected of them? Are their standards fair and attainable? Do they understand how the new plan works?

Behavior. Could they perform better if they wanted to?

Consequences. Are the consequences for performing positive? Will employees get paid or promoted regardless of how they perform? Are the consequences clearly tied to performance? Are performance evaluations effective, or is the performance-reward link broken?

CHAPTER SUMMARY

1. Of all the rewards organizations have at their disposal, none is so important, visible, or flexible than pay. We discussed two bases on which you can pay employees—increments of time, and volume of production—and noted that the overall purpose of *job evaluation* is to determine the relative worth of each job.

2. Pay based on time still seems to be the most popular method for paying employees, although most experts would agree that rewards that are not performance based do not motivate behavior. We noted however, that even time-based pay may serve to improve performance if (1) pay was too low to begin with or (2) a salaried person perceives his or her relative pay as too high given his effort.

3. Pay based on performance—financial incentives—*can* motivate improved performance. In other words, when a person's pay is tied directly to his or her output, he comes to see pay as an importance consequence of performance, and performance improves. Again, however, the *antecedents* and the *behavior* itself are also both important.

4. There are a number of reasons why incentive plans fail, but the main one seems to be that for motivation to take place, the worker must believe that effort on his or her part will lead to rewards, and the rewards must be valuable to the person. In most cases where incentive plans fail, it is because one (or both) of these conditions are not met. In other words, standards have to be fair, realistic, and attainable, and employees must believe that standards will not be raised if they are met or exceeded.

5. A performance-based pay plan is more appropriate where units of output can be measured, where there is a clear relationship between effort and output, where delays are few or consistent, where quality is less important than quantity, and where competitive conditions require that unit labor costs be definitely known and fixed in advance.

6. Promotions are also important rewards, and are similar to pay in that (1) they tend to be associated with raises in pay, and (2) can be either time-based or performance-based. The extent to which promotions are seen as performance based helps determine how important and useful promotions are for improving performance, and this in turn depends on the answers to three main questions: Will promotions be based on seniority or competence? Will the promotion system be formal or informal? and How will we measure competence? As was the case with *pay*, promotions are primarily useful for improving performance and productivity when they are seen as consequences of effective performance.

7. Financially-based benefits are usually distributed to all employees based on membership in the organization and are not performance based. However, *individualizing* benefits (perhaps through cafeteria benefit plans), may help make the benefits more valuable to each individual employee and thereby improve their usefulness as rewards. A four-day workweek does have the potential for increasing productivity, but may be disadvantageous if it leads to fatigue. Flexitime's effects on performance, morale, absenteesim, and turnover seem to be overwhelmingly positive; so flexitime seems to be one benefit that can clearly and directly improve productivity.

8. On the whole, the findings suggest that extrinsic rewards (like the ones we discussed in this chapter) often do seem to detract from intrinsic motivation by giving the person the impression that he or she is no longer exerting as much control over rewards. Therefore, considerable caution should be used before installing incentive pay plans on jobs that are inherently challenging and intrinsically motivating. For example, a person who enjoys working hard because she believes she is contributing to society's welfare, may actually produce less—not more—if told she will henceforth be rewarded in direct proportion to her performance.

DISCUSSION QUESTIONS AND PROJECTS

1. Give an example of how time-based pay can be used to improve performance.

2. Describe several types of incentive plans. Has anyone in the class ever worked under such a plan? If so, describe your experiences: Do you think it made you work harder? Did you enjoy working under the plan? Were there any drawbacks to you or the organization?

3. Describe the three promotion-related decisions that will determine what (if any) impact promotions have on motivation and performance. Has anyone in the class ever worked in an organization where promotion was based on seniority rather than competence? What effect do you think this policy had on performance in the organization?

4. The instructor should poll the class to find out how many students would prefer to work a four-day rather than a five-day week. Which did most students vote for? Why do people prefer the four-day week prefer it? What about the five-day week?

5. Explain a situation you are familiar with in which offering a person money (or some other extrinsic reward) for a job they were doing actually seemed to detract from their performance.

6. Assume that you are the newly appointed head of a typing pool and that you do not believe the typists are producing as much work as they should. Explain how you would analyze the problem with the "ABCs" of performance (What questions would you ask?), and explain some of the ways in which extrinsic rewards can be used to solve the problem.

CASE EXERCISE

The Tarnished Company Image*

The Silverstone Corporation was the brainchild of Gordon Silverstone. Gordon persuaded his older brother John, a certified public accountant, and his younger brother Tom, a computer salesman, to join him in this enterprise. Recognizing that their personal resources were insuffdcent to really get the company going, they managed to secure financial backing from Brainbridge Corporation, which became the fourth principal stockholder of the company.

The organization of the company was built around the backgrounds of the three brothers. John, the accountant, was named as president and was responsible for the financial functions. Tom, the salesman, was installed as marketing vice-president, and Gordon, the technician, was also titled vice-president with responsibility for recruiting, staffing individual accounts, and generally managing the day-to-day operations.

Early in the company's history, Tom actively searched for business and managed to line up a few small initial programming contracts. Gordon was busy prospecting for some expert technicians (whom he called "eagles") to form the core of the staff; by use of such phrases as "ground-floor opportunity" and "employee stock option plan" he was successful in attracting three capable individuals.

These "eagles" rapidly performed the work called for by the programming contracts. Estimates were consistently beaten, the company began to develop an excellent reputation, and new business was becoming plentiful. As the amount of work grew, Gordon and the other technicians invested time in recruiting new personnel. The new people brought in more people and within two years the company employed thirty systems engineers (or SEs as the technicians were called) on the payroll. The Silverstone Corporation was a profitable operation from its very first year, and the future looked bright.

Underspending estimates become expected, thereby making jobs even more profitable to the company, which usually worked on a fixed-price basis. This resulted in many unpaid overtime hours for the SEs. Sixty-hour (and more) workweeks were common. No one seemed to mind since a true team spirit had developed, and, besides, it would be worth it in the end because, as Gordon would frequently say, "This company will belong to those who build it."

Within four years, the company had grown to 100 people and expanded geographically into five cities. In a number of cases the Silverstone brothers deliberately underestimated contract bids for the purpose of securing a foothold in a new market. They felt this approach was justified by the fact that the Silverstone SEs had traditionally under-run estimates and could be counted on to do so in the future.

* Case researched and written by Paul R. Paulson.

The reason for the excellent track record the SEs had established on past contracts was primarily because of overtime effort. The effect of low-balling a contract bid, then, was to plan on this overtime effort and thereby remove the profit–loss cushion that it normally provided. Consequently, any error in the estimating procedure would result in an overrun condition even if the normal overtime effort was expended. This problem was compounded by the fact that many of the SEs were commuting (on a daily or weekly basis, depending upon distances involved) from their homes to the client's work site in another city. The travel time involved made it difficult for the SEs to apply even the normal amount of overtime, and almost impossible for them to react to major problems with extended overtime.

The first seeds of discontent among the SEs had taken root in a general pressure for improved working conditions: less traveling and less overtime, higher pay (or at least some form of compensation for overtime), and, most importantly, the as yet unseen "piece of the action" (stock options). Gordon Silverstone's reading of this situation was that he was losing control of the SEs. The company, he reasoned, had grown to the point that he could no longer effectively manage all the SEs, spread around as they were. His response was to install Fred Maxwell (an older and well-liked SE) as SE manager. Fred's responsibility was to keep the SEs happy and productive and lift from Gordon the burden of dealing with individual SE complaints.

It became apparent to both the SEs and Fred that he was not given the tools to do the job. He had no authority to grant pay increases, modify company policy with respect to overtime pay, or even discuss the stock-option question about which he knew nothing. In effect, Fred's real job was to act as a buffer to shield Gordon from the unhappy SEs. A quote attributed to Silverstone in describing Fred's function spread throughout the SE ranks. "He keeps the cattle off my back."

Within three months, five SEs left the company. Four months later a group of six SEs left to work for a client whose Silverstone contract had expired. Three weeks later all SEs were required to sign a document (the legality of which was questioned, but never tested) stating that no Silverstone SE could go to work for a current or previous Silverstone client within two years of the SEs separation from the company. There was a general acceptance of the idea that those who refused to sign (and there were some) might as well start looking for new jobs, since, although they might not be fired, they certainly had lost a lot of leverage within the company.

After much informal pressure had been brought to bear on the Silverstone brothers, primarily by the original group of SEs who had been with the company longest, the "key employee stock option plan" was announced. This was greeted with high expectations by the SEs, who assumed that their loyalty, hard work, and their long hours were finally being recognized.

As the details of the plan were made clear, however, the high expectations turned to deep disappointment. The company had, immediately before announcement of the plan, diluted the stock through a ten-for-one split. The stock was being made available to certain employees (at the discretion of the Silverstone brothers) in twenty-five share blocks. Each certificate carried on the back an agreement which said:

These shares were purchased for investment purposes only. They cannot be sold to anyone without first offering Silverstone Corporation the option to buy them at the price originally paid by the employee. In the event of termination of employment for any reason, the employee must offer the shares to Silverstone Corporation at the original purchase price. These shares cannot be used as collateral for securing any type of debt.

The employees' reaction to this plan was that it was worse than worthless. The number of shares offered was so small as to be insignificant. Even if the stock greatly appreciated in value, the employees could not realize any cash gain if the company elected to exercise its option to buy at the original purchase price. The SEs were close to outrage. They felt cheated and insulted. Distrust of the Silverstone brothers was widespread. This general condition precipitated a new wave of quits, primarily among the older, original SEs, which included Fred Maxwell.

This further depressed morale among those left, who, at the same time, were being called upon to put forth greater effort to make up for the diminishing manpower. This extra effort, for the most part, was not forthcoming. Several important accounts were lost, and six years after its birth the company suffered its first loss. The reputation of the company was severely damaged. It became increasingly difficult to secure new business and more difficult still to attract competent computer professionals to the firm.

Questions

1. How would you analyze the "ABCs" of the situation?
2. What do you think can be done to recapture the trust of the system engineers at Silverstone Corporation?
3. Why do you think the situation at the company was allowed to deteriorate so badly without somebody taking corrective action?
4. How might Gordon Silverstone have prevented the loss of effectiveness in his company?
5. What is the lesson or moral to be learned from this case?
6. Do you think the lack of a stock option plan, by itself, is what's bothering the SEs?
7. Do you think providing a stock incentive was the way to handle the problem? Why? Why not?

EXPERIENTIAL EXERCISE

Purpose: The purpose of this exercise is to give you practice in reviewing:

1. The conditions under which time- versus performance-based incentives are appropriate
2. The advantages of company-wide versus individuals incentives
3. The standards (sales, productivity, etc.) to which incentives can be tied

Required Understanding: You should be thoroughly familiar with our discussion of financial incentives and come to class prepared to discuss the following:

A Case of Incentives: *The Bonus Policy of Ezell Musical Instrument Company*
Ezell Music Instrument Company (EMI) is located in Frederick, Maryland. It is a medium-sized operation that has grown out of a family-owned company. Like many companies, it has to face tough competition at home and abroad. M. G. Ezell III is now the president of the firm.

Several years ago, when Ezell first took over, he thought about how he might build morale in the company. He felt that the company had good workers and that he would like to reward them for past services to encourage them to be more productive. EMI was not unionized. He hesitated to raise base wages since it might make the firm uncompetitive if foreign competition increased.

EMI was having an exceptionally good year, both for sales and profits. As a result, Ezell thought that the best way to reward the employees was to give them a Christmas-New Year's bonus. As he said to Abe Stick, his personnel manager: "Nothing like the old buck to make a man work harder." His bonus system was as follows:

Wages or Salary	Bonus
<$6,500	$500
$6,501–7,500	$600
$7,501–8,500	$700
$8,501–10,000	$800
>$10,000	8% of salary or wage

The bonuses were well received. Many people thanked the president, and Stick heard lots of good comments from the supervisors in January about how much harder the employees were working.

The next year, more foreign competitors entered the market. Materials were harder to get and more expensive. Sales were down 5 percent, and profits were down 15 percent. Ezell did not feel he could afford the same bonuses as last year. As a result, the bonuses were decreased as follows:

Wages or Salary	Bonus
<$6,500	$250
$6,501–7,500	$300
$7,501–8,500	$350
$8,501–10,100	$400
>$10,000	4% of salary or wage

This time, Stick heard little from the supervisors about increased productivity. He asked Harry Bell, one of the supervisors, what the reaction was to the bonuses.

Bell: To tell you the truth, Abe, I have morale problems. My people worked hard this year. It wasn't their fault sales or profits were down. Many expected last year's bonus or better. So they spent most of the old figure for Christmas gifts. When they got that letter from M. G. telling them they were getting only half of last year's on December 27, there was gloom and doom and some mumblings. Some of my people seem to be working less hard than at any time I can remember.

Stick: But that's not fair, Harry. They never received any bonuses before. Now they should be glad they received anything.

Bell: That's not the way they see it!

Stick decided not to discuss the matter with Ezell. Stick figured the problem would blow over. But, this year was even worse. Sales held but were not up to the prior years' levels. But, profits were almost nonexistent. The board of directors decided to omit the dividend.

Now, Ezell has come to Stick. Ezell says: "Abe, I don't see how we can pay any bonus this year. Do you think we can get by without causing a big drop in morale?"

How to Set Up the Exercise: Divide the class into groups of four or five students. Everyone should briefly review "A Case of Incentives."

Instructions

After discussing the case each group should develop answers to the following questions:

1. What does this case illustrate about the motivational impact of bonuses and incentives?

2. What could Mr. Ezell have done to prevent this problem in the first place?

3. Why should Mr. Bell expect that the employees would react negatively to the reduction in bonuses when they are not guaranteed as part of an employee's compensation?

4. Have rewards been accurately tied to performance by the Ezell compensation policy? If not, how might this failure be the cause of their problem?

5. What alternative formula or policy for distributing extra income to employees would you suggest?

6. What would you do now if you were Ezell? Stick?

If time permits the class should discuss their recommendations.

NOTES FOR CHAPTER 5

1. Quoted in Orlando Behling and Chester Schriesheim, *Organizational Behavior* (Boston: Allyn & Bacon, 1976), p. 230.

2. J. Richard Hackman and J. Lloyd Suttle, *Improving Life at Work: Behavioral Science Approaches to Organizational Change* (Santa Monica: Goodyear, 1977), p. 174.

3. Mason Haire, Edwin Ghiselli, and Lyman Porter, "Psychological Research on Pay: An Overview," *Industrial Relations*, 3 (October 1963), 3, quoted in Paul Pigors and Charles Myers, *Personnel Administration* (New York: McGraw-Hill, 1976), p. 333. For another perspective on pay and new techniques for developing pay plans, see Edwin Lawler III, "New Approaches to Pay Administration," *Personnel*, 53, No. 5 (September–October 1976), 11–23, reprinted in J. Richard Hackman, Edward Lawler III and Lyman Porter, *Perspectives on Behavior in Organizations* (New York: McGraw-Hill, 1976), pp. 297–306.

4. See, for example, Edward Lawler III, "Using Pay to Motivate Job Performance," reprinted in W. Clay Hamner and Frank Schmidt, *Contemporary Problems in Personnel* (Chicago: St. Claire Press, 1974), pp. 308–22.

5. Edward Lawler III, *Pay and Organizational Effectiveness* (New York: McGraw-Hill, 1971), 273–74; see also Behling and Schriesheim, *Organizational Behavior*, p. 233.

6. F. Herzberg, B. Mausner and B. Snyderman, *The Motivation to Work*, 2nd ed. (New York: John Wiley & Sons, 1959), quoted in Behling and Schriesheim, *Organizational Behavior*, p. 234.

7. For support of this idea see Grey Oldham, J. Hackman, and J. Pearce, "Conditions under which Employees Respond Positively to Enriched Work," *Journal of Applied Psychology*, 61 (August 1976), pp. 392–403.

8. See, for example, J. Stacey Adams and William Rosenbaum, "The Relationship of Worker Productivity to Cognitive Dissonance About Wage and Equity," *Journal of Applied Psychology*, 46 (1962), pp. 161–64.

9. J. K. Louden and J. Wayne Deegan, *Wage Incentives* (New York: John Wiley, 1959), p. 4.

10. Robert Rice, "Survey of Work Measurement and Wage Incentives in the U.S.A.," *Management Services* (January 1978); "Sharing the Wealth: H. R. D.'s Role in Making Incentive Plans Work," *Training* (January 1979). Keep in mind, though, that while some industries, such as basic steel, have incentive plans that cover most of their workforces, other industries reflect an almost total absence of financial incentives. As a result about 26 percent of American workers work under financial incentives.

11. Quoted in *Training* (January 1979), p. 30. For studies of the effectiveness of Financial Incentives see, for example, Gary Latham and Dennis Dossett, "Designing Incentive Plans for Unionized Employees: A Comparison of Continuous and Variable Ratio Reinforcement Schedules," *Personnel Psychology*, Vol. 31, No. 1 (Spring 1978), pp. 47–62; Todd Stevens and Wayne Burroughs, "An Application of Operant Conditioning to Absenteeism in a Hospital Setting," *Journal of Applied Psychology*, Vol. 63, No. 4 (August 1978), pp. 518–21.

12. See, for example, Opsahl and Dunnette, "The Role of Financial Compensation in Industrial Motivation," *Psychological Bulletin*, 66, No. 2 (1966), pp. 94–118; R. Marriot, *Incentive Pay Systems* (London: Staples Press, 1968); James Farr, "Incentive Schedules, Productivity, and Satisfaction in Work Groups: A Laboratory Study," *Organizational Behavior and Human Performance*, 17, No. 1 (October 1976), pp. 159–70.

13. For discussions of this see, for example, Saul Gellerman, *Motivation and Productivity* (New York: American Management Assn., 1963), p. 63.

14. For a discussion of how goal setting and monetary incentives act to complement each other see James Terbog and Howard Miller, "Motivation, Behavior and Performance: A Closer Examination of Goal Setting and Monetary Incentives," *Journal of Applied Psychology*, 63, No. 1 (1978), pp. 29–39. Also, keep in mind that while an incentive plan can be set up in such a way that employees are rewarded according to some schedule so that their behavior is in fact, "unthinkingly" modified, many (if not most) incentive plans actually assume a good deal of thinking will take place on the part of employees. (This was the criticism Locke made of actual behavior modification programs, and that we discussed in the previous chapter). As a result, some would probably prefer to view incentive plans in terms of expectancy theory, which assumes that employees think about the values of the rewards, and their abilities to obtain them.

15. See, for example, Manuel London and Greg Oldham, "A Comparison of Group and Individual Incentive Plans," *Academy of Management Journal*, 20, No. 1 (1977), pp. 34–41; for a discussion of the use of incentives for salesmen see, for example, John Steinbrink, "How to Pay your Sales Force," *Harvard Business Review* (July–August 1978), pp. 111–22; Jacob Gonik, "Tie Salesmen's Bonuses to Their Forecasts," *Harvard Business Review* (May–June 1978), pp. 116–23.

16. David Belcher, *Compensation Management* (Englewood Cliffs, N.J.: Prentice-Hall, 1974), pp. 329–31.

17. George Sherman, "The Scanlon Concept: Its Capabilities for Productivity Improvement," *Personnel Administrator* (July 1976).

18. J. D. Dunn and Frank Rachel, *Wage and Salary Administration* (New York: McGraw-Hill, 1972), p. 253; Behling and Schriesheim, *Organizational Behavior*, pp. 247–48; Belcher, *Compensation Management*, pp. 330–32.

19. See Hackman and Suttle, *Improving Life at Work*, pp. 197–289.

20. Leonard Sayles, "The Impact of Incentives on Inter-group Work Relations—A Management and Union Problem," *Personnel* (May 1967), pp. 483–90; W. Clay Hamner, "How to Ruin Motivation with Pay," *Compensation Review* (Third Quarter 1975).

21. Hamner, "How to Ruin Motivation with Pay."

22. Based on Belcher, *Compensation Administration*, pp. 309—11; see also Edward Lawler III, "Reward Systems," in Hackman and Suttle, *Improving Life at Work*, pp. 191–219.

23. See, for example, Pigors and Myers, *Personnel Administration*, p. 282.

24. Pigors and Myers, *Personnel Administration*, p. 283.

25. James Healy, "The Factor of Ability in Labor Relations," in *Arbitration Today* (Proceedings of the 8th Annual Meeting of the National Academy of Arbitrators, 1955), pp. 45–54, quoted in Pigors and Myers, p. 283.

26. Charles Halaby, "Bureaucratic Promotion Criteria, *Administrative Science Quarterly*, 23 (September 1978), pp. 466–84.

27. See, for example, Joseph Famularo, *Handbook of Modern Personnel Administration* (New York: McGraw-Hill, 1972), p. 17.

28. See for example, Edward E. Lawler III, "Reward Systems," in Hackman and Suttle, *Improving Life at Work*, pp. 176–77.

29. Adapted from National Industrial Conference Board, *Personnel Practices in Factory and Office*, Studies in Personnel Policy No. 145 (1954), pp. 12, 69.

30. Bureau of National Affairs, *Finding and Training Potential Executives*, Personnel Policies Forum, Survey No. 58 (September 1960), p. 4, quoted in Wendell French, *The Personnel Management Process* (Boston: Houghton Mifflin, 1974), p. 339.

31. See, for example, James Huck and Douglas Bray, "Management Assessment Center Evaluations and Subsequent Job Performance of White and Black Females," *Personnel Psychology*, 29, No. 1 (Spring 1956).

32. J. Brad Chapman and Robert Otteman, *Employee Preference for Various Compensation and Fringe Benefit Options* (Berea, Ohio: ASPA Foundation, 1975).

33. Janis Hedges, "New Patterns for Working Time," *Monthly Labor Review*, 96 (1973), pp. 3–8; Myron D. Fottler, "Employee Acceptance of a Four-Day Work Week," *Academy of Management Journal*, 20, No. 4 (December 1977), pp. 656–68; Randall B. Dunham and Donald Hawk, "The Four Day/Forty Hour Week: Who Wants It?" *Academy of Management Journal*, 20, No. 4 (December 1977), pp. 644–55.

34. John Ivancevich and Herbert Lyon, "A Shortened Work Week: A Field Experiment," *Journal of Applied Psychology*, 62, No. 1 (1977), pp. 34–37.

35. William F. Guleck, "Changing Hours of Work: A Review and Analysis of the Research," *The Personnel Administrator* (American Society of Personnel Administration, 1978), reprinted in William F. Glueck, *Personnel: A Book of Readings* (Dallas: Business Publication, Inc., 1979).

36. Hedges, "New Patterns," Glueck, "Changing Hours," pp. 26–30.

37. J. H. Foegan, "From Flexitime to Fringe," *Personnel Administrator* (September 1976).

38. See, for example, Edward Deci, "Notes on the Theory and Metatheory of Intrinsic Motivation," *Organizational Behavior and Human Performance*, 15 (1976), pp. 130–45.

39. Hamner, "How to Ruin Motivation."

40. The literature in this area is voluminous: see, for example, Edward Deci, "The Effect of Externally Mediated Rewards on Intrinsic Motivation," *Journal of Personality and Social Psychology*, 18 (1971), 105–15; E. Deci, "Notes on the Theory;" E. Deci, W. Cascio and J. Crussell, "Evaluation Theory and Some Comments on the Calder and Stalk Critique," *Journal of Personality and Social Psychology*, 31 (1975), pp. 81–85.

41. See, for example, Robert Pritchard, Kathleen Campbell and Donald Campbell, "Effect of Extrinsic Financial Rewards on Intrinsic Motivation," *Journal of Applied Psychology*, 62, No. 1 (1977), 9–15; J. Bobby Calder and Mary Stow, "The Interaction of Intrinsic and Extrinsic Motivation; Some Methodological Notes," *Journal of Personality and Social Psychology*, 31 (1975), pp. 599–605; William E. Scott, Jr., "The Effect of Extrinsic Motivation: A Critique," *Organizational Behavior and Human Performance*, 15, No. 1 (February 1976).

6

Job Redesign and Enrichment

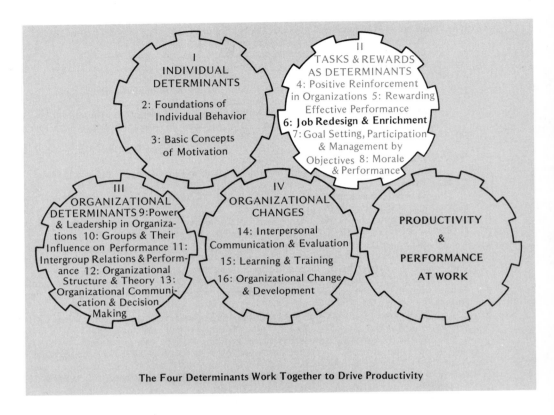

The Four Determinants Work Together to Drive Productivity

BY THE TIME YOU FINISH STUDYING THIS CHAPTER, YOU SHOULD BE ABLE TO:

1. *Compare and contrast job specialization and job enrichment.*
2. *Explain how you would enlarge a job.*
3. *Cite the arguments against job enrichment.*
4. *Answer the question: Is job enrichment effective at improving performance?*
5. *List the ingredients of an enriched job.*
6. *Explain how to use the technology for enriching jobs.*
7. *Discuss some actual job enrichment programs.*
8. *Explain how you would diagnose the need for job redesign.*

OVERVIEW

The main purpose of this chapter is to explain how to use job enrichment to improve attitudes, productivity, and performance at work. We first discuss basic approaches to job design including the "scientific management" approach of job specialization, job enlargement and job rotation, and job enrichment. We explain the arguments for and against job enrichment, and then describe a "technology" for enriching jobs. Finally, we discuss several actual job redesign programs. In the last chapter we explained how to use some important extrinsic rewards; in the present chapter we turn to building intrinsic rewards or consequences into the work, for example, by building in opportunities for challenge and creativity.

INTRODUCTION: INTRINSIC REWARDS AND MOTIVATION

Few rewards are as powerful as the sense of accomplishment and achievement that come from doing a job that you genuinely want to do, and doing it well. Thus, the person who collects stamps, builds a ham radio, or volunteers her time at the hospital generally doesn't have to be coerced or prodded into doing the job well since the job carries its own intrinsic rewards—in terms of challenge, achievement, and so on. In other words this sort of job— its content, functions, and specific duties—is "designed" in such a way so that performing it contributes to and satisfies people's "higher order" needs for achievement, recognition, and self-actualization. Needless to say, designing jobs at work to provide such intrinsic rewards can substantially increase employee morale and performance since, in the words of Katz and Kahn:

> Motivation is so internalized that performance is autonomous. The supervisor does not have to be present to wave a stick or offer candy. The activities carry their own rewards; they are so much a pattern of motive satisfaction that they need no additional incentives.[1]

BASIC APPROACHES TO JOB DESIGN

The basic issue in job design is whether jobs should be highly specialized and routine or highly "enriched" and nonroutine. Those who advocate specialized jobs argue for making jobs as simple as possible, so that each worker performs the same highly specialized task over and over again, many times a day, since in this way certain production efficiencies are obtained. Advocates of job enrichment, on the other hand, claim that such highly specialized jobs lead to unanticipated problems like boredom and animosity and that tasks should actually be recombined into more "enriched" jobs.

The Argument for Specialization

The modern argument for job specialization had its origins in the classical economic theory that developed in the early 1800s. This theory emphasized the advantages of efficiency, and it was, and still is, widely believed that highly specialized jobs are more efficient than less specialized ones. For example, one writer of the period, Charles Babbage, listed the following reasons for making jobs as specialized as possible:[2]

1. *There is less time required for learning.* When the job is highly specialized and involves, for example, always turning the same screw, it can be learned quickly, and little training is required. For example, it would probably take only two or three hours to train an assembly line worker to install a door handle on a car. However, it might take several days to train him to assemble a door and several years to train a person to assemble an entire car.

2. There is *less waste of material during the training period.* There is usually some wasted material while a person is learning how to perform a task, and this waste tends to be minimized when the job is simple and easily learned.

3. *There is less time lost in switching from task to task.* There is usually a short "warm-up" period required when a person starts a new task; as a result, there is always some time lost when a person switches from task to task. When a person can habitually perform the same task over and over again, there is no changeover time to be lost.

4. *Proficiency increases with practice.* When a person performs the same task over and over, he or she acquires a skill or proficiency that enables the person to perform the job relatively efficiently. In other words, "practice makes perfect."

5. *Hiring is made more efficient.* By dividing work into specialized jobs, the organization can hire and pay for a person who has exactly the skill level called for. Where the job is not specialized and requires the worker to perform several tasks, then he or she has to have enough skill to perform the most difficult task, and this is wasted on the simpler tasks that this person also has to perform.

6. *Parts become uniform and interchangeable.* Since each person is making the same part over and over again, the parts become more uniform and, as a result, more interchangeable.

Scientific Management. These somewhat theoretical arguments were expanded upon and applied by advocates of the Scientific Management school of thought. Scientific managers like Frederick Winslow Taylor and Frank and Lillian Gilbreth were implementers who developed principles and practices for "scientifically" analyzing tasks. In addition to using stopwatches to improve production efficiency, these experts developed various tools including "motion-study principles," "therbligs," and "micromotion study" to assist them in their quest for efficiency. Many of these tools are still used effectively today. Some *motion-study principles* include, for example:

1. The two hands should begin as well as complete their motions at the same time.
2. The two hands should not be idle at the same time except during rest periods.
3. Motions of the arms should be made at opposite and symmetrical directions and should be made simultaneously.[3]

Therbligs, another example of the tools these people used to analyze jobs, are elemental motions like "search," "grab," "hold," and "transport." (The notion of a therblig was developed by Frank and Lillian Gilbreth, who use their last name spelled backwards to come up with the name for their new tool.) Just as the 26 letters of the alphabet can be used to construct a multitude of words, any task, it was assumed, could be analyzed in terms of about 20 therbligs. It was believed that by observing and analyzing jobs one could identify redundant or unnecessary therbligs and eliminate these, thereby increasing the worker's productivity. *Micromotion study* is a similar approach to job design. It involves taking motion pictures of the worker doing his or her job and then analyzing the film by running it forward and backward at different speeds so that various details of the job can be examined and reexamined. Used in conjunction with timing devices, it was, and is, possible to determine precisely how long each component activity of a task takes a worker, and to improve the worker's performance by modifying or eliminating one or more of these activities.

The Drawbacks to Specialization. Scientific management took a purely "rational" approach to job design, and pursued technical efficiency with a single-minded abandon. It resulted in highly simplified, short-cycle jobs, jobs which consisted of performing the same activity over and over again, hundreds of times a day. The worker in this system was relegated to little more than the proverbial cog in the machine, and the worker was studied, analyzed, and prodded in a manner that many workers found increasingly demeaning and unacceptable. The worker became little more than an adjunct to a machine, and his or her responses were as completely programmed and beyond his or her control as they could be.

Almost from the onset of industrialization, however, workers rebelled (and are still rebelling) against being kept in so tight a harness and being dragged so far from the challenge that craft work provides; this rebelliousness has manifested itself in a number of ways.[4] These range from relatively harmless actions like daydreaming[5] to more serious problems like excessive absences[6] and antimanagement activities like wildcat strikes and sabotage.[7] In summary, as Sayles and Strauss point out:

> Management pays a price for the work simplification, routinization, and ease of supervision inherent in mass-production work. The cost is largely in terms of apathy and boredom, as positive satisfactions are engineered out of the jobs. Being confined physically and limited socially to contacting his own immediate supervisor, the factory worker sees very little of the total organization and even less of the total product being manufactured. It is hardly surprising that there is frequently little pride in work or identification with a job.[8]

Toward Less Specialized Jobs

Job Enlargement and Rotation. Management's initial response to problems like these was often to redesign jobs, either through job enlargement or through job rotation. *Job enlargement* involves assigning workers additional same-level tasks to increase the number of tasks they have to perform.[9] For example, if the work involved assembling chairs, the worker who previously only bolted the seat to the legs might take on the additional tasks of assembling the legs and attaching the back as well. *Job rotation*, involves systematically moving workers from one job to another. Thus, on an assembly line, a worker might spend an hour fitting doors, the next hour installing head lamps, the next hour fitting bumpers, and so on.

Both job enlargement and job rotation are similar in two ways. First, they both represent the antithesis of job specialization. With job specialization the objective is to reduce the job to its most fundamental components and to assign each component to a worker who will then perform it routinely. Job enlargement and rotation involve *recombining* simple jobs, assigning several to a worker to increase the variety of tasks he or she performs. Second, job enlargement and job rotation are not primarily aimed at injecting motivators like "challenge" into jobs. Instead, they are aimed at reducing the monotony and boredom that may be inherent in highly specialized jobs, by increasing the number and variety of simple tasks that are assigned to the worker.

Job Enrichment. *Job enrichment* is an approach to job redesign that *is* aimed at building motivators like opportunities for achievement into the job. It involves redesigning jobs—for example, by letting the person schedule her own work—to increase the opportunities for the worker to experience a feeling of responsibility, achievement, growth, and recognition by doing the job well. Job enrichment is always concerned with changing the content—the specific duties and functions—of the job rather than with hygiene factors like salary and working conditions.

Exhibit 6.1 An Outline of a Successful Job Enrichment Project

Specific changes aimed at enriching jobs	"Motivators" these changes are aimed at increasing
A. Removing some controls while retaining accountability	Responsibility and personal achievement
B. Increasing the accountability of individuals for own work	Responsibility and recognition
C. Giving a person a complete natural unit of work (module, division, area, and so on)	Responsibility, achievement, and recognition
D. Granting additional authority to an employee in his activity; job freedom	Responsibility, achievement, and recognition
E. Making periodic reports directly available to the worker himself rather than to the supervisor	Internal recognition
F. Introducing new and more difficult tasks not previously handled	Growth and learning
G. Assigning individuals specific or specialized tasks, enabling them to become expert	Responsibility, growth, and advancement

Source: Frederick Herzberg, "One More Time: How Do You Motivate Employees?"

An example of what Herzberg recalls "a highly successful job enrichment experiment" is illustrated in Exhibit 6.1. (In this case the jobs were those of people responsible for corresponding with a large corporation's stockholders—answering their questions and so on.) On the left of the exhibit are listed some of the changes that were aimed at enriching the job, such as "removing some controls while retaining accountability." On the right, are listed the motivators—such as recognition—these job changes were aimed at satisfying.

While the terms are sometimes used interchangeably, job enlargement and job enrichment are not exactly the same thing. Job enlargement usually involves a *horizontal* expansion of the worker's job, by increasing the number and variety of similar tasks he or she is assigned. Job enrichment, on the other hand, usually involves a *vertical* expansion of the worker's job in that tasks formerly carried out by his or her supervisor are now assigned to the worker. For example, he or she may be given more discretion to *schedule* the day's work, *communicate* directly with clients, and *inspect* the work that is produced.

ARGUMENTS FOR AND AGAINST JOB ENRICHMENT

The Case for Job Enrichment

Simply stated, the case for job enrichment may be summarized as follows:

> By increasing the duties and functions of a job, job enrichment replaces the sense of achievement, challenge, and accomplishment that job specialization removes and, in doing so, leads to increased employee morale and performance. Job enrichment builds motivators into the job, motivators like challenge and responsibility that can satisfy needs for psychological growth, achievement, recognition, and advancement. On the other hand, job specialization results in routine, short-cycle jobs that in turn can lead to monotony, boredom, dissatisfaction, and various behavioral consequences such as absenteeism and reduced performance.[10]

The case for job enrichment is an appealing one, for several reasons. It is, first of all *intuitively appealing*, since it just seems to make more sense to assume that people prefer interesting jobs to uninteresting ones. Related to this, job enrichment reflects what many believe is a more positive view of the *nature of man*, a view that emphasizes the importance of employees' achievement and self-actualization needs. Finally, there is also a good deal of *research evidence* that supports the usefulness of job enrichment. For reasons like these the job enrichment technique has spawned an unusual number of zealots. Their gospel was summarized as follows in a study called *Work in America*, which was written for the U.S. Department of Health, Education, and Welfare:

> Significant numbers of American workers are dissatisfied with the quality of their working lives. Dull, repetitive, seemingly meaningless tasks, offering little challenge or autonomy are causing discontent among workers at all occupational levels. . . . The redesign of jobs is the keystone of this report.[11]

Arguments Against Job Enrichment

The four arguments against job enrichment can be summarized as follows:

> *Job enrichment is expensive.* First, job enrichment increases costs for exactly those reasons that specialization reduces them. Specifically, it involves higher training and production costs, and whether or not the benefits derived can compensate for these higher costs is something that has to be evaluated for each situation. As two writers put it:

> > At some point, suggestions for enlarging jobs, increasing skills, lengthening job cycles, and rotating tasks bump into the logic which dictated the division of labor in the first place. . . . The return to craft production may be humanly desirable but is impractical. Every addition to jobs which requires workers to spend more time learning the job, or alternating tools, or which entails greater inventories or duplication of tools, is likely to raise unit costs.[12]

> *Inadequate theoretical basis.* Others argue that job enrichment's theoretical underpinnings are shaky on two counts. First, job enrichment is based largely on the work of Frederick Herzberg, and, as we saw, there are many who assert that Herzberg's theory is invalid. (For a detailed discussion of this see Chapter 3), Basic Concepts of Motivation. Second, we now believe that routine, short-cycle jobs are not automatically viewed as boring, demoralizing, or counterproductive by many (or most) workers. In many instances, researchers have found that workers actually seem to prefer the more routine jobs, and, based on the evidence, it is simply not possible to generalize about how the worker will react to a routine job without specifying his or her age, cultural background, values, needs, and other traits.[13]

> *The problem of individual differences.* A related argument is that individuals vary so widely in their values and needs that one simply cannot generalize about the effectiveness of job enrichment. For example, two researchers[14] found that workers in urban, big city factories seemed to be alienated from the work ethic and therefore did not respond well to job enrichment; those in rural settings were not alienated and did respond favorably. Furthermore, employees who have strong growth needs (for self-actualization, achievement, and recognition) and who are also satisfied with the basic hygienes of the work (pay, job security, coworkers, and supervisors) respond more positively to enriched jobs than do employees who have weak needs for growth and/or are dissatisfied with basic hygienes like pay.[15]

Natural selection: workers get what they want. One writer argues that job enrichment often fails because workers in apparently routine, "boring" jobs have intentionally chosen these types of jobs and are therefore put off by attempts to complicate them.[16]

How Successful Has Job Enrichment Been?

These arguments notwithstanding, the "bottom line" is whether or not job enrichment is effective at improving performance, and this, unfortunately, is not an easy question to answer. The main problem is that most of the studies in this area have been "uncontrolled" since, in addition to the job enrichment program, other changes were also taking place in the companies studied.

Thus, it is impossible to say for sure whether the improvements that occurred after the enrichment program resulted from the enrichment or from some other change such as a pay raise, a friendlier manager, or a tighter job market.[17] As a result, the research findings are a little sketchy, but on the whole they indicate that job enrichment can improve employee attitudes and performance (especially quality of output), if the enrichment program is implemented properly.

Herzberg reports the results of one relatively well-controlled experiment[18] that involved the stockholder correspondents of a large corporation. There "almost all indexes of performance and job attitudes were low, and exit interviewing confirmed that the challenge of the job existed merely as words"; therefore, a job enrichment program was implemented. Among other things, this involved removing some supervisory controls, increasing employees' accountability for their work, granting employees additional authority, and introducing new and more difficult tasks to those previously handled. The enrichment program was implemented in one "achieving" group, while a "control" group continued to do its job in the traditional way. (There were also two "uncommitted" groups of correspondents to ensure that attitudes in either the achieving or control groups had not changed merely because employees knew that they were part of an experiment.) The change in performance for each group is displayed in Exhibit 6.2. Performance (in terms of quality and speed of response to stockholders' letters of inquiry) improved markedly in the achieving group; attitudes improved as well.

As another example, from 1965 to 1968 a group of researchers at AT&T conducted 19 formal field experiments in job enrichment.[19] According to Robert Ford, who is an advocate of job enrichment, of the 19 studies, 9 were rated "outstandingly successful," one was a "complete flop," and the remaining 9 were "moderately successful."[20]

Exhibit 6.2 Effect of Job Enrichment in Correspondents Study

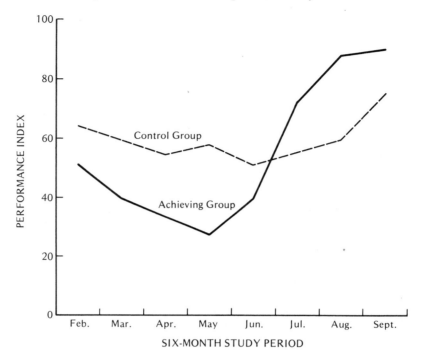

Source: Frederich Herzberg, "One More Time: How Do You Motivate Employees?", Reprinted in Harvard Business Review, *Motivation Series*, p. 61.

In another experiment, a group of researchers investigated the effects of both job enrichment and goal setting on employee productivity and satisfaction. They found that job enrichment improved satisfaction but had little effect on productivity. Goal setting (having a supervisor and an employee jointly set specific, difficult goals for the latter), on the other hand, had a major impact on productivity and a less substantial impact on satisfaction. These researchers therefore suggest using job enrichment in conjunction with goal setting.[21] :

Locke and his associates introduced a job enrichment program in three clerical work units of a federal agency. In this case, job enrichment apparently had no effect on attitudes. Productivity did increase, but, on the basis of interviews and observations, the researchers concluded that these changes could be attributed mainly to a more efficient use of manpower and elimination of unnecessary operations, not to the job enrichment program.[22]

Summary. On the whole, job enrichment does seem to result in improved attitudes and performance, but two caveats are in order. First, detractors have argued that most studies of enrichment have been uncontrolled, have used unrepresentative groups of employees, and have reflected the overoptimism of the researchers themselves.[23] Many of these arguments are valid, and enrichment advocates will have to try to deal with them. (However, from a practical point of view it may be impossible to implement an effective enrichment program without simultaneously making other improvements in the organization—such as better pay, improved staffing, and more attention to goal setting—and unscrambling the effects of all these changes may not be feasible, or particularly useful.) Second, it goes without saying that how the enrichment program is implemented will determine its effectiveness. For example, do employees want the program? Is it economically feasible in this case? and so on. We should, therefore, turn to the issue of how to implement a job enrichment program.

HOW TO ENRICH JOBS

What Are the Characteristics of "Enriched" Jobs?

In order to "set the stage" for our discussion of how to enrich jobs, it would be useful to briefly review what Herzberg, who many consider the "father" of job enrichment says are the main characteristics of an enriched job. These are as follows[24]:

> *Direct feedback:* The employee should get timely, direct, noncritical feedback concerning his or her performance.
>
> *Client relationships:* The worker should have a customer or client to serve, either external to the organization or inside it. For example, instead of typing memos for everyone on a first come first served basis, each secretary in the typing pool is assigned to a specific department.
>
> *New learning:* According to Herzberg, an essential ingredient of a good job is the opportunity for individuals to feel that they are growing psychologically. In one case, for example, laboratory technicians were previously responsible only for setting up the laboratory equipment for the research scientists. After job enrichment, they were given additional responsibility for the research reports, which created the opportunity for them to analyze and evaluate data and to learn to write scientific reports.
>
> *Scheduling:* Herzberg says that another ingredient is the opportunity to schedule one's own work. In one plant, for example workers had

previously been told when they could take coffee, rest, and lunch breaks. After enrichment, workers were held accountable for meeting quotas and could schedule their own breaks.

Unique experience: Herzberg says that "in this day of homogenization and assembly line intelligence when everyone is judged on sameness, there exists a countervailing need for some personal uniqueness at work—for providing aspects of jobs that the worker can consider as "doing his own thing.""[25]

Control over resources: Herzberg recommends giving employees or groups of employees their own "mini-budgets," and pushing cost and profit centers down as low as is organizationally feasible.

Direct communications authority: The worker should have direct access to his or her customer or client.

Personal accountability: For example, inspectors could be eliminated and the employee allowed to both assemble and inspect his or her own product.

A Technology for Enriching Jobs

A group of researchers has developed a new technology for implementing job enrichment programs.[26] These researchers say that people "get turned on to"—are motivated to perform—their work if: the activity is *meaningful* to the person, the person knows he or she is solely *responsible* for its completion, and he or she has *knowledge of results* within a few seconds.[27]

As illustrated in Exhibit 6.3, the researchers assume there are five "core job dimensions" that determine whether the person will in fact experience this *meaningfulness, responsibility,* and *knowledge of results:*

Skill variety—the degree to which the job requires the worker to perform activities that challenge his or her skills and abilities

Task identity—the degree to which the job requires completion of a "whole" identifiable piece of work

Task significance—the degree to which the job has a substantial and perceivable effect on the lives of other people, in the organization or the world at large

Autonomy—the degree to which the job gives the worker freedom and independence

Knowledge of results—the degree to which the worker gets information about the effectiveness of his or her job efforts.

Step 1—Diagnosis: The first step in developing a job enrichment program, according to these researchers, is to diagnose the problem: here one

Exhibit 6.3 Relationships Among Core Job Dimensions, Critical Psychological States, and On-the-Job Outcomes

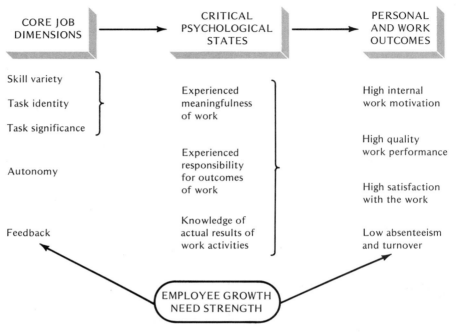

Source: J. Richard Hackman, Greg Oldham, Robert Janson, and Kenneth Purdy, "A new Strategy for Job Enrichment," California Management Review, Vol. 17, No. 4.

determines if the job is amenable to job enrichment. This process consists of answering four questions (the researchers have questionnaires to formalize this process):

1. *Are motivation and satisfaction central to the problem?* Or is there some other problem (a poorly designed production system, etc.)?
2. *Is the job low in motivating potential?* Is the *job* the source of the motivation problem identified in Step 1?
3. *What specific aspects of the job are causing the difficulty?* Here examine the job on the five "core dimensions" presented above.
4. *How "ready" are the employees for change?* As discussed above, not everyone is motivated by job enrichment. The extent to which job enrichment is effective depends on the workers' needs—for self-actualization, achievement, and so on.

Step 2—Implementation: After diagnosing the problem, the next step

Exhibit 6.4 The Full Model: How Use of the Implementing Techniques Can Lead to Positive Outcomes

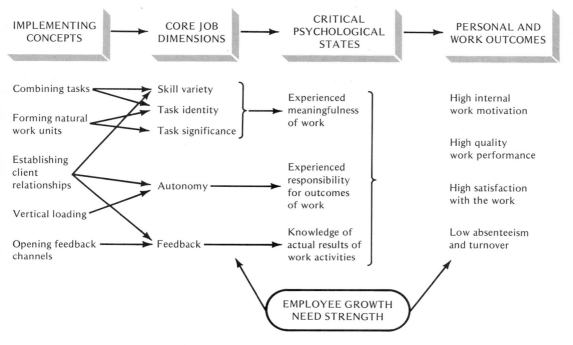

Source: J. Richard Hackman, Greg Aldham, Robert Janson, and Kenneth Purdy, "A new strategy for Job Enrichment," California Management Review, Vol. 17, No. 4.

is implementation. Here, as summarized above in Exhibit 6.4, take specific actions to enrich the jobs, for example:

1. *Form natural work groups.* Here we change the job in such a way that each person is responsible for—"owns"—an identifiable body of work. For example, instead of having the typist in a typing pool do work for all departments, we might make the work of one or two departments the continuing responsibility of each typist.

2. *Combine tasks.* For example, let one person assemble a product from start to finish, instead of having it go through several separate operations that are performed by different people.

3. *Establish client relationships.* Let the worker have contact, as often as possible, with the consumer of the product.

4. *Vertical loading.* Let the worker plan and control his or her own job, instead of having it controlled by outsiders. For example, let the worker set his or her own schedule, do his or her trouble shooting, decide when to start and stop working, and so on.

5. *Open feedback channels.* Finally, find more and better ways for the worker to get quick feedback on his or her performance.

Research Results. The researchers tested their job enrichment approach at the Travelers Insurance Company and found it to be effective. The work group chosen was a key punching operation. Here, the employees' function was to transfer the information from printed or written documents onto punched cards for computer input. Prior to enrichment work output was inadequate, error rates were high, schedules were often missed, and absenteeism and turnover were higher than average. The researchers first carried out a diagnosis, based on the steps we summarized above, and determined that there was a need for job enrichment. As a result, they took the following steps:

> *Formed natural work groups.* Each key punch operator was assigned continuing responsibility for certain accounts—for example, each worked only for particular departments.
>
> *Combined tasks.* Key punchers began doing more of their own "verifying" or inspecting to see that the cards were punched correctly.
>
> *Established client relationships.* Each operator was given several channels of direct contact with clients. The operators, not their assignment clerks, now inspect the documents for correctness and legibility. When problems arise, the operators, not the supervisor, take them up with the client.
>
> *Provided feedback.* In addition to feedback from client contact, other channels of feedback were installed. For example, the computer operators now return incorrect cards to the operators who punched them, and operators correct their own errors.
>
> *Vertically loaded jobs.* For example, operators may now set their own schedules and plan their daily work as long as they meet the schedules.

According to the researchers, the results of this experiment were dramatic. The number of operators declined from 98 to 60. In the group whose jobs were enriched, quantity of work increased by almost 40 percent, as compared with an increase of only about 8 percent in the control, no change group. Absenteeism in the enrichment group decreased by 24 percent after jobs were enriched, while in the controlled group absenteeism actually increased by almost 30 percent. Favorable attitudes toward the job increased by over 16 percent in the enrichment group, while they remained about the same in the control group. Actual savings in salary and machine rental charges during the first year totalled $64,305. Thus the application of this particular job enrichment technology apparently resulted in substantial increases in employee morale and productivity.[27]

ACTUAL JOB REDESIGN PROGRAMS

In practice, job enrichment is usually carried out in conjunction with other redesign efforts, including job enlargement, job rotation, and the instituting of self-contained work teams. Furthermore, as we'll see, job enrichment programs are often associated with increased employee participation and with an increase in hygienes like pay and working conditions. Several examples of actual job redesign programs follow.

The Stockholder Correspondent Job at AT&T

The enrichment of the stockholder correspondent's job at AT&T (which we mentioned briefly above) is one good example of job enrichment in practice.[28] Stockholder correspondents are responsible for corresponding with stockholders of the company by answering the latters' questions and informing them about such things as stockholder meetings. This would seem to be a relatively complex and challenging job, but in this case "performance and attitudes were found to be low" and, according to Herzberg, "the challenge of the job existed merely as words."[29]

As a result, a controlled job enrichment experiment was carried out that, as we discussed, proved quite successful. It involved "vertical loading"— giving the correspondents more control over their jobs—as follows:

"Subject matter experts" were appointed within each group of correspondents for other members to consult with before seeking supervisory help. (The supervisor had been answering all specialized and difficult questions.)

Correspondents now sign their own names on letters. (The supervisor had been signing all letters).

The work of the more experienced correspondents was proofread less frequently by supervisors and was done at the correspondent's desk, dropping verification from 100 percent to 10 percent. (Previously all correspondents' letters had been checked by the supervisor).

Production was discussed, but only in terms such as "a full day's work is expected." As time went on, this was no longer mentioned. (Before, the group had been constantly reminded of the number of letters that needed to be answered.)

Outgoing mail went directly to the mail room without going over supervisors' desks. (The letters had always been routed to the supervisors.)

Correspondents were encouraged to answer letters in a more personalized way. (Reliance on the form-letter approach had been standard practice.)

Each correspondent was held personally responsible for the quality and accuracy of letters. (This responsibility had been the responsibility of the supervisor and the verifier.)[30]

Job "Nesting" at AT&T

The American Telephone and Telegraph Company[31] has carried out many job enrichment programs; according to Robert Ford, who was responsible for these changes, they demonstrate that productivity and morale rise when a worker can claim "a job of my own."[32] The general strategy behind job enrichment at AT&T is summarized in Exhibit 6.5. As can be seen, improving a job involves pulling down responsibilities from above (for example, by letting employees schedule their own work, and deal directly with clients); pulling "prework" and later work stages into the job (for example, by letting key punch operators verify their own work); and pushing work down to lower job classifications (for example, having the supervisors delegate more responsibility to subordinates).

At Indiana Bell Telephone Company, for example, 33 clerical employees compiled all telephone directories for the state. The processing from clerk to clerk was laid out in 21 steps, many of which were for verification:

Exhibit 6.5 Steps in Enriching a Job at AT&T

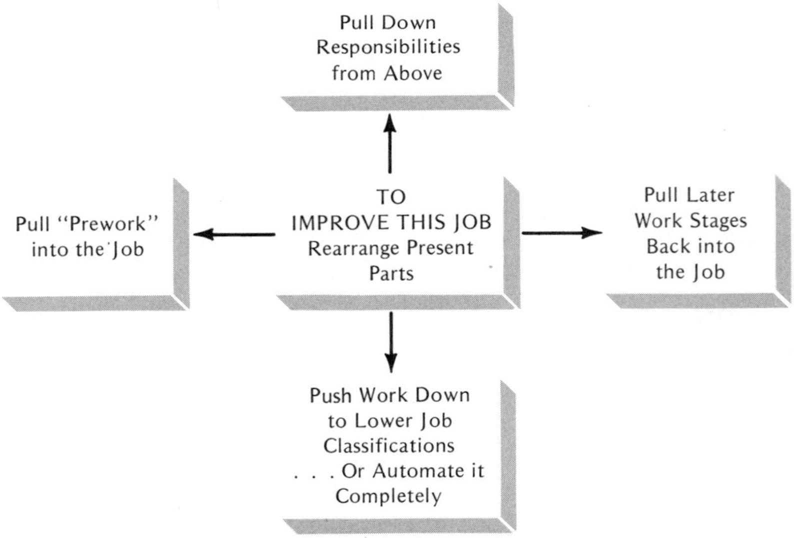

Source: Robert Ford, "Job Enrichment Lessons from AT & T," *Harvard Business Review*, January-February, 1973, pp. 96–106. Reprinted in Keith Davis, *Organizational Behavior: A Book of Readings* (New York: McGraw-Hill, 1977), p. 201.

thus, the steps included manuscript reception, manuscript verification, key punch, key punch verification, and so on, in what amounted to an assembly line operation. Morale was low, turnover was unacceptable, and a job enrichment program was instituted to alleviate these problems. Supervisors and employees were consulted, and because all agreed that employees could do error-free work, most "verification" steps were eliminated. Next, employees agreed that they could "own" their own phone books and perform all remaining steps themselves. For example, new entries to all directories had previously been made by a succession of clerks; now *all* paperwork connected with the book belonging to a clerk stayed with that clerk. According to Ford, "owning" one's own book, combined with the increased responsibility and range of tasks each clerk performs, has increased morale and performance at Indiana Bell.

Based on successes like this, AT&T has been investigating ways of going beyond enriching of individual jobs. One way they are doing this is by "nesting" several jobs to improve morale and upgrade performance. Basically, job nesting involves rearranging the physical layout of offices to reinforce the fact that each group of employees has its own particular client to serve.

For example, Southwestern Bell Telephone Company was able to substantially improve the morale and productivity of a group of its service representatives through a combination of job enrichment and job nesting. Before the job enrichment started, the service representatives' office was laid out as it appears in Exhibit 6.6. Desks were lined up in a standard, "in line" arrangement, facing the desks of the supervisors who exercised close control of the service representatives.

As part of the enrichment effort, each service representative group was assigned a geographical locality of its own, instead of being responsible for just "the next customer who calls in from anywhere in the district"; this added an "enriched" element to their jobs. At the same time, each "geographical" location group was "nested," by moving their desks and those of their supervisors to form a sort of wagon train layout. As in Exhibit 6.7, they were gathered into a more or less circular shape and were no longer directly facing the desks of the business office supervisors and unit managers. (The district manager's office was further removed too.) In total, this nesting helped to reinforce the unique identity of each service group, as well as the fact that they were not as closely supervised as before.

Production Teams at Volvo[33]

As is often the case, job redesign at Volvo Auto in Sweden began as a reaction to a number of severe personnel problems facing the company. Wild-

Exhibit 6.6 District Service Representatives Office Layout Before Job Enrichment

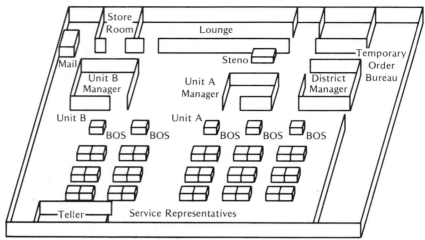

BOS-Business Office Supervisor

Note: Desks lined up in standard "in-line" arrangement, facing supervisors.

Source: Robert Ford, "Job Enrichment Lessons from AT & T," *Harvard Business Review,*
January-February, 1973, pp. 96–106. Reprinted in Keith Davis, *Organizational Behavior:*
A Book of Readings (New York: McGraw-Hill, 1977), p. 202.

cat strikes, turnover, absenteeism, and dependence on foreign workers had
become such acute problems that management was willing to experiment with
the relatively "inefficient," less specialized jobs, to restore some semblance
of continuity to its production lines.

Job redesign at Volvo included job rotation, job enlargement, and an
enrichment of employees' jobs that involved forming them into production
teams. *Job rotation* was instituted on the production line that was responsible
for sealing car bodies. The "internal sealing" job is an especially uncomfortable one, since employees have to work in cramped positions inside the car
body. In this case, jobs were rotated every other hour. The remaining jobs on
the line are rotated daily. *Job enlargement* was instituted on an assembly
line. Here employees follow the same car body for seven or eight stations
along the line for a total period of 20 minutes, performing each of the jobs
that a separate worker previously would have carried out at each station. This
results in a job for each worker that takes seven or eight times longer than
his previous, specialized job. Job rotation and enlargement is strictly voluntary
at Volvo, and about 20 percent of the employees have volunteered for these
programs.

Exhibit 6.7 Job "Nesting": Service Representatives Office Layout After Job Enrichment Program Was Implemented

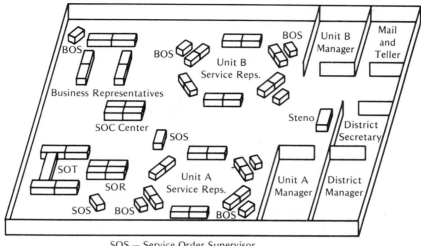

SOS — Service Order Supervisor
SOC — Service Order Control
SOR — Service Order Reviewers
SOT — Service Order Typists

Note: Desks for each area moved into "wagon train" circles, with reps no longer facing supervisors directly.

Source: Robert Ford, "Job Enrichment Lessons from AT & T," *Harvard Business Review*, January-February, 1973, pp. 96–106. Reprinted in Keith Davis, *Organizational Behavior: A Book of Readings* (New York: McGraw-Hill, 1977), p. 203.

Several Volvo plants have also instituted job enrichment, "production team" programs. At one truck assembly plant, for example, production teams of 5 to 12 men together assemble entire engines. Each group elects its own "charge hand" (supervisor), schedules its own output, distributes work among its members, and does its own quality control. The team is paid on a group piecework basis, (rather than on an individual piecework basis), and everyone in the group therefore earns the same amount, except the charge hand.

So far, the effectiveness of job redesign at Volvo is unclear. At a truck assembly plant the introduction of the production teams apparently has reduced turnover and absenteeism and improved product quality. At the auto plant (where job rotation and enlargement were introduced), turnover dropped from 40 to 25 percent. However, the introduction of job redesign coincided with an economic slowdown, which may have accounted for much of this reduction. And, when Volvo surveyed its employees to probe for the causes of turnover and absenteeism, most of the causes turned out to be external—child care, long distances traveling to the plant, and so on. As a result, Volvo instituted other changes (including extending the bus fleet and loaning money to employees to purchase apartments), and these changes probably contributed to the reduction in turnover and absenteeism.

Regardless of this, Volvo's new assembly plant at Kalmar, Sweden has been especially designed to accommodate the production team approach. The plant is shaped like a star, and in each point of the star there is a work group finishing a big share of the whole automobile—the electrical system, the safety system, the interior, and so on. Each work team of 15 to 25 persons distributes the work among themselves, and the employees determine their own work rhythm, subject to meeting overall production standards. Thus, if they decide to work hard in the morning and relax in the afternoon, the decision is theirs. As happens in the truck assembly plant, each team chooses its own boss and can deselect him if he turns out poorly. Architecturally, the building has been designed to preserve the atmosphere of a small workshop. For example, each work team has its own entrance, dressing room, rest room, and so on. Furthermore, each team is physically shielded from a view of the other teams by special walls and buffers.

Job Redesign at Saab-Scania

One of the best known job enrichment programs was instituted at the Scania division of the Saab automobile company in Sweden. As in the case at Volvo, employee turnover had been running (in 1969) about 45 percent annually, and the personnel situation was described by one expert as "horrendous":[34] it was becoming impossible to fill jobs on the shop floor and therefore to maintain an even flow of production.

As a result of these problems, several job redesign programs were initiated at Saab. For example, one plant instituted small-group assembly of auto engines. As shown in Exhibit 6.8, this plant is laid out in such a way that all the basic components for an engine—cylinder heads, engine block, spark plugs, and so on—are supplied to one of seven production teams (in the upper left of the exhibit). Each team plans its own work, makes its own assignments, and assembles its own engine; the engines are then sent to testing, and shipping. While this approach worked well enough with small car engines, it proved impossible with larger truck diesel engines. Assembling them this way was a six-hour undertaking involving 1,500 parts and was abandoned at the employees' request.

A similar program was instituted in a truck chassis assembly plant. Here production groups of 5 to 12 workers with related job duties decide among themselves how they will do their jobs. For instance, they can rotate

Exhibit 6.8 Diagram of Engine Plant, Saab-Scania

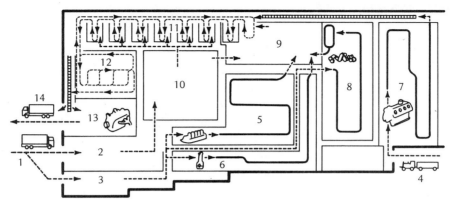

1. Goods Reception	5. Machining Cylinder heads	11. Group Assembyly
2. Arrival Inspection	6. Machining Connecting Rods	12. Engine Testing
Purchased Factory Parts	7. Machining Engine Blocks	13. Ready Stock
3. Raw Material Store	8. Machining Crankshafts	14. Engines to Trollhattan
4. Engine Blocks (Material	9. Preassembly	and Uusikaupunki
from Own Foundry)	10. Parts Store	

Source: Editor, *Organizational Dynamics*, "Job Redesign on the Assembly Line: Farewell to Blue-Color Blues?" Reprinted in Dennis Organ, *ReApplied Psychology of Work Behavior* (Dallas: BPI, 1978), p. 270.

job assignments, do many jobs or fewer, and vary their pace. Furthermore, other tasks were "pulled into" and made a part of each truck chassis assembly groups' job. For example, certain "housekeeping," simple service and maintenance, and quality control activities previously performed by staff personnel were made an integral part of the production teams' tasks.

As at Volvo, the effectiveness of job redesign at Saab is not entirely clear, although (again, as at Volvo) management thinks enough of the programs to be planning to continue and expand them. On the positive side, the production team approach means that each worker is less specialized and able to do more jobs, which makes the plant more flexible. Because automation has, in a sense, been reversed, there is less investment in complex, automated machine tools. Productivity is apparently higher than it would have been with the conventional (but troubled) assembly line, although at this point there is no absolute proof. Each engine now takes longer to assemble, and training costs have increased, but, on the other hand, quality has improved and turnover has decreased. Yet an economic downturn and other changes make it difficult to assess the extent to which improvements are a result of job redesign.

SUMMARY: CONDITIONS UNDER WHICH JOB ENRICHMENT IS MOST EFFECTIVE

The Two Main Barriers in Job Enrichment

Numerous barriers to effectively implementing job enrichment have been identified,[35] but these barriers usually fall into one of two categories. First, there is often insufficient *diagnosis* of the jobs involved, of the situation surrounding these jobs, and of the need for using job redesign to raise morale and performance. As a result, job enrichment (or some other job redesign program) is often initiated although employees do not want it, the job itself is not amenable to enrichment, or the "motivational" problem is caused not by the job but by some other problems like low pay, poor working conditions, unclear performance standards, or inadequate training. The second barrier is that the redesign is often attempted "in a vacuum," rather than as a concerted effort—one entailing improved training and appraisal, better pay, and various other associated improvements. As a result, employees (subordinates, supervisors, and managers alike), lacking in sufficient training, education, and "priming" may resist the "improvements" and further cripple the program.[36]

Diagnosis: Conditions Under Which Job Enrichment Will More Likely Be Effective

Given the need to accurately diagnose the situation before proceeding with job enrichment (or some other job redesign program), it would be useful to summarize some "guidelines for diagnosis" (based on the research findings discussed in this chapter). To diagnose the need for job redesign one should ask:

> *Is motivation central to the problem?* We have seen that job enrichment has the potential for increasing morale and performance, but this is only possible when the problem (such as high turnover, low quality, or poor productivity) stems from dissatisfaction or low motivation. In many cases, for example, employees could not do the job even if they wanted to, because they live too far from the plant, their tools are inadequate, there is interdepartmental conflict, or because of some other "nonmotivational" reason. In other words, remember our "ABCs" of performance. Do employees know what is expected of them? Could they do the job if they wanted to? What are the consequences of effective (or ineffective) performance?
>
> *Is there an easier way?* Related to the first point, it is usually a good idea to ask, "Is there an easier way to improve the situation in question?" Sometimes, for example, improved personnel testing and training might eliminate the problem.
>
> *Are the hygienes adequate?* One thing most job enrichment experts

agree on is that enrichment will not reduce problems caused by inadequate hygienes like low pay, poor working conditions, or nonacceptable leadership practices. Employees usually have to be at least adequately satisfied with these hygienes—in other words, their lower level needs must be fairly well satisfied—for job enrichment (with its appeal to higher level needs) to be effective.[37]

Is the job low in motivating potential? Here, analyze the job in terms of the skill variety, task identity, task significance, autonomy, and knowledge of results that were part of the job enrichment technology we discussed earlier in this chapter.

Is it technically and economically feasible to enrich the jobs? In some cases there are simply too many costs involved in de-automating to make job enrichment ever pay for itself. At Saab, for example, the complexity of assembling an entire diesel truck engine was so great that the employees themselves asked to have the experiment aborted. Herzberg therefore suggests zeroing in on those jobs in which "the investment in industrial engineering does not make changes too costly."[40] Richard Walton says that the particular technology and manufacturing process must provide significant room for human attitude and motivation to affect costs and, furthermore, it has to be technically and economically feasible to eliminate some (but not all) of the routinized, inherently boring work.[41]

Is quality important? There seems to be little doubt that as far as the final product is concerned it is its *quality* rather than its *quantity* that is usually the main "performance" beneficiary of job enrichment. An important question then concerns whether quality—or an increase in quality—is necessary.

Are workers ready for the change? and, Do they want it? Experts also agree that the workers that seem to benefit most from job enrichment are those whose psychological growth needs—their higher level needs for self-actualization, achievement, and challenge—are aroused. Remember, as we discussed earlier in this chapter, that for many employees (and for many different reasons) apparently boring jobs are neither boring nor dissatisfying—instead they simply "get turned on" by various nonwork interests.

Job Enrichment Must be Part of a Concerted Effort

It is also apparent that job enrichment is generally not effective unless it is part of a broader effort on the part of the organization. Specifically, it generally has to coincide with coordinated changes in pay, performance appraisal, training, and similar factors. As one expert has stated:

> Job design may generate into a mere gimmick if it is not part of both a comprehensive new policy concerning the use and development of human resources and a comprehensive new philosophy of management.

There are many nonjob factors that often have to be reappraised and possibly changed when implementing a job enrichment program.[41] These include:

Managerial assumptions and supervisor/subordinate relationships. For example, supervisors and managers have to come to understand that the employees can function effectively with their new autonomy.

Organization structure. For example, enriched jobs often permit wider "spans of control." As the tasks normally carried out by supervisors are absorbed by their subordinates, the number of supervisors may decrease, and the remaining supervisors end up with more subordinates reporting to them.

Pay. Job enrichment leads to increased responsibility and, often, to a production team approach to assembly. Changes like these demand commensurate changes in how employees are paid—for example, there may be a shift from individual incentive to group incentive plans and to higher pay in general.

Performance appraisal. As jobs become more responsible and less routine, there may have to be a shift from a more mechanical approach to appraisal (like "graphic rating forms") to a more professional approach involving mutual goal setting.[42] In general, there is often a deemphasis on closely monitoring the *means* by which employees get their tasks done and a corresponding emphasis on periodically checking the *end results.*

Communications. Job enrichment (like any organizational change), requires open, effective communications to be implemented properly. This usually involves a good deal of two-way communication between supervisors and production workers about schedules, production problems, and quality.[43]

Selection, placement, and training. The new responsibility, decision making, and involvement that are associated with job enrichment generally demand corresponding changes in the organization's selection, placement, and training procedures. Workers who have the ability to learn the new techniques have to be trained in their proper execution, new selection criteria have to be developed, and more care has to be taken in placing employees in the more demanding jobs.

JOB REDESIGN AND THE "ABC s" OF PERFORMANCE

The "ABC" approach can help you to analyze the need for, and effectiveness of, a job enrichment program. For example, it can help you to analyze whether there is a *need* for such a program. When analyzing the *behavior* component, for example, ask, "is motivation central to the problem, or is the person simply unable to do the job?" Similarly, since the challenge employees get from performing their jobs can be an important *consequence,* ask, when focusing on consequences, "Does the person get a sense of achievement from doing his job?" "Is getting a sense of achievement important in this situation?"

The "ABC" approach can also help you analyze why a job enrichment program has not been effective. For example, assume you have implemented such a program, but that productivity and performance are no better than before. Ask, for example:

> *Antecedents.* Do the employees understand the new program? Do they know how to do their new jobs? Do they understand their new standards?
>
> *Behavior.* Could they do their jobs if they wanted to? Have they received the necessary training? Do the supervisors allow them enough discretion?
>
> *Consequences?* Are the consequences for performing positive? Do the employees want the additional challenge and responsibility? Have salaries been raised to reflect the added duties?

CHAPTER SUMMARY

1. The basic issue in job design is whether the job should be highly specialized and routine or highly enriched and nonroutine. Those who advocate specialization argue that specialized jobs are more efficient—there is less time required for learning, less waste of materials, "practice makes perfect." and so on. Those who argue for job enrichment (and, to a lesser extent, for job enlargement and job rotation) claim that by increasing the duties and functions of a job, job enrichment replaces the sense of achievement, challenge, and accomplishment that job specialization removes, and in doing so "turns employees on" to their jobs and leads to increased employee morale and performance.

2. Those who argue *against* job enrichment claim that its theoretical basis (Herzberg's theory) is inadequate, that it is too expensive, and that many employees actually prefer more specialized jobs. On the whole, the evidence on job enrichment tends to show that it *does* improve attitudes and productivity. However, it is possible that these improvements are also a result of other changes—like better goal setting and improved pay—that usually are associated with job enrichment programs.

3. According to Herzberg, the ingredients of an enriched job include: direct feedback, client relationships, new learning, scheduling, unique experience, control over resources, direct communications authority, and personal accountability.

4. The technology for enriching jobs assumes that there are five "core dimensions" that determine whether the person will experience the necessary job meaningfulness, responsibility, and knowledge of results: *skill variety, task identity, task significance, autonomy,* and *knowledge of results.* To build these core dimensions into the job one can: form natural work groups; combine tasks; establish client relationships; vertically load jobs; or open feedback channels.

5. Actual job redesign programs at AT&T, Volvo, and Saab generally seem to have improved attitudes and productivity, and these companies have decided to continue their programs. Again, however, effective job enrichment programs are always associated with other changes—increased employee participation, better goal setting, increased hygienes like pay and working conditions—and it is not possible at this time to determine to what extent any improvements resulted from these changes, rather than the job enrichment itself.

6. Two main barriers to job enrichment are *inadequate diagnosis* and the failure to make the program a part of a more *concerted effort*. Diagnosis involves asking questions like "Is motivation central to the problem?" "Is there an easier way?" and "Are the hygienes adequate?" Making job enrichment part of a *concerted effort* includes changing managerial assumptions, modifying the organization structure, and improving pay and the performance appraisal system.

7. To use our terms, job enrichment may be effective because the challenge that is "built into" the job is an important *consequence* of performing the job: the job thus provides "its own rewards."

8. Having discussed some important rewards, we return, in the next chapter, to a more detailed look at Goal Setting, which is one important way in which a manager can ensure that his or her employees know what is expected of them.

DISCUSSION QUESTIONS AND PROJECTS

1. Set up a debate in a class: have two people argue for job specialization, and two argue for job enrichment. Could the two groups develop any areas of agreement between them? Over what issues?

2. Explain how Herzberg's motivation theory is related to job enrichment.

3. Answer the question: Is job enrichment useful for improving performance?

4. Would you recommend job enrichment for workers who are dissatisfied because of low pay? Why?

5. Discuss the conditions under which job enrichment will more likely fail.

6. "To believe in job enrichment, you have to believe that people do not like routine jobs." Explain why you agree or disagree with this statement.

7. Would you consider a professor's job enriched or not enriched? What would you do to make it more enriched? What would you do to make it less enriched?

8. Working in groups of four or five students, give several concrete examples of how you would enrich the following jobs: toll-booth attendant; assembly-line worker in an auto factory; directory assistance operator; bus driver.

9. Discuss the conditions under which job enrichment will more likely result in increased motivation. Based on this, would you in fact try to enrich all of the jobs listed in the preceding discussion question?

10. Working in groups of four or five, pick out a job and specify how you would go about enriching it. Indicate both what you would do to change the job and the motivators you are aiming to build into the job with the changes.

CASE EXERCISE

Memo From the General Manager

Cal Johnson, general manager of the assembly department of TMC's refrigeration division, was perplexed. For several months, a number of the men working on mechanical assembly had been grumbling about their jobs. Mostly they mentioned things like the monotony of the assembly work, long hours at the conveyor, low pay, and noisy working conditions.

The comments of two of the older and more experienced employees were typical. Sam Campanella told Cal Johnson that he was ready to ask for a transfer if something wasn't done about his job: "A guy can go crazy just screwing on doors and fitting gaskets all day with no variety!" Harry Kranz threatened to quit outright at the end of the month if things didn't get better. "Why can't we be given more different things to do? Any Lincoln Zoo monkey could do what I do! Why can't you give us bigger jobs like putting together a whole compressor assembly or even a whole refrigerator? We'd be a lot happier and turn out more and better units than we're doing now!"

As Cal Johnson reflected on these reactions from his workers, he opened a memorandum he had just received from the vice-president:

March 12, 1979

To: Production Managers and General Foremen

From: John Garrison

Subj: Work Specialization Program

Our industrial engineers tell me that we can both cut costs and speed up production through further specialization of assembly-line jobs. I have scheduled a meeting on this subject Thursday, March 29, for all concerned. Jim Carpenter of Industrial Engineering will be there to present his views.

John Garrison

Questions

1. How would you go about analyzing whether there is a need for job enrichment here, based on our discussions in this chapter?

2. If you were Johnson, would you discuss the situation with your production manager and/or with Garrison before the meeting? If so, what would you plan to say? Would you explore the problem with your assemblers?

3. What would you plan to say at the 29 March meeting? Would you be willing to compromise with industrial engineering?

4. Suggest some practical approaches to this potentially serious conflict between the needs of the company and those of the assemblers.

5. Do you think you would recommend job enrichment here? Why? Why not?

EXPERIENTIAL EXERCISE

Purpose: The purpose of this exercise is to give you practice in enriching a job.

Required Understanding: You should be thoroughly familiar with our discussion of job enrichment in this chapter, particularly the technology for enriching jobs, and the section on "Diagnosis: Conditions under which job enrichment will more likely be effective."

How to Set Up the Exercise: The class should form into groups of about 5 students each, *but* at least one member of each group should be working in (or should have worked in) a job that he or she thinks may be amenable to job enrichment. (The group is going to analyze this job, and recommend how to enrich it.)

Instructions

1. Group members should interview the "worker" to develop answers to the "diagnostic" questions (such as "Is motivation central to the problem?") discussed toward the end of this chapter. Remember to ask about the "ABCs" of behavior as part of the questioning. Write down the answers to all questions.

2. Next, using the "Enrichment Technology" as a guide (and Herzberg's comments on the characteristics of an enriched job) the group should write up specific recommendations for enriching the job.

If time permits, a spokesman from each group should present the group's recommendations to the class, along with a synopsis of the group's "diagnosis." Did the group miss any important questions in its diagnosis? Are its recommendations sound? Could the class suggest any improvements to the group's recommendations?

NOTES FOR CHAPTER 6

1. Daniel Katz and Robert Kahn, *The Social Psychology of Organizations* (New York: John Wiley & Sons, 1966), p. 345.

2. Charles Babbage, *On the economy of Machinery and Manufacturers* (London: Charles Knight, 1832), pp. 169–76, reprinted in Joseph Litterer, *Organizations* (New York: John Wiley & Sons, 1969), pp. 73–75.

3. Richard Hopeman, *Production* (Columbus: Charles E. Merrill, 1965), pp. 478–85.

4. See Leonard Sayles and George Strauss, *Human Behavior in Organizations* (Englewood Cliffs, N.J.: Prentice-Hall, 1966), pp. 42–50.

5. Daniel Bell, "Work in the Life of an American," in William Haber et al., *Man in Power in the United States* (New York: Harper & Row, 1948), p. 15.

6. Arthur Tomac and Paul Lawrence, *Industrial Jobs and the Worker* (Boston: Harvard Business School, Division of Research, 1965), pp. 35–48; Charles Walker and Robert Guest, *The Man on the Assembly Line* (Cambridge: Harvard University Press, 1952), p. 120.

7. Leonard Sayles, "Wildcat Strikes," *Harvard Business Review*, 32, No. 6 (November 1954), pp. 42–52.

8. Sayles and Strauss, *Human Behavior*, p. 47; see also J. W. Gooding, *The Job Revolution* (New York: Walker, 1972); *Work in America: Report of a Special Task Force to the Secretary of Health, Education and Welfare* (Cambridge: Massachusetts Institute of Technology Press, 1973).

9. See, for example, Chris Argyris, *Integrating the Individual and the Organization* (New York: John Wiley & Sons, 1964).

10. Richard Herzberg, "The Wise Old Turk," *Harvard Business Review* (September–October, 1974).

11. See "Work in America," reprinted in Jerome Shnee, E. Kirby Warren, and Harold Lazarus, *The Progress of Management* (Englewood Cliffs, N.J.: Prentice-Hall, 1977), pp. 119–20.

12. Sar Levitan and William Johnston, "Job Redesign, Reform, Enrichment-Exploring the Limitations," *Monthly Labor Review*, 96 (July 1973), reprinted in Karl Magnussen, *Organizational Design, Development and Behavior* (Glenview, Ill.: Scott, Foresman and Company), p. 214.

13. See, for example, Hugo Munsterberg, *Psychology and Industrial Efficiency* (Houghton Mifflin, 1913), p. 195, quoted in A. C. Mackinney, T. F. Wernimont, W. O. Galitz, "Has Specialization Reduced Job Satisfaction?" *Personnel*, Vol. 39 (1962), pp. 8–18; Patricia Smith, "The Prediction of Individual Differences in Susceptibility to Industrial Monotony," *Journal of Applied Psychology*, Vol. 39 (1955), pp. 322–329. J. E. Kennedy and H. E. O'Neill, "Job Content and Worker's Opinions," *Journal of Applied Psychology*, 42 (1958), pp. 372–75; W. Baldamus, *Efficiency and Effort* (London: Tavistock, 1961). M. Kilbridge, "Do Workers Prefer Larger Jobs?", *Personnel*, 1960, Vol. 37, p. 45–49. Similarly, Turner and Miclett interviewed 115 female assembly workers from an electronic plant. They found that even though the work was extremely repetitive and routine, most workers were satisfied with the work itself. Instead, dissatisfaction arose from the sense of being caught in a quantity-quality squeeze and from interruptions from staff and supervision personnel: A. M. Turner and A. L. Miclett, "Sources of Satisfaction in Repetitive Work," *Occupational Psychology*, 1962, Vol. 36, p. 215–31.

14. Discussed in Charles Hulin and Milton Blood, "Job Enlargement, Individual Differences, and Worker Responses," *Psychological Bulletin*, 69, No. 1 (1968), pp. 41–53. The question of whether factors like rural-urban differences, or workers' values influence the effectiveness of job enrichment is a matter of debate: many believe these factors have little or no influence. See for example: Eugene Stone, "The Moderating Effect of Work-Related Values on the Job Scope-Job Satisfaction Relationship." *Organizational Behavior and Human Performance*, Vol. 15 (April 1976), pp. 147–67; Ramon Aldag, and A. P. Brief, *Task Design and Employee Motivation* (Glenview, Ill.: Scott-Foreman, 1979), pp. 81–105.

15. G. Oldham, J. R. Hackman, and J. Pearce, "Conditions under which employees respond favorably to enriched work," *Journal of Applied Psychology*, 61, No. 4 (August 1976), pp. 395–403. Some researchers have recently found that it is, in particular, an employee's need for achievement that determines how he reacts to job enrichment, not all his higher order growth needs. See, for example, Richard Steers and Daniel Spencer, "The Role of Achievement Motivation in Job Design," *Journal of Applied Psychology*, Vol. 62 (August 1977), pp. 472–79.

16. Mitchell Fein, "Job Enrichment: A Reevaluation," *Sloan Management Review* (Winter 1974), p. 124, reprinted in Jerome Schnee, E. Kirby Warren, and Harold Lazarus, *The Progress of Management* (Englewood Cliffs, N.J.: Prentice-Hall, 1977), p. 124. William Giles, "Volunteering For Job Enrichment: A Test of Expectancy Theory Predictions." *Personnel Psychology*, Vol. 30 (Autumn 1977), pp. 427–35.

17. See, for example, Albert King, "Expectation Effects in Organization Change," *Administrative Science Quarterly* (June 1974), pp. 221–30; Fein, in Schnee, Warren, and Lazarus, *The Progress of Management*, p. 124.

18. Frederick Herzberg, "One More Time: How Do You Motivate Employees," *Harvard Business Review* (January–February 1968), reprinted in *Harvard Business Review Motivation Series* (Cambridge: Harvard University Press, 1970), pp. 54–63.

19. Robert Ford, "Job Environment Lessons from AT&T," *Harvard Business Review* (January–February 1973), pp. 96–106.

20. Robert Ford, *Motivation Through the Work Itself* (New York: American Management Association, 1969), p. 188; William Reif and Fred Luthans, "Does Job Enrichment Really Pay Off?" *California Management Review*, 15, No. 1, reprinted in Keith Davis, *Organizational Behavior* (New York: McGraw-Hill, 1977), pp. 209–220. Reif and Luthans point out that no claim is made that these 19 trials cover a representative sample of jobs and people within the Bell System: there are more than 1,000 jobs in the Bell System, not just the 9 in these studies.

21. Dennis Umstot, Cecil Bell, Jr., and Terrence Mitchell, "Effects of Job Enrichment and Task Goals on Satisfaction and Productivity: Implications for Job Design," *Journal of Applied Psychology*, 61, No. 4 (August 1976), pp. 379–94.

22. Edwin Locke, David Sirota, and Alan Wolfson, "An Experimental Case Study of the Successes and Failures of Job Enrichment in a Government Agency," *Journal of Applied Psychology*, 61, No. 6 (December 1976), p. 701.

23. See M. Fein, "Motivation for Work," in *Handbook of Work, Organization, and Society*, ed. R. Dubin (Chicago: Rand McNally, 1973); Fein, in Schnee, Warren and Lazarus, *Progress*, pp. 122–24; F. K. Foulkes, *Creating More Meaningful Work* (New York: American Management Association, 1969).

24. Herzberg, "The Wise Old Turk," pp. 70–80.

25. Herzberg, "The Wise Old Turk," p. 75.

26. J. Richard Hackman, et al., "A New Strategy for Job Enrichment," *California Management Review*, 17, No. 1, 51–71, reprinted in H. Kirk Downey, Don Hellreigel, and John Slocum, Jr., *Organizational Behavior* (St. Paul: West Publishing 1977), 304–32. For discussions of some of the work that led up to this development see A. N. Turner and Paul R. Lawrence, *Industrial Jobs and the Worker* (Cambridge: Harvard University Graduate School of Business Administration, 1965); Raymond Aldag and Arthur Brief, *Task Design and Employee Motivation* (Glenview, Ill.: Scott Foresman), pp. 45–48. J. Richard Hackman and Edwin Lawler III, "Employee Reactions to Job Characteristics," *Journal of Applied Psychology*, 55 (1971), 259–96; Wayne Cascio, *Applied Psychology in Personnel Management* (Reston Publishing Co., Reston, 1978), p. 355. For other studies in this area see, for example, R. J. Aldag and A. P. Brief, "Some Correlates of Work Values," *Journal of Applied Psychology*, 60 (1975), 757–70; A. P. Brief, M. Wallace, and R. J. Aldag, "Linear vs. Nonlinear Models of the Formation of effective responses: The case of Job Enlargement," *Decision Sciences*, 7 (1976), pp. 1–9.

27. See also, J. Richard Hackman and Greg Oldham, "Motivation Through the Design of Work: Test of a Theory," *Organizational Behavior and Human Performance*, 16, No. 2 (August 1976), pp. 250–79.

28. Based on Herzberg, "One More Time," in Motivation Series, p. 59.

29. Herzberg, "One More Time," in Motivation Series, p. 60.

30. Herzberg, "One More Time," in Motivation Series, p. 62.

31. This is based on Ford, "Job Enrichment Lessons," pp. 96–106.

32. Ford, "Job Enrichment Lessons," p. 96.

33. See Charles Gobson, "Volvo Increases Productivity through Job Enrichment," *California Management Review*, 15, No. 4 (Summer 1973), 64–66; Editor *Organizational Dynamics*, "Job Redesign on the Assembly Line: Farewell to Blue Collar Blues?" *Organizational Dynamics*, 2, No. 2 (1973), 51–67, reprinted in Dennis Organ, *The Applied Psychology of Work Behavior* (Dallas: Business Publications, Inc., 1978).

34. Organ, *Applied Psychology*, p. 269.

35. See, for example, J. Richard Hackman, "Is Job Enrichment Just a Fad?" *Harvard Business Review* (September–October, 1975), pp. 129–38; Wayne Cascio, *Applied Psychology in Personnel Management* (Reston, Va.: Reston Publishing Co., 1978), pp. 358–60.

36. See Richard E. Walton, "How to Counter Alienation in the Plant," *Harvard Business Review* (November–December 1972), p. 77.

37. Rollin Simmons and John Oriff, "Worker Behavior vs. Enrichment Theory," *Administrative Science Quarterly*, Vol. 20 (1975), p. 606; Goldham, J. Hackman, J. Pearce, "Conditions," pp. 395–403.

38. Herzberg, "One More Time," in Motivation Series, p. 62.

39. Walton, "How to Counter Alienation," p. 79.

40. Elinar Thorsrud, "Job Design in the Wider Context," in Lewis Davis and James Taylor, eds., *Design of Jobs* (Baltimore, Md.: Penguin Books, 1972).

41. Based on Cascio, *Applied Psychology*, pp. 363–67.

42. Umstot, Bell, and Mitchell, "Effective Job Enrichment," pp. 379–94.

43. M. Beer and E. F. Huse, "A Systems Approach to Organizational Development," *Journal of Applied Behavior Science*, 8 (1972), pp. 79–101.

7 Goal Setting, Participation and Management by Objectives

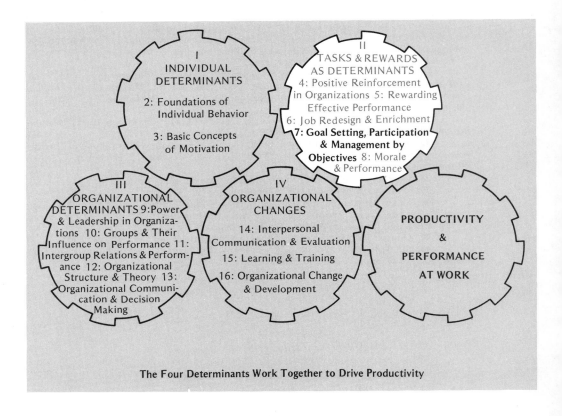

The Four Determinants Work Together to Drive Productivity

BY THE TIME YOU FINISH STUDYING THIS CHAPTER, YOU SHOULD BE ABLE TO:

1. *List the characteristics of effective goals.*
2. *Explain why participation can aid in goal setting.*
3. *Apply the Vroom/Yetton participation model.*
4. *Discuss how you would establish an organization-wide participation program.*
5. *Explain how to use management by objectives.*

OVERVIEW

The main purpose of this chapter is to explain in detail how to improve goal setting at work. In Chapter 4, Positive Reinforcement in Organizations, we explained that the antecedents of behavior—what the person thinks you expect of him or her—is an important determinant of performance. Since what you expect is often articulated in terms of standards or goals, in this chapter we discuss goal setting and two important, related processes— participation and management by objectives (MBO). We will see that both participation and MBO can help ensure the acceptability of goals that one sets, as well as the effective implementation of these goals. Remember that goal setting is an important part of the "ABCs" of performance: Employees must first understand what is expected of them before consequences like pay, promotion, job challenge (or the improved morale we discuss in the next chapter) can motivate performance in the desired direction.

GOAL SETTING AND EMPLOYEE PERFORMANCE

Why Setting Goals is Important

Setting effective goals is important for several reasons. Often, when an employee's performance is inadequate it is not because he or she does not *want* to do better, but because he or she either thinks he *is* doing what is expected, or does not know what is expected. (Sometimes, in fact, just showing an employee how he is *actually* performing relative to his standards may be enough to bring his performance back into line.) Similarly, employees have to first understand what is expected of them before consequences like pay can motivate the desired behavior. What are the characteristics of effective goals? What is the best procedure for setting goals? We focus on such questions in this chapter.

Much of what we know about goal setting in organizations resulted from studies carried out by Edwin Locke and his associates.[1] Based on his findings, Locke has developed a theory of goal setting that holds that (1) hard goals result in a higher level of performance than do easy goals and (2) that *specific* hard goals result in a higher level of performance than do no goals or a generalized goal of "do your best."[2] Basically, his theory assumes that a person's conscious intentions regulate his or her actions and that a goal is simply what the individual is consciously trying to do. Therefore, the higher and more specific are the person's goals, the harder the person will try and the higher will be his performance. A great deal of research has been carried out to test Locke's theory, and today most psychologists would probably agree that the theory is sound.

Setting Specific Goals vs. General Goals (or no goals)

We know that employees who are given specific goals usually perform better than those who are not. One study that illustrates the practical significance of this finding was carried out in a logging operation in Oklahoma.[3] As part of the logging operation, truck drivers had to load the cut logs and drive them to the mill, and these drivers were the subject of the study. An analysis of the performance of each trucker showed that they were often not filling their trucks to the maximum legal net weight. The researchers believed this was largely because these workers were traditionally urged to simply "do their best" when it came to loading the truck to its maximum weight. Therefore, as part of this study, the researchers arranged for a specific goal (94 percent of the truck's net weight) to be communicated to each driver. The drivers were told that this was an experimental program, that they would not be required to make more truck runs, and that there would be no retaliation if performance suddenly increased and then decreased. No monetary rewards or fringe benefits other than verbal praise were given for improving performance. No special training of any kind was given to the supervisors or the drivers.

As can be seen in Exhibit 7.1, the results of this study were impressive. Performance (in terms of weight loaded on each truck) rose markedly as soon as the truckers were assigned specific hard goals, and it generally remained at this much higher level. Furthermore, the researchers believe that setting the specific, hard goal was responsible for the increase, rather than other factors (like the praise the truckers were getting):

> The setting of a goal that is both specific and challenging leads to an increase in performance because it makes it clearer to the individual what he is supposed to do. This in turn may provide the worker with a sense of achievement, recognition, and commitment, in that he can compare how well he is doing now versus how well he has done in the past and in some instances, how well he is doing in comparison to others.[4]

In summary, this and other evidence clearly suggests that setting specific goals with subordinates, rather than setting no goals or telling them to do their best, can substantially increase their performance. In fact, of 11 studies surveyed in a recent article on the subject, only 1 failed to find support for this goal specificity proposition, and in this case the measure of goal setting was of "dubious validity."[5]

Exhibit 7.1 Percent Legal Net Weight of 36 Logging Trucks Over Time as a Function of a Specific Hard Goal

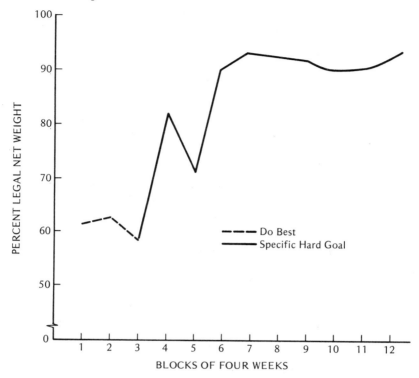

Source: Gary Latham and J. James Baldes, "The Practical Significance of Locke's Theory of Goal Setting," Journal of Applied Psychology, 1975, Vol. 60, No. 1, p. 123.

The Effect of Goal Difficulty on Performance

It is also clear that the more difficult the goal, the higher the level of performance, assuming, of course, that the goals are accepted.

Most of the early findings in this area resulted from studies conducted by Locke, in which he correlated stated goals and subsequent performance. He found that when individuals are given low, medium, and high goals, it is the people with the high goals who are consistently the most productive.[6] This assumes, however, *that the goals are attainable and acceptable and this usually means that there should be a little less than a 50/50 chance of success.*[7]

The idea that setting high, attainable goals results in better performance than setting low goals has some very practical implications. For example, some of the studies in this area have examined the effects of goal setting in the United Fund campaigns.[8] In general, researchers who have studied these campaigns have found a direct relationship between the difficulty of the goal (in terms of how far it exceeded the previous year's performance) and subsequent performance: in other words, the more difficult the goal, the more money the campaign raised. Again, however, it was found that setting high goals was only effective when they were seen as attainable and acceptable.

The Goals Must Be Attainable. A point worth repeating is that while high goals can be effective, they will not be if they are viewed as beyond the control of the employee, or as unreasonably high and unattainable. In one study the researchers set new goals at 20, 40, 60, 80, and 100 percent above what the subject had previously achieved. Performance increased with the higher goals, up to the point where goals were 80 percent higher than previously. For example, productivity increased 25 percent when goals were set 20 percent higher than previously. But when goals were set at 80 percent above previous performance, productivity went up only by 12 percent. And when goals were doubled—100 percent of the previous performance—productivity actually declined. On the whole, the best results were obtained where goals were set at about 20 percent above previous performance.[9]

Summary: Setting Effective Goals

In summary, it seems clear that *specific* goals increase performance and that *difficult* goals, *if attainable*, result in better performance than do easy goals.[10] Related to this, goals should also be *observable* and *measurable*, and the activities they cover should be *relevant:* for example, the production manager should not be evaluated on how many units the sales department sells. In practice, goals can generally be set for quantity (how many produced), quality (how well the person does it), timeliness (how long it takes), and cost (how much it costs).[11]

The overriding assumption, however, is that the goals are acceptable, and in practice ensuring such acceptability can be a complicated problem. This is because whether a high goal is viewed as acceptable or not depends on many things including your subordinate's self confidence, and his or her history of successes or failures.[12]

What is the best way to ensure that the goals that you set *are* in fact viewed as attainable? One sensible approach is to let your subordinates *participate* in developing the standards and goals by which they are to be measured.[13]

ENCOURAGING PARTICIPATION

Introduction: Why Participation?

The use of "participation" (encouraging employees to participate actively in developing and implementing decisions directly affecting their jobs) is a child of the human relations movement, and few terms are as closely related to human relations as is "participation." The use of participation grew out of the new philosophy and assumptions of the post-Hawthorne era, a philosophy and set of assumptions that held that employees do not dislike work or responsibility, and that, given adequate encouragement and support, they are capable of substantial creativity and self-control. Even today, in fact, it is useful to remember that for participation to be effective it has to be part of an underlying climate of honesty, trust, and respect for individuality, since without this participation may be perceived as little more then a gimmick.

There are basically two benefits to be derived from letting subordinates participate in decisions regarding their jobs. First, as we will see in our chapter on group decision making, participation allows one to bring to bear more points of view, and it is therefore a useful approach to obtain advice or to solve a problem where several points of view might be useful. Second, and perhaps most important, participation is generally recognized as an effective way for gaining employees' acceptance of, and commitment to, goals and for motivating them to discipline themselves to accomplish these goals.

Does Participation Lead to More Commitment?

One of the great benefits of participation is that employees who participate in decision making become "ego-involved" with the resulting decisions and develop a sense of ownership of these decisions. In other words, participation can increase the degree to which group members "own" their work practices—and therefore the likelihood that the individual and the work group will develop a norm of support for these practices.[14] Thus, the salesman who participates in setting his sales quota for next year, the vice-president who participates in setting five-year goals for her division, and the workers who participate in developing a new incentive plan or work method will likely be more committed to the new quotas, goals, or methods than they would have been if these had simply been assigned.

The research evidence clearly suggests that employees who participate in decision making do develop an ownership of their work practices and, therefore, self-control. In one study, for example, consultants were called in by the owners of an office maintenance company because the workers they employed for cleaning the offices had very poor attendance records. The consultants allowed some of the workers to develop, with the consultants help, an incentive plan that rewarded good attendance, and the incentive plan was a resounding success: attendance for those who participated in developing the plan increased almost from the start. Furthermore, communication among these workers changed from initial "shared warnings" about management to "helping members (especially new members) come to understand and believe in our plan."[15] Those who did not participate in developing the plan did not respond as well to it.

Because of findings like these, participation has been widely used in the implementation of organizational changes; participants feel they have a sense of ownership of the changes, and are therefore motivated to see these changes put into effect. One of the most famous studies of this was carried out by Coch and French. The researchers hypothesized that allowing employees to participate in planning and implementing the necessary procedural change would make a significant difference in their acceptance of the change. The researchers set up four experimental groups. In Group I (the control, or "no participation" group), employees went through the usual factory routine. Here the production department modified the job, the new piece rate was set, and the operators were called into a meeting and told about the job change. Their questions were answered, and they went back to work.

Group II was the "participation through representation group." Here, before any changes took place, a group meeting was held, and the need for change was presented dramatically. Management then presented a plan to institute the new work method, and a few representatives of the group were selected to help management work it out.

Groups III and IV were the "total participation" groups. All these employees met with management, and the need for a cost reduction was presented. All the employees in each group discussed the current methods and how they might be improved. When the new methods were agreed on, the operators were trained in them and returned to work.

The results of this study were quite definitive, and are presented in Exhibit 7.2. In Group I ("no participation") resistance developed almost immediately, and according to the researchers, 17 percent of the employers quit in the first 40 days. Grievances were filed about the piece rate, and, as you can see, productivity dropped.

At the other extreme, employees in Groups III and IV ("total participation") showed no signs of such resistance. Productivity climbed immediately, and no one quit during the experiment.

Other studies like these could also be cited; in general, they support

Exhibit 7.2 Effect of Participation on Productivity After an Organizational Change

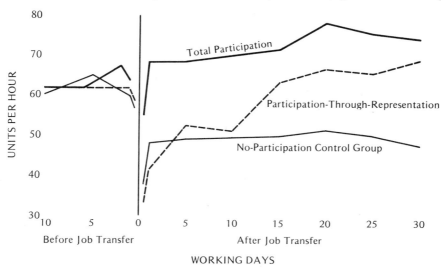

the idea that participation, handled correctly, can be a powerful tool for winning employees' acceptance for goals and changes. And, in summarizing this evidence, Lawler concludes that participation is effective because:

> People become "ego involved" in decisions in which they have had an influence. The decisions become their decisions and they develop expectancies to the effect that when the decisions are successfully implemented they will experience such intrinsic rewards as feelings of confidence and self-esteem. Because of this, they work to implement this decision even though no extrinsic rewards are involved.[16]

Does Participation Lead to Better Performance?

While participation seems to increase *commitment*, its effects on employee productivity and performance are not necessarily favorable. Sometimes, for example, it is not the participative leader who has the high performing group, but the more directive, autocratic one.

One of the most famous and comprehensive studies of how participation affects employee performance and attitudes was carried out in two clerical departments of an industrial firm. Morse and Reimer chose four work groups, and arbitrarily assigned two to a "democratic (participative) program," and two to an "autocratic program." In the democratic groups, supervisors were trained to employ more participative methods, for example, delegating more decision making to employees. In the two autocratic groups, on the other hand, those in the work group were given much less authority for making decisions, and the workers were supervised more closely. The experiment was continued for about a year and a half.

As summarized in Exhibit 7.3, productivity (as measured by cost reduction) increased much more for the autocratic groups than for the participative groups. However, the employees exposed to authoritarian leadership quickly became dissatisfied. In the more participative groups, on the other hand, satisfaction increased, and turnover and grievances decreased.

Exhibit 7.3 Comparison of Productivity and Satisfaction for Divisions: Year Preceding Introduction of Program and Year Following

Experimental Groups	Index of Productivity			Index of Satisfaction		
	Mean for Initial Year	Mean for Experimental Year	Difference	Mean for Initial Year	Mean for Experimental Year	Difference
Democratic Program						
Division A	46.3%	55.2%	+8.9*	4.16	4.32	+.16*
Division B	51.0	62.0	+11.0*	3.83	4.02	+.19
Average	48.6	58.6	+10.0*	4.01	4.18	+.17*
Autocractic Program						
Division C	50.2	63.2	+13.0*	4.04	3.80	−.24*
Division D	46.8	62.0	+15.2*	4.26	3.95	−.31*
Average	48.5	62.6	+14.1*	4.15	3.88	−.27*
	Higher Values Correspond to Higher Productivity			Higher Values Correspond to Higher Satisfaction		

*Statistically significant results.

Note: As can be seen in the two "difference" columns, the autocratic groups' productivity rose more, but they also became dissatisfied.

Source: Adapted from N. C. Morse and E. Reimer, "The Experimental Change of a Major Organizational Variable," *Journal of Abnormal and Social Psychology*, Vol. 52 (1956), 127. Copyright 1956 by the American Psychological Association. Reprinted by permission of the publisher.

In summary, we know that participation facilitates organizational changes, since it increases the employees' commitment to and "ownership" of the changes. Similarly, employees who are allowed to participate in the setting of their goals tend to be more committed to accomplishing these goals. Employees who participate more also tend to be more satisfied. However, participation does not always lead to better performance, and one of the reasons for this is that for many employees and tasks, participation is simply inappropriate. In this regard, effective participation depends on four principal factors.

1. *The time available.* Letting employees participate in decision making is inherently more time-consuming than simply making the decision yourself and imposing it on them. If there is not sufficient time for the sort of give and take that participation involves, or if the benefits derived from participation would apparently not be worth the costs in terms of lost production time, then participation would probably not be advisable.

2. *The worker's desire to participate.* At one time behavioral scientists believed that participative leadership had positive effects only on employees who had a high need for independence and strong non-authoritarian values.[17] In other words, it was believed that as a rule, certain types of people would always respond badly to participative leadership, while others—those who wanted very much to be independent—would always respond favorably to it. Today we know that these kinds of sweeping generalizations do not apply and that how any specific individual will react to being asked to participate will depend on a variety of "situational" factors like the organization's reward system.[18] On the other hand, while the employee's desire to participate may not be the major determinant of how he or she reacts to participation, there is little doubt that it is at least one of several important factors.

3. *The reward system.* One of the reasons participation is effective is that it provides employees an opportunity to become ego involved with and "own" aspects of their jobs and to derive a sense of achievement and accomplishment from these tasks. And, we know that appealing to employees' higher level needs this way can increase motivation. On the other hand, we have also seen that where employees' lower level needs are not fairly well satisfied—where there are acute morale problems due to low or inequitable pay, for instance—attempts to raise morale and productivity by appealing to higher level needs will probably not be successful.

4. *The nature of the task.* Some tasks do not lend themselves to employee participation. Probably the most important thing here is that for employees to be able to effectively participate they must also have some control over their tasks and work methods. For example, having periodic "participation" sessions with employees who are in fact required to work a rigid set of hours on a machine-paced assembly line would probably be seen as a somewhat transparent

"human relations gimmick." On the other hand, letting employees participate in decisions that they know they will in fact have some real affect on would make more sense.

The Vroom/Yetton Model

Vroom and Yetton have developed a model that can help managers analyze a task and decide how much to allow their subordinates to participate in decision making. They say there are five types of "management decision styles":

A I: You solve the problem or make the decision yourself, using information available to you at that time.

A II: You obtain the necessary information from your subordinates, then decide on the solution to the problem yourself. You may or may not tell your subordinates what the problem is when getting the information from them. The role played by your subordinates in making the decision is clearly one of providing the necessary information to you, rather than generating or evaluating alternative solutions.

C I: You share the problem with relevant subordinates individually, getting their ideas and suggestions without bringing them together as a group. Then you make the decision, which may or may not reflect your subordinates' influence.

C II: You share the problem with your subordinates as a group, collectively obtaining their ideas and suggestions. Then you make the decision, which may or may not reflect your subordinates' influence.

G II: You share a problem with your subordinates as a group. Together you generate and evaluate alternatives and attempt to reach agreement (consensus) on a solution. Your role is much like that of a chairperson. You do not try to influence the group to adopt "your" solution, and you are willing to accept and implement any solution that has the support of the entire group.

Vroom and Yetton say that the appropriate decision-making style depends on seven attributes of the "problem situation"—such as how important the quality of the decision is. These seven attributes, along with questions that can be used to diagnose the existence of such attributes, are presented in Exhibit 7.4. As an example, one could identify the importance of the quality of the decision (the first problem attribute) with the following diagnostic question: "Is there a quality requirement such that one solution is likely to be more rational than another?"

Exhibit 7.4 Problem Attributes Used in the Vroom/Yetton Model

Problem Attributes	*Diagnostic Questions*
A. The importance of the quality of the decision.	Is there a quality requirement such that one solution is likely to be more rational than another?
B. The extent to which the leader possesses sufficient information/expertise to make a high-quality decision by himself.	Do I have sufficient information to make a high-quality decision?
C. The extent to which the problem is structured.	Is the problem structured?
D. The extent to which acceptance or commitment on the part of subordinates is critical to the effective implementation of the decision.	Is acceptance of decision by subordinates critical to effective implementation?
E. The prior probability that the leader's autocratic decision will receive acceptance by subordinates.	If you were to make the decision by yourself, is it reasonably certain that it would be accepted by your subordinates?
F. The extent to which the subordinates are motivated to attain the organizational goals as represented in the objectives explicit in the statement of the problem.	Do subordinates share the organizational goals to be obtained in solving this problem?
G. The extent to which subordinates are likely to be in conflict over preferred solutions.	Is conflict among subordinates likely in preferred solutions!

Finally, Vroom and Yetton present a model for determining the best decision-making style in the form of a "decision tree," and this is presented in Exhibit 7.5. Notice that it requires the manager to identify the attributes of the problem by asking the seven diagnostic questions, each in its proper sequence. First, for example, you determine whether quality of the decision is important; then you determine if you have sufficient information to make a high-quality decision; and so forth. By answering each question "yes" or "no," you can work your way across the decision tree and identify, for the situation you find yourself in, the decision making style that is best. Thus, if you are in "Situation 1" (in column E) you decided that decision quality is *not* the requirement, and that subordinates' acceptance is *not* critical: here decision style AI is appropriate, and no other questions from Exhibit 7.4 have to be asked. Research results indicate that this model can help managers decide how much their employees should participate in decision making.[19]

In summary, participation can increase commitment, facilitate organizational changes, and increase productivity and morale. Whether it does, however, depends on several things, such as the time, the employee's preferences and the nature of the task.[20] [21]

Exhibit 7.5 The Vroom/Yetton Model: Deciding Employee's Degree of Participation

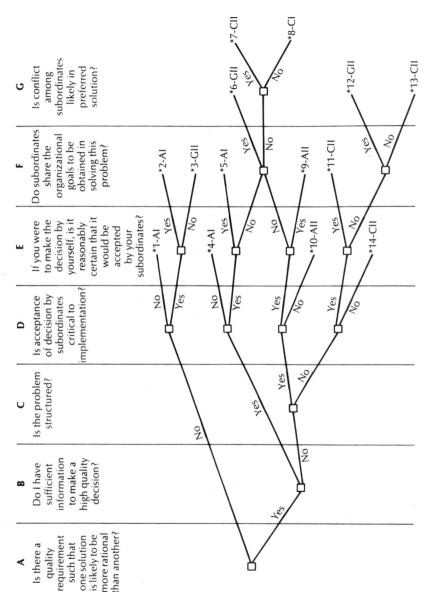

A Is there a quality requirement such that one solution is likely to be more rational than another?

B Do I have sufficient information to make a high quality decision?

C Is the problem structured?

D Is acceptance of decision by subordinates critical to implementation?

E If you were to make the decision by yourself, is it reasonably certain that it would be accepted by your subordinates?

F Do subordinates share the organizational goals to be obtained in solving this problem?

G Is conflict among subordinates likely in preferred solution?

*1-AI *2-AI *3-GII *4-AI *5-AI *6-GII *7-CII *8-CI *9-AII *10-AII *11-CII *12-GII *13-CII *14-CII

***Note:** The numbers 1-14 refer to different "problem types" or situations A1, A11, C11, etc. refer to the leadership styles (degree of participation) Vroom and Yetton recommend for each situation, and which we list in the text.

PARTICIPATION IN PRACTICE

Participation in an organization might entail any thing from an individual managers decision to let his group participate in decision making, to a formal, organization-wide program. On the individual level, many managers practice "participative leadership," and here, as Vroom and Yetton point out, there are varying degrees of participation. Participation may range, for example, from simply soliciting an employee's advice to allowing that person to arrive at the decision for you. Organization-wide support for this kind of participation is advisable, but is not mandatory for its success.

Organization-wide Participation Programs

Many companies do establish organization-wide participation plans that are aimed at gaining the active participation of all (or nearly all) their employees. Perhaps the simplest of these are the formal "suggestion boxes" many organizations set up. Others establish incentive plans that are based on employee participation. For example, the Scanlon Plan (discussed in Chapter 5) relies on worker committees for evaluating suggestions that are made by the workers themselves.

Example of an Organization-wide Program

The Advanced Circuitry Division of Litton Industries recently implemented an employee participation program that has proved quite successful.[22] When the program was first designed and implemented, employee morale was exceptionally low because of a series of layoffs and a devisive unionization attempt. In addition, the workers were being called upon to assemble new, more complex circuit boards while at the same time the division was having problems with new equipment that had been installed. The net effect of all these problems was that the usually excellent quality levels in this division were at all time lows. As a result, the participation program was aimed at improving quality, as well as at boosting productivity and morale. The program was built around a series of meetings: Level I meetings, Level II meetings, and Level III meetings.

The heart of the program is the Level I meetings, where employees are brought together once every two weeks with their immediate supervisor. The supervisor "guides" the meeting through a series of predetermined "steps," which can be interrupted at any time (and during any step) to conform to the imposed 30-minute time limit for meetings. If all the steps are not completed during one meeting, the next Level I meeting (two weeks later) picks up where the last one left off. The steps that constitute a Level I meeting are as follows:

Step 1. The supervisor introduces a general topic for discussion—such as, "Why do you think our department's product quality is low?

Step 2. The employees brainstorm all the problems they can imagine that may be causing the low quality. One such problem might be "the work area is too dirty," for example. One employee records ideas as fast as the others call them out.

Step 3. Here the employees (*not* the supervisor) rank the problems identified in Step 2.

Step 4. Here the employees again use brainstorming, this time to identify possible solutions to the problems they have ranked as most pressing in Step 3. (An average brainstorming session often produces 10 or 12 ways to solve the problem.) One solution might be "let's be sure to sweep the floor at least once each shift," for example.

Step 5. This step involves evaluating all the suggested solutions and eliminating the impractical ideas while retaining the workable approaches.

Step 6. Next, the supervisor assigns "action items" to volunteers from the group; these basically require the volunteers to explore fully the feasibility of the workable solutions identified in Step 5. In addition to encouraging group "ownership" of the final, suggested solution, this step also lets employees gain an opportunity to expand their jobs by performing tasks (like exploring the feasibility of the remaining solutions) that they had not been able to do previously.

Step 7. Finally, the group discusses and evaluates the results of their feasibility studies, and, when possible, the chosen solution is put into effect promptly. If time permits, the group now returns to Step 4 and addresses the next most important problem, again following the step-by-step method. The supervisor directs the group back to Step 1 only after a general subject has been exhausted so that a new general topic can be introduced. This whole process can take many meetings, with, for example, the group taking a full half hour just getting through Step 4 and then picking up Step 5 at the next meeting.

Level II meetings are also held every other week but are arranged so as not to conflict with Level I meetings. Whereas each work group attends its own Level I meeting and tries to solve problems relevant to the group, Level II meetings are aimed at fostering interdepartmental or intergroup coordination at the worker level. Through participation in these meetings, employees come to better appreciate some of the problems their coworkers in other groups face, become more tolerant and understanding of general conditions in the shop, and gain confidence in their coworkers.

Participants at these Level II meetings consist of representatives chosen from preselected work groups, particularly work groups that are closely associated in the production process. Also attending is a supervisor from one of these groups who has been selected from among his peers.

Level II meetings are less structured than the Level I "step" meetings but generally follow a standard format[23] where:

1. Each participant is encouraged to talk about the things that have been accomplished in their respective Level I meetings.
2. Participants then discuss problems common to the groups and are urged to communicate these matters back to their fellow employees at their next Level I meeting.
3. Ideas that cannot be implemented at the first level (because they require the cooperation of other work groups) are brought, in written form, to Level II meetings by the representatives. The supervisor in charge also acts as a "coordinator" to forward good ideas along to the Level III group.

The Level III meeting (which is held monthly and attended by the engineering, quality control, production, and industrial relations managers) functions as a review board and has three aims: first, to sort out deserving ideas from Level I meetings for further study; second, to ensure that Level I and II meetings are conducted in a timely manner; and, third, to "audit" the ideas to see that they are investigated and acted upon at the lowest possible level. (In other words, managers in this Step III meeting see to it that solutions that *can* be developed and implemented at the Step I and Step II meetings *are* implemented at these lower levels, thus reinforcing the idea that the employees are in fact being given the opportunity to participate in the problem-solving and decision-making processes.)

The program has been quite successful. Product quality rose dramatically in those departments where the program was implemented. And, during one early period, a total of 82 quality-related problems were identified, with all but 16 of them ultimately resolved in the Level I meetings. One example of the type of problems employees verbalized and then worked on during the program follows:

> In one department, employees said they could get better quality if the work area was cleaner. In discussing possible solutions, it was agreed by the employees that, if the requirement to dust and sweep the floor once per shift was followed religiously, the problem would be resolved. Supervision had experienced difficulty in assigning and following up on this particular task, but once the *employees* had identified it as a problem and voluntarily agreed to take turns, the area became, and remained, clean. The supervisor solved his problem by merely listening![24]

A successful organization-wide participation program like this cannot be implemented without some problems, but these were kept to a minimum by first carefully designing the program, and then by trying it out with six work groups on an experimental basis. To further facilitate the implementation of the program, supervisors were given six hours of introductory training, designed to acquaint them with the objectives of participative management and to teach them how to conduct the Level I "step" meetings. The most significant problem seemed to be a tendency on the part of supervisors to try to solve too many problems at one time. For example, after ranking the problems in order of their priority, some supervisors would have employees brainstorm solutions to *all* the problems one after another instead of seeing one solution through to completion. Also, management found that supervisors who strayed too far from the predetermined sequence of seven steps tended to have longer meetings. Problems like these could be solved by training, however, and, on the whole, the program has been a very successful one: it has boosted quality, productivity, and morale by gaining the active participation of employees in solving work-related problems.

USING MANAGEMENT BY OBJECTIVES

What is Management By Objectives?

Management by Objectives (MBO) is a widely used technique in which superior and subordinate jointly set goals for the latter and periodically assess progress toward these goals. While a manager could conceivably engage in a modest MBO program with his subordinates by participatively setting goals and periodically providing feedback, the term MBO almost always refers to a comprehensive *organization-wide* program for participatively setting goals.

Management by Objectives has many applications. In one respect it is a *motivation* technique, since its goal-setting, participation, and feedback components can and do enhance motivation. Yet MBO is more than just a motivation device. Especially for professionals and managers, it is also an integral part of the *performance appraisal* system the organization uses: the employees are appraised largely on the basis of how well they accomplish the jointly-set goals. Management by Objectives is also an *organizational change* technique. For example, managers can jointly assess the need for a change, set goals for changing the organization, and then periodically evaluate progress toward the targeted changes. Finally, MBO is in many respects a *planning and control* device since the jointly set goals become "control standards" that can be monitored; deviations from these goals can then be identified and rectified. Management by Objectives, therefore, is a technique that has many applications.

The MBO process itself is actually a fairly simple one and consists of five basic steps:

1. *Set organization's goals.* Organization-wide strategy and goals are established.
2. *Set departmental goals.* Department heads and their superiors jointly set goals for their departments.
3. *Discuss departmental goals.* Department heads discuss department's goals with all subordinates in the department and ask them to develop their own individual goals.
4. *Set individual goals.* Each superior and subordinate jointly set goals for the latter and assign a timetable for accomplishing same.
5. *Feedback.* There are periodic performance review meetings between superior and subordinate to monitor and analyze progress toward latter's goals.[25]

How Effective Is MBO?

One would imagine that, with its basis in participation and goal setting, MBO would be a useful management technique, but the findings on its effectiveness are somewhat contradictory. Some programs have been quite successful, some have apparently resulted in little or no performance improvement, and others have actually had to be discontinued because of the confusion they caused.[26]

These findings are especially ironic given that the MBO approach i based on some very firm foundations. For example, MBO involves mutua *goal setting*, and we saw that employees who have high, specific goals usuall perform better than those who do not. We also discussed the fact that allow ing subordinates to genuinely *participate* in establishing their own goals ca increase their commitment to these goals and thereby their performance. Gi ing employees *feedback* concerning how they are doing is a third basic con ponent of MBO. And, (as with participation and goal setting) the researc findings again suggest that providing frequent, timely feedback generally lea to increased performance.[27]

While MBO's components—goal setting, participation, and feedback can influence performance, the findings concerning the effectiveness of form organization-wide MBO programs are very mixed. One major program w implemented at the General Electric Company, where it was called "Wo Planning and Review."[82] The program grew out of attempts to improve tl firm's performance appraisal system and was quite effective. The employees operating under MBO were much more satisfied and much more likely to have taken specific action to improve performance than those operating within a traditional performance appraisal system. In another study, a researcher analyzed the performance of the subordinates of 181 MBO-involved superiors and found that the subordinates' performance had improved.[29] On the other hand, several recent studies have found that MBO programs often fail and that their apparent success is transitory and disappears within a year after introduction of the program.[30]

Making MBO Successful

While participation, goal setting, and feedback can lead to higher morale and performance, we also know that formal organization-wide MBO programs also fail, and this anomaly is probably indicative of at least two things. First, implementing an organization-wide MBO program (as we will see below) involves introducing a fairly elaborate new technology into the organization— a technology that includes instruction booklets, training, questionnaires, and so on. This technology is aimed at ensuring that the MBO program is applied consistently throughout the organization, that the program is taken seriously by all concerned, and that the goals that emerge from the MBO process are compatible with each other and with the goals of the organization. An organization-wide MBO program, therefore, introduces a whole new set of complexities and problems that would not exist if we were simply focusing on some joint goal setting between the manager and his or her subordinates. This is one source of problems.

Second, as with any technique, there is a "right" and a "wrong" way to implement MBO, and we know that there are several conditions for its success. For example, based on their analysis of an extensive MBO program at the Black and Decker Company, two researchers suggest the following conditions for success:[31]

1. *Organizational commitment.* Managers must feel that MBO is important, and that the organization and its top management is serious about it.
2. *Goals must be clear.* Organizational goals—in terms of sales quotas, production increases, and so on—must be clear, since goal setting at all lower levels is more difficult, if not impossible, without clear goals that can be fashioned into more specific departmental and individual goals.
3. *Time and resources must be adequate.* Implementing an MBO program can be a very time-consuming procedure, and managers must have the time and resources to utilize MBO.

4. *Provide timely feedback.* The subordinate has to receive timely, frequent, effective feedback. While the optimum number of feedback sessions varies from firm to firm, some managers found that four formal feedback sessions annually (between superior and subordinate) instead of just one end-of-the-period evaluation are best.[32] The *content* of the feedback session is also important. We know, for example, that those receiving more criticism tend to improve less in subsequent periods than those employees who are criticized less. Avoiding the tendency to be overly critical is especially important for those subordinates who are lower in ability, lack confidence, or are operating at lower motivation levels.[33]

When MBO programs do fail, it is often because of barriers and problems that could have been avoided. For example, MBO programs can require a great deal of time, energy, and form-completing on the part of managers, although an excellent form like that in Exhibit 7.6 can facilitate the process. You have to meet with subordinates, review their accomplishments, and discuss plans for the ensuing time period: all this can add up to a tremendous commitment of time.

Other problems arise as well. For some activities like cutting costs or increasing sales, goals are clear and measuring performance is a straightforward matter. But in many other areas, such as employee training, appraising performance is not so straightforward. Furthermore, there is often a lack of awareness on the part of managers of the rationale and value of MBO, and this can make the time spent on it seem even more exasperating. Finally, a "tug of war" often ensues in which the subordinate tries to set the lowest targets possible and the supervisor the highest.

Some Benefits of MBO

Many MBO programs are quite successful[34] and numerous benefits have been noted. Employee motivation increases (probably as a result of the participation, goal setting, and feedback components). MBO also forces and aids in planning, since, to be done properly, top management has to set plans and goals for the entire organization, and the goals of lower levels must then be tied in with these. As a result, work is directed toward organizational goals, since a "chain" of goals and plans develops that link lower and higher level work groups. Another, related benefit is that MBO provides clear standards (goals) for control purposes. Problems can thus be identified better and faster. MBO also results in (or should result in) more concrete, objective, result-oriented performance appraisal criteria, and improved appraisal conferences in which tangible progress can be discussed.

Exhibit 7.6 A Form Used in an Actual MBO Program

Black & Decker®

OVERALL PERFORMANCE WORK SHEET 19___

Birthdate_____ Grade_____ Job No._____
Job Title_____
Hire Date_____ Time in Present Job_____
Time Reporting to Present Supervisor_____

GENERAL INSTRUCTIONS

OBJECTIVES

To ensure you understand what's expected of you in the job.

To convert and communicate Black & Decker's goals and unit objectives into your job targets for the year.

To establish criteria for evaluating your job progress and for measuring your results.

To promote continuing coaching, counseling and understanding between you and your supervisor.

To provide guidance for your personal and professional career development.

To ensure a more objective and effective basis for appraising your overall performance.

AT THE BEGINNING OF THE YEAR

Briefing
The supervisor of your division, department or section will meet with you and your peers in a group briefing session to discuss the overall objectives of the group. During this session your supervisor will also discuss how the group's objectives can be converted to individual job targets.

Preliminary Target Setting
After the briefing session you should review the group's objectives and determine what your own job targets should be to help your group achieve its objectives. You should prepare the first three parts of the Worksheet — Parts A, B & C. Your supervisor will do the same.

Final Target Setting
Finally, your supervisor should meet again with you to mutually agree on your Key Job Responsibilities and Specific Job and Career Development Targets for the year. Included in this discussion should be an agreement on the criteria both of you will use for measuring and evaluating results achieved. Consideration may also be given to developing an action plan for Part D.

DURING THE YEAR

Your supervisor should schedule and hold periodic meetings with you to:

a. Coach and counsel you on your Key Job Responsibilities.

b. Review your Specific Job Target progress providing any help needed.

c. Make changes in your Key Job Responsibilities and Targets — based on changes in the work situation.

d. Discuss your job skills and provide mutually agreed upon action plans for improving your job performance. (Part D).

AT YEAR-END

Your supervisor will complete Parts A through E: reviewing, evaluating and appraising how well you performed. In cases where significant accomplishments beyond the requirements of the job have been made, or in cases of inadequate job performance, your supervisor will also record and consider them in appraising your overall performance.

Your supervisor will then meet with you to discuss your overall performance appraisal for the year.

A. **INSTRUCTIONS**

1. Describe, as specifically as possible, the type of work you would be interested in doing both in the near future (2-3 years) and in the long term.

2. Establish a list of the dominant personal and professional strengths on which you can build your career and achieve your aspirations.

3. Identify those characteristics, skills, knowledge deficiencies, etc., where further development will be needed.

4. Discuss career development with your supervisor considering each of the areas above — your aspirations, strengths and limitations. Develop a plan which will help you attain your career aspirations. Select those several items which you feel are most essential in helping you achieve your career plan. One of your targets should relate to a task or a skill that may be required of you in the future. Both you and your supervisor should discuss what criteria will be used to measure and evaluate how well you accomplish these targets.

A. CAREER DEVELOPMENT

Career Aspirations:_____
_____
_____
_____
_____
_____
_____

Greatest Strengths:_____
_____
_____
_____
_____
_____
_____

Improvement and Development Needs:_____
_____
_____
_____
_____
_____
_____

Career Development Targets . . .   Criteria for Measuring . . .   Results:
_____
_____
_____
_____
_____

Exhibit 7.6 *(continued)*

B. INSTRUCTIONS

1. You and your supervisor should develop your current list of job responsibilities. Then, with your supervisor, select (and list to the right) those Key Job Responsibilities which both of you agree are currently the most important in your job.

2. For each Key Job Responsibility, discuss, agree and list the specific criteria which will be used to evaluate how well you perform the responsibilities during the year. (See OPA Guide for examples.)

3. During the year, your supervisor will guide, counsel and coach you to ensure these key responsibilities are effectively carried out. If necessary, your supervisor will also discuss with you any condition which may require a change in the primary focus and/or responsibilities of your job function.

4. At year-end, your supervisor will make a statement on how well you performed each Key Job Responsibility.

B. KEY JOB RESPONSIBILITIES

C. INSTRUCTIONS

1. Identify the Specific Job Targets (projects, programs, assignments) you expect to accomplish during the year. Discuss these targets with your supervisor to ensure mutual agreement and understanding. Also, to the extent possible, indicate priorities, completion times, and results expected. If a target is complex or requires a prolonged period of time for completion, break it into separate phases showing when certain elements are to be completed. For lengthy targets, staple an additional sheet(s) to the Worksheet.

2. Agree with your supervisor on the specific criteria which will be used to evaluate how well you achieve each target. List the criteria in the space provided. (See OPA Guide for examples.)

3. During the year, your supervisor will meet periodically with you to:
   - Review progress toward target completion.
   - Discuss any help needed to achieve targets.
   - Change priorities, adding or deleting targets which reflect changes in current business situation, etc.
   - Record periodic coaching and guiding comments.

4. At year-end, your supervisor will evaluate the results you accomplished using the measurement criteria established during the target setting sessions. Your supervisor will also note any positive or negative outside factors beyond your control which may have helped or hindered your target achievement. This will all be discussed with you during your year-end appraisal interview.

C. SPECIFIC JOB TARGETS

Exhibit 7.6 (*continued*)

CRITERIA FOR EVALUATING PERFORMANCE	PERIODIC COACHING, GUIDING, AND COUNSEL

CRITERIA FOR EVALUATING PERFORMANCE	PERIODIC COACHING,

Exhibit 7.6 *(continued)*

ING COMMENTS	HOW WELL WERE THESE KEY RESPONSIBILITIES PERFORMED?

GUIDING, AND COUNSELING COMMENTS	TARGET RESULTS

Exhibit 7.6 *(continued)*

D. APPLICATION OF SKILLS AFFECTING CURRENT JOB PERFORMANCE

D. INSTRUCTIONS

1. During the year, your supervisor will analyze how you apply the variety of skills which affect your overall performance. They include, but are not necessarily limited to, INTERPERSONAL SKILLS (e.g., resolving conflict, motivating people, etc.); INFORMATIONAL SKILLS (e.g., communicating, gathering and disseminating information, etc.); DECISIONAL SKILLS (e.g., managing change, resource allocation, delegation, etc.), OTHER MANAGERIAL SKILLS (e.g., planning, organizing, controlling, etc.) and PROFESSIONAL SKILLS AND KNOWLEDGE you are expected to bring to the job. (See OPA Guide for elaboration.)

2. After analyzing the skills you bring to the job, your supervisor will:

   a. Discuss and identify with you those skills you are using effectively as well as those which reduce your effectiveness.

   b. Develop a SITUATION ANALYSIS with you of your current work, describing those skills that especially affect your overall performance, i.e. those that both enhance and/or limit your current job performance.

   c. Help you describe below the nature of the needed improvement(s), if any . . . JOB IMPROVEMENT AREA(S).

   d. Develop with you, and state below, an AGREED PLAN OF ACTION that will help improve both your personal and professional performance. This plan should be broken down in step-by-step sequence showing the action to be taken. (See OPA Guide for example.)

3. At year-end, you and your supervisor should make COMMENTS on the results of the action you have taken, noting the improvements made and, if needed, the additional work yet required. The factors identified should also be considered when you establish next year's Overall Performance Worksheet.

Situation Analysis: _____

_____

_____

_____

_____

Job Improvement Area(s): _____

_____

_____

_____

_____

Agreed Plan of Action: _____

_____

_____

_____

_____

Comments: _____

_____

_____

_____

_____

Exhibit 7.6 *(continued)*

E. OVERALL PERFORMANCE APPRAISAL

Appraise each of the factors below and give an Overall Performance Rating.

☐ If individual is learning new job and is too new to rate, check box

1. ELEMENTS OF EVALUATION

APPRAISAL FACTOR:	PERFORMANCE GRADIENT: ▲	Unsatisfactory	Satisfactory	Good	Exceeds At Times	Consistently Exceeds
		Results achieved failed to meet requirements in several major areas. Performance: *Unsatisfactory*	Results achieved met most requirements but were marginal in some areas which will need improvement. Performance: *Satisfactory*	Results achieved met overall requirements. Performance: *Good*	Results achieved at times exceeded overall requirements in most major areas. Performance: *Exceeds at Times*	Results achieved were excellent and continually exceeded overall requirements in all major areas. Performance: *Consistently Exceeds*
(a) CAREER DEVELOPMENT						
(b) KEY JOB RESPONSIBILITIES						
(c) SPECIFIC JOB TARGETS						
(d) SKILL APPLICATIONS						
OVERALL PERFORMANCE RATING:						

2. COMMENTS ON RATING: _____

3. PERSONAL DEVELOPMENT AND CAREER PATH DIRECTION: _____

4. INDIVIDUAL'S COMMENTS: (attach additional sheets if needed)

SIGNATURES:

Individual Rated: _____ Date: _____

Rater: _____ Date: _____

Rater's Superior: _____): _____

Form No. 15020   8-75

Source: Courtesy of Black and Decker.

Finally, MBO reduces role conflict and ambiguity. We say that *role conflict* exists when a person is faced with conflicting demands from two or more supervisors. *Role ambiguity* exists when a person is uncertain as to how he will be evaluated, or what he has to accomplish. We know that both role conflict and role ambiguity can result in lower morale, higher tension, and decreased performance. Since MBO is aimed at providing each manager with clear targets and their order of priority, MBO should reduce role conflict and ambiguity.

MBO in Practice

MBO applications range from informal two-person goal setting and feedback sessions to formal organization-wide programs. With respect to the former, many managers meet periodically with their subordinates to jointly set goals, and subordinate performance is then measured in terms of these goals.

On the other hand, it would seem that to fully take advantage of MBO's benefits a more formal organization-wide program is in order. It is only in this way, for example, that one can ensure that the goals set are compatible with those in other departments. And, it is likely that the effectiveness of the program is enhanced when employees recognize top management's commitment to the program.

One of the most successful company-wide applications to date was implemented at the Black and Decker Company. The heart of their program is the form presented in Exhibit 7.6. As you can see, the Black and Decker program consists of an initial departmental briefing session in which the department's goals are presented by the manager. Then, each employee sets some preliminary targets for himself, with final targets set at a meeting between manager and subordinate. During the year the manager coaches and counsels each subordinate, and each subordinate reviews his or her own progress. Then, at year end, the supervisor completes parts A–E of the form, thus reviewing each worker's progress, performance, development needs, and so on. Then the manager and subordinate meet to discuss the latter's overall appraisal for the year.

GOAL SETTING AND THE "ABCs" OF PERFORMANCE

The question of whether goals have been effectively set is always and integral part of any "ABC" analysis, and particularly of the antecedents stage. Thus, if an employee is performing inadequately, analyzing the antecedents might entail asking: Does the person know what is expected of him? Are his or her goals specific? Are the goals high enough? Are the goals viewed as attainable? Could the problem be solved by having the person participate in the formulation of his or her goals?

Furthermore, as is usually the case, the "ABCs" can also be used to analyze why some change—in this case, for example, a new Management by Objectives program—is not having the desired effect on performance. Ask, for example:

> *Antecedents.* Do the employees understand the new system? Are the goals they are developing specific and attainable?
>
> *Behavior.* Could the employees make the plan work if they wanted to? Do they have enough time to meet and set goals? Do they have the necessary forms? Did they have the training necessary to participate in the program?
>
> *Consequences.* Are the consequences for participating in the program positive or negative? Are those who do *not* take the program seriously rewarded anyway?

CHAPTER SUMMARY

1. *Goal setting* is important because a person's conscious intentions regulate his or her actions and because unless a person knows what is expected of him he is unlikely to perform up to par. Research indicates that (1) setting specific goals results in better performance than setting general goals or no goals, (2) that more difficult goals result in higher performance, and (3) that goals must be attainable, observable, measurable, and relevant to improve performance and productivity.

2. One way to ensure that goals *are* viewed as attainable is to allow employees to participate in their development. Participation does lead to more commitment to the goals, but it seems that whether it leads to better performance depends on many things like the time available and whether or not the worker wants to participate.

3. The Vroom/Yetton model describes the situational considerations a manager should take into account before deciding on the degree to which his or her employee should participate in the decision. The situational considerations ("problem attributes") include the importance of the quality of the decision and the extent to which the problem is structured.

4. Some organizations have implemented organization-wide participation programs. At Litton Industries for example, a program was built around a series of meetings: Level I meetings, Level II meetings, and Level III meetings. The former is the "heart" of the program: here the supervisor and his or her employees meet to determine work-related problems and solutions.

5. Management by Objectives (MBO) can be viewed as a formal organization-wide participation program in which superior and subordinate jointly set goals for the latter and periodically assess progress toward these goals. These programs can be successful, but since they involve introducing a fairly elaborate new technology into the organization (booklets, training, etc.) they can also fail; for success, they require a good deal of organizational commitment, time, resources, and "breaking in" of employees to the new methods.

DISCUSSION QUESTIONS AND PROJECTS

1. Evaluate the goals your instructor established for this course in terms of the criteria for effective goals we discussed in this chapter and in Chapter 4.

2. Do you think there would have been any benefit in having the instructor discuss the goals for the course with the students before establishing them? Why? Why not?

3. Divide the class into groups of four or five students. Each group should determine which of Vroom and Yetton's management decision styles it would use for each of the following situations: the business school dean has to decide how to allocate his school's budget amongst his department chairmen; the general has to decide whether he and his five commanders should attack the town or not; the new president has just taken over at Apex Corporation and has to decide how to cut 20 percent of the corporation's expenses; the foreman has just been told that his work group will have to work overtime on Saturday although he promised them this would never happen again. Each group should be able to defend its positions in terms of the problem attributes used in the Vroom/Yetton model. (See Exhibit 7.4.)

4. What part do you think participation plays in the "ABCs" of performance? In other words, can participation conceivably influence antecedents, behavior, and/or consequences, and if so how?

5. Explain how you would use the information in this chapter on goal setting, participation, and management by objectives to solve a problem in each of the "ABCs" of performance.

6. Explain how you would go about establishing a management by Objective's program.

7. Divide the class into groups of four or five students. Each group should develop an MBO program that the instructor can use to set goals for individual students in this class and evaluate their progress.

CASE EXERCISE

Participation in Milestone Engineering's Planning

The Milestone Engineering Company manufactures a standardized line of machine tools and a wide range of custom-built equipment and machinery of a complex, technical nature for industrial users. Last year, the president decided to introduce widespread participation in the annual planning and budgeting process at all levels in the organization. Company operating and budgeting plans were to be formulated through a process referred to as "grass-roots" budgeting, and this new company administrative philosophy was referred to as "bottom-up management."

More specifically, the process of formulating annual plans was to begin by top management's issuance of tentative objectives for overall company profits, revenues, costs, and expenses for the coming year.

On the basis of these tentative objectives—which were to flow downward through the organization—each department, division, shop, section, and work group was to prepare its own tentative plan or budget for the following year. These tentative plans and budgets were to be channeled upward in the organization, starting with work teams in the plant and the company salesmen. Differences in opinion and inconsistencies in the plans at each level would be worked out between the appropriate superiors through close consultation with their subordinates. In the event that the initial tentative objectives issued by the top executives were either overly optimistic or pessimistic, appropriate adjustments would be made in these overall objectives.

The president and his top-level staff all seemed convinced that this approach to planning would motivate managers and employees at all levels to strive for challenging but realistic plans and budgets. Moreover, those carrying out the plans would be in the best position to estimate their capabilities and resource needs.

Planning participation has not worked out according to the president's expectations, however, and he is greatly disappointed and disturbed. The planning process has turned out to be one of intense bargaining, gamesmanship, and politicking at all levels in the organization. As the plans flow upward, the lower-level managers and work groups are condemned for formulating plans and budgets that are too easy to fulfill and that include a great deal of "slack" or "fat" in terms of capabilities and resource needs. Subsequently, the lower-level plans are tightened substantially by the higher-level managers after a great deal of time has been expended on hard bargaining and politicking.

The lower levels compile masses of data, reports, and charts to defend their draft plans. The higher levels make little, if any, use of this data. They tend to revise the plans upward and to cut proposed budgets on the basis of performance achieved to date, plus an arbitrary "improvement" factor for the following year. Managers and other employees at various levels in the organization admit that they do tend to incorporate some "fat" into their draft plans and budgets, because they know that their superiors will tighten them up almost automatically, and they certainly do not want to inadequately fulfill their plans or exceed their budgets.

Questions

1. How would you analyze the problems in this case, in terms of the "ABC" of performance?

2. What conditions existing in the company do you feel might be major causes of such planning behavior?

3. Does this incident suggest that widespread participative planning of the type introduced by Milestone Engineering cannot prove worthwhile and effective in any company? If not, how can widespread planning participation be made more effective in this or any other company wishing to introduce such a process?

4. In general, what are some of the other changes that should be carefully considered if a company desires effective introduction of "participation" at one or more levels in the organization?

NOTES FOR CHAPTER 7

1. See, for example, Edwin Locke, "Toward a Theory of Task Motivation and Incentives," *Organizational Behavior and Human Performance*, 3 (1968), 157–89; Edwin Locke, N. Cartledge, and C. S. Knerr, "Studies of the Relationship between Satisfaction, Goal Setting, and Performance," *Organizational Behavior and Human Behavior*, 5 (1970), pp. 135–58.

2. See Gary Latham and Gary Yukl, "A Review of Research on the Application of Goal Setting in Organizations," *Academy of Management Journal*, 18, No. 4 (1965), p. 824.

3. Gary Latham and J. James Baldes, "The Practical Significance of Locke's Theory of Goal Setting," *Journal of Applied Psychology*, 60, No. 1 (February 1975).

4. Latham and Baldes, "The Practical Significance," p. 124.

5. Latham and Yukl, "A Review of Research," p. 830.

6. Locke, "Toward a Theory," pp. 168–71.

7. Edward Lawler III and John Rhode, *Information and Control in Organizations* (Pacific Palisades: Goodyear, 1976), pp. 69–72.

8. A. Zander and T. T. Newcomb, Jr., "Group Levels of Aspirations in United Fund Campaigns," *Journal of Personality and Social Psychology*, 6 (1967), pp. 157–62; see also A. Zander, J. Foreword, and R. Albert, "Adaption of Board Members to Repeated Failure or Success by the Organization," *Organizational Behavior and Human Performance*, 4 (1969), pp. 56–76.

9. Mukul K. Day and Gurmin D. D. Kaur, "Facilitation of Performance by Experimentally Induced Ego Motivation," *Journal of General Psychology*, 73 (1965), pp. 237–47.

10. Latham and Yukl, "A Review of Research," p. 840.

11. See Thomas Connellan, *How ot Improve Human Performance* (New York: Harper & Row, 1978), p. 67.

12. Latham and Yukl, "A Review of Research," p. 841.

13. The advantages of participatively set goals have recently been studied: see, for example, Gary Latham and Gary Yukl, "Assigned versus Participative goal setting with Educated and Uneducated Woodsworkers," *Journal of Applied Psychology*, 60, No. 3 (June 1975); and Gary Latham, Terence Mitchell, and Dennis Dosett, "Importance of Participative Goal Setting and Anticipated Rewards on Goal Difficulty and Job Performance," *Journal of Applied Psychology*, 63, No. 2 (April 1978), pp. 163–71. However, several exceptions to the idea that participatively set goals are superior to assigned goals or unspecified goals have been found. In one study, for example, Latham and Yukl found that only for uneducated loggers was there a superiority of participative over assigned goal setting. There were no significant differences in the accomplishment of task goals for the educated loggers sampled. In another study, with salesmen, Ivancevich found that both the participative and assigned goal-setting participants were more effective than was the control group in improving performance and satisfaction for at least nine months after the goals were set. The improvement, however, was generally not found twelve months after training. See Latham and Yukl, "Assigned versus Participative Goal Setting"; and John Ivancevich, "Effects of Goal Setting on Performance and Job Satisfaction," *Journal of Applied Psychology*, 61, No. 5 (1976), pp. 605–12. Keep in mind that participation is only a means to an end—that end being the setting of attainable, acceptable goals. The important thing is that the goals be attainable and acceptable, and if this can be arranged in some nonparticipative way, performance would probably not suffer much.

14. J. Richard Hackman, Edward Lawler III, and Lyman Porter, *Behavior in Organizations* (McGraw-Hill, 1975), p. 419.

15. See Kenneth Scheflen, Edward Lawler III, and J. Richard Hackman, "Long-Term Impact of Employee Participation in the Development of Pay Incentive Plans: A Field Experiment Revisited," *Journal of Applied Psychology*, 55 (1971), pp. 182–86; and Edward Lawler III and J. Richard Hackman, "Impact of Employee Participation in the Development of Pay Incentive Plans: A Field Experiment," *Journal of Applied Psychology*, 53 (1969), pp. 467–71.

16. Edward Lawler III, "Control Systems in Organizations," in Marvin Dunnette, *Handbook of Industrial and Organizational Psychology* (Chicago: Rand McNally, 1976), p. 1281. See also Joseph Alutto and Donald Redenburgh, "Characteristics of Decisional Participation by Nurses," *Academy of Management Journal*, 20, No. 2 (1977), pp. 341–47.

17. Victor Vroom, "Some Personality Determinants of the Effects of Participation," *Journal of Abnormal and Social Psychology*, Vol. 59 (1959), pp. 322–27.

18. See, for example, Ahmed A. Abdel-Halim, Kendrith M. Rowland, "Some Personality Determinants of the Effects of Participation: A Further Investigation," *Personnel Psychology*, 29, No. 1 (Spring 1976); J. Kenneth White, "Generalized Ability of Individual Difference Moderators of the Participation in Decision Making and Employee Response Relationship," *Academy of Management Journal*, 21, No. 1 (March 1958), pp. 36–43.

19. Victor Vroom, "A New Look at Managerial Decision Making," *Organizational Dynamics* (Spring 1973); reprinted, by permission of the publisher, from *Organizational Dynamics* (Spring 1973), © 1973 by AMACOM, a division of the American Management Association. All Rights reserved. Victor Vroom and Arthur Jago, "On the validity of the Vroom-Yetton model," *Journal of Applied Psychology*, Vol. 63, No. 2 (1978), pp. 151–62.

20. Hackman, Lawler, and Porter, *Behavior in Organizations*, p. 420; see also H. G. Kaufman, "Individual Differences, Early Work Challenge, and Continuing Education," *Journal of Applied Psychology*, Vol. 60, No. 3 (June 1975); G. Latham and G. Yukl, "Assigned versus Participative Goal Setting."

21. Lawler, "Control systems in Organizations."

22. H. B. Curtis, "Employee Participation in Solving Production Problems," *Personnel Administrator* (June 1977), pp. 33–49.

23. From Curtis, "Employee Participation," p. 35.

24. Curtis, "Employee Participation," p. 36.

25. Steven Carroll and Henry Tosi, *Management by Objectives* (New York: Macmillan, 1973).

26. Steven Carroll and Henry Tosi, *Management by Objectives* (New York: Macmillan, 1973), p. 140.

27. Clive Seligman and John Darely, "Feedback as a Means of Decreasing Residential Energy Consumption Level," *Journal of Applied Psychology*, 62, No. 4 (1977), pp. 363–68.

28. J. R. P. French, Jr., E. Kay, and H. H. Meyer, "Participation and the Appraisal System," *Human Relations*, Vol. 19 (1966), pp. 3–19.

29. John Ivancevich, "Changes in Performance in a Management by Objectives Program," *Administrative Science Quarterly* (December 1974).

30. See, for example, Tosi et al., "How Real Are Changes Induced by Management by Objectives?" *Administrative Science Quarterly*, 21, No. 2 (June 1976), pp. 276–306; Bruce Kirchoff, "A Diagnostic Tool for Management by Objectives," *Personnel Psychology*, 28, No. 3 (Autumn 1975), p. 31.

31. Carroll and Tosi, *Management by Objectives*, pp. 45, 105.

32. John Ivancevich, J. H. Donnelly, and H. L. Lyon, "A Study of the Impact of Management by Objectives on Perceived Need Satisfaction," *Personnel Psychology*, 23, No. 2 (Summer 1970), pp. 139–51.

33. Carroll and Tosi, *Management by Objectives*.

34. Henry Tosi, John Hunter, Rob Chesser, Jim Tarter, and Steven Carroll, "How Real are Changes Induced by Management by Objectives?" *Administrative Science Quarterly*, Vol. 2, No. 2 (June 1976).

8 *Morale and Performance*

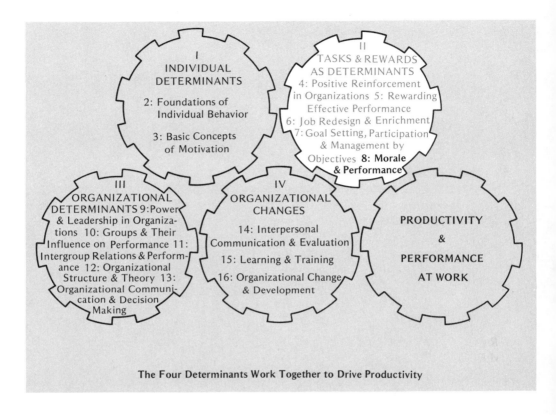

The Four Determinants Work Together to Drive Productivity

*BY THE TIME YOU FINISH STUDYING THIS CHAPTER,
YOU SHOULD BE ABLE TO:*

1. *Define job satisfaction.*
2. *Answer the question: How are satisfaction and performance related?*
3. *Explain the relationship between satisfaction and performance in terms of the "ABCs" of performance.*
4. *Discuss how satisfaction can influence an organization's performance.*
5. *Give examples of how to measure job satisfaction.*
6. *Summarize how a manager can influence his or her employees' satisfaction.*
7. *Explain the involvement approach to surveys.*

OVERVIEW

The main purpose of this chapter is to explain how morale—employee satisfaction—affects employee attendance and performance. We will see that while there is generally no clear relationship between morale and performance the effects of morale on attendance are clearly favorable and that, therefore, improving morale can definitely improve an organization's "bottom line." High satisfaction may improve attendance because it is a consequence of coming to work: Thus, if the person is happy at work, then coming to work will result in a positive consequence (feeling good because of being satisfied at work), and better attendance should result. We first discuss job satisfaction in organizations, including what it is and how it is related to performance. We next discuss satisfaction's relation to attendance and other factors. We explain several methods (such as questionnaires) for measuring job satisfaction and then explain how to influence job satisfaction by (1) taking into account individual differences and (2) modifying situational determinants of job satisfaction. Finally, we discuss an involvement approach to attitude surveys, which can be used to identify morale problems and generate solutions for them.

INTRODUCTION: WHY JOB SATISFACTION IS IMPORTANT

Job satisfaction is an important topic for managers and management students. Most adults spend about half their waking hours in job-related activities, and it probably would not be exaggerating to say that the satisfaction they derive from their jobs is an important consequence of coming to work, as well as a major determinant of their behavior both on and off the job. On the job, for example, we know that satisfied employees usually have better attendance and turnover records, less union activity, and (sometimes) better performance than do less satisfied employees. (We will discuss the research findings in this regard later in this chapter.) Job satisfaction also leads to *non*job satisfaction, in that being satisfied with one's work seems to make most people more satisfied with their nonwork endeavors as well. Many contemporary writers believe that workers have what amounts to an inalienable right to be able to satisfy important personal needs through their experiences in the organization, and, indeed, "employee satisfaction" is a veritable cornerstone of the human relations and organizational behavior movement.[1] What exactly is job satisfaction? How is it related to employee performance and attendance? How can we measure and influence job satisfaction? These are the main questions addressed in this chapter.

JOB SATISFACTION IN ORGANIZATIONS

What is Job Satisfaction?

"Job satisfaction" generally refers to how happy a person is with his or her job. "Happiness," however is not an easy thing to measure; so we will define job satisfaction as the degree to which one's important needs for health, security, nourishment, affiliation, esteem, and so on are fulfilled on the job or as a result of the job. Thus if we wanted to measure how satisfied an organization's employees are, we would usually start by measuring their satisfaction with important facets of the job such as pay, promotions, and recognition, and then add our results to obtain some measure of the employee's overall job satisfaction. Some of the items for which researchers normally obtain satisfaction measures are presented in Exhibit 8.1 and include the work itself, pay, working conditions, and supervision.

Exhibit 8.1 Measures of Job Satisfaction

Researchers typically measure employees satisfaction with at least the following job dimensions:

Work: including how interesting it is, its variety, opportunity for learning, difficulty, amount, chances for success, and control over pace and methods

Pay: including amount, fairness or equity, and method of payment

Promotions: including opportunities for, fairness of, and basis for

Recognition: including praise for accomplishment, credit for work done, and criticism

Benefits: such as pension, medical, annual leave, paid vacations, and cafeteria

Working conditions: such as hours, rest pauses, equipment, temperature, ventilation, humidity, location, and physical payout

Supervision: including supervisory style, and technical, human relations, and administrative skill

Coworkers: including confidence, helpfulness, and friendliness

Company and management: including concern for employees as well as pay and benefit policies

---

Source: Edwin A. Locke, "Nature and Causes of Job Satisfaction," in Marvin Dunnette, *Handbook of Industrial and Organizational Psychology*, p. 1302.

Relation of Job Satisfaction to Performance

There are two basic theories of how employee satisfaction and performance are related.[2] The first theory is that *Satisfaction* leads to performance; in other words, that the way to improve employees' performance is to "boost their morale." This approach was popularized by the Human Relations movement, the essence of which was that managers could increase productivity by increasing the morale of their employees.[3] The Human Relations movement, you may recall, emerged out of the Hawthorne studies and was an integral part of the evolving behavioral approach to management.

While the idea that "happy workers are better workers" is intuitively appealing, the research findings generally fail to support it.[4][5] In other words, sometimes satisfied workers perform better, and sometimes they do not. And so, taking actions to boost morale will not necessarily lead to better performance.

The second theory is that rewards which are based on performance lead to both satisfaction and subsequent performance.[6] According to this theory it is the reward—either extrinsic or intrinsic—that causes both performance and satisfaction: the expectation of a reward leads to performance, and the reward itself (which results from performance) then results in satisfaction.[7] As illustrated in Exhibit 8.2, Porter and Lawler, who have studied this theory, thus argue that the relationship between satisfaction and performance is reciprocal: performance leads to rewards and satisfaction, and the expectation of rewards then leads to further performance.

The research evidence supports this theory.[8] In one study the researchers had two groups of subjects: those whose rewards were based on how well they performed and those whose rewards were not. Subjects who performed

Exhibit 8.2 Lawler-Porter Model of the Relationship of Performance to Satisfaction

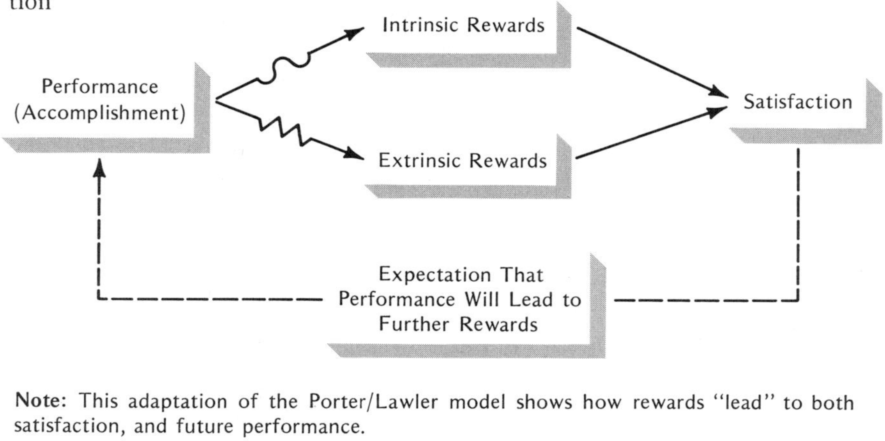

Note: This adaptation of the Porter/Lawler model shows how rewards "lead" to both satisfaction, and future performance.

Source: From Lawler, E. E., and Porter, L. W., "The Effect of Performance on Job Satisfaction." in *Industrial Relations*, 1967, 7, 20–28. Reprinted by permission of the publisher, Industrial Relations.

well *and were rewarded for doing so* expressed greater satisfaction immediately and subsequently performed better than did subjects whose rewards were not tied to their performance. Similarly, subjects who were paid based on performance and who did *not* perform well, (and who were therefore denied rewards), subsequently improved their performance, although they were initially dissatisfied. On the other hand, when a low performer was rewarded anyway (where pay was *not* contingent on performance), the person expressed high satisfaction, but his or her subsequent performance continued at a low level.[9]

In summary, the evidence suggests that "boosting morale" may have some positive effects on the organization but that it will not necessarily lead to better performance. In other words, taking actions that can raise morale (like giving everyone a raise, or telling all employees they no longer have to work week ends) may raise morale, and may even improve performance, but as often as not performance will remain about the same. It is when the reward—and therefore the satisfaction—is seen as a *consequence* of good performance that satisfaction seems to "lead" to good performance.

Satisfaction and Its Relation to Attendance and Other Factors

Satisfaction may not "cause" performance, but every manager knows that a lack of satisfaction is one sure sign that all is not well in the organization. For example, employees who are more satisfied generally have better attendance records than those who are not; participate less in unionization activities; and tend to be more satisfied off their jobs as well.

Satisfaction and its Relation to Attendance and Turnover. Behavioral scientists have long sought to understand the relationship between satisfaction and attendance, but their efforts have been plagued by several problems. Perhaps the most obvious of these is that attendance depends not just on an employee's satisfaction, but on many other things as well. For example, an employee who fears that staying home may jeopardize her job will probably come to work regardless of whether she's satisfied with her job or not. Similarly, economic and market conditions, the reward system, work group norms, a person's ability to attend, and whether or not the company penalizes nonattendance also affect the person's attendance.[10]

As a rule, for example, we might expect that where attendance is compulsory, rather than voluntary, and absences are penalized, satisfaction and attendance would not be related. In these situations it is not so much the employee's *satisfaction* that determines whether or not he attends, but instead the fact that attendance is compulsory and he will be penalized if absent. On the other hand, where attendance is more or less voluntary and absences are not penalized, we might expect employee satisfaction to have a considerable effect on whether or not employees come to work.

One recent study provides some fascinating insights into this question.[11] As part of this study, the researcher administered a morale survey to over 3,000 salaried employees in a major retailer's Chicago headquarters. For comparison purposes, satisfaction data were also obtained from 340 salaried employees in the company's New York headquarters office. The survey measured employees' satisfaction with supervision, kind of work, amount of work, career future and security, financial rewards, and company identification.

As it was originally envisioned, the study was simply aimed at determining how (if at all) satisfaction and attendance were related. The satisfaction data were supposed to be related to attendance data that the personnel department collected on April 3, about three months after the satisfaction data had been obtained. However, as it turn out, there was a severe snowstorm in Chicago on April 2, 1975, and this storm greatly hampered the city's transportation system. Now, in this company, occasional absenteeism by managerial people is not subject to financial penalty and is relatively free of social and work group pressure. Furthermore, good attendance following a crippling snowstorm is especially unique because attendance actually requires considerable personal effort. As a result, we would expect to find a rather strong relationship between satisfaction and attendance among the employees in the Chicago office: here, after all, occasional absence was not penalized, and the snowstorm provided a perfect "built-in" excuse for those employees who did not want to come to work. In the New York office, on the other hand, we might expect to find much less of a relationship between satisfaction and attendance: here, employees are also not penalized for an occasional absence, but there was *not* a built-in excuse (the snowstorm) for their staying home.

The results of this study are presented in Exhibit 8.3. As you can see, in Chicago there *was* a significant relationship between all six facets of job satisfaction and attendance. In New York, on the other hand, there was much less of a relationship between satisfaction and attendance. In summary, satisfied employees do have better attendance records—especially when absences are not penalized or are relatively easy to "get away with."

If satisfaction *is* related to attendance, how much money could a company save by increasing the satisfaction of its employees? Mirvis and Lawler used cost accounting techniques to apply costs in dollars to absenteeism and turnover. As you can see in Exhibit 8.4, they found, for example, that the total cost of an employee being absent one day was computed to be $66.45.

The researchers then correlated employee attitudes with both attendance and turnover. Based on this, they were able to predict what effect improved attitudes would have on attendance and turnover and, therefore, costs. This particular study involved 160 tellers in a Midwestern bank, and the researchers concluded that a slight increase in job satisfaction would result in an expected *direct* cost savings of over $17,000 per year.

Exhibit 8.3 Correlations Between Job Satisfaction and Attendance in Chicago and New York Groups

Scale	Chicago[a] (n = 27)	New York[b] (n = 1.3)
Supervision	.54*	.12
Amount of Work	.36*	.01
Kind of Work	.37*	.06
Financial Rewards	.46*	.11
Career Future	.60*	.14
Company Identification	.42*	.02

*Statistically significant

[a]Group following storm, April 1975.
[b]Group, April 1975.

Note: that satisfaction and attendance were significantly related in Chicago, where the storm made it "easier" for employees to stay home. In New York there was no such "built in" excuse for staying home, and satisfaction did not seem to matter as much.

Source: Frank Smith, "Work Attitudes as Predictors of Attendance on a Specific Day," Journal of Applied Psychology, 1977, Vol. 62, No. 1, p. 18.

Exhibit 8.4 Cost per Incident of Absenteeism and Turnover

Absenteeism		Turnover	
Variable	Cost (in dollars)	Variable	Cost (in dollars)
Absent employee		Replacement acquisition	
Salary	23.04	Direct hiring costs	293.95
Benefits	6.40	Other hiring costs	185.55
Replacement employee:		Replacement training	
Training and staff time	2.31	Preassignment	758.84
Unabsorbed burden	15.71	Learning curve	212.98
Lost profit contribution	19.17	Unabsorbed burden	682.44
		Lost profit contribution	388.27
Total variable cost	23.04	Total variable cost	293.95
Total cost	66.45	Total cost	2,522.03

Source: Philip Mirvis and Edward Lawler, "Measuring the Financial Impact of Employee Attitudes," *Journal of Applied Psychology*, Vol. 62, no. 1, pp. 1–8. Copyright 1977 by the American Psychological Association. Reprinted with permission.

How would you account for the fact that satisfaction seems to improve attendance? Our discussion of positive reinforcement may provide one clue. Recall that we said that behavior followed by positive consequences tends to be repeated, while behavior followed by negative consequences diminishes. In this case the "behavior" we are interested in is "coming to work." Now, if the person comes to work and is unhappy at work, then coming to work will be associated with a negative consequence, and it is a good bet that the person will avoid work wherever he or she can. On the other hand, if the person is happy at work, then coming to work will result in a positive consequence (feeling good because of being satisfied at work), and better attendance should result.

The Relation of Satisfaction and Unionization Activity. There is little doubt that job dissatisfaction is a major reason why workers turn to unions. One study involved almost 88,000 salaried, clerical, sales, and technical employees from 250 units of a large organization.[12] As part of its normal personnel procedures, this company administered an attitude survey to employees in these 250 units. The survey was carried out prior to any history of unionization activity, but, several months later, attempts were made to unionize employees in 125 of these units, and the employees in 31 of them finally opted to "go union." As a result, the researchers could correlate *job satisfaction* (with supervision, kind of work, amount of work, career future, security, financial reward, physical surroundings, and company identification) and whether or not employees in a unit *decided to join the union.*[13]

The results of this study show quite clearly that employees who were more dissatisfied were more prone to engage in unionization activity and to unionize. For example, *in all cases* the units with no unionization activity had employees who were more satisfied than did the units with unionization activity. Furthermore, the company had enough information from the attitude survey to *predict* the degree of future union activity.

Dissatisfaction with *which aspects* of their jobs leads workers to unionize? In one recent study, a survey of job satisfaction was made just after the union representation election (the election results were kept secret until all questionnaires were completed and returned).[13] The subjects in this study were 59 production employees working for a medium-sized company in the Midwest, and the survey measured three things: (1) eight types of job satisfaction; (2) "union attitudes" (the employees' attitudes toward the local union and toward unions in general); and (3) the question, "How did you vote in the union election which was just conducted?"

The results of this study are presented in Exhibit 8.5. As it illustrates, employee dissatisfaction and pro-union voting seemed to go hand in hand, since (in most cases) there was a significant *inverse* relationship between satisfaction and pro-union voting. Also notice that it did *not* seem to be *non-economic* factors (like "how much variety the job provided") that were the culprits. Instead, dissatisfaction with "hygienes"—"bread and butter" facets like security and pay—was associated with pro-union voting.

Exhibit 8.5 Degree of Relationship Between Each Attitude and Pro-union Voting

Variable	r
Attitude toward the local union	.57*
Attitude toward unions in general	.51*
Total noneconomic satisfaction	−.38*
Independence satisfaction	−.36*
Variety satisfaction	−.04
Creativity satisfaction	−.17
Achievement satisfaction	−.36*
Total economic satisfaction	−.74*
Security satisfaction	−.41*
Company policy satisfaction	−.55*
Pay satisfaction	−.60*
Working conditions satisfaction	−.76*
Total noneconomic and economic satisfaction	−.64*

*Significant correlations:

Note: That there was a significant inverse relationship between most measures of job satisfaction, and pro-union voting.

Source: Chester Schriesheim, "Job Satisfaction, Attitudes toward Unions, and Voting in a Union Representation Election," Journal of Applied Psychology, 1978, Vol. 63, No. 5, p. 550.

Job Satisfaction, Nonwork Satisfaction, and the Quality of Work Life. An argument often made in favor of trying to raise morale is that being more satisfied is simply a better state of affairs than being dissatisfied and that employees tend to be more satisfied off the job and have a better "quality of life" when they are satisfied with their jobs. While this argument is somewhat altruistic, it is nevertheless an attractive one (to many people, at least), and the evidence seems to support it.

In one study, for example, 73 supervisors were surveyed, and the results suggested that job satisfaction seemed to enhance *nonjob* satisfaction, rather than the other way around.[14] In other words, a person's job satisfaction seems to "spill over" and influence his or her satisfaction off the job as well; many people would view this as a good argument for the benefits of high job satisfaction.

Furthermore, being satisfied with one's job seems to have implications that go far beyond just nonjob satisfaction: thus, researchers at the Survey

Research Center of the University of Michigan have found that job satisfaction can influence how a person feels about his or her life as a whole. In one study these researchers interviewed almost 1,300 people.[15] For each person, the researchers measured three things: the person's job satisfaction, leisure satisfaction, and quality of life. *Job satisfaction* reflected the person's satisfaction with things like coworkers and pay. *Leisure satisfaction* reflected, for example, satisfaction with "things you and your family do together." *Quality of life* was measured by responses to the question, "How do you feel about your life as a whole?"

The researchers found that both job satisfaction *and* leisure satisfaction influenced how these people perceived their quality of life, although the latter seemed to be the more potent influence. However, job satisfaction was also quite important. And here, the satisfaction the person "derived from the work itself and from pay, fringe benefits, and security were the most relevant *job* items in predicting life quality."[16]

Summary. While job satisfaction may not have any direct influence on performance, its relationship to other important factors is clear and consistent. Employees who are more satisfied with their jobs have better attendance and turnover records than do those who are not, and this is especially true in those cases where employees have more discretion or control over their attendance. Job satisfaction is also a major determinant of unionization activity, since dissatisfied employees are much more prone to unionize than satisfied ones. Employee satisfaction, therefore, can have a substantial effect on an organization's productivity and "bottom line."

While these reasons by themselves might be sufficient for trying to increase the satisfaction of one's employees, there is also another reason, in this case noneconomic: high job satisfaction simply seems to be a better state of affairs for employees, at least insofar as it effects their nonjob satisfaction and their perceived quality of life.

As a result, questions concerning employee satisfaction or morale can usefully be included in your "ABCs" analysis. For example, if attendance is poor, ask:

> *Antecedents.* Do employees understand what is expected of them in terms of good attendance?
>
> *Behavior.* Could employees come to work if they wanted to? Are there impediments like poor transportation?
>
> *Consequences.* What are the consequences of coming to work? Are employees happy at work? Is job satisfaction so low that employees prefer to stay home whenever they can? Are there negative consequences—like an inconsiderate boss—that make coming to work unattractive? Are employees penalized for non-attendance?

National Trends in Job Satisfaction

There is conflicting evidence as to whether employees today are more or less satisfied with their jobs than were their counterparts of 5 or 10 years ago.

Much of the evidence suggests that workers are less satisfied today, and the main reference here is *Work in America*, published by the Department of Health, Education, and Welfare.[17] This report argues that there is a growing problem of job alienation because an increasingly younger and better educated labor force cannot derive the self-esteem and sense of meaning and purpose that work should provide. As a result, it concludes, job satisfaction is decreasing.[18]

Yet not all researchers agree that employees are less satisfied today. For example, one group compared the findings of seven national surveys of job satisfaction and concluded that overall job satisfaction had not changed significantly over the past decade.[19] It said that if all the national surveys are carefully analyzed, the results actually indicate that job satisfaction remained about the same between 1958 and 1973. The results of these surveys are presented in Exhibit 8.6. This evidence suggests that the level of job satisfaction has remained about constant over the past few years. (This does not mean, however, that some segments of the workforce (like women) haven't grown more dissatisfied, while others (like men) have become more satisfied.)

Viewed as a whole, at least two conclusions are warranted. First, regardless of the direction of the trend, most workers (about 90 percent) report that they *are* fairly satisfied with the work that they do. (Of course, if 10 percent of the work force is therefore dissatisfied, this is still a very large number of dissatisfied workers—about 10 million.) Second, the evidence seems to suggest that job satisfaction in this country is not decreasing, or at least has not decreased substantially since 1958. Conversely, employees are clearly not more satisfied today than they have been in the past.

MEASURING JOB SATISFACTION

There are several methods of measuring job satisfaction; these include questionnaires, interviews, observations, and the use of secondary and unobtrusive measures.

Questionnaires

Satisfaction questionnaires (also sometimes called "attitude" or "morale" surveys) come in many shapes and formats; they range from short forms that

Exhibit 8.6 Percentage of "Satisfied" Workers, 1958–1973, Based on Seven National Surveys

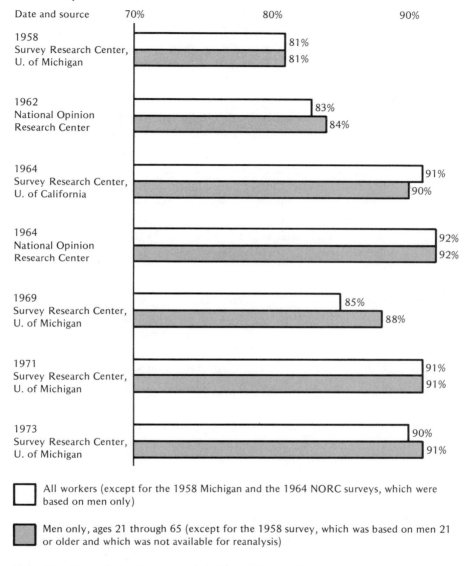

Date and source

| | 70% | 80% | 90% |

1958
Survey Research Center,
U. of Michigan
— 81%
— 81%

1962
National Opinion
Research Center
— 83%
— 84%

1964
Survey Research Center,
U. of California
— 91%
— 90%

1964
National Opinion
Research Center
— 92%
— 92%

1969
Survey Research Center,
U. of Michigan
— 85%
— 88%

1971
Survey Research Center,
U. of Michigan
— 91%
— 91%

1973
Survey Research Center,
U. of Michigan
— 90%
— 91%

☐ All workers (except for the 1958 Michigan and the 1964 NORC surveys, which were based on men only)

▨ Men only, ages 21 through 65 (except for the 1958 survey, which was based on men 21 or older and which was not available for reanalysis)

Note: "Don't know" answers were excluded from the percentage bases.

Source: Robert Quinn, Graham Staines, and Margaret McCullough, "National Trends in Job Satisfaction, 1958–1973," Reprinted in Dennis Organ, *The Applied Psychology of Work Behavior* (Dallas: BPI, 1978), p. 115.

are useful for providing management with a quick glimpse of employee satisfaction to relatively complicated forms that tend to be more research oriented.

Texas Instruments Questionnaire. A version of the attitude questionnaire presented in Exhibit 8.7 has been used successfully by the Texas Instruments Company for several years. Notice that it is designed to be filled out quickly and easily and that it provides information concerning satisfaction with a wide range of factors including hours of work, promotion possibilities, top-management attitudes, freedom of expression, and pay.

Job Description Index (JDI). Another popular questionnaire is called the Job Description Index and taps five facets of job satisfaction: satisfaction with the work itself, pay, promotion, supervision, and coworkers. Developed by Smith and her associates, it has the advantage of being very easy to fill out; at the same time it has a good track record of accurately measuring employee satisfaction.[20] For each of the five categories (work, pay, promotions, supervision, coworkers) a series of adjectives are listed. The employee then has to indicate, with a **Y** (for yes), **N** (for no), or **?** (for cannot decide), whether that adjective relates to his or her job. A few example are given below:

WORK:	**PROMOTIONS:**	**COWORKERS:**
_____Fascinating	_____Good opportunity for	_____Stimulating
_____Routine	advancement	_____Intelligent
_____Challenging	_____Promotion on ability	_____Lazy
	_____Dead-end job	

PAY:	**SUPERVISION:**
_____Bad	_____Impolite
_____Barely live on	_____Tactful
income	_____Knows job well
_____Highly paid	

In practice there are at least nine, and usually more adjectives for each of the five job satisfaction categories.[21]

The Porter Questionnaire. One possible drawback to the Texas Instruments and JDI questionnaires is that they fail to take the relative importance of each facet of job satisfaction into consideration. Thus, "pay satisfaction" may be more important to most people than is "satisfaction with supervision," but most questionnaires weight these factors equally. Some psychologists also say that it is not enough to just ask an employee what his or her satisfaction *is now* with some job facet like pay, or supervision. Instead, writers like Porter define satisfaction as the difference between responses to a "how much *is*

Exhibit 8.7 Texas Instruments Incorporated—Attitude Questionnaire

This questionnaire is designed to help you give us your opinions quickly and easily. There are no "right" or "wrong" answers—it is your own, honest opinion that we want. Please do not sign your name.

DIRECTIONS:
Check ( ) one box for each statement to indicate whether you agree or disagree with it. If you cannot decide, mark the middle box.

EXAMPLE:

I would rather work in a large city than in a small town .... Agree 2☐ ? 1☐ Disagree 0☐

Each item below has columns: Agree 2☐ ? 1☐ Disagree 0☐

1. The hours of work here are O.K.
2. I understand how my job relates to other jobs in my group.
3. Working conditions in TI are better than in other companies.
4. In my opinion, the pay here is lower than in other companies.
5. I think TI is spending too much money in providing recreational programs.
6. I understand what benefits are provided for TIers.
7. The people I work with help each other when someone falls behind, or gets in a tight spot.
8. My supervisor is too interested in his own success to care about the needs of other TIers.
9. My supervisor is always breathing down our necks; he watches us too closely.
10. My supervisor gives us credit and praise for work well done.
11. I think badges should reflect rank as well as length of service.
12. If I have a complaint to make, I feel free to talk to someone up-the-line.
13. My supervisor sees that we are properly trained for our jobs.
14. My supervisor sees that we have the things we need to do our jobs.
15. Management is really trying to build the organization and make it successful.
16. There is cooperation between my department and other departments we work with.
17. I usually read most of Texins News.
18. They encourage us to make suggestions for improvements here.
19. I am often bothered by sudden speed-ups or unexpected slack periods in my work.
20. Qualified TIers are usually overlooked when filling job openings.
21. Compared with other TIers, we get very little attention from management.
22. Sometimes I feel that my job counts for very little in TI.
23. The longer you work for TI the more you feel you belong.
24. I have a great deal of interest in TI and its future.
25. I have little opportunity to use my abilities in TI.
26. There are plenty of good jobs in TI for those who want to get ahead.
27. I often feel worn out and tired on my job.
28. They expect too much work from us around here.
29. The company should provide more opportunities for employees to know each other.
30. For my kind of job, working conditions are O.K.
31. I'm paid fairly compared with other TIers.
32. Compared with other companies, TI benefits are good.
33. A few people I work with think they run the place.
34. The people I work with get along well together.
35. My supervisor has always been fair in his dealings with me.
36. My supervisor gets employees to work together as a team.
37. I have confidence in the fairness and honesty of management.
38. Management here is really interested in the welfare of TIers.
39. Most of the higher-ups are friendly toward us.
40. I work in a friendly environment.
41. My supervisor lets us know what is expected of us.
42. We don't receive enough information from top management.
43. I know how my job fits in with other work in this organization.
44. TI does a poor job of keeping us posted on the things we want to know about TI.
45. I think TI informality is carried too far.
46. You can get fired around here without much cause.
47. I can be sure of my job as long as I do good work.
48. I have plenty of freedom on the job to use my own judgment.
49. My supervisor allows me reasonable leeway in making mistakes.
50. I really feel part of this organization.
51. The people who get promotions in TI usually deserve them.
52. I can learn a great deal on my present job.

(PLEASE CONTINUE ON REVERSE SIDE)

Exhibit 8.7 *(continued)*

	Agree	?	Disagree
53. My job is often dull and monotonous	2☐	1☐	0☐
54. There is too much pressure on my job	2☐	1☐	0☐
55. I am required to spend too much time on the job	2☐	1☐	0☐
56. I have the right equipment to do my work	2☐	1☐	0☐
57. My pay is enough to live on comfortably	2☐	1☐	0☐
58. I'm satisfied with the way employee benefits are handled here	2☐	1☐	0☐
59. I wish I had more opportunity to socialize with my associates	2☐	1☐	0☐
60. The people I work with are very friendly	2☐	1☐	0☐
61. My supervisor welcomes our ideas even when they differ from his own	2☐	1☐	0☐
62. My supervisor ought to be friendlier toward us	2☐	1☐	0☐
63. My supervisor lives up to his promises	2☐	1☐	0☐
64. We are kept well informed about TI's business prospects and standing with competitors	2☐	1☐	0☐
65. Management ignores our suggestions and complaints	2☐	1☐	0☐
66. My supervisor is not qualified for his job	2☐	1☐	0☐
67. My supervisor has the work well organized	2☐	1☐	0☐
68. I have ample opportunity to see the end results of my work	2☐	1☐	0☐
69. My supervisor has enough authority and backing to perform his job well	2☐	1☐	0☐
70. I do not get enough instruction about how to do a job	2☐	1☐	0☐
71. You can say what you think around here	2☐	1☐	0☐
72. I know where I stand with my supervisor	2☐	1☐	0☐
73. When terminations are necessary, they are handled fairly	2☐	1☐	0☐
74. I am very much underpaid for the work I do	2☐	1☐	0☐

	Agree	?	Disagree
75. I'm really doing something worthwhile in my job	2☐	1☐	0☐
76. I'm proud to work for TI	2☐	1☐	0☐
77. Many TIers I know would like to see the union get in	2☐	1☐	0☐
78. I received fair treatment in my last performance review	2☐	1☐	0☐
79. During the past six months I have seriously considered getting a job elsewhere	2☐	1☐	0☐
80. TI's problem-solving procedure is adequate for handling our problems and complaints	2☐	1☐	0☐
81. I would recommend employment at TI to my friends	2☐	1☐	0☐
82. My supervisor did a good job in discussing my last performance review with me	2☐	1☐	0☐
83. My pay is the most important source of satisfaction from my job	2☐	1☐	0☐
84. Favoritism is a problem in my area	2☐	1☐	0☐
85. I have very few complaints about our lunch facilities	2☐	1☐	0☐
86. Most people I know in this community have a good opinion of TI	2☐	1☐	0☐
87. I usually read most of my division newspaper	2☐	1☐	0☐
88. I can usually get hold of my supervisor when I need him	2☐	1☐	0☐
89. Most TIers are placed in jobs that make good use of their abilities	2☐	1☐	0☐
90. I receive adequate training for my needs	2☐	1☐	0☐
91. I've gone as far as I can in TI			
92. My job seems to be leading to the kind of future I want	2☐	1☐	0☐
93. There is too much personal friction among people at my level in the company	2☐	1☐	0☐
94. The amount of effort a person puts into his job is appreciated at TI	2☐	1☐	0☐
95. Filling in this questionnaire is a good way to let management know what employees think	2☐	1☐	0☐
96. I think some good will come out of filling in a questionnaire like this one	2☐	1☐	0☐

97 Please check on term which most nearly describes the kind of work you do: 1 ☐ Clerical or office 2 ☐ Production

3 ☐ Technical 4 ☐ Maintenance 5 ☐ Manufacturing 6 ☐ R & D 7 ☐ Engineering 8 ☐ Other

98 1 ☐ Hourly 2 ☐ Salaried **99** 1 ☐ Male 2 ☐ Female **100** Do you supervise 3 or more TIers? 1 ☐ Yes 2 ☐ No

Name of your department:

Please write any comments or suggestions you care to make in the space below.

there now" item and a "how much *should there be"* item. For each satisfaction item, the researcher then subtracts the employee's response to the question "How much is there now?" from his response to the question "How much should there be?" and thus derives what is actually a measure of the deficiency in need fulfillment, or dissatisfaction.[22] An example of one such item, which also includes a rating by the employee of *how important* the item is to him or her, would be as follows:

The pay I receive for doing my job:

A. How much is there now?		1	2	3	4	5	6	7
B. How much should there be?		1	2	3	4	5	6	7
C. How important is this to me?		1	2	3	4	5	6	7

                         None   A great deal

Pros and Cons. Questionnaires (and we have only presented a few of many) have a number of advantages and disadvantages. The responses can be quantified and easily summarized, and questionnaires are relatively easy and inexpensive to use with large numbers of employees. On the other hand, questionnaires tend to be an impersonal way of collecting information, and, related to this, the predetermined sequence of questions may miss important issues. Good, unambiguous, questionnaire items are also difficult to develop and test, and while many organizations use "packaged" forms, others choose to develop special ones for themselves. Analyzing the responses also usually requires the use of a computer, especially where large numbers of respondents are involved—and where there are *not* large numbers, some other method, such as interviewing, will often suffice.

Other Methods for Measuring Job Satisfaction[23]

Interviews. Interviewing employees is perhaps the most obvious and direct way of finding out whether or not they are satisfied with their jobs, and there are several ways to interview them. For example, interviews may be *formally* arranged and held periodically, or when an employee leaves the company; or they may be *informal* and just involve a conversation between the manager and employee over lunch or at the workplace. Interviews can be *structured;* as where the interviewer follows a predetermined sequence of questions, or *open-ended* in that the response to each question determines what the interviewer asks next. Interviews can also be carried out either by *outside* consultants or by *in-house* staff.

Interviews have a number of advantages and disadvantages. Most importantly, they are *adaptive* in that the interviewer can follow promising lines of inquiry. They also tend to be a source of *"rich" data,* since the employee has an opportunity to indicate the degree to which he is satisfied, and also *why* he is satisfied (or dissatisfied) with different aspects of the job. On the other hand, interviews tend to be *time-consuming* and, thus, an expensive way of measuring job satisfaction, especially where many employees are involved. There is also always the possibility that the interviewer may knowingly or unknowingly *bias responses*, for example, by asking "leading" questions. Similarly, there is more chance in these "face to face" meetings that the interviewee will give slanted answers, perhaps by telling the interviewer what he or she thinks that person wants to hear. And, interview data are also very difficult to quantify.

Observations. Observing the actual behavior of the employees in the organization is another useful way to measure their satisfaction. By observing them, for example, one might notice that employees seem "down," or annoyed, or antagonistic and from this deduce that a survey or some interviews are called for.

There is often no real substitute for such direct observation. Because data on *actual* behavior rather than on reports of behavior can be collected, the information tends to have a clear, "real-time" validity that information obtained through interviews or questionnaires might not. On the other hand, observation also has some major limitations: *interpreting* the observations; deciding *which employees* or operations to sample; deciding if the observer is *biased* and so "reading into" the situation his or her own interpretations; and deciding if the "observees" *know* they are being watched and are therefore acting unusually are the main ones.

Secondary Data and Unobtrusive Measures. Information that is (usually) already available in the organization's existing personnel files can also be a valuable source of job satisfaction data. For example, data on attendance, turnover, and grievances tend to be fairly sensitive barometers of job satisfaction. In addition, measures of accidents, productivity, reject rates, repairs, complaints, costs, and so on can also provide valuable, indirect information about employee satisfaction.

Indirect, unobtrusive measures like the above can be useful. When employees know they are being questioned or observed, there is always a possibility they will tell you what they think you want to hear, or only what they want you to hear; with nondirect, unobtrusive measures there is little or no chance for such a "response bias." This type of information also tends to be easily quantified, since you can, for example, graph historical accident rates, reject rates, and turnover. (This is important where you want to compare different units in your organization, or monitor one unit over time.) However, assessing, retrieving, and compiling this data can sometimes be a problem.

Important advantages and disadvantages of different methods of measuring job satisfaction are summarized in Exhibit 8.8.

Exhibit 8.8 A Comparison of Different Methods of Data Collection

Method	Major advantages	Major potential problems
Interviews	1. Adaptive—allows data collection on a range of possible subjects 2. Source of "rich" data 3. Process of interviewing can build rapport	1. Can be expensive 2. Interviewer can bias responses 3. Coding/interpretation problems 4. Self-report bias
Questionnaires	1. Responses can be quantified and easily summarized 2. Easy to use with large samples 3. Relatively inexpensive 4. Can obtain large volume of data	1. Predetermined questions may miss issues 2. Response bias
Observations	1. Collects data on behavior rather than reports of behavior 2. Real-time, not retrospective 3. Adaptive	1. Interpretation and coding problems 2. Sampling is a problem 3. Observer bias/reliability 4. Costly
Secondary data/unobtrusive measures	1. Nonreactive—no-response bias 2. High-face validity 3. Easily quantified	1. Access/retrieval posibly a problem 2. Potential validity problems 3. Coding/interpretation

Source: David Nadler, *Feedback Organization Development: Using Data-Based Methods* (Reading: Addison-Wesley, 1977), p. 119.

INFLUENCING JOB SATISFACTION

Introduction: Factors That Influence Satisfaction

An organization can improve it's employees' satisfaction by improving, controlling, or adjusting either *individual* or *situational* factors. Individual factors (like age) are important because even on the same job and with the same rewards and leader, some employees will be more satisfied than others. *Situational* factors (like pay, and leader behavior) are important because they satisfy (or fail to satisfy) employees' important needs.

The Effect of Individual Differences on Job Satisfaction

Age. A person's age is one factor that determines how satisfied he or she is, and until recently most management writers believed there was a "U" shaped relationship between age and satisfaction. Psychologists believed that satisfaction was highest when people started on their jobs, but subsequently declined until people reached their late twenties or early thirties. Then satisfaction again began to rise.[24] The assumption was that workers came to their jobs enthusiastically but that as their aspirations conflicted with the realities of their job and their abilities they slowly grew more dissatisfied. As they grew older, however, they began to lower their aspirations so that as a result older workers became relatively satisfied with the realities of their jobs.

Today many experts believe that employee age and satisfaction are *directly* related: that, other things equal, older employees are more satisfied than younger employees.[25] For example, the researchers in one study analyzed data from over 1,000 males and over 400 females who had taken part in surveys conducted by the National Opinion Research Center in 1972, 1973, and 1974. In this survey, employees had to respond to the following question: "On the whole, how satisfied are you with the work you do—would you say you are very satisfied, moderately satisfied, a little dissatisfied, or very dissatisfied?" The findings of this study indicated that for both males and females job satisfaction varies (or recently has varied) directly with age: that, generally speaking, employees tend to grow more satisfied the older they get.

Yet while we know that age and satisfaction are often directly related, the reasons for the association are not understood. Many explanations have been proposed,[26] but perhaps the most reasonable has been put forth by Herzberg. He says that employees who have realistic expectations about their jobs should be more satisfied than those with unrealistic expectations. And, probably, as employees grow older, they gradually lower their aspirations and bring them into line with their abilities. Thus, to the extent that older workers have more realistic expectations, they are more satisfied.[27]

Other "Individual Difference" Determinants of Job Satisfaction. Other "individual difference" factors also influence satisfaction. For example, there is often, an inverse relationship between educational level and employee morale, although the findings here are not entirely consistent.[28] Thus, *other things equal*, it appears that the higher the educational level of an employee, the lower his or her job satisfaction, particularly with pay. One possible explanation is that people with higher educational levels also have higher "reference groups." These are groups both inside and outside of the company with which an employee compares his or her own attainments. And, the higher a person's reference point—the higher he thinks he should be—the less satisfied he may be at any particular point. (Managers intuitively know this, and thus resist hiring people they believe are "overqualified" for a job.) There is also a direct relationship between *occupational level* and employee satisfaction. Thus, executives are, on the whole, more satisfied than managers; managers are more satisfied than subordinates; and so forth.[29] Employees for whom work is a "central life interest" also tend to have the highest job satisfaction, while those with a nonwork-oriented central life interest have the lowest job satisfaction.[30]

Implications. A number of individual difference items influence employee job satisfaction: these include age, occupational level, educational level, and central life interests.

All are factors that a manager cannot easily change or manipulate once an employee is on the job. However, it *is* possible to manipulate these factors earlier, when the "man-requirements" for each job are drawn up, and when employees are hired and assigned. For example, on especially boring, dissatisfying jobs, one could probably make a case for seeking out workers who are somewhat older, less educated, and who are "company men" in that work in general and your company in particular are important, central factors in their lives.

Situational Factors that Influence Job Satisfaction

To understand why and how situational factors influence job satisfaction one has to remember that employees bring to their jobs many needs that they want to have satisfied. These needs include a number of basic, existence needs for health, security, and pay, and a number of higher level "growth" needs like the needs to achieve, to be recognized, and to self-actualize.

Whether or not these needs are satisfied depends largely on situational factors. The nature of the work itself, for example, will determine whether the job provides the challenge and sense of achievement that can satisfy the worker's needs for achievement and self-actualization. The leader's style will influence whether the person's need to be treated as a valuable, unique individual will be satisfied. The reward system and company policy will influence whether the person's needs for food, shelter, and security are satisfied. And the person's work group will help determine if his or her affiliation need is met. Situational factors like these therefore all have a direct bearing on employee satisfaction.

What do workers look for in their jobs? What situational, job-related factors make a job "good" or "bad" from the point of view of employees? A recent study sheds some light on this question. The subjects here included over 57,000 job applicants of the Minnesota Gas Company.[31] As a part of their application, these people filled out a Job Preferences Questionnaire, and data were available for a 30-year period from August 1945 to August 1975. The questionnaire asked the applicant to indicate his or her preferences for certain job characteristics by ranking these from 1 (high) to 10 (low).

The results of this study were fairly clear-cut. For the men there was an orderly progression from security (most important) to working conditions (least important) with the factors ranked as follows:

Security (highest)
Type of work
Advancement
Company
Pay
Coworkers
Supervisor
Benefits
Hours
Working Conditions (lowest)

The results for the women applicants were different. Here "type of work" was by far the most important factor in determining, "What makes a job good or bad?" The next eight factors were fairly close to each other in importance, and "benefits" stood alone in tenth place.

On the whole, job preferences were remarkably consistent over the 30-year period, but some trends were apparent. For men, "type of work" increased in importance over the period. For both men and women, "pay" increased in importance, and "advancement" decreased in importance.

The results of this study are informative for many reasons. First, most people tend to assume that "pay" is the most important factor in determining what makes a job good or bad. From this study, however, it seems that many factors, including security, type of work, and opportunities for advancement are also important in determining what makes a job good or bad. Second, men and women currently seem to have rather different preferences when it comes to determining what makes a job good or bad: thus men ranked "security" first, while women ranked "type of work" first. Third, while some trends were noted during the 30-year period, the rankings for men and women did not change very much although life-styles and the political, social, and economic environments changed markedly between 1945 and 1975.

From this and similar studies, we know that employee satisfaction is influenced by many situational factors, factors over which management usually has a good deal of control; these include job security, type of work, advancement, pay, and leader style. Workers who have more considerate, supportive leaders are generally more satisfied than those who do not.[32] Employees who are members of cohesive work groups similarly tend to be more satisfied.[33] The organization's "climate"—the perceptions the individual has of the kind of organization he is working in, and his "feel" for the organization in terms of such dimensions as autonomy, structure, rewards, consideration, warmth and support, and openness—will also influence whether or not he is satisfied with his job. *Pay* is another important factor, and from our earlier discussions we know that it is not just the adequacy of the pay but whether or not it is perceived as equitable that determines whether or not the person is satisfied with it.

The nature of a person's job also has a direct bearing on his or her job satisfaction. Recall that many believe that people have needs to be challenged, to achieve, and to feel important, and that routine, simplified jobs lead to monotony, boredom, and, finally, dissatisfaction.[34] Often the prescription for dealing with this problem is to redesign the job, enriching it so that the employee has a more varied set of tasks to perform, preferably ones that include some responsibilities for planning and checking his or her own work.

An Involvement Approach. Many situational factors influence job satisfaction. These include supervisory style, organizational climate, pay, working conditions, and the work itself. A person interested in increasing the satisfaction of his or her employees would typically use interviews, questionnaires, observations, or unobtrusive measures to identify satisfaction problems and would then act to eliminate the sources of those problems. Solutions may range from job redesign and leadership training to providing a better benefits package and better food in the company cafeteria.

Meyers has proposed what he calls an involvement approach to ferreting out attitude problems and solving them.[35] At the Texas Instruments Company, where this approach was developed, a questionnaire (like that in Exhibit 8.7) is administered to a 10–20 percent sample of employees throughout the company. Profiles (such as Exhibit 8.9) are prepared from the results and delivered to each of the approximately 160 department managers. The heavy solid line shows the *company* average for the year, and is the same on every department's profile. The thin solid line is this year's *department* results, while the dotted line is last year's results. As you can see each department manager can therefore compare his or her department results for each item to both the total company results and to his or her last year's profile. In this way management can identify problems—be they low pay, inadequate benefits, poor benefits, or nonsupportive leader style—and work with employees in solving them.

Exhibit 8.9 Employee Attitude Profile

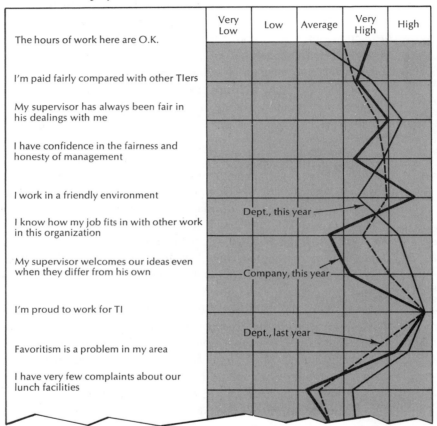

Source: Dale Beach, *Managing People at Work: Readings* (New York: Macmillan, 1971).

To avoid making department managers defensive, survey results are fed directly back to them (rather than back to top management). The department head presents and discusses these results in general terms in a group meeting of his or her department and then hands them to a committee of employees. These five or six people meet as often as necessary to analyze the results and make recommendations to the department managers. The department manager, in turn, analyzes these recommendations with his boss, and final recommendations are transmitted back to departmental employees. Some examples of "problems" and "recommendations" are presented in Exhibit 8.10.

Exhibit 8.10 Problems and Committee Suggestions

Committee Report for XYZ Department

Problems	Recommendations
1. New employees are sometimes hired for good jobs that old employees are qualified to fill.	1. Post job openings on bulletin boards and explain procedure for bidding on these jobs.
2. Sometimes employees are not told till Friday night that they are expected to work on Saturday.	2. Give at least two days' notice of the requirement to work on weekends.
3. Some believe that salary comparisons with other companies do not take into consideration overtime pay practices in effect in other companies.	3. Define the normal work week for salaried personnel which serves as the basis for salary comparisons with other companies.
4. We sometimes read about company events in local newspapers before we hear about them in the company.	4. Let employees hear first about company events through department meetings, newspaper, bulletins and supervisors.
5. We are often pulled off a job before it's finished and put on another rush job.	5. Better planning and more consideration on the part of supervision could correct most of this.
6. Some items on attitude survey are confusing.	6. Give Corporate Personnel a list of confusing items with suggested changes.
7. Because the attitude survey is done on a sample basis, a lot of people feel "left out."	7. Increase the size of the samples or explain why you can't.

Source: Beach, *Managing People at Work: Readings.*

CHAPTER SUMMARY

1. Job satisfaction reflects the degree to which important needs for health, security, esteem, and so on are satisfied on the job or as a result of the job. It is typically measured on at least the following dimensions: work, pay, promotions, recognition, benefits, working conditions, supervision, coworkers, company, and management.

2. Two theories have been advanced for explaining how satisfaction and performance are related: satisfaction causes performance; and rewards cause both satisfaction and performance. Today we generally believe that when an employee successfully performs a task his or her satisfaction will increase, so long as he receives some reward for performing the task—it is the reward (either extrinsic or intrinsic) that causes satisfaction, not performance. Therefore, tying rewards to performance increases employee satisfaction at once and also leads to further increases in the level of performance.

3. While job satisfaction may not have any direct influence on performance, its relationship to other important factors is clear and consistent. Employees who are more satisfied with their jobs have better attendance and turnover records than do those who are not, and this is especially true in those cases where employees have more discretion or control over their attendance. Job satisfaction is also a major determinant of unionization activity, since dissatisfied employees are much more prone to unionize than are those who are not.

4. There are several methods of measuring job satisfaction: these include questionnaires, interviews, observations, and the use of secondary and unobtrusive measures. The important advantages and disadvantages of different methods of measuring job satisfaction are presented in Exhibit 8.8.

5. There are basically two ways in which an organization can improve its employees' satisfaction. First, it can fit individual differences to the task. For example, we know that, generally speaking, younger and older employees tend to have higher morale than do those of middle age, and that those with higher educational levels will not be quite as satisfied in a given job as will a person with a lower educational level. Second, an organization can modify situational factors, for example, by training leaders to be more considerate and by making specific changes that will increase employees' needs satisfaction—for example, by making their jobs more secure, by improving the type of work, by providing better pay, and so on.

6. The involvement approach to attitude surveys can be very useful. Organizations can use this approach to identify the specific sources of low morale and then to get the employees involved in mapping out the necessary changes.

DISCUSSION QUESTIONS AND PROJECTS

1. List the dimensions along which you would measure satisfaction in an organization. Then, meet in groups of four or five students and develop (in each group) a satisfaction questionnaire for measuring the satisfaction or morale of the students in this class. Remember, you do not have to actually measure the students' satisfaction; just develop the questionnaire for doing so. The groups should then compare questionnaires and discuss them.

2. Explain why a manager should aim at keeping his or her employees' morale high.

3. Based on the evidence we discussed in this chapter, how (if at all) are job satisfaction and employee performance related?

4. Explain how satisfaction and attendance are related. Do you find that this relationship also holds with respect to students coming to class? Can you explain this relationship in terms of the "ABCs" of performance?

5. Can you think of any experiences that would support (or not support) the argument that job satisfaction affects non-job satisfaction?

6. Discuss the pros and cons of various methods for measuring job satisfaction.

7. Do you think that it is true that a person's age and satisfaction are curvilinearly related? Can you cite any examples? What, if anything do you think this has to do with what some psychologists call the "mid-life crisis"?

8. Write a short essay entitled: "How I as a manager can influence the morale of my employees."

CASE EXERCISE

Allison Auto Parts

In 1927, Henry Allison opened his first auto parts store in connection with his garage and service station. He sold high quality products at fair prices and in the years that followed developed a reputation as a reliable source for replacement parts.

With continued growth in the auto parts business, he sold his garage and service station and in 1934 opened a mail-order auto parts store. By 1954, his staff had grown to 60 salesmen, 15 warehousemen, and 5 office employees.

Mr. Allison was an iron-fisted man who ran a "tight" shop. His word was law, and everyone knew it. His hiring practices were simple. If an applicant for a job wore a hat, he concluded that the man would make a good salesman. If he did not wear a hat, Mr. Allison, depending on his mood, might consider him as a possible warehouseman. He always asked a prospective employee, "Do you repair your own car?" If the prospect answered "no," he was turned down for the job. When an applicant was hired, Mr. Allison personally took him into the store or warehouse, depending on his assignment, and told him precisely what he wanted him to do. Then he turned the employee over to the supervisor. Any worker who contradicted or strongly disagreed with Mr. Allison was fired without question.

Allison Auto Parts had no formal system of pay or merit increases. Instead, every employee was paid what Mr. Allison thought he was worth, and his pay was increased whenever Mr. Allison thought it should be increased. Mr. Allison was a firm believer in hard work and didn't "baby" his employees with fringe benefits, paid vacations, or sick leave.

In 1967, Mr. Allison's son, Dick, came to work in the business as vice-president and general manager. In school, Dick had taken some courses in personnel and human behavior and felt that the company's personnel practices were not ideal. His first act was to devise an application blank for all employees. One was filled out for each applicant, and to complete the files, he also had one made out for each old employee. In addition, he made arrangements with a local physician to give every new employee a physical examination to determine his physical fitness for the work. Dick also wanted to install an employee as well as supervisory training program, but he was not able to convince his father of its need.

Labor turnover during the past ten years increased from 6 to 26 percent, and absences had increased in proportion. Although most employees who left the company said they did so because the work was too hard, they also stated their dissatisfaction with their jobs, and some complained about pay. When Dick checked the average wage, however, he found that it was above the community average for similar work.

In trying to figure out the cause of the trouble, Dick decided that what was needed was a system of job specifications (which list the human traits and abilities required for performing each job), and also indicated that he thought morale could be improved by an employee suggestions system. Mr. Allison, however, vetoed the idea of job specifications but agreed tentatively to an employee suggestions system. Accordingly, Mr. Allison placed on the company bulletin board an announcement indicating that a suggestions systems was in effect and that employees should make their suggestions to their supervisors. If an employee's suggestion was adopted, he would be awarded a cash bonus to be determined by the value of the suggestion to the company.

After a month and a half had passed with no suggestions, Dick found that several had been made but that the supervisor thought they were of no value and, therefore, had not passed them on to Mr. Allison. Dick then got his father's permission to install a new suggestion system, and during the next month, over 41 suggestions were received covering such topics as changes in manufacturing methods, changes in plant layout, job classifications, employee leaves, vacations with pay, a system of promotions and transfers, and materials handling. Mr. Allison patiently read each suggestion aloud to his son and explained why it could not be adopted. When employees heard nothing from their suggestions, they stopped submitting them within two months. Labor turnover continued to increase, up to 32 percent.

Dick Allison knew that his employee relations and morale were getting out of hand, but he could not decide what steps he should take next.

Questions

    1. What, if anything, do you think this case tells you about the relationship between morale and profits?

    2. How would you analyze the problem here if you were a consultant? What *is* the problem? What behavior do you want to change here?

    3. What do you think of the company's suggestion system?

    4. What would you do to correct the situation at Allison.

NOTES FOR CHAPTER 8

1. For a discussion of the importance of permitting members of an organization to satisfy their important personal needs see J. Richard Hackman and J. Lloyd Suttle, *Improving Life at Work: Behavior Science Approach to Organizational Change* (Santa Monica: Goodyear, 1977), p. 4.

2. For two reviews in this area see Arthur Brayfield and Walter Crockett, "Employee Attitudes and Employee Performance," *Psychological Bulletin,* 52 (September 1955), 396–424; Donald Schwab and Larry Cummings, "Theories of Performance and Satisfaction: A review," *Industrial Relations,* 9, No. 4 (October 1970), pp. 408–30.

3. Victor Vroom, *Work and Motivation* (New York: John Wiley & Sons, 1964); L. L. Cummings and W. E. Scott, *Readings in Organizational Behavior and Human Performance* (Homewood, Ill.: Irwin, 1969), ch. 3.

4. Dennis Organ, "A Reappraisal and Reinterpretation of the Satisfaction Causes performance hypothesis," *Academy of Management Review,* 2, No. 1 (1977), 46–53.

5. John Wanous, "A causal correlational analysis of the job satisfaction and performance relationship," *Journal of Applied Psychology,* 59, No. 2 (1974), pp. 139–44; J. E. Sheridan and J. W. Slocum, Jr., "The direction of the causal relationship between job satisfaction and work performance," *Organizational Behavior and Human Performance,* 14, No. 2 (October 1975), 159–72; Edward Lawler III, and Lyman Porter, "The Effect of Performance on job satisfactions," *Industrial Relations,* 7 (October 1967) 20–28; George Strauss, "Human Relations—1968 style," *Industrial Relations,* 7 (May 1968), p. 264.

6. D. Bowen and J. P. Siegel, "The relationship between satisfaction and performance: the question of causality," *Proceedings of the Annual Convention of the American Psychological Association* (1970); C. N. Greene, "A causal interpretation of the relationships among pay, performance, and satisfaction," (paper presented at the annual meeting of the midwest Psychological Association, 1972, Cleveland, Ohio). See also J. P. Siegel, D. Bowen, "Satisfaction and Performance: causal relationships and moderating effects, *Journal of Vocational Behavior,* 7 (1971), pp. 263–69.

7. Some of the recent evidence suggests that other factors like the employee's self-esteem and the leader's behavior influence the degree to which performance leads to satisfaction. See for example, C. N. Greene, "The reciprocal Nature of Influence between leader and subordinate," *Journal of Applied Psychology,* 60 (1975), pp. 187–93; H. K. Downey, J. E. Sheridan, and J. W. Slocum Jr., "The Path-Goal Theory of Leadership: A longitudinal analysis," *Organizational Behavior and Human Performance* (1976); Jeffrey Greenhaus and Irwin Badin, "Self-esteem, performance, and satisfaction: some tests of the theory," *Journal of Applied Psychology,* 62, No. 4 (1977), pp. 417–21.

8. Charles Greene and Robert Craft, Jr., "The satisfaction-performance controversy revisited," in Kirk Downey, Don Hellreigel and John Slocum, Jr., *Organizational Behavior: Readings* (St. Paul: West Publishing, 1977), pp. 187–201.

9. D. J. Cherrington, H. J. Reitz, and W. E. Scott, Jr., "Effects of Contingent and Noncontingent reward on the relationship between satisfaction and task performance," *Journal of Applied Psychology,* 55 (1971), pp. 531–36. See also Greene and Craft, "The satisfaction-performance," p. 189; D. A. Kesselman, M. T. Wood, and E. L. Hagen, "Relationship between performance and satisfaction under contingent and noncontingent reward systems," *Journal of Applied Psychology,* 59 (1974), pp. 374–76: these researchers attempted to replicate the findings of Cherrington et al. ,and their findings were less conclusive. These findings also include the findings on behavior modification discussed in chapter 4; C. N. Greene, "Causal connections between managers' pay, job satisfaction and performance," *Journal of Applied Psychology,* 58 (1973), pp. 95–100; Wanous, "A causal correlational analysis," pp. 139–44; R. A. Sutermeister, "Employee performance and employee need satisfaction—which comes first?" *California Management Review,* 13 (1971), pp. 43–47.

10. For a model describing how these other factors influence attendance, see Richard Steers and Susan Rhodes, "Major influences on employee attendance: a process model," *Journal of Applied Psychology,* 63, No. 4 (1978), pp. 391–407.

11. Frank J. Smith, "Work Attitudes as predictors of attendance on a specific day," *Journal of Applied Psychology,* 62, No. 1 (1977), pp. 16–19.

12. W. Clay Hamner and Frank Smith, "Work Attitudes as predictors of unionization activity," *Journal of Applied Psychology*, 63, No. 4 (1978), pp. 415–21. For some earlier research, see J. G. Getman and S. B. Goldberg, "The Behavioral Assumptions" underlying NLRB regulation of campaign misrepresentations: an empirical evaluation," *Stanford Law Review*, 28 (1976), pp. 263–84; W. J. Bigoness, "Correlates of faculty attitudes toward collective bargaining," *Journal of Applied Psychology*, 63, 228–33.

13. Chester Schriesheim, "Job satisfaction, attitudes toward unions, and voting in a union representation election," *Journal of Applied Psychology*, 63, No. 5 (1978), pp. 548–52.

14. Christopher Orpen, "Work and nonwork satisfaction: a causal-correlational analysis," *Journal of Applied Psychology*, 68, No. 4 (1978), pp. 530–32.

15. Manuel London, Rick Crandall and Gary Steals, "The contribution of job and leisure satisfaction to quality of life," *Journal of Applied Psychology*, 62, No. 3 (1977), pp. 328–34.

16. M. London, R. Crandall, and G. Steals, "The contribution . . .," p. 332.

17. *Work in America: a report of the special task force of the secretary of Health, Education and Welfare* (Cambridge: Massachusetts Institute of Technology Press).

18. For other studies that suggest that job satisfaction is decreasing see, for example: "job satisfaction and productivity," *Gallup Opinion Index*, report no. 94 (1973), pp. 8–9; Frank Smith, Kenneth Scott, and Charles Hulin, "Trends in job related attitudes of managerial and professional employees," *Academy of Management Journal*, 20, no. 3 (September 1977), pp. 454–60; Frank Smith, Carlene Roberts, and Charles Hylin, "Ten year job satisfaction trends in a stable organization," *Academy of Management Journal*, 19, no. 3 (1976), pp. 462–69.

19. Robert Quinn, Gram Stanes, and Margaret McCullough, *Job satisfaction: is there a trend? Manpower Research Monograph, no. 30* (Manpower Administration, U.S. Department of Labor, 1974).

20. See, for example, Bernard Gillet and Donald Schwab, "Convergent and discriminant validities of corresponding job descriptive index and Minnesota satisfaction questionnaire scale," *Journal of Applied Psychology*, 60, no. 3 (1975), pp. 313–17.

21. The job description index is copyrighted by Dr. Patricia C. Smith, Bowling Green State University. Researchers wishing to use those scales are asked to obtain permission from Dr. Patricia Smith, Psychology Building, Bowling Green University, Bowling Green, Ohio, 43404.

22. Lyman Porter and Vance Mitchell, "Comparative study of need satisfactions in military and business hierarchies," *Journal of Applied Psychology*, 51, no. 2 (1967), pp. 139–44.

23. See David Nadler, *Feedback and Organization Development: using data-based methods* (Reading, Mass.: Addison-Wesley, 1977), pp. 118–43.

24. John Hunt and Peter Saul, "The relationship between age, tenure, and job satisfaction in males and females," *Academy of Management Journal*, 18 (December 1975), pp. 690–702.

25. Hunt and Saul, "The relationship of age, tenure, and job satisfaction," Norval Glenn, Patricia Taylor, and Charles Weaver, "Age and job satisfaction among males and females: multivariate, multisurvey study," *Journal of Applied Psychology*, 62, no. 2 (1977), pp. 189–93.

26. See, for example, Glenn, Taylor, and Weaver, "Age and Job Satisfaction."

27. See, for example, Frederick Herzberg et al., *Attitudes: review of research and opinion* (Pittsburgh: Psychological services of Pittsburgh, 1957).

28. See J. Maher, "Educational level and satisfaction with pay," *Personnel Psychology*, 19 (1966), 195–208; Michael Gordon and Richard Arvey, "The relationship between education and satisfaction with job content," *Academy of Management Journal*, 18, no. 4 (December 1975).

29. Lyman Porter and Edward Lawler III, "Properties of organization structure in relation to job attitudes and job behavior," *Journal of Applied Psychology*, 64 (1965), pp. 23–51.

30. Robert Dubin and Joseph Champouy, "Central life interest and job satisfaction," *Organizational Behavior and Human Performance*, 18, no. 2 (April 1977), pp. 366–77.

31. Clifford Jurgensen, "Job preferences (what makes a job good or bad?)," *Journal of Applied Psychology*, 63, no. 3 (June 1978), pp. 267–76.

32. See, for example, Rensis Likert, *New Patterns of Management* (New York: McGraw-Hill, 1961), p. 101.

33. Paul Adams and John Slocum, "Work groups and employee satisfaction," *Personnel Administration*, 34, no. 2 (March–April 1971), pp. 37–43.

34. Charles Hulin and Milton Blood, "Job enlargement, individual differences and worker responses," *Psychological Bulletin*, 69, no. 1 (1968), pp. 41–55.

35. M. Scott Meyers, "How attitudes surveys help you manage," *Training and Development Journal*, 21 (October 1967), pp. 34–41, reprinted in Dale Beach, *Personnel*; see also Robert Solomon, "An examination of the relationship between a survey feedback O.D. technique and the work environment," *Personnel Psychology*, 29, no. 4 (Winter 1976).

ORGANIZATIONAL DETERMINANTS OF PERFORMANCE

The main purpose of this part of the book is to explain the effects on performance of organizational factors like leadership, groups, intergroup conflict, organization structure, and organizational communication.

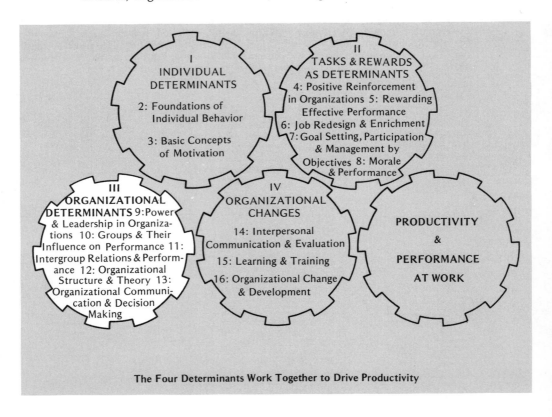

I
INDIVIDUAL
DETERMINANTS

2: Foundations of
Individual Behavior

3: Basic Concepts
of Motivation

II
TASKS & REWARDS
AS DETERMINANTS
4: Positive Reinforcement
in Organizations 5: Rewarding
Effective Performance
6: Job Redesign & Enrichment
7: Goal Setting, Participation
& Management by
Objectives 8: Morale
& Performance

III
ORGANIZATIONAL
DETERMINANTS 9: Power
& Leadership in Organiza-
tions 10: Groups & Their
Influence on Performance 11:
Intergroup Relations & Perform-
ance 12: Organizational
Structure & Theory 13:
Organizational Communi-
cation & Decision
Making

IV
ORGANIZATIONAL
CHANGES

14: Interpersonal
Communication & Evaluation

15: Learning & Training

16: Organizational Change
& Development

**PRODUCTIVITY
&
PERFORMANCE
AT WORK**

The Four Determinants Work Together to Drive Productivity

Organizational factors like these can have profound effects on employee performance. Work groups for example, can pressure their members to reduce (or increase) their output. Similarly, uncontrolled conflicts between, say, Sales and Production can undermine the performance of members of each department.

To get a better perspective on how factors like these can affect performance, consider their potential effects on the "ABCs" of performance. For example, assume that a work group's performance is well below the average for the rest of the plant, and that you want to determine why. Ask, for example:

Antecedents. Does the group know what is expected of it? Does the group have it's own *norms* or standards that conflict with those set by you? Has the group's *leader* made it clear to the group how they should be proceeding?

Behavior. Could the group do a better job if it wanted to? Are there any intergroup *conflicts* that are inhibiting performance? Is the organization's *structure* adequate—for example, is the work of the group coordinated with that of other groups on which it depends? Is there adequate *communication*—for example, can the group get the information, say, on sales forecasts, that it needs to function? Is the group's *leader* effective?

Consequences. What are the consequences of performing? Is the organization *structure* or division of work so unclear that another department gets credit for the group's successes? Does the group's *leader* make it clear to the group how performance and rewards are related?

In Chapter 9 we discuss *leadership and power* in organizations, and explain some of the traits and behaviors that characterize high performing leaders. In Chapter 10, Groups and Their Influence on Performance, we explain how and why groups form, how they influence the performance of their members, and how a manager can improve the performance of the members of his or her work group. In Chapter 11, Intergroup Relations and Performance: Managing Organizational Conflict, we discuss the causes of intergroup conflict in organizations and explain some specific techniques for managing these conflicts. In Chapter 12, Organization Structure and Theory, we explain how the "structure" of an organization—its formal pattern of relationships—can influence employee performance, and we discuss the rudiments of organizing. Finally, in Chapter 13 we explain how to improve *communications and decision making in organizations.*

9 Leadership and Power in Organizations

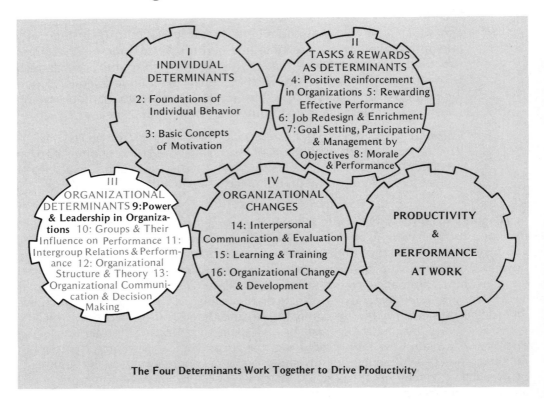

The Four Determinants Work Together to Drive Productivity

*BY THE TIME YOU FINISH STUDYING THIS CHAPTER,
YOU SHOULD BE ABLE TO:*

1. *Explain why leadership theory alone cannot explain leader effectiveness.*
2. *Cite the traits of effective leaders.*
3. *Distinguish between the two basic styles of leadership and give examples of each.*
4. *Explain the importance of considerate leadership.*
5. *Describe the situational forces you should consider before deciding on a leadership style.*
6. *Identify the leadership style which might be "best" 1) on an assembly line, 2) in a research laboratory, and 3) for a staff manager.*
7. *Give several examples of how you would increase your power in an organization.*

OVERVIEW

The main purpose of this chapter is to explain some important determinants of leader effectiveness. We discuss three theories of leader effectiveness: trait theory (which explains leader effectiveness in terms of the leader's traits); behavioral styles theory (which explains leadership in the basis of what the leader does); and situational or contingency theory (which says the leader has to be appropriate for the situation). Finally, we explain why power is an essential ingredient of leadership and discuss its important sources.

WHAT IS LEADERSHIP?

"Leadership" is an easy concept to define but a difficult one to study and understand. It is easy to define since "leadership occurs whenever one person influences another to work toward some predetermined objective."[1] It is difficult to study and understand because effective leadership actually entails all the activities we discuss in this book (positive reinforcement, goal setting, managing intergroup relations, and so on): in other words, it is the leader who is charged with motivating employees, helping them set their goals, engaging in management by objectives, and ensuring that they understand the consequences of their behavior, and so to a very large extent a leader's effectiveness depends on how well he or she performs all these component activities.

Nevertheless, a considerable amount of information has been gathered in the area known as leadership theory. This is the body of knowledge that aims to understand, explain, and predict why some leaders are more effective than others. Basically three types of theories have emerged, and these are called trait theory, behavioral style theory, and contingency theory. Each theory has its own proponents, and each theory contributes to our understanding of what makes an effective leader. We will discuss these theories in this chapter, but as you read them do not forget that each theory—and all three theories combined—can only provide us with part of the explanation of why some leaders are more effective than others: the rest of the explanation (perhaps most of it) lies in the leader's ability to successfully apply the kinds of concepts we discuss in this book.

TRAIT THEORY: WHAT ARE THE TRAITS
OF EFFECTIVE LEADERS?

Background

The idea that some leaders are characterized by certain "traits" was initially inspired by a "great man" concept of leadership. Basically this concept held that people like Winston Churchill, Dwight Eisenhower, or Joan of Arc were great leaders because they were born with certain definable traits that made them so. Early researchers felt that if they studied the personality, intelligence, and attitudes of great leaders, they would sooner or later stumble on the combination of traits that made these people outstanding leaders.

This trait approach to leadership developed out of work done by the American Psychological Association at the beginning of World War I.[2] A group of psychologists was appointed to assist the U.S. Army in screening and selecting military personnel, and a number of useful tools like the Army Alpha Test of Intelligence were developed at this time. After the war it seemed logical to try and apply the same techniques in industry, and the trait approach to leadership grew out of this personnel testing movement.

Early Findings

On the whole, early attempts to find that bundle of traits that characterize effective leaders were inconclusive. On the one hand, researchers who studied specific companies often found that certain traits did characterize effective leaders *in those companies*. Even today, for example you might find that more effective leaders in certain Wall Street banks all have Ivy League educations and are from upper-class backgrounds. On the other hand, none of these studies found traits that were related to leader effectiveness in a *variety* of different organizations. Thus, people with certain traits might be very effective leaders in one kind of organization but ineffective in another. These kinds of findings led one researcher to conclude that "(our) investigation showed no support for the hypothesis that management effectiveness, as evaluated by subordinate managers, is a function of the personality characteristics of the individual."[3]

The Ghiselli Study

In one important multi-company study, however, a researcher did find that effective managers in many companies seemed to be characterized by certain traits. In this study, Professor Edwin Ghiselli studied over 300 managers from 90 different businesses in the United States. All of his subjects were middle managers in firms including those in the transportation, finance, insurance, manufacturing, utilities, and communications industries.[4]

To measure traits Ghiselli used a test called the Self Description Inventory, a portion of which is presented in Exhibit 9.1. In this test subjects are asked to describe themselves by checking which of a series of adjectives applies to them. For example, a person might describe himself as discrete, thorough, cooperative, and cheerful. Based on this test, Ghiselli identified a number of traits which he called:

Supervisory ability	Maturity
Intelligence	Affinity for working-class values
Initiative	Need for self-actualization
Self assurance	Need for power over others
Decisiveness	Need for high financial rewards
Masculinity/Femininity	Need for job security

Exhibit 9.1 Portion of "Self-description Inventory"

The purpose of this inventory is to obtain a picture of the traits you believe you possess, and to see how you describe yourself. There are no right or wrong answers, so try to describe yourself as accurately and honestly as you can.

In each of the pairs of words below, check the one you think *most* describes you.

1. ___ capable
   ___ discreet

2. ___ understanding
   ___ thorough

3. ___ cooperative
   ___ inventive

4. ___ friendly
   ___ cheerful

5. ___ energetic
   ___ ambitious

6. ___ persevering
   ___ independent

7. ___ loyal
   ___ dependable

8. ___ determined
   ___ courageous

9. ___ industrious
   ___ practical

10. ___ planful
    ___ resourceful

11. ___ unaffected
    ___ alert

12. ___ sharp-witted
    ___ deliberate

13. ___ kind
    ___ jolly

14. ___ efficient
    ___ clear-thinking

15. ___ realistic
    ___ tactful

16. ___ enterprising
    ___ intelligent

17. ___ affectionate
    ___ frank

18. ___ progressive
    ___ thrifty

19. ___ sincere
    ___ calm

20. ___ thoughtful
    ___ fair-minded

Ghiselli found that several of these traits characterized effective managers in a wide range of companies. *Supervisory ability*—the capacity to direct the work of others and to organize and integrate their activities so that the goal of the work group can be attained—was the most significant leadership trait.

Next in importance was a cluster of five traits. As might be expected, effective managers were more *intelligent,* and *decisive* than less effective managers as well as more *self-assured.* More effective managers were also more *achievement oriented* in that they seemed driven to achieve high-level positions. Finally, more effective managers had a high need for *self-actualization* in that they seemed to need and seek the opportunity to utilize their talents to the fullest extent.

In Summary. Ghiselli found that six traits (supervisory ability, achievement, intelligence, self-actualization need, self-assurance need, and decisiveness) characterized effective managers. Similarly, researchers have isolated several other traits that seem to characterize effective leadership, including: aggressiveness, self-reliance, persuasiveness, education, and dominance. While these findings may not be conclusive, they do suggest that trait theory can be useful in predicting leader effectiveness. In other words, a leader may be effective although he or she does not exhibit one or more of these traits and may be ineffective while exhibiting all of them. Yet, generally speaking, it would seem that a person's chances to be an effective leader would be enhanced if he or she did exhibit these traits.

THE IMPORTANCE OF THE LEADER'S "STYLE"

Behavioral or "style" leadership theories focus on what the leader does and how he behaves in carrying out his leadership functions, rather than on traits like intelligence or initiative. Trait theory attempts to explain leadership on the basis of what the leader *is,* behavioral theory on the basis of what the leader *does.*

Bales carried out a famous study some years ago in which he established a series of five-man discussion groups that had to arrive at a single solution to human-relations problems within a specified time. Group members were relative strangers, and the group met four times. After each session, members had to answer a number of simple questions, such as, Whom do you like? Whom do you dislike? Who did most to guide the discussion? Who contributed the most ideas?

Bales found that after the first session, the best liked member was usually the one who had contributed the most ideas or guidance. However, by the end of the last session, he was no longer the person best liked; in fact, the one who contributed the most was usually the most disliked man.[5]

Bales' findings draw attention to a major assumption underlying the behavioral leadership theories. Specifically, there are two major functions that leaders can perform—accomplishing the task and satisfying the needs of group members—and the same person will not necessarily fill both roles. Bales found that as the task leader continued to force people to focus on their jobs, certain of their needs (for affiliation, for example) were frustrated. What emerged was a social leader, one whose role was to reduce tension and make the job more pleasant. The behavior of this leader helped boost morale and crystallize and defend the values, attitudes, and beliefs of the group. Most experts believe that the task and people dimensions of leader behavior are not mutually exclusive. In other words, they are usually thought of as independent, with most leaders exhibiting degrees of both people and task orientation simultaneously.[6]

There are a number of different leadership styles typically associated with these basic "task" and "people" dimensions. Writers distinguish between structuring and considerate leaders and close and general leaders, for example. A great deal of research has been addressed to the questions of how each of the styles are related to employee morale and performance, and we turn to these questions next.

Structuring and Considerate Styles

Initiating structure and *consideration* are two of the most frequently used descriptions of leader behavior. These two factors were developed out of research begun in 1945 at Ohio State University that was aimed at constructing an instrument for describing various leadership styles.[7] On the basis of conversations with various specialists, researchers developed a list of nine dimensions or categories of leadership behavior. Descriptive items were then written for each, and a final instrument, known as the Leader Behavior Description Questionnaire (LBDQ) was produced; it included a total of 150 descriptive items. This questionnaire was then further refined, and today usually focuses on just two dimensions of leader behavior, *consideration* and *initiating structure*. Consideration has been defined as "behavior indicative of mutual trust, friendship, support, respect, and warmth." Initiating structure has been defined as "leader behavior by which he organizes the work to be done; and defines relationships or roles and the channels of communication, and the ways of getting jobs done."[8] Some of the descriptive items used to measure consideration and initiating structure are presented in Exhibit 9.2.

Leader Consideration and Employee Morale and Performance. Considerate leadership usually results in higher employee satisfaction, but its effect on employee performance is still unclear. In one major study, for example, Stogdill surveyed over 1,000 managers in 27 organizations, including

Exhibit 9.2 Selection of Items Representing Consideration and Initiating Structure

	Ratings by Judges*	
	Consideration	Initiating Structure
Consideration		
1. He expresses appreciation when one of us does a good job.	1.48	3.15
2. He stresses the importance of high morale among those under him.	1.39	4.55
3. He treats all his foremen as his equals.	1.97	5.21
4. He is friendly and can be easily approached.	1.53	4.61
Initiating Structure		
1. He rules with an iron hand.	5.85	1.48
2. He insists that his foreman follow standard ways of doing things in every detail.	5.39	1.48
3. He insists that he be informed on decisions made by foremen under him.	4.30	2.30
4. He "needles" foremen under him for greater effort.	6.30	1.94
5. He decides in detail what shall be done and how it shall be done.	4.85	1.12

*On a scale from 1.0 (always characteristic) to 7.0 (never characteristic)

Source: A. E. Lowin, W. J. Hrapchak, and M. J. Kavanagh, "Consideration and Initiating Structure: An Experimental Investigation of Leadership Traits," *Administrative Science Quarterly*, Vol. 14 (1969), 239–40.

those in the metals, chemicals, textiles, aircraft, and retail store industries and in government agencies. While few relationships (between leadership and morale or performance) were found that characterized *all* the organizations of a given type, leader consideration was generally related to employee satisfaction and, especially, to how satisfied he or she was with freedom on the job.[9] No consistent relationship was found between consideration and employee performance. Thus, a more considerate, people-oriented leader may or may not have more productive employees: whether or not he or she does probably depends on other, "situational" factors like how dissatisfied his employees were to begin with.[10] On the other hand, as one expert has put it, "The research literature indicates that in most situations, considerate leaders will have more satisfied subordinates."[11]

    Initiating Structure and Employee Morale and Performance. The effects (if any) of *initiating structure* on subordinates' satisfaction and performance are inconsistent. While literally thousands of studies have attempted to determine how a more "structuring" style on the part of the leader affects employee satisfaction and performance, no consistent findings have emerged. Instead, initiating structure has been found to be both positively and negatively (and often ot at all), related to satisfaction and performance.[12] Here, too, it therefore seems that whether or not a more structuring style is beneficial (from the point of view of the organization) depends on other, "situational," factors like how much guidance the employees need. In fact, one of these situational factors seems to b leader consideration itself. For example, researchers have found that where a leader was relatively inconsiderate then his or her attempts to structure subordinates' tasks often led to employee grievances. On the other hand, where consideration was high, leader structure and grievances were unrelated.[13]

Production-Centered and Employee-Centered Leadership Styles

At about the same time that researchers at Ohio State were undertaking the construction of their LBDQ, a similar program was being started at the University of Michigan's Survey Research Center.[14] This line of research led to the identification of two dimensions of leader behavior, which were called *employee orientation* and *production (job) orientation*. The former reflects behavior by a leader that indicates he views his employees as human beings of intrinsic importance and accepts their individuality and personal needs. Production orientation is behavior that stresses production and the technical aspects of the job and reflects an assumption that employees are simply means to an end.

This line of research was developed by Rensis Likert of the University of Michigan. Likert and his associates have carried out many studies to determine which leadership style appears most effective. He concludes:

> Supervisors with the best record of performance focus their primary attention on the human aspects of their subordinates' problems and on endeavoring to build effective work groups with high performance goals.[15]

There are three important things to remember about Likert's findings. First, on the whole his own findings do indicate that the most effective leaders are generally (but not always) those that are more employee centered—they treat their employees as ends, rather than as means; they are supportive; and they treat their people as individuals. Second, however, even Likert has found that there are times when it is the *production*-oriented leader that has the high-performing group: we will have more to say on this in a moment. Finally, it is important to understand that there is much more

to Likert's employee-centered leader than just considerateness and supportiveness. To Likert, in other words, an effective employee-centered leader is
not just a "nice guy" who relies on the morale and good nature of his or her
subordinates to get the job done. Instead, according to Likert, *the employee-
centered leader also sees to it that subordinates have clear, high performance
goals,* and this, as we have seen, may help explain part of this leader's effectiveness. Of course, a production-oriented leader may also set high production goals for subordinates, but the way in which he does it—his "style"—
is different from that of the employee-centered leader. The production-
oriented leader is the kind that leads employees to believe that he is not
interested in them as people but only as means to an end, and he does not
treat them with the supportiveness and individuality that most people seem
to desire.

Close and General Styles of Leadership

Other experts distinguish between close and general styles of leadership and
this line of research also evolved out of work begun at the University of
Michigan.[16] *Close supervision* was conceptualized as "one end of a continuum
that describes the degree to which a supervisor specifies the roles of subordinates and checks up to see that they comply with the specifications.[17]
The *laissez-faire* leader who takes a completely hands-off policy with his or
her subordinates, would be at the other extreme, with a *general* leader somewhere in the middle of the continuum.

The research findings concerning the effects of close versus general
styles on employee morale and performance are much clearer with respect
to morale then they are with performance. Generally speaking, they indicate
that most people do not like being closely supervised or having, in effect,
someone constantly watching them and telling them what to do. Close supervision is usually therefore associated with low employee morale.[18] Related
to this, close supervision also seems to lead to employees becoming more aggressive against peers and the supervisor.[19] On the other hand, there seems to
be no consistent relationship between close (or general) styles of leadership
and employee *performance*. Here, again, other factors apparently determine
whether performance is high or low and what effect if any the leader's style
will have on performance.

Common Elements of Leadership Styles

We have discussed these various pairs of leadership styles individually, but in
practice they have much in common. For example, many writers place the
employee-centered, general, and considerate styles into one category and the

production-centered, close, and structuring styles into a second.[20] On the whole, in fact these several pairs of styles do have much in common, and there seems to be a good deal of sense in reducing them to two broad—"people" and "task"—leadership styles. We have to be careful, however, not to carry such categorizations too far. For example, employee-centered leadership need not be devoid of initiating structure, and a "close" leadership style need not be an inconsiderate one.

Summary: *Leadership Style and Employee Satisfaction and Performance*

We can draw four conclusions from the research on behavioral styles theories of leadership. First, there seems little doubt that considerate, employee-centered, supportive leadership usually leads to higher employee morale. In other words, leaders who support the individuality of their subordinates and who treat these people as valued, important individuals have subordinates who are more satisfied with work, as might be expected. Of course, this is not to say that this is *always* the case. For example, if the leader is "considerate" but also so inept that subordinates do not have clear goals or for some other reason can't get their jobs done, then this ineptness may itself lead to frustration and low morale. Second, employee-centered leadership (as defined by Likert) is *usually* related to higher employee performance. Keep in mind, though that Likert's employee-centered leader is actually a bit exceptional, in that he or she is not only considerate and supportive but also has the knack for setting clear, attainable goals and ensuring that employees can get their jobs done. Third, it would be unwise to assume that employee-centered leadership will always lead to the best performance. The style that is best for one situation (like managing a group of research scientists) would probably be quite different than for some other situation (like leading a group of marines), and, in any case, the leader's effectiveness (in getting subordinates to perform) depends on many things other than "style"—such as goal setting, providing rewards, and resolving conflicts. Fourth, and finally, it should also be apparent from what we have said that in many situations production-centered leadership—leadership that focuses on the technical aspects of getting the job done—can be (and often is) more effective than employee-centered leadership. Of course subordinates here may not be as satisfied as they might otherwise be, but if the job is such that the supervisor can closely supervise the work and use tight controls, then he or she probably will be effective. In this regard, the following comments by Likert are useful:

> Although the research findings show that (employee-centered leadership) is *more often* characteristic of the operation of the high-producing managers than the low, the results do *not* show that *all* high-producing managers adhere to this pattern. Technically compe-

tent, job-centered, insensitive, and tough management can achieve relatively high productivity. The evidence clearly indicates that if this kind of supervision is coupled with the use of tight controls on the part of the line organization, impressive productivity can be achieved. Members of units whose supervisors use these high pressure methods, however, are more likely to be among those who have the least favorable attitudes toward their work and their supervisors and are likely to display excessive waste, scrap loss, and turnover. In general, these are the work groups which showed the greatest hostility and resentment toward management, the least confidence and trust in their supervisors, the largest number of grievances that go to arbitration, and the greatest frequency of slowdowns, work stoppages, and similar difficulties.

It is important also to recognize that the research findings . . . do *not* support the conclusion that *every* organization in which there are high levels of confidence and trust, favorable attitudes, and high levels of job satisfaction will be highly productive. Even though a manager may have built his department into an organization with these qualities, his department will not achieve high productivity unless his leadership and the decision-making processes used by the organization result in the establishment of high performance goals by the members for themselves. High performance goals as well as favorable attitudes must be present if an organization is to achieve a high degree of productivity.[21]

CONTINGENCY THEORIES: THE IMPACT OF THE "SITUATION"

Behavioral scientists have long recognized the importance of "situational" factors in explaining leader effectiveness. We saw, for example, that leaders with certain traits might be successful in one organization but unsuccessful in another. Similarly, we saw that no one style of leadership has been found to be universally effective—a fact that led two experts to conclude that "effective leadership depends on the leader, his followers, and the situation, and the interrelationships between them."[22] Part of the reason for these inconsistencies, as we have said, is that there is more to effective leadership than having the right traits or style. Instead, effective leaders also have to effectively carry out all the other activities we discuss in this book, such as goal setting, appraising performance, and providing rewards. Beyond this, we have seen that leadership experts are now fairly well convinced that a leadership style that might be appropriate in one situation might be inappropriate in another.

Intuitively, this kind of "situational" approach makes a good deal of sense. It seems intuitively obvious, for example, that while a general, supportive kind of leader might be just the thing' for running a research lab, he or she might be a disaster if a "take charge" structuring sort of leader is called for—for example say, to organize an emergency airlift during a hurricane. In fact, two situational theories of leadership that tie the appropriateness of a leader's style to the situation have emerged, and they both provide some insights into what makes a leader effective.

Fiedler's Contingency Theory of Leadership

In 1951, Fred Fiedler began a program of research that almost from its inception focused on the situational nature of leader effectiveness.[23] At the base of Fiedler's theory are three situational factors that determine how much power and influence the leader has. And, he says, together they determine whether a more democratic and people-oriented leader or a more autocratic and task-oriented leader is called for. The situational factors are as follows:

Leader-Member Relations. This refers to the extent to which the leader "gets along" with his men and the extent to which they have confidence in and are loyal to him. According to Fiedler, leaders presumably have more power and influence if they have a good relationship with their subordinates than if they have a poor one. Similarly, they have more power and influence if they are liked, respected, and trusted than if they are not. Fiedler's research suggests that leader-member relations is the most important determinant of whether a people- or task-oriented style is appropriate.

Task Structure. This refers to how routine and predictable the work group's task is. According to Fiedler, tasks or assignments that are highly structured, spelled out, or programmed give the leader more influence than tasks that are vague, nebulous, and unstructured. It is easier, for example, to be a leader whose task it is to set up a sales display according to clearly delineated steps than it is to be the chairman of a committee preparing a new sales campaign.

Position Power. This is "the degree to which the job itself enables the leader to get his group members to comply with and accept his direction and leadership." According to Fiedler, leaders will have more power and influence if as part of their job they are able to hire, fire, discipline, reprimand, and so on. Position power, as used by Fiedler, is determined by how much power the job gives the leader over his subordinates. If the janitor foreman can hire and fire, he has more position power in his own group than the chairman of the board of directors, who, frequently, cannot hire or fire—or even reprimand—his board members.

Fiedler's Model: As illustrated in Exhibit 9.3, Fiedler distinguishes between eight types of situations, depending upon whether leader member relations are good or poor, task structure is structured or unstructured, and leader position power is strong or weak. In Cell II, for example, leader member relations are good, the task is structured, and leader position power is weak. In Cell IV leader member relations are good, the task is unstructured, and the leader's position power is weak. To Fiedler, the critical question is, "What kind of leadership style does each of these different situations (cells) call for?"

Exhibit 9.3 Effective Leadership Style Varies With the Situation

	I	II	III	IV	V	VI	VII	VIII
Leader-Member Relations	Good	Good	Good	Good	Poor	Poor	Poor	Poor
Task Structures	Structured		Unstructured		Structured		Unstructured	
Leader Position Power	Strong	Weak	Strong	Weak	Strong	Weak	Strong	Weak

For these kinds of tasks, a more considerate leader is called for, according to Fiedler.

For these kinds of tasks, a more structuring leader is called for.

Source: Adapted from Fred Fiedler, *A Theory of Leadership Effectiveness* (New York: McGraw-Hill 1967) p. 176.

Exhibit 9.3 summarizes Fiedler's findings. Basically, Fiedler says that the more task-oriented leaders tend to perform better than people-oriented leaders in situations that are favorable for the leader (Situations I, II, and III) and in those that are unfavorable (VIII). On the other hand, people-oriented leaders tend to perform better than task-oriented leaders in situations that are neither very favorable, nor unfavorable (Situations IV, V, VI, and VII).

Fiedler explains his findings as follows. He says that in the very favorable conditions (where the leader has power, informal backing, and a well-structured task) the group is ready to be directed, and his subordinates expect to be told what to do. On the other hand, in the relatively unfavorable situation the group will fall apart without the leader's active intervention and control. Thus in both favorable and unfavorable situations a more autocratic, task-oriented leadership style is called for. In the middle range, says Fiedler, the situation is not so clear-cut, and here the leader must provide a non-threatening, permissive environment—he must be democratic and people oriented—because it is important that he coax his employees to work with him.

   The Status of Fiedler's Theory: Just how useful is Fiedler's leadership theory? The findings here are mixed. On the one hand, the results of many studies contradict Fiedler's theory. For example, Fiedler's says a task-oriented leader is best in Situation III, but others have found that the more democratic leader does best here.[24] Others criticize Fiedler's measure of leadership style, which he calls the LPC. The LPC is aimed at determining how critical a person is of his or her subordinates. A person filling it out (it is presented as part of the Exercise at the end of this chapter) has to describe his or her "least preferred coworker" by choosing adjectives like "smart," "lazy," and so on. Fiedler believes that a high LPC score means that the person is a considerate, people-oriented leader. A low LPC score means that the person is an autocratic, task-oriented leader.[25] At the present time, however, there is some controversy over what exactly the LPC is measuring.[26]

   Yet other findings do support Fiedler's theory[27] and, it seems to make sense based on actual practice. (For example, the first few months that a new college Dean is on board is usually a "honeymoon period"—a highly favorable situation during which he or she can make many more unilateral decisions than is usual.) In summary, Fiedler's work probably does help to explain what situational factors determine which leadership style is "best." And his evidence clearly shows that no single set of traits or style of leadership will be effective in all situations. On the other hand, it is likely that other "situational" factors not incorporated in his model—such as the leader's intelligence, and decisiveness—are also important determinants of how successful he or she is .Fiedler's theory thus contributes to our understanding of what makes a leader effective but does not by itself explain leader effectiveness.

House's Path-Goal Approach to Leadership

   Robert House has also proposed a "situational" theory of leadership. He calls it a "path-goal theory," because he says a leader's main functions are to set important *goals* for subordinates and to clear their *paths* to these goals.

   House's basic thesis is a simple one. He says that ambiguous, uncertain situations can be frustrating and that in such situations the structure provided by a more task-oriented leader will be viewed as legitimate and satisfactory by subordinates. On the other hand, in routine situations (such as might be encountered on assembly lines), the additional structure provided by a task-oriented leader might be viewed as redundant by subordinates and here the task-oriented leader's attempts to further structure employees' tasks (by closely supervising them, telling them in detail what to do and when to do it, and so on) might be annoying and dissatisfying.

What does this mean in practice? For one thing, it means that if subordinates are confused as to what to do next, it may be best to structure their jobs for them: that way, the leader gives them a clear path to follow. It also means that if subordinates' tasks are already very clear—as they might be on an assembly line—then the leader wants to "stay out of their hair." In this case, their "paths" are already clear enough. The path-goal theory also assumes that setting clear goals for subordinates and explaining to them why these goals are important are basic functions all leaders should perform.

In total, the findings suggest that this theory of leader effectiveness is useful.[28] For example, we know that ambiguity and uncertainty are closely associated with individual stress, tension, anxiety, and dissatisfaction[29]: in these situations a more autocratic, task-oriented leader is often most appropriate. And, as we have seen, clarifying employee's expectations—making sure they know what is expected of them—is a basic aspect of the "ABCs" approach to behavior, and one that is especially important when they do not, in fact, know what is expected of them.

POWER AND INFLUENCE IN ORGANIZATIONS

Power and Leadership

The concepts of power and leadership are closely related, and, in fact, some experts all but equate the two. Etzioni, for example, defines power as "an actor's ability to induce or influence another actor to carry out his directives or any other norms he supports"—a definition that is similar to our definition of leadership.[30] To most experts, however, power is not equivalent to leadership: instead, it is an essential *ingredient* of leadership, one without which the leader is usually doomed to ineffectiveness.

The idea that the leader, to be effective, has to have "clout" with his superiors and with others is now fairly well established. Fiedler, for example, argues that a leader's *position power* helps to determine how favorable the situation is for the leader and, thereby, that leader's effectiveness. Similarly, Likert has found that the amount of influence that a supervisor has with his own superior affects the results the supervisor can expect to get from his subordinates because:

To function effectively, a supervisor must have sufficient influence with his own superior to be able to affect the superior's decision when required. Subordinates expect their supervisors to be able to exercise influence upward in dealing with problems on the job and handling problems which affect them and their well-being.[31]

What this all boils down to is this: A leader without power—power to influence his superiors, power to distribute rewards, power to mete out punishment, and so on—is really not much of a leader. Leadership involves getting others to work toward predetermined objectives, and people usually do not allow themselves to be influenced just because the leader has the right traits or leadership style. Instead, they allow themselves to be influenced because the leader wields some power over them, such as the power to reward and to punish. Therefore, we ought to discuss the topic of "power" to round out our discussion of leadership.

Authority, Power, and Influence. Although we are going to use the terms more or less synonymously, experts usually distinguish between the interrelated concepts of authority, power, and influence. *Influence* is usually defined as the act of producing an effect—of somehow getting someone or something to take some action. *Power*, on the other hand, is usually viewed as the possession of the *potential* for influencing others. To Weber, for example, "power is the probability that one actor within a social relationship will be in a position to carry out his own will despite resistance . . . ."[32]

A person's power can (but need not) stem from "illegitimate" sources, sources that violate prevailing norms of acceptability. For example, a thief might have power over a victim because of the gun he holds. *Authority*, like power, refers to a person's potential for influencing others, but the word authority "has implicit in it the notion of legitimacy or ethical sanctification."[33]

What are the Sources of Power in Organizations?

What of the sources of a leader's power in organizations? According to French and Raven, there are five sources or "bases" of social power. They call these reward power, coercive power, legitimate power, referant power, and expert power.[34]

Reward power is defined as power whose basis is the ability to reward. In other words, a person has power over another to the extent that he or she can significantly influence the positive rewards or consequences (such as money) accruing to the other person and can significantly reduce the "negative" rewards or consequences (such as poor working conditions) the other person might otherwise have to endure.

Coercive power is similar to reward power in that it also involves one person's ability to manipulate the attainment by another of positive (or negative) rewards or consequences. The coercive power of one person over another, however, stems from a real or imagined expectation on the part of the latter that he will be punished if he fails to conform. In organizations, coercive power is a familiar ingredient in group pressure. Groups are famous, for example, for keeping "rate busters" in line by coercing them with fears of ostracism or physical violence.

Legitimate power is characterized by the feeling of "oughtness" on the part of a person. Legitimate power is defined as stemming from internalized values in a person that dictate that another has a legitimate right to influence him and that he has an obligation to accept this influence. The actual source of this legitimate power, and the reason subordinates feel they ought to obey, might be tradition (as in the case of a monarch) or may derive from the office the superior holds (as in Fiedler's position power). As an example, on agreeing to join an organization, its salesmen accept the right of the sales manager to assign them work, since this is a legitimate right of the office of "sales manager" in the organization structure. Similarly, "a judge has a right to levy fines, a foreman should assign work, a priest is justified in prescribing religious beliefs and it is the management's prerogative to make certain decisions."[35]

Referent power is based on the fact that one person identifies with and is highly attracted to another. A verbalization of such power might be, "I want to be like that person, and therefore I shall behave or believe as he does."

Expert power derives from the fact that one person is viewed as an expert in some area and others must therefore depend on him or her for advice and counsel. Expert power in an organization often stems from a person's position in the communications network and from that person's ability to control access to coveted information. Thus, even an organization's president may find herself deferring to one of her firm's research scientists in those cases where the scientist has the knowledge and expertise to solve some critical problem with one of the firm's products. Similarly, an air-base commander may find himself partly at the mercy of the maintenance clerk whose years of experience have given him access to, and control of, sources of airplane parts.

Two kinds of power. What are the sources of a leader's power or influence? We have discussed five (reward, coercive, legitimate, referent, and expert) but we might actually classify these even further, by saying that any source of power stems ultimately from either *dependence* or *legality*. A leader's power stems first from the fact that his subordinates are *dependent* on him, perhaps because he can reward or coerce them, or because he is an expert in some area and thus controls access to coveted information or persons.

The second source of power might be termed *legality*. It derives from the feeling of a person that another person (in this case the leader) has a *legitimate right* to demand obedience. French and Raven's legitimate power is an example of this, as perhaps is their referent power. This "legal" base of power is extremely important in organizations. One familiar example is the acceptance by a subordinate of the authority of a superior, authority legally sanctioned by the organization and accepted by the subordinate as one of the conditions of continued employment. In other words, in organizations a leader is given the right (by his or her own superiors) to give orders in certain areas, and subordinates accept these orders as a condition of employment—at least as long as the orders remain "legitimate."

Milgram's Study of Legitimate Power. To what extent do subordinates obey authority because they view that authority as legitimate, and obeying as part of the job? Stanley Milgram carried out a study that shed some startling light on this question.[36] Milgram's experiments were originally conducted at Yale in 1962–63, and set out to answer the following question: "In a laboratory situation, if an experimenter tells a subject to act with increasing severity against another person, under what conditions will the subject comply and under what conditions will he disobey?"

Basically, what Milgram did was as follows. He had two subjects come into his laboratory. One was designated the "teacher." The other, the "learner," is strapped into a chair, and an electrode is attached to both of his wrists. (The "learner" is actually one of the researcher's assistants, and the "electrodes" are not really attached to any power source). The "teacher" is then told he is to "teach" the learner by giving him an electric shock whenever the latter gives the wrong answer to a question. The shocks range from low (one that reads "15 volts") to severe (one that reads "450 volts"). The point of the experiment is actually to see how far the "teacher" will go in following the researcher's "legitimate" orders to administer the shocks. (Actually, of course, the learner is not being shocked at all, although he shrieks appropriately as the "shocks" get more severe).

According to Milgram, the results of his study "are both surprising and dismaying." Although many of his subject "teachers" experienced stress and protested to the experimenter, a substantial portion of them—almost two-thirds—fell into the category of obedient subjects, continuing to the last shock on the generator although the learner was by this time shrieking frantically. These "teachers," remember, were not some "sadistic fringe of society," but were "ordinary people drawn from working, managerial, and professional classes." Milgram found that "the ordinary person who shocked the victim did so out of a sense of obligation—a conception of his duties as a subject—and not from any peculiarly aggressive tendencies."

Milgram's findings paint a vivid picture of the adjustments through which obedience to legitimate authority takes place. The subjects, he found, became so absorbed in the "narrow technical aspects" of the task that they lost sight of its broader consequences. (One is reminded of the Watergate affair, which was to follow these studies by ten years). Furthermore, the obedient subject begins to see himself as not responsible for his own actions, as he "divests himself of responsibility by attributing all initiative to the experimenter, a legitimate authority." Obedient subjects saw themselves not as people acting in a morally accountable way, but as the agents of external authority: When asked after the experiment why they had gone on, the typical reply was, "I wouldn't have done it by myself. I was just doing what I was told." And, Milgram believes, this was not just a "thin alibi concocted for the occasion":

> Rather, it is a fundamental mode of thinking for a great many people once they are locked into a subordinate position in a structure of authority. The disappearance of a sense of responsibility is the far-reaching consequence of submission to authority.

It further appeared that people working under authority did not lose their "moral sense," but instead shifted it to a consideration of how well they were living up to the expectations that *the authority* had for them. Most subjects also saw their behavior in a larger context—the pursuit of scientific truth. Some devalued the victim as a consequence of acting against him, making comments like, "He was so stupid and stubborn he deserved to get shocked."

What Milgram found, therefore, was that people were much more willing than one might have imagined to "just follow orders." People obeyed simply because they had elected to join the organization (the experiment) and viewed following legitimate orders as part of their jobs.

Summary: Sources of Power

In summary, *legitimate* power, the power a leader has because his subordinates think they *ought* to obey him, combined with the subordinate's *dependence* on the leader (for rewards, avoiding punishment, and so on) together largely explain the sources of a leader's power, a power without which, in fact, he or she could hardly be called a leader.

How to Accumulate Power

Based on what we have said, there are many specific actions a leader can take to bolster his or her power. One is to insist that there be no bypassing of the chain of command. In other words, no subordinates are to discuss any substantive matters with the leader's boss, unless they have the leader's permission. This ploy requires the active approval (or at least consent of the leader's boss. Once in effect, this policy means that the leader's power is greatly enhanced since he or she becomes the sole conduit of pay raises, benefits, and punishment for subordinates.

Another, related tactic is to insist that subordinates eliminate all or most sources of outside income—for example, a college dean might insist that faculty members cannot consult more than one day per week. This may cause some good employees to leave, but those that stay are that much more dependent on the dean for rewards.

Other leaders work hard at currying favor with those in power. By doing so the leader can build a "pipeline" to a higher level source of rewards and favors, and his or her subordinates therefore come to view the person as a more influential source of rewards. Others—leaders, and nonleaders alike—develop some expertise, preferably one not shared by others in the organization, and thus make others dependent on them.

Some leaders also work hard at bolstering the trappings of their positions, and thereby other's perception of their legitimate power. For example, some are careful to always wear an expensive suit and to negotiate the most impressive office possible. In sum, there are many actions a leader can take to bolster his or her power (or others' perception of that power) and we have only mentioned a few representative ones.

LEADERSHIP, POWER, AND THE ABCs OF PERFORMANCE

The "ABCs" approach can be used to analyze leadership effectiveness problems. For example, assume that several months ago you appointed a new supervisor to a work group, and that the group's performance has subsequently declined. You believe the new supervisor is not an effective leader, and you want to analyze what he is doing wrong as a leader. Ask, for example:

> *Antecedents.* Does the leader know what is expected of him and his group? (And does he see to it that his subordinates know what is expected of *them?*)
>
> *Behavior.* Could the leader do a better job if he or she wanted to? Does he have the necessary traits? For example, does he make good decisions? Is he self assured? Does he have sufficient influence with his boss? Is the leader supportive enough? Is he *too* supportive, given the situation? (And, does he or she see to it that the subordinates *could* do their jobs if they wanted to?)

Consequences. Is the leader rewarded if his work group performs better? (And, does he see to it that his subordinates understand that *their* rewards are tied to their performance?)

CHAPTER SUMMARY

1. The trait theory of leadership explains leader effectiveness on the basis of what the leader *is*—his or her traits or characteristics like need for power, decisiveness, and job security. We concluded that a leader may be effective although he or she does not exhibit one or more of Ghiselli's traits (supervisory ability, achievement, intelligence, self-actualization needs, self-assurance needs, and decisiveness), but that it would seem that a person's chances to be an effective leader would be enhanced if he or she did exhibit these traits.

2. Behavioral or "style" leadership theory focuses on what the leader does and how he or she behaves in carrying out the leadership functions, rather than on traits like intelligence or initiative. We discussed the people and task dimensions of leadership, and specifically, *structuring and considerate* styles, *production-centered and employee-centered* styles, and *close and general* styles. A more people-oriented style usually seems to lead to better employee attitudes, but there is no clear-cut relationship between structuring leadership and employee attitudes or performance. One important point, however, is that for the more considerate, employee-centered leader to be effective he or she has to set clear, high, production standards.

3. The work of Fiedler and House serves to underscore the importance of fitting the leader to the task. Fiedler, for example, says that leader member relations, task structure, and position power determine the kind of leader that is appropriate. House says that ambiguous, uncertain situations can be frustrating and that in such situations the structure provided by a more task-oriented leader would be viewed as legitimate and satisfactory by subordinates.

4. To most experts, power is not equivalent to leadership: instead, it is an essential ingredient of leadership. We discussed five sources of power: reward power, coercive power, legitimate power, referent power, and expert power. On the whole, we said that power stems either from *dependence* or *legality*. Accumulating power therefore involves taking actions that enhance the "legal" power of a person's position (like getting a bigger office), while at the same time increasing subordinates' dependence on the leader (for example by making the leader the sole arbiter of their rewards).

DISCUSSION QUESTIONS AND PROJECTS

1. Explain why leadership is an easy concept to define but a difficult one to study and understand.

2. You have just read in a newspaper that an army colonel was passed over for a promotion because he had "failed to exert leadership." What does it mean to "fail to exert leadership"?

3. Discuss the traits possessed by successful leaders.

4. Compare and contrast the two basic styles of leadership. How are each related to employee performance? Satisfaction?

5. Your boss has just asked you to give a short lecture to a group of new supervisors on "how to be an effective leader." What would you tell them?

6. Do you think it is more important for a leader to be respected, or to be popular? Why?

7. Explain the situational forces which a manager should consider before he or she decides on adopting a leadership style.

8. What leadership style would you exhibit under the following conditions? (The class might want to divide into groups of four or five students to develop answers to this question.)

> a) You have just been given a job as director of marketing services for an organization, and have been told by the president to "get those division managers to use some up-to-date marketing tools." He has also told you that you have no position power or authority over these division managers. How would you act as a leader?
> b) You have just been named the new manager of a large division. It has had four managers in three years, profits are declining, morale is at an all time low, and the recent consultants' report states that "nobody knows what he is doing or what he is supposed to be doing." How would you act as a leader?
> c) The president of Central Steel wants to get his company into some new businesses, and has asked you to take charge of a recently organized new-ventures department. The steel company has always been highly centralized, with top management making virtually all important decisions. Everyone has always "played it by the rules," and requests for deviations from standard practices traditionally have to be funnelled through the chain of command—a process which could take up to one year. How would you act as the leader?

9. Write an essay entitled, "The Most Effective Leader I Have Ever Met." Make sure to discuss his or her leadership style and personality traits as well as any conditions that contributed to this person's being effective.

10. Working in groups of four or five students, skim through a biography of some famous leader—Dwight Eisenhower, John F. Kennedy, etc. Using our discussions from this chapter and any other information we discussed so far in this book write an essay describing why you think the person was such an effective leader.

11. Working in groups, speak to persons responsible for hiring managers. Find out how they go about identifying leadership potential and leadership ability. Discuss your findings in class.

12. Divide the class into groups of four or five students. Each group should come up with ten concrete examples of how a person can accumulate power in an organization.

CASE EXERCISE

A Foreman's Success at Jackson & Co.

George Tucker was the new production manager at Jackson & Co., and he wanted to do the best possible job. It had taken him ten years to work himself up to this position. For him, however, this was only the beginning. He had plans of moving into a vice-presidency before he retired. This, he knew, meant performance. It was an established fact in the company that only the most successful managers were moved up. George felt that productivity was a major factor in this respect and that good supervision on the production line was important. What does a successful foreman do that an unsuccessful one does not? George sought to isolate the factors that were involved.

For the first month, he decided that it would be wise to spend most of his time observing the workers and the foremen. He asked the foremen many questions about their supervisory techniques. George was a little apprehensive at first, feeling that the foremen would believe he was wasting their time with his questions. Fortunately, it did not turn out this way. In fact, the foremen seemed to like George's queries, for it gave them an opportunity to verbalize some of their pet theories of management.

George recorded the ideas gained from his talks with the foremen. Within a month's time, he had been able to talk with all of them. He then began to look at past productivity records to determine which of the foremen was most successful in terms of output.

He also wrote down the names of the foremen who had the least amount of output. In terms of productivity extremes, two foremen stood out. The first was Hal Tendling, whose productivity was the lowest in the company. Hal's comments on supervision were as follows:

> In this business, it's dog eat dog. The workers are really a bunch of goof-offs. Now don't misunderstand me. There are good workers and then there are goldbricks. It's this last bunch you have to watch carefully. Take my group. About 80 percent of them are going to quit working the minute I go out for a cup of coffee. Do you know that between 10:00 A.M. and 10:15 A.M., foreman coffee-break time, I get less output than any other time period of the morning. The same is true for my afternoon coffee break. This goldbricking is nothing more than the men's way of testing you. That's why I adhere to two rules. One, always keep the emphasis on productivity. The men like this. It lets them know that you are not going to sit still for horsing around.
>
> Second, when someone does something wrong, chew them out good and proper. If you don't, the men think you've gone soft. Believe me, the workers appreciate a boss they can't shove around. It creates a kind of respect, and they'll do a better job for you. Now, my productivity record isn't very good but can you imagine how much worse it would look if I tried treating these people softly? No sir, there's no one in this company who could get as much productivity out of those men as I do."

The second foreman Steve Jessup, who, for the past six months, had the highest productivity record in the company, summarized his supervisory approach as follows:

> My approach to managing people is to take it easy with them. The workers want to do a good job. Now, that isn't to say that you won't get a goof-off from time to time. But you are going to face that situation regardless of what position you are in. The question is how to live with it. I find that the men are basically conscientious. Therefore, the first rule I employ is to never jump on them about output. I spend most of my time trying to be helpful. If they need assistance in repairing a machine, I call maintenance. If they have a family problem, I tell them to check out early. The men don't need to be told that output is important. They know this.
>
> Secondly, if someone goofs up, never scream and shout at him. It only embarrasses the fellow, and it serves no real useful purpose. If you can't be helpful, say nothing. Believe me, the men like this easy style.

Questions

1. Summarize briefly the leadership style of Steve Jessup. Then contrast it to that of Hal Tendling. What do you see the basic difference to be?

2. In addition to information given in the case, why else might Steve Jessup be so effective as a foreman?

3. Are there any times when Hal Tendling would be a more effective manager than Steve Jessup? If yes, when? If no, why not?

EXPERIENTIAL EXERCISE

Purpose: The purpose of this exercise is to teach you something about your leadership style by having you fill out Fiedlers LPC.

Required Understanding: You should be thoroughly familiar with our discussion of Fiedler's leadership theory and should study exhibits 9.4 and 9.5. Then, read this:

You are the associate director of city hospital. Having just taken a course in leadership at your local university you've decided to try and apply Fiedler's contingency theory to your own job. You use the "position power questions," and "group atmosphere scale" shown in case exhibits 9.4 and 9.5 to measure leader member relations and position power. And, you believe that since your employees' tasks are fairly routine and repetitive, that the task is a structured one. In this way you have come to the conclusion that according to Fiedler's model the situation is as in Cell II: Leader member relations are good, task structure is structured, and leader position power is weak.

Exhibit 9.4 LPC Questionnaire and Group Atmosphere Scale

Think of the person *with whom you can work least well.* He may be someone you work with now, or he may be someone you knew in the past. He does not have to be the person you like least well, but should be the person with whom you had the most difficulty in getting a job done. Describe this person as he appears to you.

	8	7	6	5	4	3	2	1	
Pleasant	:	:	:	:		:	:	:	: Unpleasant
Friendly	:	:	:	:		:	:	:	: Unfriendly
Rejecting	:	:	:	:		:	:	:	: Accepting*
Helpful	:	:	:	:		:	:	:	: Frustrating
Unenthusiastic	:	:	:	:		:	:	:	: Enthusiastic*
Tense	:	:	:	:		:	:	:	: Relaxed*
Distant	:	:	:	:		:	:	:	: Close*
Cold	:	:	:	:		:	:	:	: Warm*
Cooperative	:	:	:	:		:	:	:	: Uncooperative
Supportive	:	:	:	:		:	:	:	: Hostile
Boring	:	:	:	:		:	:	:	: Interesting*
Quarrelsome	:	:	:	:		:	:	:	: Harmonious*
Self-Assured	:	:	:	:		:	:	:	: Hesitant
Efficient	:	:	:	:		:	:	:	: Inefficient
Gloomy	:	:	:	:		:	:	:	: Cheerful*
Open	:	:	:	:		:	:	:	: Guarded

*These scales should be reversed; higher score = higher LPC (more "people oriented").

Group Atmosphere Scale

Describe the atmosphere of your group by checking the following items.

	8	7	6	5	4	3	2	1	
1. Friendly	:	:	:	:	:	:	:	:	: Unfriendly
2. Accepting	:	:	:	:	:	:	:	:	: Rejecting
3. Satisfying	:	:	:	:	:	:	:	:	: Frustrating
4. Enthusiastic	:	:	:	:	:	:	:	:	: Unenthusiastic
5. Productive	:	:	:	:	:	:	:	:	: Nonproductive
6. Warm	:	:	:	:	:	:	:	:	: Cold
7. Cooperative	:	:	:	:	:	:	:	:	: Uncooperative
8. Supportive	:	:	:	:	:	:	:	:	: Hostile
9. Interesting	:	:	:	:	:	:	:	:	: Boring
10. Successful	:	:	:	:	:	:	:	:	: Unsuccessful

Exhibit 9.5 Position Power Questions

1. Can the supervisor recommend subordinate rewards and punishment to his boss?
2. Can the supervisor punish or reward subordinates on his own?
3. Can the supervisor recommend promotion or demotion of subordinates?
4. Can the supervisor promote or demote subordinates on his own?
5. Does the supervisor's special knowledge allow him to decide how subordinates are to proceed on their jobs?
6. Can the supervisor give subordinates a general idea of what they are to do?
7. Can the supervisor specifically instruct subordinates concerning what they are to do?
8. Is an important part of the supervisor's job to motivate his subordinates?
9. Is an important part of the supervisor's job to evaluate subordinate performance?
10. Does the supervisor have a great deal of knowledge about the jobs under him but require his subordinates to do them?
11. Can the supervisor supervise and evaluate subordinate jobs?
12. Does the supervisor know both his own and his subordinates' jobs so that he could finish subordinate work himself if it were necessary and he had enough time?
13. Has the supervisor been given an official title by the company which differentiates him from his subordinates?

The number of "yes" answers indicates the score.

Instructions

1. Break into groups of four or five students, and, *with each group member working individually*, fill out the LPC questionnaire in exhibit 9.4. Then, each person should determine if he or she is a "high" or "low" LPC (4.5 is the breakpoint).

2. Then, the group should evaluate the LPCs of one or two volunteers in the group to determine if he or she has the right leader style for the task, and, if not, what sorts of tasks the person's style is more appropriate for.

NOTES FOR CHAPTER 9

1. Gary Dessler, *Management Fundamentals* (Reston: Reston Publishing Co., 1978), p. 301; see also Jeffrey Pfeffer, "The Ambiguity of Leadership," *Academy of Management Review*, Vol. 2, No. 1 (January 1977), pp. 104–112; Steven Kerr and John Jermier, "Substitutes for Leadership: Their meaning and measurement," *Organizational Behavior and Human Performance*, Vol. 22, No. 3 (December 1978), pp. 375–403.

2. Ralph Stogdill, "Historical Trends in Leadership Theory and Research," *Journal of Contemporary Business*, Vol. 3, No. 4 (Autumn 1974), pp. 1–17.

3. Walter Palmer, "Management Effectiveness as a Function of Personality Traits of a Manager," *Personnel Psychology*, Vol. 27 (1974), pp. 283–95.

4. Ralph Stogdill, *Managers, Employees, Organizations* (Columbus: Bureau of Business Research, Ohio State University, 1965).

5. Robert Bales, "The Equilibrium problem in small groups," in *Working Papers in Theory of Action*, eds. T. Parsons et al. (New York: Free Press, 1953).

6. However, the matter of whether the dimensions are independent of each other is still under debate. See, for example, Peter Wissenbert and Michael Kavanagh, "The Independence of Initiating structure and consideration: a review of evidence," *Personnel Psychology*, 25 (1972), pp. 119–30.

7. R. M. Stogdill and A. E. Coons, eds. *Leader Behavior; Its Description and Measurement* (Columbus: Ohio State University, Bureau of Business Research, 1957).

8. F. W. Halpin and B. J. Weiner, "A factorial study of leader behavior description," in Stogdill and Coons, *Leader Behavior.*

9. Ralph Stogdill, *Managers, Employees, Organizations* (Columbus: Ohio State University, Bureau of Business Research, 1965).

10. Robert J. House, "A Path Goal Theory of Leadership," in E. A. Fleishman and J. G. Hunt (Eds.), *Current Developments in the Study of Leadership* (Carbondale: Southern Illinois University Press, 1973.

11. Gary Yukl, "Toward a Behavioral Theory of Leadership," *Organizational Behavior Performance*, 6, No. 4 (July 1971), pp. 414–440, reprinted in W. E. Scott and L. L. Cummings, *Readings in Organization Behavior and Human Performance* (Homewood, Ill.: Richard D. Irwin, 1973).

12. See Chester Schrieschem, Robert J. House, and Steven Kerr, "Leader Initiating Structure: A Reconciliation of Discrepant Research Results and Some Empirical Tests," *Organizational Behavior and Human Performance*, 15, No. 2 (April 1976); and M. N. Petty and Gordon Lee, Jr., "Moderating Effects of Sex of Supervisor and Subordinate on Relationship between Supervisory Behavior and Subordinate Satisfaction," *Journal of Applied Psychology*, 6, No. 5 (October 1975); see also Tamas Motsui, Yoshie Ohtsuka, and Akio Kiguchi, "Consideration and Structure Behavior as Reflections of Supervisory Interpersonal Values," *Journal of Applied Psychology*, Vol. 63, No. 2 (April 1978), pp. 259–62; David Gilmore, Terry Beehr, and David Nichter, "Effects of Leader Behaviors on Subordinate Performance and Satisfaction: A Laboratory Experiment with Student Employees," *Journal of Applied Psychology*, Vol. 24, No. 2 (April 1972), pp. 166–172.

13. E. A. Fleishman and E. F. Harris, "Patterns of Behavior Related to Employee Grievances and Turnover," *Personnel Psychology*, 15 (1962), pp. 43–56.

14. Rensis Likert, *New Patterns of Management* (New York: McGraw-Hill, 1961).

15. Likert, *New Patterns*, p. 7.

16. D. Katz and R. L. Kahn, "Leadership Practices in Relation to Productivity and Morale," in D. Cartwright and A. Zander, *Group Dynamics* (Evanston, Ill.: Rowe Peterson, 1960), pp. 550–70.

17. Robert Day and Robert Hamblin, "Some Effective Close and Punitive Styles of Leadership," *American Journal of Psychology*, 69 (1964), pp. 499–510.

18. See, for example, Nancy Morse, *Satisfactions in the White Collar Job* (Ann Arbor: University of Michigan, Survey Research Center, 1953).

19. Day and Hamblin, "Styles of Leadership."

20. See, for example, Allen Filley, Robert House, and Steven Kerr, *Managerial Process and Organizational Behavior* (Glenview, Ill.: Scott Foresman, 1976), pp. 399–405.

21. Likert, *New Patterns*, pp. 58–59.

22. Robert Tannenbaum and Warren Schmidt, "How to Choose a Leadership Pattern," *Harvard Business Review*, 36 (March–April 1958), pp. 95–101. Stephen Green and Delbert Nebekser, "The Effects of Situational Factors and Leadership Style on Leader Behavior," *Organizational Behavior and Human Performance*, Vol. 19, No. 2 (August 1977), pp. 368–77.

23. Fred Fiedler, *A Theory of Leadership Effectiveness* (New York: McGraw-Hill, 1967). See also, for example, Stan Weed, Terence Mitchell, and Weldon Moffitt, "Leadership Style, Subordinate Personality, and Task Type as Predictors of Performance and Satisfaction with Supervision," *Journal of Applied Psychology*, Vol. 61, No. 1 (February 1976).

24. G. Graen, K. Alvarez, J. B. Orris, and J. A. Martella, "Contingency Model of Leadership Effectiveness: Antecedent and Evidential Results," *Psychological Bulletin*, Vol. 74 (1970), pp. 285–96. See also, Graen, Orris, and Alvarez, "Contingency Model of Leadership Effectiveness: Some Experimental Results," *Journal of Applied Psychology*, Vol. 55 (1971), pp. 196–201.

25. Fiedler, *A Theory of Leadership Effectiveness*, p. 45.

26. For example, see Martin M. Chemers and Robert W. Rice, "A Theoretical and Empirical Examination of Fiedler's Contingency Model of Leadership Effectiveness," in *Contingency Approaches to Leadership*, ed. J. G. Hunt and L. Larson (Carbondale: Southern Illinois University Press, 1974), 91–123. Mitchell, et al., "The Contingency Model: Criticisms and Suggestions." The literature on the LPC is voluminous. In addition to the studies mentioned, see, for example, Martin G. Evans, "A Leader's Ability to Differentiate the Subordinate's Performance," *Personnel Psychology*, Vol. 26 (1973), pp. 385–95; Joe E. Stinson and Lane Tracy, "Some Disturbing Characteristics of the LPC Score," *Personnel Psychology*, Vol. 27 (1974), pp. 477–85; Martin G. Evans, and Jerry Dermer, "What Does the Least Preferred Co-worker Scale Really Measure," *Journal of Applied Psychology*, Vol. 59, No. 2 (1974), pp. 202–6; Lars Larson and Kendrith M. Rowland, "Leadership Style and Cognitive Complexity," *Academy of Management Journal*, Vol. 17, No. 1 (March 1974), pp. 37–45; Marshall Sashkin, F. Carter Taylor, and Rama C. Tripathi, "An Analysis of Situational Psychological Measures," *Journal of Applied Psychology*, Vol. 59, No. 6 (1974), pp. 731–40; Robert P. Vecchio, "An Empirical Examination of the Validity of Fiedler's Model of Leadership Effectiveness," *Organizational Behavior and Human Performance*, Vol. 19, No. 1 (June 1977), pp. 180–206.

27. See, for example, Martin Chemers and Robert Rice, "A Theoretical and Empirical Examination of Fiedler's Contingency Model of Leadership Effectiveness" in *Contingency Approaches to Leadership*, ed. J. G. Hunt and Lars Larsen (Carbondale: Southern Illinois University, 1974), pp. 91–123. Louis S. Csoka and Paul M. Bons, "Manipulating the Situation to Fit the Leader's Style: Two Validation Studies of LEADER MATCH," *Journal of Applied Psychology*, Vol. 63, No. 3 (June 1978), pp. 295–300. Fred Fiedler and Linda Mahar, "The Effectiveness of Contingency Model Training: A Review of the Validation of LEADER MATCH," *Personnel Psychology*, Vol. 32, No. 1 (Spring 1979), pp. 45–62.

28. Gary Dessler and Enzo Valenzi, "Initiation of Structure and Subordinate Satisfaction: A Path Analysis Test of Path-Goal Theory," *Academy of Management Journal*, Vol. 20, No. 2 (1977), pp. 251–59; Enzo Valenzi and Gary Dessler, "Relationships of Leader Behavior, Subordinate Role Ambiguity, and Subordinate Job Satisfaction," *Academy of Management Journal*, Vol. 21, No. 4 (December 1978), pp. 671–78; Charles Greene, "Questions of Causation in the Path Goal Theory of Leadership," Vol. 22, No. 1 (March 1972), pp. 22–42.

29. R. C. Kahn, D. M. Wolfe, R. P. Quinn, J. D. Snoek, and R. A. Rosenthal, *Organizational Stress* (New York: John Wiley, 1964).

30. Amitai Etzioni, *Complex Organizations* (New York: Free Press, 1961), pp. 3–22.

31. Likert, *New Patterns of Management*, p. 94.

32. Quoted in Sanford Dornbush and W. Richard Scott, *Evaluation and the Exercise of Authority* (San Francisco: Jossey Bass, 1975), p. 51.

33. Robert Peabody, "Perceptions of Organizational Authority: A Comparative Analysis," *Administrative Science Quarterly*, 6, No. 4 (1962), p. 514.

34. John French, Jr. and Bertram Raven, *Studies in Social Power* (Ann Arbor: Institute for Social Research, 1959), reprinted in Henry Tosi and W. Clay Hamner, *Organizational Behavior and Management* (Chicago: St. Clair Press, 1977), pp. 442–56.

35. John French, Jr. and Bertram Raven, *Studies in Social Power*.

36. Stanley Milgram, *Obedience to Authority: An Experimental View* (New York: Harper and Row, 1974), pp. 1–12; reprinted in Jerome E. Schnee, E. Kirby Warren, and Harold Lazarus, *The Progress of Management* (Englewood Cliffs, N.J.: Prentice-Hall, 1977), pp. 427–36.

10 Groups and Their Influence on Performance

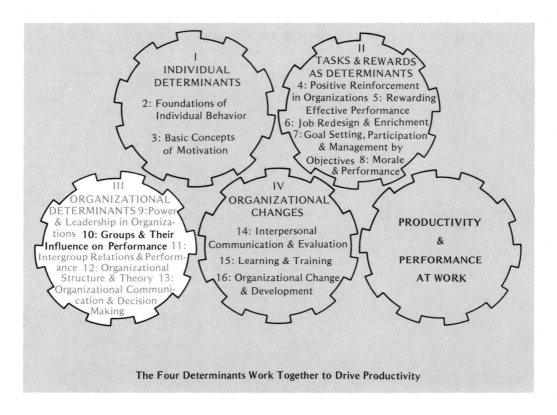

I
INDIVIDUAL DETERMINANTS

2: Foundations of Individual Behavior

3: Basic Concepts of Motivation

II
TASKS & REWARDS AS DETERMINANTS
4: Positive Reinforcement in Organizations 5: Rewarding Effective Performance 6: Job Redesign & Enrichment 7: Goal Setting, Participation & Management by Objectives 8: Morale & Performance

III
ORGANIZATIONAL DETERMINANTS 9: Power & Leadership in Organizations **10: Groups & Their Influence on Performance** 11: Intergroup Relations & Performance 12: Organizational Structure & Theory 13: Organizational Communication & Decision Making

IV
ORGANIZATIONAL CHANGES

14: Interpersonal Communication & Evaluation

15: Learning & Training

16: Organizational Change & Development

PRODUCTIVITY & PERFORMANCE AT WORK

The Four Determinants Work Together to Drive Productivity

BY THE TIME YOU FINISH STUDYING THIS CHAPTER, YOU SHOULD BE ABLE TO:

1. *Discuss several types of work groups.*
2. *Answer the question: "Why do people join groups?"*
3. *Explain how groups influence performance.*
4. *Diagram the Homans model.*
5. *Cite the characteristics of effective work groups.*
6. *More effectively use groups to solve problems.*

OVERVIEW

The main purpose of this chapter is to explain how a manager can improve the performance of his work group—and thereby that of his subordinates. We first discuss different types of groups and the factors that lead to group formation. Next, we explain how groups effect their members' performance through their effects on the antecedents of performance, their members' abilities, and the consequences of performance. Next, we explain how to improve a group's performance, for example, by practicing "group-centered leadership," and ensuring that the group is not too large. Finally, we discuss the fact that problem-solving groups are important examples of work groups and we explain how a leader can better manage such groups.

INTRODUCTION: GROUPS AND EMPLOYEE PERFORMANCE

Groups—two or more persons interacting with one another in such a way that each influences the other—play a critical role in organizations. Perhaps the most obvious reason for this is that groups influence the performance of their members, a process known as *group dynamics*. Many examples of this influence could be cited: a company institutes an incentive pay plan only to have it fail because employees don't wish to exceed the informal production quota set by their work groups; intergroup conflicts arise because group members identify more with the aims of their own groups than with those of the organization as a whole; and so on. The important point is that one cannot understand or predict an employee's performance without understanding the dynamics of the group or groups to which he or she belongs; understanding why and how groups function is therefore an important human relations skill.

Types of Groups[1]

Formal and Informal Groups. In practice there are actually several types of work groups. First, most writers distinguish between formal and informal groups. Formal groups are a product of the formal structure and work flow of the organization, both of which define specific groups of persons who are *required* to work interdependently on a task. On the other hand, informal groups emerge without plan. A major difference between the two is that, with formal groups, behavior is (or should be) specified and directed toward organizational goals. In the informal group, behavior is directed toward the *group's* goal (be it resisting management, providing a friendly atmosphere at lunch, or whatever) and this behavior may or may not support the goals laid down by management. Instead, the informal group serves other functions, functions which may or may not be job related. For example, informal groups can help satisfy their members' needs for affiliation and provide their members with a sense of security, particularly from perceived threats from the group's environment, including management, customers, and other groups. Informal groups also have their own "norms" that provide members with a standard or yardstick with which to evaluate themselves as group members.

Command and Task Groups. Two types of formal work groups are command groups and task groups. The *command group* is composed of the supervisor and his or her immediate subordinates. The *task group* is composed of employees who work together to complete the task or project. Any formally designated task, such as putting together an automobile, requires certain stable, predictable interactions among the workers themselves, i.e., a task group.

Why Do People Join Groups?

When it comes to joining *formal* work groups, of course, employees usually do not have much choice. Here, membership in some group is generally dictated by the requirements of the job, and the person's work mates and supervisor are simply assigned.

The question of why employees join *informal* groups—and why these groups evolve at work—is considerably more complex, however. In general, there are two basic ingredients—*opportunity* and *desire*—and without both of these such groups simply don't emerge.

First, *proximity* and *contact* are prerequisites for group formation because they provide an opportunity for individuals to interact, and because without them there would be no opportunity for the individuals to become attracted to one another.[2] In other words, proximity and contact provide the necessary *opportunity* for people to get to know each other and to determine if the basis for a positive relationship exists. Without this opportunity there is little likelihood of a group forming. On the other hand, proximity and contact are no guarantee that the people will discover they like each other, and if the individuals should find they have little in common the effects could be just the opposite.

Will people who *are* in contact form a group? The answer to this question depends partly on whether there is an *interpersonal attraction* between the people involved, and we know that such attraction is largely a function of how *similar* the people are in terms of attitudes, or goals. In other words, individuals are usually attracted to a group because they find the activities or goals of the group attractive, rewarding, or valuable or because they believe that through the group they can accomplish something they could not accomplish themselves. Thus, a person might join a hunting club, or a bridge club, or a political party because the activities and/or goals of the group are attractive to him. At the workplace, individuals often band into groups in the hopes of protecting themselves from what they perceive as threats from "outsiders" such as management, customers, and other groups. At the extreme, such groups can evolve into what Schachter has dubbed "frozen groups." These are groups of employees who have banded together for the purpose of protecting themselves from what they see as a hostile management and who resist mandated changes with an almost mindless determination.

HOW GROUPS INFLUENCE
EMPLOYEE PERFORMANCE

How Groups Affect the ABCs of Performance

Groups influence the performance of their members in three ways. First, groups often have their own production standards or norms, and in the minds of group members these may conflict with (and supercede) the standards, or *antecedents*, set by management. Groups can also influence their members' *ability* to do their jobs, for example, by providing (or withholding) informal training and assistance on the job. Finally, and perhaps most importantly, groups influence the *consequences* of performance and therefore the performance itself. To many people, for example, having friendly relations with one's peers far outweighs the attractiveness of a small raise in pay. Similarly, ostracism from one's peers is often a more powerful consequence than is praise from one's supervisor or the prospect of a raise. In summary, groups influence (in our terms) the "ABCs" of performance, and therefore performance itself.

Groups and the Antecedents of Performance

One way a group influences its members' performances is by substituting its own standards or *norms* for the standards set by management. These norms are "rules of conduct, proper ways of acting, which have been accepted as legitimate by members of a group and which specify the kinds of behavior that is expected of group members."[3] Norms such as "don't produce more than eight units per hour" are useful guidelines that group members agree on and that tell group members how they are expected to act in various situations. Group members are usually highly motivated to conform to these norms, either because as active members of the group the norms are, in a sense, their own, or because they fear the consequences of not conforming to them.

In any case, group performance is influenced in two ways by these norms. First, because the group norm tends to be the "target" that all members shoot for, group performance is generally *less variable* than it might otherwise be. Thus, all members produce about the same amount, and output tends to stay level from hour to hour and day to day. Second, the *level* of performance may be either high or low, depending on whether the group as a whole sets high or low production norms.[4] As a result, some managers have learned that they cannot just ask, "Does the employee know what is expected of him?" Instead, they also ask, "Does the employee's work group have it own production norms, and do these disagree with mine?"

Groups and Their Members' Ability

An employee's work group can also affect his or her ability to perform the job well. In many cases, for example, an employee could not perform up to standard *even if he or she wanted to,* because other group members on whom the person relies won't provide the necessary help or assistance.

This can especially be a problem where the jobs are interdependent— where, for example, one person has to supply a bolt, another has to hold it, and another has to tighten it. Here, if the group as a whole so chooses, it can easily undermine the ability of even the most highly motivated member, by simply withholding the necessary assistance.

There are also other, less obvious ways in which a group can undermine a member's ability. For example, few training programs are so complete that the new employee does not have to depend to some extent on the "informal" training provided by others in his or her work group. And where, for some reason, this training and advice is withheld, the employee's ability to perform well will suffer. In summary, groups also influence their members' *ability* to perform their tasks.

Groups and the Consequences of Performance

Groups are also an important source of positive and negative consequences— of rewards and punishment. Employees who violate group norms for, say, production quotas, usually find themselves exposed first to "education," and then to ostracism or physical abuse. (In one of the earliest documented examples of this, researchers in the Hawthorne studies reported how "rate busters" were exposed to "binging"—being hit on the wrist by others in the work group—if they exceeded the group's own production standard).

Again, however, a person's work group also provides many "consequences" that are neither so obvious or so direct. A person's work group, for example, can be a source of tremendous satisfaction to a person, as well as a buffer that protects him from (and helps him to live with) job-related tensions that might otherwise be unbearable. In such a case the friendship of one's peers (or the loss thereof) can be a much more important reward than a supervisor's praise or the promise of a raise.

The "Homans Model"

What is the process through which groups influence their members? Many theories have been proposed but the most famous of these was developed by George Homans and is called the "Homans Model." It is illustrated in Exhibit 10.1.

Homans says that all group behavior consists of three "basic elements," and he calls these elements "activities," "interactions," and "sentiments."

Activities. Activities refer to things that people do, such as planting, cutting, smoking, or walking. To be precise, says Homans, all activities "refer in the end to movements of the muscles of men."[5]

Interactions. Interactions refer to communications of any sort between individuals. These communications need not be verbal and in fact may be nonverbal:

"Perhaps the simplest example of interaction, . . . is two men at opposite ends of a saw, sawing a log. When we say that the two are interacting, we are not referring to the fact that both are sawing—in our language, sawing is an activity—but to the fact that the push of one man on the saw is followed by the push of the other. In this example, the interaction does not involve words."[6]

Sentiments. Sentiments are "internal states of the human body" and include motives, drives, emotions, feelings, and attitudes. Sentiments thus range from fear and hunger to affection. Unlike activities and interactions sentiments cannot be seen or observed.

According to Homans, group behavior can be described in terms of an external system, and an internal system (see Exhibit 10.1). Each system contains its own activities, interactions, and sentiments.

The "external" system is comprised of the *required* activities, interactions, and sentiments which the group must carry out to survive. For

Exhibit 10.1 The Homans Model

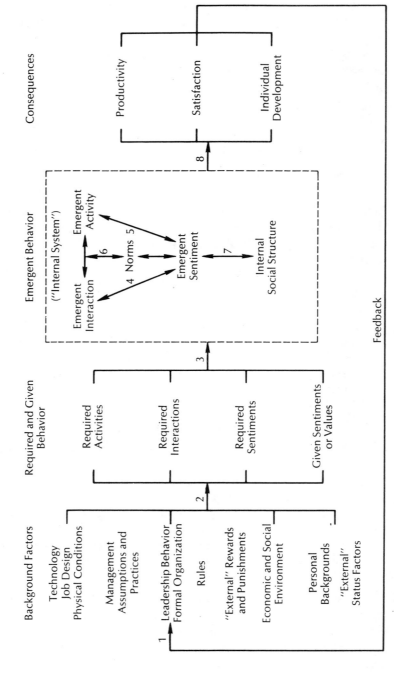

example, there are certain activities, interactions, and sentiments that are required of a flight crew on a passenger jet. Activities include flying the plane, checking fuel levels, and navigating. Interactions include communication between the navigator and pilot concerning wind speed and direction. Required sentiments include professional concern over the safety of passengers.

On the other hand, "internal" activities, interactions, and sentiments *emerge* from the work group itself. A work group's control of production levels is a good example of this. Groups often establish norms (which are types of sentiments) that say "no group member should produce more than X number of units per day." This norm is communicated to new and existing group members through various kinds of interactions: verbal admonitions, frowns, and so on. As a result, the emergent activity of the group—in this case its production level—is often much lower than what management planned for the group.

IMPROVING GROUP PERFORMANCE

Groups are a double-edged sword from the point of view of employee performance. On the one hand, a close knit, cohesive work group that supports management's aims can induce its members to perform better than they might otherwise. Unfortunately, however, the reverse is also true. A cohesive group that has learned to mistrust management's motives and resist its attempts at productivity improvements can drastically reduce the performance of its members by threatening "ratebusters" with ostracism, punishment, or abuse.[7]

This being the case, it is to everyone's advantage for the manager to try to win the group's support, and there are a number of specific group-centered actions he or she can take to accomplish this. These include: practicing group-centered leadership; analyzing the ABCs of group problems; making sure the group is the right size; and developing high group cohesiveness.

Practice Group-centered Leadership

First, according to Likert, the leaders of effective work groups practice what he calls "group-centered leadership," an approach to leadership that is analogous to the "employee-centered leadership" we discussed in chapter 9. These leaders, you may recall, treat their employees as ends, rather than means, they are supportive, and they treat people as individuals. In all of their actions, in other words, they treat each employee of their work group in a way that builds and maintains his or her sense of personal worth and importance.[8] Furthermore, according to Likert, effective group leaders see that all problems involving the group are dealt with by the group—they are generally *participative*, in other words, where the situation permits being so.

Analyze the "ABCs" of Performance

Group-centered leadership is important, but it is as (or more) important to remember to analyze the group's behavior when performance is inadequate. For example, after determining that a new incentive plan is not working because the work group is resisting it (by keeping output low), ask: do the group members know what is expected of them under the new plan? Do they fully understand the plan? Could they perform better if they wanted to? Are there organizational impediments (like poor maintenance) prohibiting improved performance? What are the consequences of performing better? Does the group as a whole believe that improved performance will be detrimental to their well being?

The Size of the Group is Important

The number of persons in a group—its size—is one of its most important characteristics, and it is one that can both improve or undermine group performance.

Group Size and Member Participation. We know that as the size of a group increases—say, above 5 or 6 members—significant changes take place in the degree to which members participate in the group's activities. For one thing, there is less time available for each member to participate in the group's activities, and group members also tend to feel more inhibited when the group is large. As a result, there is usually a decrease in the overall amount of participation as the size of the group increases: there is less talking and discussion and more subgrouping (cliques) for example.[9]

In addition to the fact that there is less total participation in the group's activities, the *pattern* of participation also changes as the size of the group increases. For example, as the group becomes larger, most people tend to participate less, but at the same time a few members tend to dominate the discussion, and communications are increasingly directed toward the group as a whole rather than to specific members of the group.[10]

Group Size and Group Performance. Increasing the size of the group introduces opposing forces as far as group performance is concerned. On the one hand, an increase in the size of the group means that more knowledge, skills, and abilities can be brought to bear in carrying out the group's activities. On the other hand, we have seen that in large groups this benefit may never materialize because members usually participate and contribute less to the group's activities.

As a result of these opposing forces, whether or not larger groups perform better or worse than smaller ones depends on at least two factors. The first of these is the *kind of task* the group has to perform. For example, in an "additive" task like a tug-of-war, the contributions of each member tend to be additive, and so performance and size thus tend to be directly related, at least up to a point. On the other hand, where the task is not additive— for example, where a group is measured by how fast it completes a ten-mile hike—a less effective (in this case slower) member will detract from the group's performance, and the larger the group is, the more chance there is that there will be such less effective members.[11]

In addition to the nature of the task, the *skills of the group's leader* can also affect whether increasing the group's size raises or lowers its performance. For example, if the leader has well-developed conference leader skills (we discuss these in a moment) and is able to ensure that all group members participate in the group's discussions and present their different points of view, group performance is more apt to increase as more members are added. Without such a leader, communications may simply break down as more people are added, and chaos will reign.[12]

Group Size and Member Attitudes. The size of the group also has implications for how the members view the group, as well as for the group's cohesiveness. As the group becomes larger, most members are able to participate less in the group's activities, and one side effect is that their satisfaction drops. And, generally speaking, as the size of the group increases, there is greater disagreement among its members and greater antagonism toward each other.[13]

Related to this, group cohesiveness—the ability of its members to "stick together"—tends to decrease as the size of the group increases. In fact, this reduction in cohesiveness is one of the forces that tends to reduce group performance as the size of the group increases. Group cohesiveness is a very important characteristic of effective groups, and so we will discuss it in more detail.

Improve the Group's Cohesiveness

A group's cohesiveness is another of its important characteristics. Group formation and functioning are important topics for managers because groups influence the thinking and behavior of their members, and it stands to reason that the more cohesive is the group—the more the group has a tendency to stick together, and the more reluctant are group members to leave—the more influence the group can bring to bear on its members.

Many factors influence a group's cohesiveness. First, all of those things that contributed to the formation of the group in the first place also contribute to the group's cohesiveness. These include an ability for group members to interact (proximity), and the extent to which each group member finds the activities and goals of the group to be attractive, rewarding, and valuable. Generally speaking, the more attractive (and important) are the goals to the members, the more cohesive the group will be. The size of the group (to repeat) also influences its cohesiveness, with larger groups generally being less cohesive than smaller ones.

Intragroup and intergroup competition are also important factors. Intragroup competition amongst members of the group generally undermines group cohesiveness, as might be expected. On the other hand, intergroup competition between competing groups can either increase or decrease group cohesiveness. In one study, groups were assigned problems and were then arranged in pairs of groups that had to compete with one another in a situation in which only one group could win.[14] The researchers found that the newly created competitive environment increased group cohesiveness. In addition, however, they found that whether the group won or lost had important implications for its cohesiveness: in the losing groups tensions emerged that tended to undermine group relationships and cohesion.

USING GROUPS TO SOLVE PROBLEMS: IMPROVING GROUP PROBLEM SOLVING

"Problem-solving groups" or committees are important examples of work groups, although the "work" they perform is not tangible as is building a car or constructing a house. Instead, the product of a problem-solving group is—or should be—a better decision for the organization, whether the decision involves where to build the new plant, whether to lease or buy the machine, which ad campaign to choose, or something else. Whatever the decision, problem-solving groups are important work groups in organizations, and knowing how to lead or "chair" an effective problem-solving group is an important human relations skill.

Do Groups Make Better Decisions than Individuals?

Virtually all organizations use groups like committees to analyze and solve problems,[15] and it might therefore be useful to consider whether groups arrive at better decisions than would their members working individually.

Do groups make better decisions than individuals? The evidence here suggests that while bringing individuals together can result in better decisions, the way most group meetings are held they usually result in worse—not better —decisions than the individuals would have arrived at separately. Surprisingly, for example, there seems to be a tendency for more ideas to emerge when persons work on a problem separately, since working in face-to-face groups apparently inhibits the exchange of ideas, *unless such an exchange is specifically nurtured and encouraged* in a nonthreatening atmosphere.[16]

In other words, group decision making experts know that groups do not necessarily have to inhibit the production of ideas, at least not if the meeting is run by a person who has what Norman Maier calls "effective conference leader skills."[17] For example, Maier says that there are certain *assets* and *liabilities* inherent in using groups to solve problems and that if the liabilities can be overcome the group *will* produce much better decisions.

Assets and Liabilities in Group Problem Solving[18]

Maier's findings help shed some light on the assets and liabilities of group decision making. He says that the decision-making *assets* of the group are:

1. *The greater sum total of knowledge and information.* There is more information in a group than in any one of its members. Thus problems that require the utilization of knowledge should give the groups an advantage over individuals.
2. *A greater number of approaches to a problem.* Since group members do not have identical approaches (to solving the problem), each can contribute by knocking others out of ruts in thinking.
3. *Participation in problem solving increases acceptance.* Insofar as group problem solving permits participation, it helps to make the resulting solutions more acceptable to the participants.
4. *Better comprehension of the decision.* The chances for communication failures are greatly reduced when the individuals who must work together in executing the decision have participated in making it.

The decision-making *liabilities* to watch out for include:

1. *Social pressure.* The desire to be a good group member and to be accepted tends to silence disagreement and favor consensus.
2. *"Valence" of solutions.* Each solution (or alternative) receives both critical and supportive comments. When a solution receives about 15 more positive than negative comments ("valence"), it tends to be accepted *regardless* of its quality. This is because a turning

point between the *idea-getting* and *decision-making* steps occurs here.

3. *Individual domination.* In many groups a dominant individual emerges and captures more than his share of influence on the outcomes.

4. *Conflicting secondary goal: winning the argument.* When groups are confronted with a problem, the intial goal is to obtain a solution. However, the appearance of several alternatives causes individuals to have preferences, and once these emerge the desire to support a position is created. More and more the goal becomes that of winning the argument.

Groups Make Riskier Decisions

One of the most interesting affects that a group has on its members is that the decisions the group arrives at are usually more risky than the decisions its members advocated in private. In many of the best-known studies of this "risky shift" phenomenon, the subjects were asked first to answer a set of questions individually and then to discuss the questions as a group and arrive at a consensus.[19] In most of these studies the subjects were asked to serve as "advisors" to hypothetical persons who have two alternatives to choose between; one alternative is less attractive but safe, while the other is more attractive but less likely to succeed. (As an example, one hypothetical advisee is an engineer who may remain at his current job at a modest but adequate salary, or take a new job that offers a much higher potential income but no assurance of long-range security.) Each subject first indicated how he or she would advise the hypothetical person (in this case, the engineer). Then, the subjects met in a group, and the group made its own group recommendation. In almost all such studies the group ends up making more risky decisions (it advises the person to pursue the riskier option) than did the members of the group when they individually made their decisions.

   Why do groups make riskier decisions than would their individual members? At this point no one knows for sure, but several reasonable explanations have been advanced. First, many experts believe that when people meet in a group it is easier for any one person to shirk his or her responsibility since, in a sense, the responsibility for the decision is diffused or spread among all the members of the group: people therefore just feel safer making riskier decisions when they know there are others to share in the blame for them. (It is also easier to make a riskier decision when you know others support it as well.) A second explanation is that taking moderate risks is something that is valued in our society, and when people meet in groups they therefore want to seem as willing as their peers to take risks and not be too cautious. Whatever the explanation, though, it is apparent that groups usually make riskier decisions, and this is something to take into consideration when evaluating a group's advice and recommendations.

Guidelines: How to Lead a Problem-solving Group

To a large extent, whether or not a group is able to capitalize on the assets of group problem solving and avoid the liabilities depends on the skills of the leader. With this in mind, some guidelines for leading a group problem-solving meeting effectively include the following.

Make Sure That Everyone Agrees on How to Define the Problem. Very often groups spend enormous amounts of time developing "solutions" to the wrong problems. At first glance it might seem that identifying the problem is a fairly straightforward matter, but this is not the case. Perhaps the most common fallacy here is to emphasize the obvious or to be misled by symptoms. For example, take the case of a consulting team that was retained by the owners of a large office building. The office workers in the building were disturbed because they had to wait so long for an elevator to pick them up, and many tenants were threatening to move out. The owners called in a consulting team, and told them that the "problem" was that the elevators were running too slowly.

How would you have attacked the problem if you were one of the consultants? If you assume, as did the owners, that the problem could be defined as "slow-moving elevators," then the alternative solutions are fairly obvious. The elevators were running about as fast as they could, given the number of people that had to use them; so one solution might be to request that the tenants stagger their work hours. But that could cause more animosity than the slow-moving elevators. Another solution might be to add one or two more elevators, but this would be tremendously expensive.

The point of this example is that the alternatives the group develops and the decision it makes are tied to the way it defines the basic central problem. What the consultants actually did in this case was to disregard "slow-moving elevators" as the problem and instead defined it as "tenants are upset because they have to wait for an elevator." Then, the solution the consultants hit on was to have full-length mirrors installed by each bank of elevators so that tenants could admire themselves while waiting! The solution was both inexpensive and satisfactory, and the complaints all but disappeared.

The point is this: as the leader of a group discussion, you have to be very careful about how the group defines the problem. Peel away the obvious "problems" until you hit on the heart of the matter. Then the group will be ready to begin developing useful alternative solutions.

See That All Group Members Participate. It is the discussion leader's job to see to it that all members of the group actively participate in the discussion. After all, two of the main assets in using a group to solve problems are that it brings to bear different points of view and approaches and helps gain acceptance for the final decision by allowing people to participate in developing that solution. If everyone does *not* have an opportunity to express his or her point of view, and if conflicting points of view are not aired, then, in all likelihood, the meeting will result in relatively poor decisions.

Distinguish Between Idea Getting and Idea Evaluation. Professor Maier says that the "idea-getting" process should be separated from the idea evaluation process because the latter inhibits the former.[20] Identifying problems or developing solutions each involve both idea getting and idea evaluation. The trouble is that in most group meetings the participants do not clearly distinguish between the idea-getting and idea evaluation phases. Instead, as one person presents an idea, the others begin discussing its pros and cons, and as a result fewer new ideas are presented and members become increasingly apprehensive about suggesting new ideas. One technique that is often used to generate new ideas is called *brainstorming*. The brainstorming approach to group problem solving means that everyone has to follow certain ground rules. Most importantly, (1) no one is permitted to criticize an idea until all ideas are presented, and (2) the members are asked to suggest anything that occurs to them, even if it seems silly or humorous.[21]

In summary, the discussion leader's task is to see to it that all the ideas are "out on the table" before the evaluation of each idea begins; there has to be a clear distinction between idea getting and idea evaluation.

Do Not Respond to Each Participant or Dominate the Discussion. One of the main liabilities of group problem solving is that too often a dominant individual emerges and overly influences the outcome. And, ironically, this dominant person often turns out to be the discussion leader, the very person who should be helping the group to avoid this liability. *The leader's main task in running a problem-solving meeting is to elicit ideas from the group, not to supply them.* The trouble is that the role of leader makes it relatively easy for the person to respond to and become *argumentative with each person* that tries to make a comment, and, in addition, there is always the natural tendency for discussion leaders to try to "sell" their own ideas. To run an effective group problem-solving meeting, however, the leader has to keep these natural inclinations under control. Instead the person ought to remember that he or she is there to elicit ideas through the full participation and cooperation of all group members.

See That Effort is Directed Toward Overcoming Surmountable Obstacles. Many problem-solving groups make the mistake of becoming embroiled in discussions concerning who is to blame for the problem or what should have been done to avoid the problem. Maier says that such discussions cannot lead to solutions, since the past cannot be changed. Instead, the leader has to ensure that the group focuses on obstacles that can be overcome and on solutions that are implementable.[22]

Summary. In summary, Maier says that "openmindedness"—a willingness to look for a best solution rather than to sell a particular alternative—is an important prerequisite to effective group problem solving. In line with this, it is imperative that the leader ensure that all facts and alternatives are out on the table before the group starts criticizing alternatives and zeroing in on a solution. Most importantly, therefore, capitalizing on group problem-solving assets and avoiding problem-solving liabilities, involves ensuring that: (1) people with different points of view are represented in the group; (2) the problem is carefully identified; (3) all group members are encouraged to get all possible alternatives out on the table; (4) the pros and cons of all alternatives are then discussed; and (5) the best alternative is then chosen, perhaps by combining several of the alternatives that were discussed.

CHAPTER SUMMARY

1. We distinguished between formal and informal groups and command and task groups and explained that people join groups if there is both the *opportunity* and the *desire*. Most importantly, however, individuals are usually attracted to a group (*desire* to join a group) because they find the activities or goals of the group attractive or rewarding.

2. Groups influence the performance of their members in three ways. First, groups often have their own production standards or norms, and in the minds of group members these may conflict with and (supercede) the standards or *antecedents* set by management. Groups can also influence their members' *ability* to do their jobs, as well as the perceived *consequences* of performance.

3. The Homans model is based on the idea that all group behavior consists of three basic elements—activities, interactions, and sentiments.

4. Improving work group performance involves ensuring that there is: the right size, cohesiveness, a group-centered leadership style, and an analysis of the "ABCs" of the group's performance.

5. Groups often make riskier (and inferior) decisions than would their members working individually, but an effective conference leader can vastly improve the performance of a problem-solving group. For example, it is essential that: the problem is defined correctly, that all group members participate, that the participants distinguish between idea getting and idea evaluating, that no participant dominate the discussion, and that effort is directed toward overcoming obstacles that *can* be eliminated.

DISCUSSION QUESTIONS AND PROJECTS

1. Explain why people join groups. Then, list some specific ways in which you would (1) encourage group formation and (2) discourage group formation. How would you go about undermining group cohesiveness? Increasing group cohesiveness?

2. Explain how groups effect the "ABCs" of performance.

3. What are the characteristics of effective work groups? Explain how you would go about increasing a work group's effectiveness if you were its manager. (Be specific)

4. You are a manager and have just instituted a new piece-rate incentive system only to find that your employees' performance is no higher than it was before the plan, when they were paid an hourly wage. Analyze the problem using our "ABCs" of performance (in other words, indicate what specific questions you would ask in analyzing whether the problem lay in the antecedents, behavior, or consequences), and indicate where you think your organization's work group may fit into the problem.

5. The instructor should choose five students to form a "problem-solving group" and appoint one person to be the group discussion leader. The instructor should then assign some problem to this group (such as, "analyze the case exercise for this chapter"). The group discussion leader should apply his or her knowledge of group problem-solving leadership skills and try to get the group to solve the problem. The class should then discuss the group leader's effectiveness.

CASE EXERCISE

The Unstoppable Coffee Klatch

Jim Lyons, the newly appointed manager of operations at Gulf Coast Insurance Company, confided to Wendy McPherson, his executive secretary, "We're going to see a lot of changes around here. Last year the company just about broke even. I don't see any need to lay off people, but I do see a need for us to become more efficient.

"What irks me the most is the time being wasted in the office while people sit around in coffee klatches. Around ten in the morning, the place is deserted. About ninety percent of the staff is down in the cafeteria whiling away time, drinking coffee. We could get by on less staff if we could cut down on those coffee breaks. We could lose about five percent of our office staff due to attrition and not have to replace them if we could stop the time leak created by the coffee break."

Jim's first management action to curtail the coffee break was to prepare an edict that from now on no coffee breaks would be allowed in the cafeteria. Instead, coffee- and tea-vending machines would be installed at two key locations in the office building. Any employee who wanted coffee or tea could purchase a beverage in the machine and take it back to his or her work station.

One month later the vending machines were installed and the cafeteria was declared off limits to employees except during their lunch break. Shortly thereafter, Jim received a phone call from Mickey, the head of maintenance.

"Mr. Lyons," said Mickey excitedly, "I think we have a major fire hazard on our hands. Since you ended the cafeteria coffee break and installed the vending machines, the employees have found a new way to serve coffee. All of a sudden we have a collection of hot water heaters, Silexes, and those new coffee makers around the office. I first got on to it when one of them shorted and blew a fuse. I understand that the vending machine is losing money. That's what the route man told me."

"Mickey, I appreciate your having brought this problem to my attention," replied Jim, "I'll get on it right away."

The next day Jim Lyons had a memo affixed to every bulletin board and sent to every supervisor. It read in part, "From now on, no unauthorized coffee- or tea-making equipment will be brought into this office. Any employee caught using unauthorized coffee-making equipment will be subject to suspension."

Two weeks later, Jim asked Mickey to make a secretive night inspection of the office. His task was to discover if any coffee pots were still being used in the office. Mickey's investigation turned up no such evidence. Jim also phoned a few supervisors to see if the edict was receiving full compliance. Again, the report was positive. Jim thought to himself that the coffee klatch problem had finally been resolved. Three weeks later, Jody, the personnel manager, came forth with a disconcerting comment:

"Jim, I thought your edict might have been a little heavy handed. And I told you so. I now have evidence that your removal of the coffee pots has created a new problem."

"What's that? I haven't heard of any problems," said Jim.

"Perhaps, then, you haven't been making recent tours of the office at any time from nine to eleven in the morning. You can find little pockets of people drinking coffee in the strangest of places. We found five women from underwriting sitting on the steps of a fire exit. Three fellows and two gals from the claims department were found gathered around the Xerox machine drinking coffee. Worst of all, five people were sitting under a tree on the front lawn with paper cups in their hands. That's hardly what you had in mind with your no coffee pot edict."

"Jody, let me think about this problem for a while longer," mused Jim. Three days later, he sent out a new memo:

"Because of disappointment with certain aspects of the service, the coffee-vending machine will be removed from the building. Therefore, all employees who so desire are allowed a fifteen-minute break per morning to have coffee or other beverage in the cafeteria. Please make sure that this fifteen-minute limit is not exceeded."

Questions

1. Why didn't Jim Lyon's plan to stop the time spent on coffee breaks work?

2. How sound was Jim's decision to reinstate the cafeteria coffee break?

3. What does this case tell us about informal groups?

4. What does this case tell us about Jim's managerial skills?

5. How do you think Jim's actions affected the morale in the office?

6. How would you have gone about analyzing and solving the problem with our "ABCs" of of performance? What is the *desired* behavior?

NOTES FOR CHAPTER 10

1. See, for example, Gary Dessler, *Organization and Management* (Englewood Cliffs, N.J.: Prentice-Hall, 1976), pp. 231–32.

2. See Marvin E. Shaw, *Group Dynamics* (New York: McGraw-Hill, 1976), ch. 4.

3. A. P. Hare, *Handbook of Small Group Research* (New York: Free Press, 1962), pp. 24–25.

4. S. Schachter, N. Ellertson, D. McBridge, and D. Gregory, "An Experimental Study of Cohesiveness and Productivity," *Human Relations* (Fall 1951), pp. 229–38.

5. G. C. Homans, *The Human Group* (New York: Harcourt, Brace and Company, 1950).

6. G. C. Homans, *The Human Group*, pp. 25–40, 90–107, 108–13, 118–19.

7. For a classic explanation of this, see George Homans, *Fatigue of workers: It's relation to Industrial Production* (New York: Rineholt, 1941), pp. 77–86.

8. Rensis Likert, *New Patterns of Management.*

9. See, for example, P. B. Indik, "Organization Size and Member Participation: Some Empirical Tests of Alternatives," *Human Relations* 18 (1965), pp. 339–50.

10. Shaw, *Group Dynamics*, pp. 156–57.

11. I. P. Steiner, *Group Process and Productivity* (New York: Academic Press, 1972).

12. See, for example, N. R. F. Maier, *Psychology in Industrial Organizations* (Boston: Houghton Mifflin, 1973), pp. 610–39.

13. J. W. O'Dell, "Group Size and Emotional Interaction," *Journal of Personality and Social Psychology*, 8 (1968), pp. 75–78.

14. Robert Blake and Jane Mouton, "Reactions to Intergroup Competition under Win-Lose Conditions," *Management Science*, 7 (1961), p. 432.

15. As one example, a study carried out by a consulting firm some years ago found that five vice-presidents in an insurance firm were each spending 26 hours per month—exclusive of preparation time—in committee meetings, and from other studies this seems to be more the rule than the exception. Charles T. McCormick, *The Power of People* (New York: Harper and Row, 1949), p. 18.

16. See, for example, A. Van de Ven and A. L. Delbecq, "Nominal vs. Interacting Group Processes for Committee Decision Making Effectiveness," *Academy of Management Journal*, 14 (1971), pp. 203–12.

17. See, for example, Warren Street, "Brainstorming by Individuals, Coacting and Interacting Groups," *Journal of Applied Psychology*, 59, No. 4 (1974), pp. 433–36; L. R. Hoffman and Norman R. F. Maier, "Quality and Acceptance of Problem Solutions by Members of Homogeneous and Heterogeneous Groups," *Journal of Abnormal and Social Psychology*, 62 (1961), pp. 401–07.

18. This is based on Norman R. F. Maier, "Assets and Liabilities in Group Problem Solving: The Need for an Integrative Function," *Psychological Bulletin*, 74, No. 4 (July 1967), pp. 239–49.

19. See, for example, Russell D. Clark III, "Group-Induced Shift toward Risk: A critical Appraisal," *Psychological Bulletin*, 76, No. 4 (1971), pp. 251–70.

20. Maier, *Psychology*, pp. 610–39.

21. See Maier, *Psychology*, p. 621.

22. See R. F. Maier and E. P. McRay, "Increasing Innovation in Change Situations through Leadership Skills," *Psychological Report*, 31 (1972), pp. 30–43, 354.

11 *Intergroup Relations and Performance: Managing Organizational Conflict*

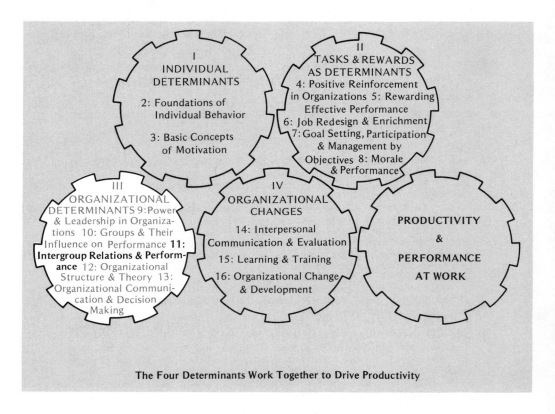

The Four Determinants Work Together to Drive Productivity

BY THE TIME YOU FINISH STUDYING THIS CHAPTER, YOU SHOULD BE ABLE TO:

1. *Explain the pros and cons of conflict.*

2. *Answer the question: "Do you have an abrasive personality?"*

3. *Cite the causes of line-staff conflict.*

4. *Describe the causes of intergroup conflict.*

5. *Present a model of organizational conflict.*

6. *More effectively manage organizational conflicts.*

OVERVIEW

The main purpose of this chapter is to explain how to manage intergroup conflicts—between the sales and production departments, for example, or the nursing and purchasing departments. These types of conflicts can seriously reduce employees' performance, by causing them to divert their efforts from their jobs to inter unit squabbling, maneuvering, and hiding of information. We first discuss different types of conflict and the causes of intergroup conflict, noting that four factors create most of the problems: interdependencies, differences in goals, authority imbalances, and ambiguities. We then discuss a model of conflict that explains the emergence of intergroup conflict as a predictable sequence of stages. Next we describe how to use three types of techniques for managing organizational conflict: setting superordinate goals, modifying the structure of the organization, and using conflict resolution behaviors like confrontation meetings. Finally, we explain how intergroup conflicts can be better managed by analyzing their antecedents, behavior, and consequences.

INTRODUCTION

Conflict is a familiar characteristic of organizational life. One fundamental cause is the self-interest of individuals in the organization, a self-interest that often manifests itself in competing objectives, philosophies, or methods, and in associated struggles of one or more levels or departments to dominate others. Conflict may be interpersonal in nature and emerge out of the visceral, apparently "irrational" and selfish desires of some individuals to have their own way. Some people seem to be characterized by such tendencies and seem predisposed to aggression and a tendency to respond to threatening or frustrating situations with anger and abrasiveness. We will touch on this sort of conflict, but in most of this chapter we are especially concerned with *intergroup* conflict, conflict that stems from the structure of the organization and that results in differences in objectives, goals, and so forth between departments, divisions, or other units in the organization.

TYPES OF CONFLICT

Pros and Cons of Conflict

Anyone who has ever worked in an organization is aware that conflict exists and that it can have an extremely dysfunctional effect on the organization and the people that comprise it. Opposing parties tend to put their own aims above those of the organization, and the organization's effectiveness suffers as the antecedents or standards that *should* be guiding performance become superseded by those of the opposing groups. Time that could have been used productively is wasted as the opposing parties hide valuable information from each other and jockey for position, each thereby preventing the other from carrying out its assigned tasks; and those involved in the conflict can become so personally enwrapped in the tensions it produces that, left unbridled, it can drastically undermine their emotional and physical well-being. Perhaps the most insidious effect of organizational conflict is that it doesn't remain organization-bound for long: instead its effects are observed by customers and stockholders and are taken home by the opponents whose innocent families are often caught in the fallout.

Despite its adverse effects, most experts today view conflict as a potentially useful aspect of organizations since it can, if properly channeled, be an engine of innovation and change. According to Robbins the idea that conflicts are inherently destructive has been replaced with what he calls the "interactionists'" view. This view recognizes the necessity of conflict and explicitly encourages a certain amount of controlled conflict in organizations. The basic case for this view is that some conflict is necessary if an organization is to avoid stagnation and myopic decision making, and an example often cited is a paper by Janis called "Group-Think." In this paper, Janis describes how potential critics of the abortive Bay of Pigs invasion in Cuba were put under tremendous pressure not to express their opposing viewpoints. For example, then Attorney General Robert Kennedy at one point took Arthur Schlesinger aside and asked him why he was opposed to the invasion. According to Janis, Kennedy listened coldly and then said, "You may be right or you may be wrong, but the President has made his mind up. Don't push it any further. Now is the time for everyone to help him all they can."[1]

Janis feels that if Kennedy and his staff had encouraged the expression of more criticism, many of their questionable assumptions would have been challenged and much better decisions would have resulted. As Robbins puts it:

> Constructive conflict is both valuable and necessary. Without conflict, there would be few new challenges; there would be no stimulation to think through ideas; organizations would be only apathetic and stagnant.[2]

This generally positive picture of conflict appears to be supported by surveys of current management practice. In one recent survey of top and middle managers, for example, managers rated "conflict management" as of equal (or slightly higher) importance than topics like planning, communication, motivation, and decision making. The managers spent about 20 percent of their time on conflicts; yet they did not consider the conflict level in their organization to be excessive. Instead, they rated it as about right—that is, at the midpoint of a scale running from "too low" to "too high."[3]

Individual, Personal, and Organizational Conflict

At least three different kinds of conflict can be identified in organizations. "Role conflict" is a familiar example of conflict within the *individual*. Role conflict occurs when a person is faced with conflicting orders, such that compliance with one would make it difficult or impossible to comply with the other. Sometimes role conflict arises out of obviously conflicting orders, as when a corporal receives orders from a captain that would force him to disobey an order from his sergeant. Sometimes, however the source of the role conflict is not quite so obvious, as when obeying an order might force a person to violate his own cherished values and sense of right and wrong. In any case, role conflict is a serious problem in organizations, one that can be stressful to the persons involved, and one that can adversely affect their morale and performance.[4]

Conflicts in organizations can also be *interpersonal* and occur between individuals, or between individuals and groups. Sometimes, of course such conflicts arise from "legitimate" sources, as when there are real differences in goals or objectives between the parties involved. Often, however interpersonal conflicts arise not from legitimate differences, but as a result of the "personalities" involved. Some people are simply more aggressive and conflict prone than others, for example, and others are so hypersensitive that every comment is viewed as an insult. For example, Levinson says that some people have "abrasive personalities" and that these people seem to have "a natural knack for jabbing others in an irritating and sometimes painful way."[5] He says that people like this are often very bright and highly motivated but that their abrasiveness eventually so reduces their ability to work with others that their effectiveness is seriously impaired.

Finally, there are *intergroup* organizational conflicts, conflicts, for example, between line and staff units, or between production and sales departments. We will focus on the causes and management of intergroup conflicts in the remainder of this chapter.

Conflict Between Line and Staff (Advisory) Units

Most writers distinguish between managers who are *line* and those who are *staff* managers in an organization. Line managers are authorized to direct the work of subordinates—they are always someone's boss—and, in addition, they are in charge of accomplishing the basic goals of the organization. (Production managers and sales managers are almost always line managers, for example.) Staff managers, on the other hand, are authorized to *assist and advise* line managers in accomplishing these basic goals. These ideas are illustrated in Exhibit 11.1. Here (as is usually the case) the personnel manager is a *staff* manager. He or she is responsible for advising line managers (like those for production and marketing) in areas like recruiting, hiring, and compensation. The managers for production and marketing are *line* managers. They have direct responsibility for accomplishing the basic goals of the organization. They also have the authority to direct the work of various subordinates.

Exhibit 11.1 Line and Staff Authority

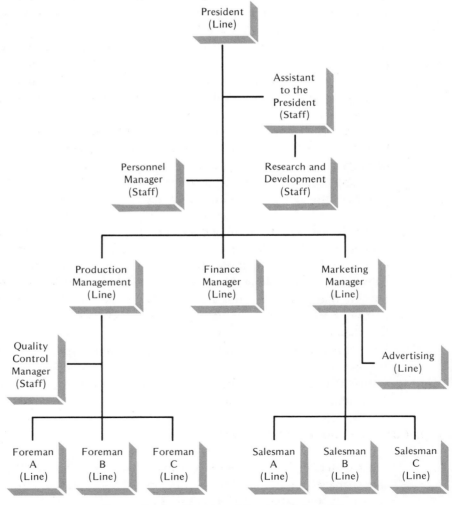

Source: Dessler, *Management Fundamentals*, p. 111

Line and staff managers are usually highly interdependent, since they each need each other for carrying out their tasks. For example, the sales manager needs the personnel manager when it comes to recruiting and testing salesmen, and the personnel manager cannot do his job unless people like the sales manager are willing to accept his help and advice.

The existence of these two kinds of managers, each of whom is dependent on and must work with the other, is a frequent source of "line-staff" conflict in organizations, and there are several reasons for this:[7]

1. Staff personnel tend to be *younger*, more educated, of a higher social status class, and more ambitious and restless than line managers.
2. The older, more experienced line managers tend to dislike having to take advice from younger staff managers. They fear being "shown up."
3. Line managers tend to view staff as *agents on trial* and as people who must constantly prove themselves. The staff person, on the other hand, views himself as an expert.
4. Line managers frequently feel that staff is *encroaching* on their duties and prerogatives, and that the creation of a staff unit tends to diminish the line manager's authority.
5. Line managers also complain that staff does not give sound advice, *steals credit*, and fails to see the "whole picture."
6. Staff managers, on the other hand, feel that line managers are "bull-headed," don't give staff enough authority, and resist new ideas.

With such differences in points of view, it is no wonder that the line-staff structure is often a source of tension, bickering, and conflict. On the one hand, these are managers that necessarily have to work together to achieve their own aims and those of the organization. On the other hand, there are often a number of real or imagined differences between line and staff managers, and the net result is often that the staff managers are made to feel like "second class citizens."

One of the symptoms of line-staff conflict may be the lower levels of satisfaction generally found among staff managers. Three studies by the Opinion Research Corporation reported that engineers and scientists in staff positions were less satisfied with their jobs than were engineers and scientists in line positions.[8] Another study surveyed almost 2,000 managers and found that although staff vice-presidents were about as satisfied as line vice-presidents, line managers below the vice-presidential level were consistently more satisfied than staff managers.[9] Similarly, another researcher found that staff managers in the three plants he studied had a turnover rate between two and four times that of line managers.[10]

Reducing or managing conflict between line and staff managers is therefore a serious problem. Generally speaking, many of the conflict-management techniques we discuss toward the end of this chapter (techniques like establishing common or "superordinate" goals that both the line and staff managers can agree on) can be useful in managing line-staff conflicts, as well as other types of intergroup conflicts. However, there are also some specific things one can do to reduce line-staff conflict.

Ask Do You Really Need the Staff? You usually need a fairly high volume of business to support staff personnel. This is because staff provides specialized assistance and advice but is otherwise "nonproductive"—it must be supported by the volume generated by line managers. Thus, for a staff person to be viewed as helpful there must be a sufficient volume of business so that the expert assistance and advice of the staff manager is justified. For example, if the sales manager hires only two or three salesmen per year and has no basic need for the specialized recruiting and hiring assistance of a separate personnel manager, it stands to reason that he will be more skeptical about the personnel manager's contribution than if he had to hire 30 or 40 salesmen per year and found the job too time-consuming.

Make Job Assignments Clear. It is also important to avoid the sorts of "power vacuums" that often occur when job assignments are not clear, and when authority is "up for grabs." Remember that the staff person usually ends up doing some of the tasks formerly assigned to the line manager. And unless it is made very clear where staff's authority ends and line's begins, the stage is set for conflict and "power plays."

Beware of the Staff "Gatekeeper." Try to avoid ending up with a staff person who plays "gatekeeper" to you or to others. If it is the plant's personnel manager, for example, make sure he knows that he is supposed to try working out "personnel" problems with the foreman before running to the plant manager. Or, if it is your own "assistant-to" make sure he or she does not end up as an impenetrable barrier between you and your other subordinates.

WHAT ARE THE CAUSES OF INTERGROUP CONFLICT?

Many factors contribute to the conflicts that often emerge between different departments and groups in organizations. In one recent study, for example, the researchers listed the following sources of conflict:

> Misunderstanding (communication failure)
> Personality clashes

Value and goal differences
Substandard performance
Differences over method
Responsibility issues
Lack of cooperation
Authority issues
Frustration and irritability
Competition for limited resources
Noncompliance with rules and policies[11]

But although there are obviously many sources of intergroup conflict, research findings suggest that four factors create most of the problems: interdependencies and shared resources; intergroup differences in goals, values, or perceptions; authority imbalances; and ambiguities.

Interdependencies and Shared Resources

Groups (or individuals) who work interdependently, or who are required to compete for scarce resources may eventually come into conflict. Conversely, groups that do not have to depend on each other, or compete for scarce resources, will generally not get involved in intergroup conflicts.[12]

Examples of how interdependence or competition for scarce resources lead to conflict abound. For example conflicts are a way of life for members of quality control and production departments, and sales and production departments, departments which depend on each other and which are interdependent. On the other hand, intergroup conflict is less likely to occur between, say, the finance and quality control departments, since the people in these departments are not too interdependent. Similarly, competition for scarce resources—such as when two or more departments must compete for limited funds, or for the services of a typing pool—generally leads to "office politics," hiding of information, and conflict.

Of course interdependence does not have to *necessarily* lead to intergroup conflicts—just the opposite. If the situation is managed correctly, or if the groups' overall aims are similar, interdependence can provide an incentive for collaboration rather than conflict; this is one reason why the conflict management techniques we discuss later in this chapter are important.[13]

Intergroup Differences in Goals, Values, or Perceptions

Persons who are in agreement in terms of their goals, values, or perceptions are less likely to find themselves arguing than are those with fundamental differences.

Differences in Goals. Differences in goals are a familiar source of intergroup conflict. Walton and Dutton, for example, have found that the preference of production departments for long, economical runs conflicted with the preference of sales units for quick delivery for good customers, and that these differing goals often led to intergroup conflict.[14] Other fundamental differences in goals that have been found to lead to intergroup conflicts include an emphasis on flexibility versus stability, on short-run versus long-run performance, measurable versus intangible results, and on organizational goals versus societal needs.[15] In summary, when the goals of two groups are similar or identical, there is little chance of serious conflict arising; but when there *is* a fundamental difference in goals conflicts will likely arise.

Differences in Values and Perceptions. Similarly, when two groups differ in terms of their values or how they perceive a situation, conflicts are more likely to arise. One good example of this are the sorts of differences that lead to line-staff conflicts, differences which we listed above. For example, staff personnel tend to be younger and of a higher social status class than line managers. Line managers tend to view staff managers as agents on trial, while the staff people view themselves as proven experts.

Organizational Differentiation. Lawrence and Lorsch say that what they call "organizational differentiation" is a frequent source of intergroup conflict.[16] Basically, they found that as each department in an organization tries to cope with the unique demands of its own environment, it necessarily develops its own types of procedures, cherished values, and point of view. For example, a research department in a chemical firm might be run very democratically, and its personnel might develop a rather long-term time perspective since most of the things they are working on will not reach fruition for years. On the other hand, the production department might be run more autocratically, and its managers might be expected to put a much greater emphasis on immediate results. Lawrence and Lorsch believe that the greater the differentiation between departments, the more *potential* for conflict there it. However they found that whether conflict in fact emerges depends on several things, including how departments settle their differences.

Authority Imbalances

We also know that when a department's actual authority is inconsistent with its prestige, intergroup conflicts are more likely to develop. Seiler diagnosed interdepartmental conflicts in several firms, and his findings are summarized in Exhibit 11.2. He concluded that intergroup conflicts arise either because points of view are in conflict (the "differences in goals, values, and perceptions" problem we discussed above) or because a department's authority is inconsistent with its prestige. As an example of the latter, Seiler found that in one company, the production department had to accept instructions from a production engineering department composed of men with skills no greater than (and in fact quite similar to) those possessed by production employees. As a result, "production managers spent an inordinate amount of time checking for consistency among the various items produced by production engineering."[17]

Exhibit 11.2 Summary of Seiler's Findings on Organizational Conflict

	Where Points of View Are Closely Allied	*Where Points of View Are in Conflict*
Where authority* is consistent with prestige differences	We will tend to find . . . . . . collaboration and productive conflict	We will tend to find . . . . . . Energies absorbed by efforts to force points of view on other groups. Relations will be formal and often arbitrated by outsiders.
Where authority is inconsistent with prestige differences	We will tend to find . . . . . . Energies devoted to regaining a "proper" authority relationship. Relations will usually be distant and between low hierarchical levels of the two groups (e.g. messengers).	We will tend to find . . . . . . Energies initially expended on forcing points of view and righting authority relations. But the task will be so patently fruitless that the groups will break off contact rather than expose themselves to further threat.

*As indicated by work flow.

Source: John A. Seller, "Diagnosing Interdepartmental Conflict," *Harvard Business Review*, September-October, 1963, pp. 121–32.

Ambiguity

Finally, difficulty in assigning credit or blame between two departments increases the likelihood of conflict between units. For example, if both the quality control and production departments can claim credit for the cost savings resulting from a change in production procedures, a conflict may well result. Similarly, if it is difficult to place the blame for a problem, conflicts will emerge as departments attempt to shed themselves of the blame, for, say, a cost overrun or machine breakdown. Conflict is also a familiar phenomenon in organizations where departmental responsibilities are not clearly delineated, and where "power vacuums" arise and intergroup conflicts ensue as each department fights to fill those vacuums by taking on increased responsibilities.

A MODEL OF ORGANIZATIONAL CONFLICT

What is the process through which organizational conflicts arise? Do conflicts between departments go through a predictable sequence of stages? We address these questions next.

Experts in intergroup conflict have developed a number of models to explain and describe the emergence and process of intergroup conflict. A full explanation of all of these models is beyond the scope of this book, but it will be useful to review at least one of these models since it can help to put into perspective the process through which intergroup conflicts emerge.

Lewis Pondy has developed a model that assumes that intergroup conflict is a sequence of interlocking "conflict episodes."[18] He says that whether the conflict involves groups at different levels in the organization, or groups at the same level there are usually five fairly distinct stages through which the conflict evolves.

Stage I: The Latent Conflict Stage

Pondy says that each episode of conflict usually begins with a "latent conflict" stage. At this stage the basic prerequisites (such as competition for scarce resources, or differences in goals between departments) are present, but the conflict has not yet emerged.

Stage II: The Perceived Conflict Stage

For one thing, whether or not these prerequisites (like differences in goals) lead to conflict depends on the *perceptions* of the people involved. Prerequisites of conflict like mutual dependence are always present to some degree between departments, but it is only when the differences are seen as significant that they lead to conflict. For example, if two departments have to share a water cooler, conflicts would probably not likely arise even if the sharing caused some waiting. On the other hand, if the departments had to share a typing pool, and reports were often late because of it, there would probably be more likelihood of conflicts emerging as each department tried to get its work typed first.

Conversely, conflict may be *perceived* even though the basic conditions of conflict—what Pondy calls latent conflict—do not exist. One familiar example of this occurs when there is a "communications breakdown" or misunderstanding between groups with respect to each other's true position. Here basic sources of conflict like competition for scarce resources and differences in goals do not actually exist. However due to misunderstandings group members misperceive the true positions of the members of the other group and so conflicts may arise.

Stage III: The Felt Conflict Stage

The next stage that most conflicts go through may be called the "felt conflict" stage. Pondy says that even though people perceive that there is a basis for conflict, conflicts will usually not arise unless the differences become personalized or internalized ("felt"). In other words, Pondy argues that for conflicts to emerge the people in each group usually have to become "ego involved" in a conflict relationship, in that each of them becomes so intent on "winning" that the best interests of the organization are forgotten. Often what results is literally a feud in which the people in each department identify so completely with the goals and values of their own groups that they view each and every action of the competing group personally. Like the hillbilly feuds of some years ago the members of each group may continue trying to "pick off" the opposing group's projects and people, although to an outsider the conflict seems baseless and irrational.

Stage IV: The Manifest Conflict Stage

The next stage, according to Pondy, is characterized by open conflict. Open, violent aggression is the most extreme example of such behavior, but would be unusual in work organizations. However, the motivation driving such aggression may remain, and may manifest itself in sabotage, defensive coalitions, apathy, or rigid, blind adherence to rules, all of which, of course, reduce the organization's effectiveness.[19]

Stage V: Conflict Aftermath

Assuming that the conflict does manifest itself, how it is managed and resolved has important implications for whether it results in a more cooperative relationship, or in continued aggravation and conflict. Pondy says (and many experts would agree) that if the conflict is confronted and resolved to the satisfaction of all participants, the basis for a more cooperative relationship may be laid. On the other hand, "if the conflict is merely suppressed but not resolved, the latent conditions of conflict may be aggravated and explode in more serious forms until they are rectified or until the relationship dissolves."[20]

This legacy of conflict, a legacy that may be either a force for cooperation or continued conflict, is what Pondy calls "conflict aftermath." In summary, the aftermath of conflict may be either positive or negative for the organization, depending on how the conflict is confronted and resolved. With this in mind, we turn to a discussion of techniques for managing organizational conflict.

TECHNIQUES FOR MANAGING ORGANIZATIONAL CONFLICT

There are many techniques for managing or resolving conflicts but they generally fall into one of three categories. The first involves establishing *superordinate goals* and thus creating an area of commonality between the previously competing groups—for example by convincing each that they share a common enemy. Second, there are various *structural approaches* that involve, for example, reducing the interdependencies between the competing groups or referring the disagreement to a common superior. Finally, different *conflict resolution behaviors* can be used: these include behaviors like avoiding the problem, confronting the problem, or negotiating a solution.

Using Common Goals to Manage Conflicts

One of the most familiar and sensible ways of short-circuiting conflicts is to find some common ground that the parties can agree on. In labor-management negotiations, for example, arbitrators generally begin their work by finding some point that both sides can agree on, and then build a solution from that one point of agreement. As another example, national leaders often use the ploy of claiming that their countries are about to be attacked to bring about (at least) a temporary unification of the opposing factions in their own countries.

Sherif carried out a classic series of experiments in intergroup conflict using groups of boys in a summer camp some years ago, and his findings help illustrate the usefulness of superordinate goals.[21] His basic hypothesis was that "when two groups have conflicting aims—i.e., when one can achieve its end only at the expense of the other—their members will become hostile to each other even though the groups are composed of normal, well-adjusted individuals."[22] To test this hypothesis his research team produced friction between the groups of boys by arranging a tournament of games including baseball, touch football, a tug-of-war, and a treasure hunt. They found that the tournament started in a spirit of good sportsmanship but that as it progressed the good feelings soon evaporated. *Between* the groups, members began calling their rivals "snakes" and "cheaters." They refused to have anything to do with individuals in the opposing group, and boys often turned against buddies they had chosen as "best friends" when they first arrived at camp. The rival groups made threatening posters and planned raids against each other. Name calling, scuffles, and raids were the rule of the day.

Within each group solidarity increased, and there were other important changes. One group deposed its leader because he could not "take it" in the contest with the adversary. Another group made something of a hero of a big boy who had previously been regarded as a bully. Generally speaking, morale and cooperativeness within each group became stronger.

Sherif and his associates then set about creating a series of "urgent and natural" situations, which would face the competing groups with the need to work together to accomplish superordinate, common goals. In one case the researchers rigged a breakdown in the water supply to the camp. (Water normally came to the camp in pipes from a tank about a mile away.) The researchers arranged to interrupt the water flow, and then called the boys together to tell them of the crisis. Both of these initially hostile groups promptly volunteered to search the waterline for the trouble. According to the researchers, both groups worked together harmoniously, and before the end of the afternoon had located and corrected the difficulty. On another occasion the two groups were taken on an outing some distance from the camp. A truck was to go to town for food, but when everyone was hungry and ready to eat, the truck would not start—a situation that had been conveniently arranged by the researchers. The two groups of boys (who had previously been hostile to one another) got a rope, and all pulled together to start the truck. As a result of these joint efforts the bickering and name calling between the two groups diminished, new friendships developed between individuals in the two groups, and in the end the groups were actually seeking opportunities to mingle, to entertain, and "treat" each other.[23] Therefore,

> what our limited experiments have shown is that the possibilities for achieving harmony are greatly enhanced when groups are brought together to work toward common ends. Then favorable information about a disliked group is seen in a new light, and leaders are in a position to take bolder steps toward cooperation. In short, hostility gives way when groups pull together to achieve overriding goals which are real and compelling to all concerned.[24]

Using Reward Systems. An organization's reward system can either breed a "win-lose" mentality in the organization, or can help ensure that different departments work together to accomplish a goal that they share.

The Sears Roebuck Company recently revised the method used in rewarding store managers and the change is a good example of the use of reward systems to reduce intergroup conflict. For years Sears store managers were rewarded based on the sales of their own stores. In recent years it became apparent that this reward system was breeding conflictful behavior on the part of store managers. For example, managers in the same geographical area were generally not inclined to advertise area-wide sales, and they resisted transferring merchandise from store to store. Under the new reward system, store managers are rewarded, not only on the basis of sales of their own store, but on the sales of all Sears stores in their area, and this has resulted in a marked increased in collaborative behavior on the part of store managers.

In Sum: Common Goals and the "ABC s". Analyzing our "ABCs" of behavior can help ensure that common goals exist and it can thereby assist in analyzing the sources—and cure for a conflict. Thus, suppose you find that two groups in your organization are in conflict, and want to determine the cause of this behavior, and how to change it.

Focusing on *antecedents* by asking, for example, "Do the groups know what is expected of them?" and "Do they know that their goals are compatible?" can be useful because two groups that share the same ultimate goals (as did Sherif's groups) ultimately have fewer conflicts. Related to this, it is useful to ask (when faced with conflicting groups), "What are the *consequences of* cooperating?" Often (as in the Sears example), intergroup cooperation is actually discouraged by the reward system. On the other hand, rewarding both groups based on their joint accomplishment can go far towards eliminating intergroup conflicts.

Structural Approaches to Conflict Management

One can also use various *structural* approaches to managing and resolving intergroup conflicts, for example, by having the groups appeal to a common superior.[25]

Appeal to a Common Superior. The most common way of resolving disagreements between departments is still to refer the disagreements to a common superior. For example, if the vice-presidents for sales and production cannot reach agreement on some point, they would typically refer their disagreement to the president for a final, binding decision.

Stagner has made a study of how executives in major corporations typically resolve their conflicts. First, he found that conflicts were usually *not* resolved on the basis of logical arguments concerning profitability and so on, although the arguments were often couched in economic terms. Instead, most conflicts were resolved by resorting to power, power that was based on things like ability to provide rewards. Thus, the opponent that had the most "clout" was typically the one that prevailed. Second, Stagner found the power of the chief executive to be the most widely used arbiter of disagreements. In some cases the chief executive simply resolved the conflict through decree, while in other cases he acted as a mediator, or arbitrator. As an alternative, some corporations let the executive vice-president arbitrate the conflict: this left open the possibility of appealing the decision to the president if necessary. While Stagner's study focused on the actions of executives, one would assume that the same general approach would work at lower levels in the organization. For example, if the managers for quality control and production disagree, referring the disagreement to the plant manager for a decision would probably be a logical step.[26]

Reduce Interdependencies and Shared Resources. Remember that it is generally only when two groups must depend on each other, or share scarce resources that intergroup conflicts arise. It seems logical, therefore that one way to reduce the potential for conflict is to reduce the interdependencies or the need to compete for scarce resources. Sometimes the changes here are as simple as just separating the units physically so that the members of each group no longer have to confront each other each day.[27] Another change is to increase the available resources so that *both* groups can get basically what they want. Sometimes the conflicting groups can be separated *organizationally* so that they no longer need to depend on each other. In fact this is one of the advantages of the "profit-center" approach to organization that many companies like General Motors have set up. Each division or profit center is basically a self-contained company with its own sales, manufacturing, and personnel employees, and the head of each division thus is not forced to go outside of his own group for the resources needed to run his business.

Create Special "Integrators." Lawrence and Lorsch, in the study we mentioned above, found that many companies have reduced interdepartmental conflict by setting up special liaisons between the conflicting departments. In the high-technology plastics industry, for example, successful companies set up special departments whose job it was to coordinate the work of the research, sales, and manufacturing departments. In the food industry (where technical changes were not as frequent), *individuals* were assigned the task of coordinating the work of the separate departments. On the other hand, in some industries, such as the container industry, where technical changes are few, special liaisons were not necessary at all; conflicts were ironed out by referring them up to a common superior.

Interpersonal Conflict Resolution Techniques: (How Do We Settle the Argument?)

There are different ways of settling an argument, and some are much better than others. For example, having both parties meet to *confront* the facts and hammer out a solution is usually more effective than simply *smoothing* over the conflict by "pushing the problems under a rug."

Lawrence and Lorsch in their study of conflict resolution found that managers used either *confrontation, smoothing,* or *forcing* to resolve conflicts. They present the following as actual examples of each:

> *Confrontation.* "In recent meetings we have had a thrashing around about manpower needs. At first we did not have much agreement, but we kept thrashing around and finally agreed on what was the best we could do."
>
> *Smoothing.* "I thought I went to real lengths in our group to cause conflict. I said what I thought in the meeting, but it did not bother anybody. I guess I should have been harsher. I could have said I won't do it unless you do it my way. If I had done this, they couldn't have backed away, but I guess I didn't have the guts to do it. I guess my reaction was—well, I made a fool of myself in the meeting and nothing happened so I'll sit back and feel real comfortable. I guess I didn't pound the bushes hard enough."
>
> *Forcing.* "If I want something very badly and I am confronted by a roadblock, I go to top management to get the decision made. If the research managers are willing to go ahead (my way), there is no problem. If there is a conflict, then I take the decision to somebody higher up."[28]

Of these methods, a confrontation approach often gets the best results, especially when the conflict involves major issues like salaries and promotions.[29] In other words, when it comes to important issues, it seems that the wisest strategy is to confront the issues head-on and hammer out an agreement. On the other hand, smoothing over problems seems to work well enough for relatively minor issues, although for major ones it has insidious effects on the organization. Managers who are prone to smoothing over problems (by not taking definite stands and trying to "laugh off" disagreements) eventually find that the cumulative effect of their mismanagement is an explosive situation they can no longer control.

The Confrontation Meeting. Some organizations have used a technique called *the confrontation meeting* to "clear the air" and resolve intergroup conflicts.[30] The technique usually requires the use of a special outside consultant (sometimes called a "change agent") who is skilled in its use. Confrontation meetings seem to be especially useful when misperceptions are at the root of the intergroup conflict, such as when each group misperceives or misunderstands the opposing group's true position. The typical confrontation meeting lasts from four to eight hours and usually begins with the consultant discussing in general terms such topics as organizational communication, the need for mutual understanding, and the need for members of the management team to share responsibility for accomplishing the organization's goals. In such a meeting, the discussion might turn to an analysis of the organization's operating problems, including how advertising budgets are arrived at, how sales commissions are computed, and how financial controls are imposed. On the other hand, some types of confrontation meetings focus exclusively on human relations problems like conflict between line and staff personnel.

Bennis describes a confrontation meeting that was supposed to deal with an intergroup conflict. The meeting took place during a State Department conference held at the Massachusetts Institute of Technology and involved conflict between the foreign service officers and the administrative staff of the State Department. The problem was that the stereotyping and mutual distrust, if not downright hostility, blocked communication and reduced effectiveness enormously, for each "side" perceived the other as more threatening than any realistic overseas enemy.

The two groups of officers were assigned to separate rooms and were asked to discuss three questions:

1. What qualities best describe our group?
2. What qualities best describe the other group?
3. What qualities do we predict the other group would assign to us?

Each group was asked to develop a list of words or phrases that they felt best described their answers to each question. The results were as follows:[31]

The Foreign Service officers saw themselves as being:

1. Reflective
2. Qualitative
3. Humanistic, subjective
4. Cultural, with broad interests
5. Generalizers
6. Interculturally sensitive
7. Detached from personal conflicts

The Foreign Service officers saw administrative officers as being or having:

1. Doers and implementers
2. Quantitive
3. Decisive and forceful
4. Noncultural

5. Limited goals
6. Jealous of us
7. Interested in form more than substance
8. Wave of the future! [exclamation mark theirs]
9. Drones but necessary evils

The Foreign Service officers predicted that the administrative officers would see them as being:

1. Arrogant, snobbish
2. Intellectuals
3. Cliquish
4. Resistant to change
5. Inefficient, dysfunctional
6. Vacillating and compromising
7. Effete

The administrative officers saw themselves as being or having:

1. Decisive, guts
2. Resourceful, adaptive
3. Pragmatic
4. Service oriented
5. Able to get along
6. Receptive to change
7. Dedicated to job
8. Misunderstood
9. Useful
10. Modest! [added by the person doing the presenting]

The administrative officers saw the Foreign Service officers as being:

1. Masked, isolated
2. Resourceful, serious
3. Respected
4. Inclined to stability
5. Dedicated to job
6. Necessary
7. Externally oriented
8. Cautious
9. Rational
10. Surrounded by mystique
11. Manipulative
12. Defensive

The administrative officers predicted that the Foreign Service officers would see them as being or having:

1. Necessary evils
2. Defensive, inflexible
3. Preoccupied with minutiae
4. Negative and bureaucratic
5. Limited perspective
6. Less culture (educated clerks)
7. Misunderstood
8. Practical
9. Protected
10. Resourceful

The two groups of officers then assembled together and proceeded to discuss their own lists as well as those developed by the other group. They questioned each other about the lists, and after several hours "it appeared as if each side moved to a position where they at least understood the other side's point of view."

Improving Interpersonal Relations. Last, but not least, remember that conflicts are highly personal in nature, and so their resolution always calls for all the interpersonal and "human relations skills" a manager can bring to bear. While the basic *causes* of a conflict may not be "personal" in nature, more often than not for the conflict to get out of hand—for the basic prerequisites like mutual dependence, and differences in goals to manifest themselves in conflict—there have to be heavy doses of miscommunication, misunderstanding, abrasiveness, and clashes of personalities.

It therefore stands to reason that managing conflict involves more than setting common goals, reorganizing, or holding confrontation meetings. Instead, working out disagreements and seeing that conflicts are a positive, not a negative, force in your organization requires all the skill that you can muster, and an application of the concepts and techniques covered in almost all the chapters in this book. It will involve, for example "active listening" (see Chapter 14): here your main objective is to get "inside" the person you are listening to—to grasp the feelings and real meaning behind what he is saying from his point of view. And, it involves understanding that each person has a need to be made to feel that he or she is a unique and valuable individual, one that has earned your respect and support. In summary, remember that somewhere along the line most conflicts become *personal* and that their origin, management, and resolution therefore depends largely on one's "human relations" skills.

Summary: Conflict Management and the "ABC s" of Performance

Intergroup conflict can be viewed as a special type of (intergroup) performance problem, and it's cause can be analyzed with our "ABCs" of performance. For example, if faced with conflicting groups, one can ask:

> *Antecedents.* Do the groups know that the conflict exists and what
> effects it is having on their performance? Do they know that manage-
> ment expects them to cease conflicting, and instead work together
> cooperatively? Do the groups share important goals? Do they know
> that management expects them to *confront* problems as they arise?
>
> *Behavior.* Could the groups settle their problems if they wanted to?
> Is the boss they share willing to make hard decisions and act as arbi-
> trator, settling the disagreements?
>
> *Consequences.* What are the consequences of cooperating? Are they
> rewarded based on their joint efforts? Does one group lose if the other
> gains?

CHAPTER SUMMARY

1. Despite the fact that it can have adverse effects, more experts today view
conflict as a potentially useful aspect of organizations since it can, if properly
channeled, be an engine of innovation and change.

2. Conflict between line and staff units is a special example of intergroup conflict in organizations. As with any type of intergroup conflict, it arises between
interdependent groups who have important differences in values and goals.

3. Many factors contribute to the conflicts that often emerge between different
departments and groups in organizations, but four factors create most of the
problems: interdependencies and shared resources; intergroup differences in goals,
values, or perceptions; authority imbalances; and ambiguities.

4. Pondy presents a model that assumes that intergroup conflict is a sequence of
interlocking "conflict episodes" ranging from "latent conflict" to "conflict aftermath." Pondy's model emphasizes that conflict may be perceived even though
the basic conditions of conflict do not exist and, conversely, that the basic conditions for conflict may exist but the parties may not perceive them as the bases
for conflict. This is one reason why the confrontation meeting is often useful
for managing conflicts, since in these meetings each group has a chance to clarify
how the other group actually views it.

5. We discussed three categories of techniques for managing organizational conflicts: establishing superordinate goals, structural approaches, and using different
conflict resolution behaviors.

DISCUSSION QUESTIONS AND PROJECTS

1. Explain the pros and cons of conflict. Do you think it is true that a certain amount of controlled conflict in an organization is healthy? Why? Why not?

2. What are the main sources of intergroup conflicts? Has any student in the class experienced a situation in which intergroup conflicts emerged? In retrospect, could they be explained in terms of interdependencies, intergroup differences, authority imbalances, and/or ambiguity?

3. Assume that you have identified a performance problem between two groups and that you want to rectify it. For example, suppose you are the vice-president of your company and want to stop the arguing and backbiting that has been going on between your sales staff and production staff. In other words, you want to *change the behavior of the groups* and get them to work together cooperatively. Explain what questions you would ask in analyzing the "ABCs" of performance in this case and suggest some ways in which you would manage the conflict.

CASE EXERCISE

Chaos at Prebuilt

The Prebuilt Company was founded 20 years ago by William Ross, and originally manufactured a patented construction panel consisting of a honeycomb core to which two steel faces were laminated. The firm's first customers were door manufacturers, who used the sturdy, lightweight panels to manufacture their product.

Since that time, however, the range of products and services offered by Prebuilt has expanded considerably, and especially rapidly during the last four years. Expansion of the product line began 15 years ago when the firm developed the capability to manufacture doors. In addition, at about that time, an engineer by the name of Bob Roan became affiliated with the firm and developed a system whereby Prebuilt's panels could be structurally connected into complete shelters (houses and the like). About 4 years ago, the firm was approached by a representative of the Egyptian government who asked if Prebuilt could provide his government with what amounted to a complete town—one thousand homes, a commissary, a small hospital, a school building, and other structures. Prebuilt took the contract and, in doing so, had to add a variety of new services to those already offered, including "buyouts" (buying and providing the electrical equipment, washing machines, and so on needed to complete the house), transportation of all goods and materials from the United States to Egypt, and on-site supervision and construction (laborers were recruited from Taiwan). This Egyptian order was followed by similar orders of about the same size from several other customers. However, numerous unanticipated crises have occurred in filling these orders and there is considerable doubt as to whether Prebuilt can convince any new, larger customers to use its services. Amongst the crises were the following: a great deal of work has to be redone when, for example, it is determined that the ceilings do not conform to the customer's specifications, or electrical equipment is not compatible with the voltage available in the client country; incoming material gets lost in the company's warehouse with no record kept of its location; no clear records are kept of exactly how much material (how many panels, say) is shipped to the customers, and the company usually cannot prove its case when a customer complains that it hasn't received all the necessary material.

William Ross did not know what the source (or sources) of these problems was, but he did know there seemed to be endless bickering and back biting between the sales, engineering, purchasing, and manufacturing departments in his company. He did some investigating and found that a common occurrence was for sales and the client to meet and develop a project based on a set of "standard" designs with little or no input from engineering, and for the sales department to then estimate the project's cost. Engineering was then brought in "after the fact" to develop the project, a situation that seemed to put it on the defensive and generally resulted in its identifying required project modifications. Engineering then sent a list of required material to purchasing, often making assumptions about quality of components, etc., without input from sales. Someone in engineering then would find a mistake (or someone in sales would stumble on one), and orders would have to be changed. Occasionally someone in purchasing would decide that he could get a "better deal" on some component and change the specification, without communicating this change to the people in engineering or sales. Because of these sorts of changes, manufacturing would usually get its production orders late, and end up making unauthorized changes to the specification in order to speed up prodction. On several occasions Ross tried to find out what department was to blame for the resulting mistakes, but his meetings with the department managers all turned into shouting matches, with each manager trying to put the blame on the other departments.

Ross is beginning to wonder whether the problem lies not with his subordinates, but with the way he is managing the company. Because his firm has grown so quickly, he never bothered to have an organization chart drawn up, nor are there specific job descriptions indicating what each manager is responsible for. There are no policies or procedures detailing who is to communicate with whom, whose approval is needed before an order is accepted or changed, and so on. It appears that projects are often sold, engineered, purchased, and shipped without any one identifiable person or group of people having both the authority and responsibility for managing them from start to finish. Also, each manager is rewarded based on the results he obtains in his own department. For example, the sales manager is rewarded based on the sales revenue his department produces, and the manufacturing manager is rewarded based on the efficiency of his department. Customers are beginning to find the situation at Prebuilt unacceptable, and Ross knows that if he does not do something to get his managers working together, he may soon find himself out of business.

Questions

1. How would you analyze the "ABCs" of performance in this case?

2. What are the antecedents of conflict in this case?

3. Do you think the conflict is being managed effectively? Why? Why not?

4. Specially, what conflict management techniques would you use to improve conflict management at Prebuilt?

EXPERIENTIAL EXERCISE

Purpose: To study the causes and possible ways of resolving intergroup conflict.

Required Understanding: The reader should be familiar with the sources and methods relating to intergroup conflict.

How to Set up The Exercise: Set up groups of four to five students for the 45-to-60-minute exercise. The groups should be separated from each other and asked to converse only with their group members. Before forming the groups, each person is asked to complete the exercise by themselves and then to join the group and reach a decision. At this point, read this:

> Assume that you are employed by a medium-sized corporation specializing in the manufacture and marketing of commodity and specialty chemicals. Your particular position is manufacturing manager: Plastics. You report to the vice-president of manufacturing, who, in turn, reports to the divisional vice-president.

Currently, your firm is experiencing a relatively high growth rate in sales and profits due to the recent introduction of new product lines, of which your products represent a major portion of this high growth rate. To provide better coordination of new-product development and marketing efforts, the president of your firm has decided to establish *product planning teams* for each new product or product lines. Each team will be responsible for the effective planning and coordination of efforts necessary to bring the new product through the pilot plant, plant construction, and initial marketing phases.

Last year, a product planning team was established to coordinate the introduction of a new, extremely durable, but expensive plastic to be used in the electronics industry. The team consists of yourself, and representatives from engineering, research, and marketing departments. The representative from engineering has been appointed as chairperson of the planning team. Pilot plant studies have been concluded, and the team will be meeting shortly to discuss the various aspects of construction of the new plant.

This morning, the planning team conducted a meeting at which you presented a plan for the construction of the new plant. The plan contained material, equipment, and capacity details and a proposed construction time schedule. Incorporated in your plan was the use of new processing equipment that will provide considerable manufacturing cost savings over existing equipment. The delivery time of this newer equipment, however, is estimated to be 12 months longer than equipment that is currently available.

During the team meeting, the marketing representative voiced strong opposition to your plan, indicating that the primary emphasis should be on placing this new product on the market as soon as possible. You, however, pointed out that the *long-term* benefits of your plan, in terms of manufacturing cost savings, outweigh *short-term* marketing considerations. The discussion becomes increasingly heated and tense as each of you becomes further entrenched in your positions. In addition, the engineering representative believes that you have the most valid point and decides to go along with the original plan. The research representative, however, agrees with the marketing representative, which results in a stalemated meeting with no decision being made.

After the meeting as you reflect on what has happened, you are clearly upset and disturbed. You are aware that the views expressed by you and the marketing team member represent not only your personal views, but the positions of the total manufacturing and marketing departments.

Because you believe that this is a serious problem between the two departments, you decide that something must be done quickly to ensure the success of the project. You see the alternatives as follows:

1. You can rework your plan to go along with the objections of the marketing representative and do the best you can with the long-term manufacturing cost considerations of the plan.
2. You can have a meeting with the marketing representative, at which time you can stress the positive aspects of the project and point out that the new equipment will make the company the foremost producer of the product in the world.
3. You can send a letter to the president resigning your position on the team.
4. You can tell the marketing representative that if he or she goes along with your position now, you will give full support to his or her new marketing plan that is to be presented to the team in the near future.
5. You can go to the divisional vice-president and request that he or she intercede for your position.
6. You can ask the marketing representative to meet with you for a full day next week in order to work out your differences and come up with an alternative solution.
7. You can ask a member of the divisional vice-president's staff to sit in on all team meetings and act as the new chairperson and arbitrator of all problems.
8. You can send the marketing representative a letter (with copies to all team members, the division vice-president, and president) indicating that his or her opposition to your plan is holding up a potentially profitable project.
9. You can ask the divisional vice-president to attend the next team meeting in order to stress the importance of this project to the continued growth of the company.
10. You can immediately walk into the marketing representative's office and ask him or her to justify their position to you.

Instructions

1. *Individually*, group members should: (a) Identify the cause(s) of the present conflict situation. (b) Rank the 10 possible alternatives from one (the most desirable) to ten (the least desirable).

2. Form into the preassigned groups and answer question 1 as a group.

3. A spokesperson from each group should give the instructor the group's decision and a rationale for its decision. Did all groups come to about the same conclusions?

NOTES FOR CHAPTER 11

1. I. L. Janis, *Victims of group think* (Boston: Houghton Mifflin, 1972), Steven Robbins, "Managing Organizational Conflict," in Jerome Schnee, E. Kirby Warren and Harold Lazarus, *The Progress of Management* (Englewood Cliffs, N.J.: Prentice-Hall, 1977), pp. 163–76.

2. Steven Robbins, "Managing Organizational Conflict."

3. Kenneth Thomas and Warren Schmidt, "A Survey of Managerial interests with respect to conflict," *Academy of Management Journal* (June 1976), pp. 315–18.

4. See, for example, John Rizzo, Robert J. House, and Sydney I Lirtzman, "Role conflict and ambiguity in complex organizations," *Administrative Science Quarterly*, 15 (June 1970), pp. 150–63.

5. Harry Levinson, "The Abrasive Personality," *Harvard Business Review* (May–June 1978), pp. 86–94.

6. Levinson, "The Abrasive Personality," p. 94.

7. Numbers 1, 2, and 3 are based on Melville Dalton, "Conflict between staff and line managerial officers," *American Sociological Review*, 15, No. 3 (June 1950), pp. 342–50; numbers 4, 5 and 6 are based on Lewis Allen, "The line-staff relationship," *Management Record*, 17, No. 9 (September 1955), pp. 346–49, 374–76.

8. Opinion Research Corporation, *The Conflict between the scientific and the management mind* (Princeton, N.J.: ORC, 1959).

9. Lyman W. Porter, "Job Attitudes in Management: III. Perceived Deficiencies in need fulfillment as a function of line versus staff types of jobs," *Journal of Applied Psychology*, 47 (1963), pp. 267–75.

10. Dalton, "Conflict."

11. Thomas and Schmidt, "Survey of Managerial Interest," pp. 315–18.

12. See, for example, Richard Walton and John Dutton, "The Management of Interdepartmental conflict: a model and review," *Administrative Science Quarterly*, 14, No. 1 (March 1969), pp. 73–84.

13. Walton and Dutton, "Management of Interdepartmental conflict," pp. 73–84.

14. John Dutton and Richard Walton, "Interdepartmental conflict and coopera-tion: two contrasting studies," *Human Organization*, 25 (1966), pp. 207–20.

15. H. A. Lansberger, "The Horizontal Dimensions in a Bureaucracy," *Administra-tive Science Quarterly*, 6 (1961), pp. 298–333.

16. Paul Lawrence and Jay Lorsch, *Organization and Environment* (Boston: Har-vard University, Graduate School of Business Administration, division of research, 1967).

17. John A. Seiler, "Diagnosing Interdepartmental conflict," *Harvard Business Review* (September–October 1963), pp. 121–32.

18. Lewis Pondy, "Organizational conflict: concepts and models," *Administrative Science Quarterly*, 12, No. 2 (1967), pp. 296–320. For a description of other models of the conflict process see, for example, Walton and Dutton, "Management of Interdepart-mental conflict," pp. 73–84; Stewart Schmidt and Thomas Kochan, "Conflict: Toward conceptual clarity," *Administrative Science Quarterly*, 17 (1972), pp. 359–70; Thomas Ruble and Kenneth Thomas, "Support for a two-dimensional model of conflict behavior," *Organizational Behavior and Human Performance*, 16 (June 1976), pp. 143–55.

19. Dalton, "Conflict"; David Mechanic, "Sources of Power of lower participants in complex organizations," *Administrative Science Quarterly*, 7, No. 3 (December 1962), pp. 349–64.

20. L. Pondy, "Organizational conflict: concepts and models."

21. Muzafer Sherif, "Experiments in group conflict," in Stanley Coppersmith (ed.), "Frontiers of Psychological Research," *Scientific American* (November 1956), pp. 112–16.

22. Sherif, "Experimentus," p. 115.

23. Sherif, "Experiments," p. 116.

24. Sherif, "Experiments," p. 116. For an example of a study in which superordi-nate goals did not seem to reduce intergroup conflict see Lewis Stern and Brian Sternthal, "Strategies for Managing interorganizational conflict: a laboratory paradigm," *Journal of Applied Psychology*, 60, No. 4 (August 1975), pp. 472–82.

25. Ross Stagner, "Corporate Decision making: an empirical study," *Journal of Applied Psychology*, 53 (1969), 1–13; Georg Wieland and Robert Ullrich, *Organization: Behavior, Design, and Change* (Homewood: Irwin, 1976), pp. 271–73.

26. R. Stagner, "Corporate Decision making."

27. Eric Neilson, "Understanding and managing intergroup conflict," in Paul Lawrence, Lewis Barnes, and Jay Lorsch, *Organizational Behavior and Administration* (Homewood: Irwin, 1976), p. 294.

28. Lawrence and Lorsch, *Organization and Environment*, pp. 74–75.

29. See, for example, Patricia Renwick, "Impact of Topic and Source of disagreement on conflict management," *Organizational Behavior adn Human Performance*, 14 (December 1975), pp. 416–25.

30. Warren Bennis, *Organization Development: It's nature, origins, and prospects* (Reading, Massachusetts: Addison-Wesley Publishing Company, 1969), pp. 4–6.

31. W. Bennis, *Organizational Development*.

32. W. Bennis, *Organization Development*.

12 *Organization Structure and Theory*

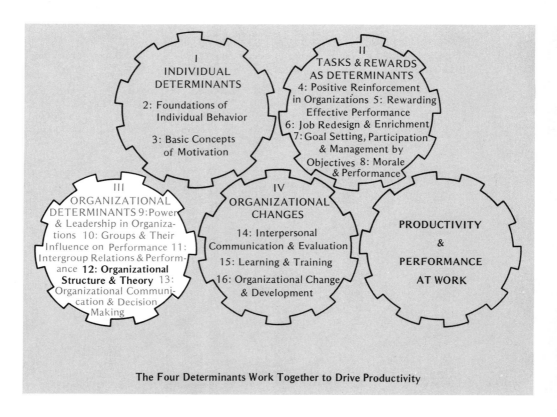

I
INDIVIDUAL DETERMINANTS

2: Foundations of Individual Behavior

3: Basic Concepts of Motivation

II
TASKS & REWARDS AS DETERMINANTS
4: Positive Reinforcement in Organizations 5: Rewarding Effective Performance
6: Job Redesign & Enrichment
7: Goal Setting, Participation & Management by Objectives 8: Morale & Performance

III
ORGANIZATIONAL DETERMINANTS 9: Power & Leadership in Organizations 10: Groups & Their Influence on Performance 11: Intergroup Relations & Performance **12: Organizational Structure & Theory** 13: Organizational Communication & Decision Making

IV
ORGANIZATIONAL CHANGES

14: Interpersonal Communication & Evaluation

15: Learning & Training

16: Organizational Change & Development

PRODUCTIVITY & PERFORMANCE AT WORK

The Four Determinants Work Together to Drive Productivity

BY THE TIME YOU FINISH STUDYING THIS CHAPTER, YOU SHOULD BE ABLE TO:

1. *Develop an organizational chart.*
2. *Compare and contrast "purpose" departmentation and "process" departmentation.*
3. *Explain departmentation by product, customer, location, marketing channel, and business function.*
4. *Discuss the span of control concept.*
5. *Compare and contrast "universal" and "contingency" organization theories.*

OVERVIEW

The main purpose of this chapter is to explain the basics of organizing. First, we explain that an organization's structure influences the antecedents, behavior, and consequences of performance—that, in other words, changing an organization's structure can actually change what employees see as their goals, as the consequences of their performing, and as their ability to do their jobs. We then discuss "fundamentals" of organizing, including organization charts, departmentation, span of control, and decentralization. Finally, several "organization theories" have been proposed for explaining how to best structure an organization and we discuss these at the end of this chapter.

INTRODUCTION: STRUCTURE AND ITS EFFECTS ON PERFORMANCE

Having discussed groups and intergroup relations, our next step is to take a look at the organization as a whole (rather than at its constituent groups) and at the topic of *organization structure*. Organization structure is the pattern of relationships or activities in the organization.[1] An organization's structure (as depicted in, say, its "organizational chart") shows, for example, how the sales group relates to the production group (i.e., can their managers communicate directly, or only through the president?) and how the managers relate to each other (i.e., who gives orders to whom?).

The structure of an organization effects the performance of its employees. For example (as we will see in this and the next chapter) how an organization is structured largely explains whether communication in the organization will be adequate, and whether people that *should* get information about things *do* get that information. (Thus, in an organization that is overly "bureaucratic" or "mechanistic" it may take the president so long to find out about a problem that by the time he does it is usually too late for him to do much about it.) As another example, some organizations are famous for having everyone "stick to the chain of command," and this aspect of their structure helps explain why their employees often seem "bureaucratic" and difficult to deal with. The structure, as we have seen, can also help explain why intergroup conflicts do (or do not) occur, and how much "position power" any particular leader has. Organization structure is therefore important to our discussion of human behavior for many reasons. Perhaps 'most importantly, though, no organization could function for long without a stable, predictable pattern of relationships for its members—a *struc-*

ture. In other words, unless employees know what their jobs are, and who they have to interact with to get their jobs done even the most motivated employees might not be able to get their jobs done, or done well.

Organization Structure and the ABCs of Performance

To get a different perspective on how structure can influence behavior, it would be useful to see how structure can influence the "ABCs" of performance. For example, suppose we have the following performance problem: our customers are increasingly upset because the quality of the products we are sending them is quite poor, and, we have a quality control manager, who should be preventing this problem. We might analyze this problem as follows:

> *Antecedents:* Does the quality control manager know what is expected in terms of product quality? Here, we interview this person and find that he does know what the company's quality control standards are; however, his boss, the production manager, has told him these standards are "too tough."
>
> *Behavior:* Could the manager control quality better if he wanted to? Are there any impediments to his doing his job better? Here we find that in our organization structure the quality control manager reports to the production manager. The latter is his boss. This makes it difficult for the quality control manager to "blow the whistle" when production turns out some poor quality products. As a result, the company's vice-president—who is the production manager's boss—never finds out about the quality problem until it's too late, and he does not have the time to notify the sales manager, or customer, that the product does not meet its specifications. We decide to rectify this problem by *reorganizing*—by having the quality control manager report to the vice-president, instead of the production manager.
>
> *Consequences.* What are the consequences facing the quality control manager for reporting the low-quality items? Are they positive, or negative? Before we reorganized, the consequences facing the quality control manager for doing his job were mostly negative. If he reported the products as poor, he was often "chewed out" by his boss the production manager, who said he was being "too picky," and that "there's no way we're going to waste all that time reworking the material." Now, the vice-president praises the quality control manager for doing his job and for saving the company the embarrassment of having customers complain and send back merchandise.

In summary, an organization's structure—its pattern of formally approved reporting relationships—affects performance in the organization in several ways. It influences what each employee recognizes as his or her standards or goals, since employees tend to adopt the goals and values of the group they belong to, and those of their boss. It also influences whether the person can perform effectively—for example: Does the person's boss prevent him from reporting problems? Is there a lack of effective coordination between departments because they should, but do not, share a common boss? And, does the president fail to get timely warnings on problems because there is too great an emphasis on "sticking to the chain of command?" Structure also influences the consequences of performing, since it is usually a person's boss that decides on his or her rewards. In summary, an organization's structure has a substantial effect on its performance (and that of its members), and understanding how to design organizations is therefore an important human relations skill.

FUNDAMENTALS OF ORGANIZING[2]

The Purposes of Organization

The purposes of organization are to give each person a separate, distinct job and to ensure that these jobs are coordinated in such a way that the organization accomplishes its goals. Except on the very rarest of occasions, organizations are never ends in themselves, but are means to an end—that "end" being the accomplishment of the organization's goals. Thus:

> An organization consists of people who carry out differentiated jobs that are coordinated to contribute to the organization's goals.

Organization Charts

The usual way of depicting an organization is with an organization chart, as shown in Exhibit 12.1. Organization charts are snapshots of the organization at a particular point in time and show the skeleton of the organization structure in chart form. They provide the title of each manager's position and, by means of connecting lines, show who is accountable to whom and who is in charge of what department.

The organization chart does not tell you everything about the organization, any more than a road map tells you everything about the towns along its routes. Organization charts do not provide job descriptions (such as the one illustrated in Exhibit 12.2). Nor does the organization chart show the actual patterns of communication in the organization. It also does not show how closely employees are supervised or the actual level of authority and power that each position holder in the organization, has. What it *does* show are the position titles and the "chain of command" from the top of the organization to the bottom.

Exhibit 12.1 An Example of an Organization Chart

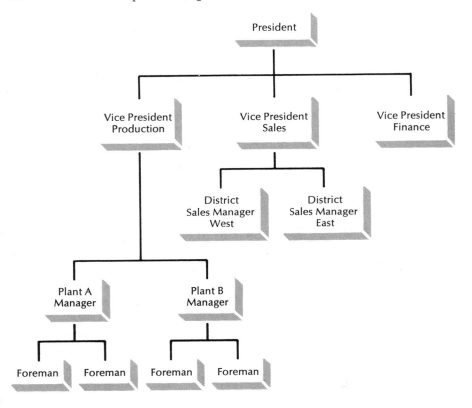

Most organizations have, or should have, organization charts because they are helpful in informing employees what their jobs are and how these jobs relate to others in the organization. On the other hand, many organizations have been quite successful without organization charts, while others have failed in spite of them.

In summary: Organization charts are useful because they:

1. Show titles of each manager's job.
2. Show who is accountable to whom.
3. Show who is in charge of what department.
4. Show what sorts of departments have been established.

Exhibit 12.2 Job Description for a Production Control Manager*

TITLE	Production Control Manager
REPORTS TO	Assistant Plant Manager
SPECIAL REQUIREMENTS	High school graduate, college degree preferred. Background in production classes, construction, machine capacities. Ability to understand specifications. Ability to coordinate and supervise.
SUPERVISORY RESPONSIBILITY OVER:	Assistant Production Control Manager, Production Control Supervisor, Production Control Schedulers, Clerks, Hourly employees, and such other operations as designated by Plant Manager.
JOB SUMMARY	Directs the activities of: scheduling plant production; procuring raw materials; and maintaining inventory for production and shipping.
DUTIES	Receive, review, enter and promise all orders. Schedule machinery, manpower and materials in such a way that the maximum amount of efficiency is obtained from the operating departments. Prepare production schedules in accordance with customer requirements and applicable specifications. Coordinates production control with technical and production operations and maintenance. Supervises procurement of raw materials and inventory control. Responsible for all production schedules including machine operation, overtime, vacation, etc. Prepares forthcoming schedules and advises Plant Manager, Production Manager, and Department Managers of these schedules. Supervises and coordinates packing, shipping, traffic, freight consolidation operations to insure most economical freight rates and best delivery. Confers with sales offices. Follows up rush and delinquent orders. Confers with Plant Manager, Production Manager, and Plant Accountant in maintaining accurate backlogs by product class. Assist in operations report. Receives, reviews, and compiles daily production reports of plant's progress per department. Performs special projects as required. Has authority to hire, fire, promote, demote, train, discipline and supervise employees under his jurisdiction. Responsible for plant safety, housekeeping, scrap and usage where applicable to his sphere of plant influence. Implements cost reduction and efficiency improvement programs. May be responsible for execution of Union agreement.

Source: Professor Robert Miller

5. Show the "chain of command."
6. Let each employee know his or her job title and "place" in the organization.

But, organization charts do *not* show you:

1. Job descriptions of specific day-to-day duties and responsibilities.
2. Actual patterns of communication in the organization.
3. How closely employees are supervised.
4. The actual level of authority and power each position holder has.

Departmentation

Every organization has to carry out certain activities to accomplish its goals. These usually include activities like manufacturing, selling, and accounting. Departmentation is the process through which these activities are grouped logically into distinct areas and assigned to managers: it is the organization-wide division of work. It results in "departments"—logical groupings of activities—which also often go by such names as divisions, branches, units, groups or sections.

Departmentation is a very important process. In fact, when most people think of "organization structure" they are usually thinking about departmentation. This is because it is the departments—like "sales" and "production"—that stand out on organization charts.

Departmentation is also a very common phenomenon. The work of the federal government, for example, is divided at its highest levels into the executive, judicial, and legislative branches. The executive branch itself is divided at its highest level into a number of departments, such as those for commerce, labor, and defense. Hospitals typically have such "departments" as intensive care and radiology units. Many companies, like General Motors, have separate "product divisions," such as those for Buicks or Pontiacs; and most also have separate departments for production, sales, and finance. However, though there are many ways to departmentalize organizations, most types of departments are built around either "end use" *purposes* like "industrial customers," or *processes* like marketing.

Departmentation by Purpose. First there are four popular *purposes* around which departments can be built: products, customers, market channels, and locations.

Departmentation by Product. Departmentation by product is illustrated in Exhibit 12.3, which presents part of the organization chart of the General Motors Corporation. Notice how, at the operating divisions level, the car and truck group is organized around product lines. The division is managed by an executive vice-president, and there are separate product divisions for Buick, Oldsmobile, Pontiac, and so forth.

Departmentation by Customer. Departmentation by customer is illustrated in Exhibit 12.4, which shows the General Electric Company organization chart. Notice how the company is organized to serve as a supplier for many different purposes or "customers." These include aerospace, construction, consumer products, and power generation.

Departmentation by Market Channel. Market channel departmentation is illustrated in Exhibit 12.5. A market channel is a conduit (wholesaler,

Exhibit 12.3 Product Departmentation at General Motors

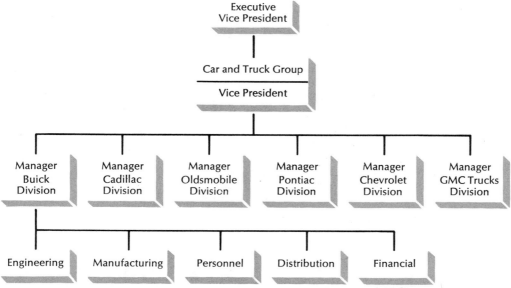

Note: The GM Car and Truck Group is departmentalized by product, and there are separate divisions for Buick, Cadillac, etc.

drugstore, grocery, etc.) through which a manufacturer distributes his products to his ultimate customers.

This type of departmentation is similar to customer departmentation, but there are several differences. In customer departmentation, each customer-oriented department is usually responsible for *both* manufacturing and selling its own products to its own customers. In marketing channel departmentation, the same product (such as a brand of facial soap) is typically marketed through two or more different channels. Thus, a decision is usually made as to which department will manufacture the product for all the other marketing channel departments. This is illustrated in Exhibit 12.5.

Departmentation by Location or Area. This is illustrated in Exhibit 12.6. Many agencies of the federal government are departmentalized by area. For example, the Federal Reserve System is divided into twelve geographical areas centered in cities like Boston, New York, and San Francisco.

Departmentation by Process or Business Function. Next, there are *process* types of departmentation: here closely related processes like advertising, selling, and sales promotion are grouped together into a single department such as marketing.

Exhibit 12.4 Customer Departmentation at General Electric

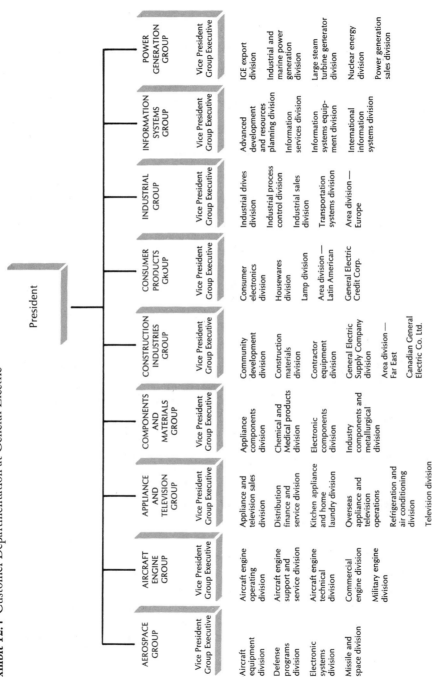

Note: Departments are built around such "customers" as aerospace, appliances and televisions, and construction.

Source: Adapted from *Corporate Organization Structures*, National Industrial Conference Board, Inc. No. 210 (1968), p. 59; Reproduced in James Gibson, John Ivancevich, and James Donnelly, Jr. *Organizations* (Dallas: Business Publications, Inc., 1973) p. 139.

Exhibit 12.5 Market Channel Departmentation at Apex Face Soap Company

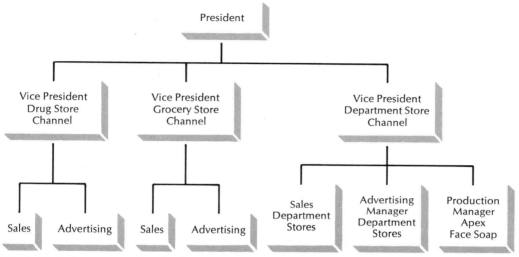

Note: 1. Only the department-store channel produces the soap, and 2. Each channel may sell to the same *ultimate* consumers.

Exhibit 12.6 Departmentation by Area or Location

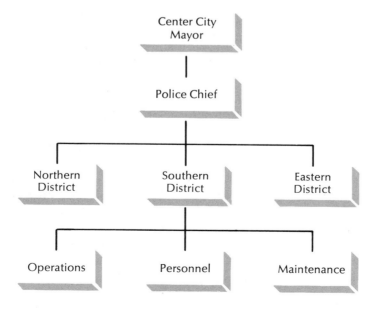

This type of departmentation is typically the basis on which a new business is organized. The head of a new company asks himself, "What basic functions ("or processes") will have to be performed if the business is to survive?" In a manufacturing business these "basic functions" usually would include (at least) manufacturing, sales, and finance and accounting. Thus, departmentalizing a company by business function is probably the most familiar form of departmentation. It is depicted in Exhibit 12.7. Here activities are grouped around business functions such as production, marketing, and finance.

Exhibit 12.7 Departmentation by Business Function

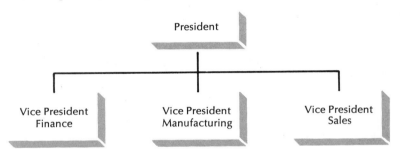

Purpose and Process Departmentation Compared. Purpose and process types of departmentation each have their own advantages and disadvantages. Whether you build departments around products, customers, market channels, or locations, *purpose* types of departmentation all result in units that are self-contained, in that there are separate sales, production, personnel, etc., departments *for each* product, customer, or location. Here a single manager is in charge of all functions (like sales and production) related to the purpose. For example, the manager of a publisher's high-school division might have his own editing, manufacturing, and distribution departments. As a result, this division could usually respond quickly to the changing needs of high-school students since the manager in charge doesn't have to rely on (or seek the approval of) editing, manufacturing, or distribution managers who are not in his own division. The main disadvantage here is that purpose types of departmentation breed duplication. The very fact that each product, customer, market channel, or area department is self-contained implies that there are several production plants instead of one and several sales forces instead of one and so on.

Process-based departments usually have single, large departments like sales, production, and personnel which serve *all* the company's products. As a result, the volume of business done in each department is relatively high, and with this volume typically increasing returns are to scale—employees become more proficient and thus more productive, and there is less duplication, for example. Building a department around processes therefore tends to work best where efficiency is very important. The main disadvantage is that responsibility for overall coordination lies squarely on the shoulders of one person, usually the president. This may not be a serious problem when the firm is small or where there is not a diversity of products. But as size and product diversity increases the job of coordinating the various functions may prove too great for a single individual: your organization can lose its responsiveness.

Span of Control

The "span of control" is the number of subordinates reporting directly to a supervisor. In Exhibit 12.8, the span of control of the president is eight, and the span of control of the production vice president is four.

Exhibit 12.8 Span of Control

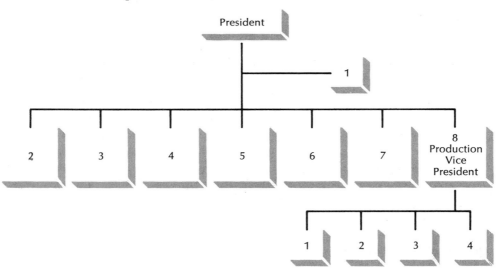

Note: The span of control of the President is 8; that of the Production Vice President is 4.

Arguments over what the "best" span of control is have been going on for decades. Early writers recommended a "narrow" span of only 5 or 6 subordinates. The assumption was that the boss could then keep a closer eye on each subordinate. But studies of spans in actual companies clearly show that spans are often much wider. Dale, for example, found that the number of managers reporting to the chief executive in 100 companies varied from 1 to 24. Half the chief executives had spans greater than 9 and half less than 9. Only about a quarter of the companies had spans as narrow as 6.

Many factors combine to determine the best span of control. We know, for example, that the spans of control of lower level managers like foremen are usually much wider than those of top level executives. The reason seems to be that the former's jobs (and those of their subordinates) are less complex. Similarly we know that jobs that are very routine (such as those on assembly lines or in the bookkeeping units of government bureaus) allow for much wider spans of control than nonroutine jobs (such as managing a research staff).

DELEGATION AND DECENTRALIZATION

Delegation

Organizing departments and jobs would be impossible without delegation, which we will define as the pushing-down of authority from superior to subordinate. This is because the assignment of responsibility for some department or job usually goes hand in hand with the delegation of adequate authority to get the task done. For example, it would be inappropriate for you to assign a subordinate the responsibility for designing a new product, and then tell him he hasn't the authority to hire designers or choose the best design.

It should be clear, though, that while *authority* can be delegated *responsibility* cannot. You can assign responsibility to a subordinate. However, most managers and management writers agree that you are still ultimately responsible for seeing to it that the job gets done properly. Since you retain the ultimate responsibility for the performance of a job, delegation of authority also usually entails the creation of *accountability*. Thus, your subordinate automatically becomes accountable to you for the performance of the tasks assigned to him.

Decentralization Defined

The way many people use the term, decentralization means about the same thing as delegation—simply pushing authority down to subordinates. Decentralization, according to them, is the opposite of "centralization" in which all, or nearly all, of the authority to make decisions and take action is retained by top management.

But decentralization is and was always meant to be much more than simply delegation. Decentralization is a philosophy of organization and management, one that implies both selective disbursal and concentration of authority. It involves selectively determining what authority to push down into the organization; developing standing plans (such as policies and rules) to guide subordinates who have this authority delegated to them; and implementing selective but adequate controls for monitoring performance. Thus, according to Koontz and O'Donnell:

> Decentralization is a philosophy of organization and management which involves both selective delegation of authority, as well as concentration of authority through the imposition of policies and selective and adequate control.[3]

Example: The organization of the General Motors Corporation provides a good example of "decentralization in practice."

When former President Alfred Sloan first developed GM's decentralized structure his approach was based on two principles.[4]

1. First, he said that the responsibility attached to the top manager of each division should in no way be limited. Each division was to be headed by a top manager and be complete "in every necessary function" so that it could exercise "its full initiative and logical development."
2. However, "certain central organization functions are absolutely essential for the logical development and proper control of the corporation's activities."

In other words, Sloan believed that each of his division managers (like those for the Buick, Chevrolet, and Cadillac divisions) should head complete, self-contained divisions. Each of these divisions would be "self-contained" in that it would do its own manufacturing, marketing, hiring, and so forth.

But Sloan knew that delegating this much authority to his top managers could result in matters getting "out of control." He therefore said that certain "organization functions" would have to be controlled *centrally*. To implement this, Sloan expanded the company's central office and created (or expanded) many special staff functions for monitoring and controlling the firm's operating divisions. For example, he expanded the "finance committee," and made it responsible for authorizing dividend rates, top management salaries, and major appropriations. In this way, GM's central-office staff groups ended up controlling things like:

> *Capital appropriations.* For example, all projects requiring capital expenditures had to be submitted to an appropriations committee func-

tioning under the finance and executive committees. Each request was given uniform treatment, and funds were approved for projects on the basis of their relative value to the corporation.

Cash. A system was set up whereby all incoming cash receipts were deposited in certain specified banks. The operating divisions (Buick, Cadillac, etc.) had no control over cash withdrawals or transfers, and all accounts were administered by the headquarter's financial staff.

Inventory. A new inventory control system was established that was tied to division managers' forecasts of the number of cars and trucks to be produced. These forecasts were submitted to corporate headquarters for approval on a monthly basis, and inventory levels had to be kept within the quantities required by the approved forecasts.

Division profitability. A system of interlocking financial ratios was established whereby each division was measured in terms of profits relative to invested capital. Each division, in other words was evaluated in terms of its overall profitability on the assumption that "if we had the means to review and judge the effectiveness of operations, we could safely leave the prosecution of those operations to the men in charge of them."

Decentralization at GM therefore represented a shrewd balance between decentralized autonomy and centralized control. On the one hand, division managers had considerable autonomy and the means for designing, producing, and marketing their cars. On the other hand, Alfred Sloan was able to maintain control of this far-flung company by centralizing—retaining control over—such things as capital appropriations, cash allocations, and inventory levels. This is why we call decentralization "a philosophy of organization and management which involves both selective delegation of authority through the imposition of policies and selective but adequate controls."

ORGANIZATION THEORY

The Purpose of an Organization Theory

What determines how a company (or hospital, city, school, etc.) should be organized? In other words, what determines whether one should use departmentation by product or function? A wide or narrow span of control? Centralized or decentralized decision making?

Organization theory is aimed at answering questions like these. Specifically, it is aimed at helping us to *understand* and *explain* how to structure an organization, and how to *predict* how some change-like switching from functional to product departmentation-may influence the rest of the organization.

Organization theories can be categorized as either *universal* or *contingency* theories. The former argue that there is "one best way" to organize regardless of the situation—whether one is organizing an electronics firm or a rayon mill, for example. *Contingency* theory holds that the organization structure has to "fit" the situation. We discussed the schools of management that spawned these theories in chapter one; in the remainder of this chapter we look in more detail at the organization theories themselves. After reading this material you should be able to explain why:

1. Clear lines of authority and adherence to the chain of command are appropriate for some companies, but not others;
2. Some companies make use of staff personnel, and others do not;
3. Some companies departmentalize by process, and others do so by purpose;
4. Jobs in some companies are highly specialized, and in others they are self-contained, and "enriched";
5. Why some companies are far more decentralized than others;
6. Why some companies have narrow spans of control, and some have wide ones.
7. Why some companies use special liasons to coordinate their departments.

Universal Organization Theories

The classical and behavioral writers both argued for *universal* organization theories, since each felt their own methods of organizing could be used for *any* organization.

The Classical Approach to Organizing. As we explained in chapter one, the classical approach was characterized by an almost total emphasis on the technical aspects of efficiency. To these writers an efficiently designed job and organization were of prime importance, and they focused their efforts on developing analytical tools and principles that would better enable managers to design these. Human work behavior was not unimportant to the classical writers; instead they simply assumed its complexities away by arguing that financial incentives would suffice to ensure motivation. Their approach, you may recall, evolved at a time when belief in the hard work ethic and in man's desire to maximize his wealth made it easy to assume that man did, indeed, "live by bread alone."

As you might imagine, the organizations these writers (like Frederick Taylor, Henri Fayol, and Max Weber) prescribed reflected this somewhat mechanical view of the world. Fayol, for example, developed management principles that held, among other things, that: "each employee should have a separate, specialized job"; "an employee should receive orders from one superior only"; and "there should be a clear, unbroken chain of command ranging from the highest to the lowest levels in the organization." Similarly, Max Weber, another classical writer, argued that what he called "Bureaucracy" was the ideal form of organization. A bureaucracy, said Weber, has a rigid chain of command, specialized jobs, centralized decision making, and a system of impersonal rules that tell each employee how to do his or her job.

The Behavioral Approach to Organizing. Whereas the classicists emphasized technical efficiency, behavioral writers like McGregor, Likert and Argyris started with the worker as their focal point. The classical writers, for example, stressed efficient jobs and assumed that workers would perform if paid. The behavioralists, on the other hand, stressed the importance and complexity of motivating employees and of building an organization and designing jobs for that purpose. The organization and its jobs, in other words, had to be designed in order to satisfy employees' needs, since it is only in this way (these writers assumed) that effective employee performance could be ensured in the long run. Like the classicists, the behavioral writers prescribed a "universal" approach to organizing, one that they too, thought would fit any type of firm. But whereas the classicist prescribed making everyone adhere to a rigid chain of command, the behavioralist prescribed letting employees decide (within reasonable bounds) who they had to talk to in the organization to get their jobs done. In a similar vein, the behavioralists argued for less specialized, more enriched jobs, more decentralized, "lower level" decision-making, and a self-contained, purpose-oriented departmentation.

Comparing Classical and Behavioral Organization Theories. Although both the classical, and behavioral writers believed they had each come up with the one best "universal" plan for organizing, their theories were obviously poles apart. To see just how divergent these two "universal" theories are, it would be useful to study Exhibit 12.9: This summarizes the differences between the two theories. As you can see, the classicists believed that the "one best way" to organize required: rigid adherence to the chain of command, centralized decision making; functional departmentation; narrow spans of control; and very specialized jobs. Behavioralists, on the other hand, argued for: less preoccupation with the chain of command; more delegation of authority; departments built around self-contained purposes; wide spans of control; and very unspecialized, enriched jobs.

A Contingency Approach to Organization

Why a "Contingency" Approach? The classical and behavioral theories of organization each arrived at very different conclusions about how

Exhibit 12.9 A Comparison of Two "Universal" Organization Theories: Classical and Behavioral

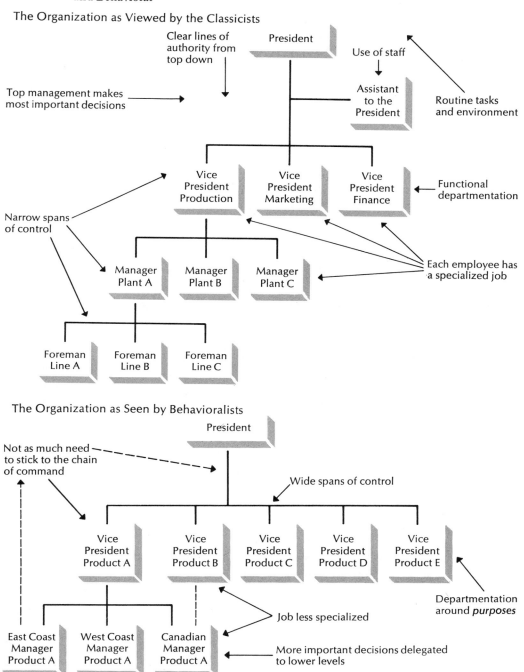

The Organization as Viewed by the Classicists

Clear lines of authority from top down

President

Use of staff

Top management makes most important decisions

Assistant to the President

Routine tasks and environment

Vice President Production

Vice President Marketing

Vice President Finance

Functional departmentation

Narrow spans of control

Manager Plant A

Manager Plant B

Manager Plant C

Each employee has a specialized job

Foreman Line A

Foreman Line B

Foreman Line C

The Organization as Seen by Behavioralists

President

Not as much need to stick to the chain of command

Wide spans of control

Vice President Product A

Vice President Product B

Vice President Product C

Vice President Product D

Vice President Product E

Departmentation around *purposes*

East Coast Manager Product A

West Coast Manager Product A

Canadian Manager Product A

Job less specialized

More important decisions delegated to lower levels

organizations should be structured. However, they both had one important thing in common. Both were "universal" theories, since their proponents prescribed them as the "best" type of organization regardless of the situation. Whether you were organizing a production plant, a hospital, or a city, *classical* theorists generally recommended centralization, high degrees of specialization, and functional departmentation. *Behavioral* theorists recommended decentralization, purpose-types of departmentation, and enlarged jobs.

In the past few years a third type of organization theory has developed. This "contingency" theory holds that the "best" organization structure varies from situation to situation. The "contingency" theory does not render useless the classical, or behavioral theories; it merely helps to place them in their proper perspective.

The Woodward Studies. Almost from their outset, the studies by Joan Woodward and her associates were aimed at trying to understand why organization structure seemed to have no relation to success for the companies they studied. Her research team spent months analyzing volumes of data on each company's history, size, and policies and procedures. None of these factors seemed to explain why some successful firms had classical, mechanistic structures, while others had behavioral, organic ones. Finally the Woodward team decided to classify the companies according to their "production technologies," as follows:

1. *Unit and small-batch production.* These companies produced one-at-a-time prototypes and specialized units to customers' requirements (like fine pianos).
2. *Large batch and mass production.* These companies produced large batches of products on assembly lines (like Ford cars).
3. *Process production.* These companies produced things liks paper and petroleum products through continuously running facilities.

Once the firms were classified it became clear that a *different type of organization structure was appropriate for each type of technology.* Some of Woodward's findings are summarized in Exhibit 12.10. Notice that organic, behavioral-type structures prevailed in the unit and process productions firms; mass production firms had classical, mechanistic structures.

Explanation: Woodward was never able to fully explain her findings. For example, why was the chain of command in unit and process production firms "not clear," while that in the mass production firms was "clear"? Why were the organizations in unit, and process production firms "organic," while those in the mass production firms were "mechanistic." A recent study of 110 New Jersey manufacturing plants has provided some answers. [5]

Exhibit 12.10 Summary of Joan Woodward's Research Findings

	Unit and Small Batch Firms *(Example: Custom Built Cars)*	*Large Batch and Mass Production* *(Example: Mass-Produced Cars)*	*Process Production* *(Example: Oil Refinery)*
Chain of command	Not Clear	Clear	Not Clear
Line-Staff	No distinction	Clear distinction	No distinction
Span of Control	Narrow	Wide	Narrow
Departmentation	Purpose	Process	Purpose
Overall Organization	Organic	Mechanistic	Organic

Note: Summary of data showing how production technology and organization structure are related.

In this study, sociologist Peter Blau found that many features of the tasks in mass production firms are quite different from those in either unit or process production firms. In mass production plants, for example, the work is much more routine and the labor force tends to have a low skill level. In unit production plants, on the other hand, products are built on a "one at a time" basis, employees are highly skilled craftsmen, and, the tasks are *not* very routine. Similarly, in process production plants (like oil refineries) the tasks generally involve monitoring and maintaining complex equipment. The tasks here are also non-routine (since machine-breakdowns can cause enormous problems), and these plants are also usually staffed by a highly skilled work force.

Blau and his associates therefore believe that Woodward's findings can be explained in terms of *employee professionalism* and *work-task routineness*. In Woodward's unit, and process production firms tasks were *not* "routine" and many unforeseen problems were always arising. And employees in these firms were generally highly skilled. Therefore, these organizations had to be more flexible so they could adapt to unforeseen problems. And, because employees were highly skilled, they did not have to be closely supervised. In unit and process firms, therefore, structures were more organic, the chain of command was not rigidly adhered to, and departments were built around "purposes."

In mass production firms, on the other hand, jobs were quite routine and employees were less skilled. Here structures were "mechanistic," there was a rigid chain of command, and departments were built for efficiency around processes like production, and quality control.

The Burns and Stalker Studies. Tom Burns and G. M. Stalker studied about 20 companies in the United Kingdom. They sought to determine what type of organization structure was best for different types of industries. The companies studied came from a variety of industries, and included a rayon mill and several electronics firms.

Rayon Mill: The rayon mill was at one extreme. In order to be successful in this highly competitive industry, the firm had to keep costs to a minimum and be as efficient as possible. Therefore, their very existence depended on keeping unexpected occurrences to a minimum and maintaining steady, high volume production runs.

The researchers found that this organization was a "pyramid of knowledge." It was highly centralized and run on the basis of elaborate policies, procedures, and rules. Job descriptions were carefully defined, and everyone from the top of the organization to the bottom had a very specialized job to do.[6]

Electronics Firms: The electronics firms were at the other extreme. These firms' existences depended on their ability to continuously introduce new and innovative electronic components. They also had to be constantly on the alert to new innovations by their competitors. Flexibility and creativity (rather than efficiency) were paramount for these companies.

Here the researchers found that there was a "deliberate attempt to avoid specifying individual tasks." Not only did employees not have highly specialized jobs; their jobs often changed from week to week and day to day. These firms usually did not even have organization charts, and there was no careful adherence to the chain of command. When a problem arose, an employee simply took it to the person he or she felt was in the best position to solve it. This often meant bypassing the "formal" chain of command. Decision-making authority was pushed down to the lowest levels, where the employees were in the best position to cope with problems as they arose.

Their analyses of these different firms led Burns and Stalker to distinguish (as we saw in Chapter 1) between two different types of organization which they called *Mechanistic* and *Organic.* The rayon mill was typical of Mechanistic, classical-type organizations; the electronics firms were typical of the Organic, behavioral-type ones.

The Lawrence and Lorsch Studies—Departmentation and Coordination. Paul Lawrence and Jay Lorsch set out to determine "what kind of organization does it take to deal with various economic and market conditions."[7] They studied two important aspects of organization structure: "differentiation" (the division of work of the organization into departments) and "integration" (coordination). They focused on several firms in both the plastics and container industries.[8] Each firm was comprised of certain basic departments or "subsystems," including marketing, research, and production. Their findings, which we turn to next, are summarized in Exhibit 12.11.

Exhibit 12.11 Summary of Lawrence and Lorsch Findings

	Production Departments	*Marketing Departments*	*Research Departments*
Plastics Firms	Very predictable tasks	Very predictable tasks	Very *unpredictable* tasks
	"Classical" organization structures	"Classical" organization structures	*"Behavioral"* organization structures
	Much "Differentiation"; coordination achieved by special committees, departments and individuals		
Container Firms	Very predictable tasks	Very predictable tasks	Very predictable tasks
	"Classical" organization structures	"Classical" organization structures	"Classical" organization structures
	Little "Differentiation"; coordination achieved by use of the "chain of command," and standing plans		

Container Firms: In the *container* firms the tasks which the marketing, research, and production departments had to accomplish were all quite routine. Here, there was little difficulty in determining what kinds of products should be developed, manufactured, and sold, and all departments could usually get quick feedback concerning how well they were performing. *All* departments, therefore, had similar structures. Furthermore, employees in each department tended to have similar points of view—they all stressed short term performance, for example. Since unexpected problems were few, and the departments were similar coordination was a straightforward matter. Coordination was accomplished through the company's chain of command. The manager of each department brought his problems to the president, who saw to it that the three departments were working in unison.

Plastics Firms: In the *plastics* firms, on the other hand, only the production and marketing departments faced such "unchanging" tasks. And they, too, had the more efficient mechanistic structures.

But the research departments faced much uncertainty. The employees could not accurately predict what would be the best type of product to develop. It took them much longer to get feedback on the success of their job performance than it did the people in the production and marketing departments. *The structures of the research departments were therefore much different from those of the other departments.* They were structured for flexibility and creativity and had "behavioral," organic-type structures. Their employees also tended to take a much longer term view of things than did employees in production, and marketing, and they put more emphasis on being allowed to participate in decision making.

Because of these differences between departments in the plastics firms, and because these firms had to deal with so many more unexpected problems, special coordinating committees and departments were needed. Instead of relying on one man—the president—special full-time coordinators were appointed. They cut across the hierarchy and kept the lines of communication open between employees in the marketing, production, and research departments.

Summary: A Contingency Approach. These "contingency" findings can help us to understand why different organization structures are appropriate for different tasks. At one extreme are organizations for performing predictable, routine tasks, such as assembling autos or bookkeeping. Here efficiency is emphasized and successful organizations are classical or *mechanistic.* They stress adherence to rules and to the chain of command; highly specialized jobs; close supervision; and functional (process) departmentation.

At the opposite extreme, organizations such as research labs and new product development departments have unpredictable, nonroutine tasks. Here creativity and entrepreneurial activities are emphasized. To facilitate such activities these organizations are behavioral or *organic.* They do not urge employees to "play it by the rules," or to closely abide to the formal chain of command. Jobs are more enlarged and self-contained, and departments are organized around purposes.

CHAPTER SUMMARY

1. The purpose of organization is to give each person a separate, distinct job and to ensure that these jobs are coordinated in such a way that the organization accomplishes its goals. The usual way of depicting an organization is with an organization chart. This provides the title of each manager's position and, by means of connecting lines, shows who is accountable to whom and who is in charge of what department.

2. Departmentation is the process through which the organization's basic activities (such as manufacturing) are grouped logically into distinct areas and assigned to managers: it is the organization-wide division of work. We distinguish between purpose and process departmentation. The former includes departmentation by product, customer, market channel, and location. Departmentation by business function is an example of *process* departmentation. With purpose departmentation, departments are "self-contained" and each can give its continuous and undivided attention to the "purpose." Process types of departments tend to be more specialized (and efficient) than purpose types.

3. We defined *delegation* as the pushing down of authority from superior to subordinate. *Decentralization* is a philosophy of organization and management.

It involves both selective delegation of authority as well as concentration of authority through policies and selective controls.

4. The "universal," classical organization theories of Weber and Fayol prescribed clear unbroken lines of authority, functional departmentation, highly specialized jobs, minimum delegation and decentralization, and a narrow span of control.

5. The behavioral organization theories of Likert and McGregor were also "universal" theories, but they prescribed: less emphasis on clear lines of authority, purpose types of departmentation, less specialization of jobs, more delegation and decentralization, and wider spans of control.

6. Contingency organization theory helps us to put the classical and behavioral prescriptions into perspective. The work of people like Woodward, Burns and Stalker, and Lawrence and Lorsch clearly show that the "best" type of organization varies from situation to situation. At one extreme are mechanistic organizations: these are best for performing routine, predictable tasks such as assembling orders or bookkeeping. Here efficiency is emphasized. At the other extreme are organic organizations: these are best for accomplishing the creative, entrepreneurial tasks carried out in units such as research labs and new-product development departments.

DISCUSSION QUESTIONS AND PROJECTS

1. What items are typically included in the organization chart? What items are not shown on the chart?

2. Compare and contrast purpose departmentation and process departmentation; make sure to discuss the advantages and disadvantages of each and where each seems most appropriate.

3. Explain departmentation by: product, customer, location, marketing channel, and business function.

4. In groups of 5 or 6 students obtain and analyze the organization chart of a local organization. What type of departmentation does it have? Which departments are "process" and which "purpose"? Why do you think it chose its form of departmentation?

5. "It is up to you," your boss tells you. "You can either have the ten salesmen reporting to you, or you can hire two sales managers to report to you. They, in turn will manage five salesmen each." What do you think are the pros and cons of a narrow versus wide span of control? What will you tell your boss in this case?

6. Interview a manager to determine how he or she monitors and controls delegated activities. What are some techniques he or she uses?

7. "You can talk about delegating all you wish. Some managers will always delegate too much, and some will delegate too little. It all depends on their personalities." Discuss whether you agree or disagree with this statement, and why.

8. "Delegation is essential for organizing. You simply cannot have an organization without delegation." Discuss whether you agree or disagree with this statement and why.

9. In groups of 5 or 6 students choose one very familiar organization that you feel is either organic or mechanistic. Look closely at the management functions in this organization. Pay particular attention to dimensions of organization structure, like departmentation and span of control. What makes this organization particularly appropriate for dealing with its tasks? If you chose an organic organization, why do you think it would be *in*appropriate for routine tasks? If you chose a mechanistic organization, what is it about this organization that you think would make it particularly *in*appropriate for dealing with entrepreneurial, creative tasks?

CASE EXERCISE 1

Mad Ludwig

The Fullfeder Pen Company was organized about 10 years ago by Ludwig Fullfeder, an engineer who simultaneously became its president and general manager of all operations. Initially the firm had about a dozen employees engaged in the manufacturing and assembly of a full line of high-quality ball point and felt tip pens, which Ludwig designed and patented. As sales expanded, Ludwig kept adding both additional plant facilities and employees to handle the increased business which resulted mainly from customers seeking specialized pens for advertising purposes.

In 1973 Fullfeder Pen was purchased by Macro Pen Industries. Fullfeder's was thereupon reorganized and Ludwig elected president of the new company. At the time Macro Pen also recommended that he develop an organization structure. Fullfeder never felt one was necessary. "I've always done the thinking here," he once remarked to a friend.

Ludwig, a rather stolid individual accustomed to managing his own shop on an informal basis, nevertheless and grudgingly, set up the following case (Exhibit 12.1) as an organizational Chart without consulting the Macro Pen management.

This organizational structure was put into effect and seemed to work satisfactorily for about a year. During this period "Mad Ludwig," as the production workers nicknamed him after a television program on Bavarian King Ludwig II, labored frantically to make the chart work. He worked 12 to 14 hours each day, much of the time out in the plant supervising the production line. And when not supervising the manufacturing process, he would move from department to department solving one problem after another.

Case Exhibit 12.1

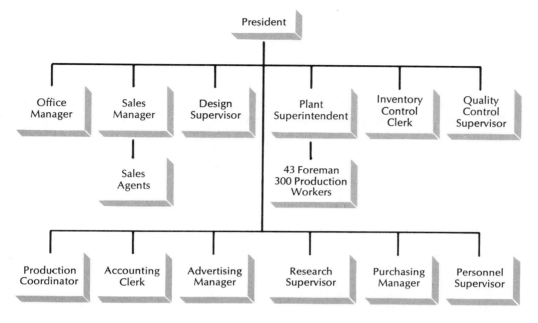

One one such typical day Ludwig:

1. Told purchasing to change suppliers of the basic plastic stock for pen barrels.
2. Hired a new accounts receivable clerk to work in the office.
3. Reviewed and made corrections on advertising copy for a trade journal.
4. Expedited a shipment of pens for a long-time account.

After a year of this kind of managing, Ludwig realized that his structure was not functioning properly. There were continual production breakdowns, sales were down, and profits were off; and to complicate things, his family physician gave him orders to slow down.

The problem, Ludwig felt, was the friction between the department heads. They were just not cooperating. Ludwig felt there was only one solution— dismiss the "troublemakers" in charge of several of the departments and hire new and more cooperative ones.

Questions

1. Identify, using our "ABCs," Ludwig's problems. Would dismissing several "trouble-makers" remedy the situation?
2. Assume you are a management consultant to Fullfeder. How would you handle Ludwig?
3. What sort of departmentation would you suggest? (Develop a new organization chart for Fullfeder.)

CASE EXERCISE 2

Nationwide Container Company

Until a few years ago Nationwide container corporation had an organizational structure that looked something like the chart below.

In the old organization, the departmental organization of the plastics, glass, and paper divisions was exactly the same as in cans. (There is no space on the chart to show it.) Not all departments are portrayed in either structure.

OLD

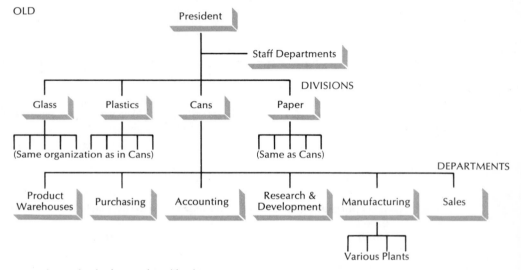

It was changed to look something like this:

NEW

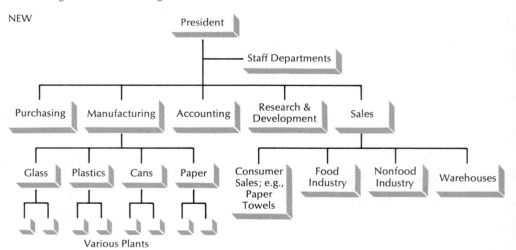

Questions

1. What are the relative advantages and disadvantages of the new organization compared to the old? Why do you think the change was made?

2. Which organization is more centralized? Why?

3. What changes are needed in the behavior and personality of the president to make the new system work?

4. List the most important forms of adjustment required by managers at levels to make the new organization work.

5. Which form of organization will adjust more easily to technological change? Why?

6. Which sort of organization is more likely to engage in "far out" research?

EXPERIENTIAL EXERCISE

Purpose: The purpose of this exercise is to give you practice in analyzing organization structures, and in distinguishing between organic and mechanistic structures.

Required Understanding: You should be thoroughly familiar with our discussions of organization structure and theory in this chapter.

How to Set up the Exercise: The class should break into groups of four or five students.

Instructions for the Exercise.

1. The members of each group should read the nationwide container company case, and then the group as a whole should develop answers to the 6 questions at the end of the case.

2. Then, if time permits, a spokesperson from each group should present the groups' answer to *one* of the questions (group one does question 1, group two question 2, etc.) and the class should discuss the groups' answers to the questions.

NOTES FOR CHAPTER 12

1. Jeffrey Pfeffer, *Organizational Design* (Arlington Heights, Ill.: AHM, 1978), p. 24.

2. Gary Dessler, *Personnel Management* (Reston: Reston Publishing Company, 1978), pp. 23–55.

3. Harold Koontz and Cyril O'Donnell, *Management* (New York: McGraw-Hill, 1976), p. 375.

4. Joan Woodward, *Industrial Organization: Theory and Practice* (London: Oxford, 1965).

5. Peter Blau, Cecilia Falbe, William McKinley, and Phelps Tracy, "Technology and Organization in Manufacturing," *Administrative Science Quarterly*, March 1976.

6. Tom Burns and G. M. Stalker, *The Management of Innovation* (London: Tavistock Publications, 1961).

7. Paul Lawrence and Jay Lorsch, *Organization and Environment* (Cambridge: Harvard University Press, 1967).

8. They also studied several food industry companies.

13 *Organizational Communication and Decision Making*

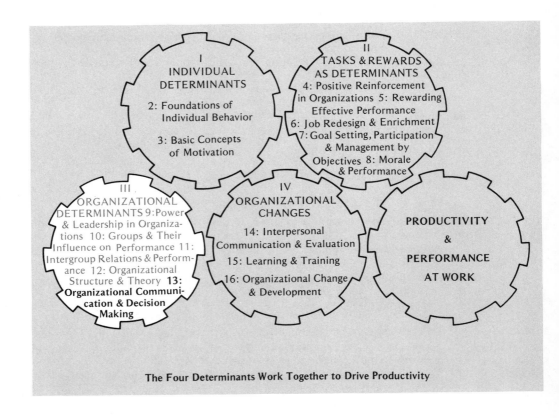

The Four Determinants Work Together to Drive Productivity

*BY THE TIME YOU FINISH STUDYING THIS CHAPTER,
YOU SHOULD BE ABLE TO:*

1. *Present a basic model of communication.*
2. *Distinguish between formal and informal communications and give examples of each.*
3. *Discuss the "communications network experiments."*
4. *Improve an organization's interdepartmental and upward communications.*
5. *Answer the question: "How rational are decision makers?"*
6. *Describe the basic decision-making process.*
7. *Improve an organization's decision making.*

OVERVIEW

The main purpose of this chapter is to explain how to improve organizational communication and decision making. These topics are important because virtually every action taken in an organization is based on decisions, and good decisions, in turn, require effective communications. First, we discuss the nature of organizational communications (including formal versus informal communications) and different patterns of communication. We then explain how to improve organizational communications both laterally (between departments) and upward (from subordinate to superior). (Downward communication will be discussed in the following chapter.) Finally, we discuss decision making in organizations, and particularly rationality in decision making, the decision-making process, and how to improve decision making through the "ABCs" of performance.

INTRODUCTION: THE IMPORTANCE OF ORGANIZATIONAL COMMUNICATION AND DECISION MAKING

No organization can perform effectively without adequate communications and decision making, and there are two reasons for this. First, virtually every action an organization takes—like building a new plant—involves decisions such as whether to build the plant, where to build it, and how much to spend on it. Therefore, in a very real sense, the performance of each employee and of the organization as a whole depends on the quality of the decisions made and on the extent to which each decision is "right" from the point of view of the organization.

Second, the quality of an organization's decisions depends in turn on the quality of its communications. Decision making, after all, requires information—on competitors' actions, new products, price levels, the company president's intentions, and so on—and unless this information is communicated clearly, quickly, and without distortion, the decisions that emerge will suffer. Good decisions and communication are thus essential for effective organizational performance, and we therefore turn to these topics in this chapter.

THE NATURE OF ORGANIZATIONAL COMMUNICATION

Communication is the exchange of information and the transmission of meaning, and it is the very essence of an organization.[1] Managers operate on the basis of information—about competitors' tactics, supplies of labor and materials, or delays on assembly lines. And it is not the *actions* themselves (of competitors, decreasing supplies, or delays) that prompt managerial action, but rather the *information* that is communicated about these things.

Steps in Communication

A basic model depicting the communication process was developed by Claude Shannon and Warren Weaver and is presented in Exhibit 13.1.[2] According to them, any communication involves five basic steps. First, there is an *information source*, which provides the "raw materials" for the message—for example, a machine breakdown on a production line. Next, there is a *transmitter* (or what some writers call an *encoder*). This monitors the information source and changes or encodes the information into a form (language, a production report, telegram, or other) that can then be transmitted along a communications channel to the receiver. The plant manager who discovers the machine breakdown and telegrams a report to company headquarters is an example of a transmitter. The information is then transmitted along a communication *channel*, which in this case may be the telegraph wires over which the production report is transmitted. Next there is a communication *receiver* or *decoder*. The receiver (for example, the company's head of production) decodes the message and then transmits it in a more useful form (perhaps with a list of production delay implications) to the *ultimate* destination, which might be the company president. (Note from the model that the message received may also be filtered or distorted by "noise" from outside the system.)

Exhibit 13.1 Model of the Communication Process

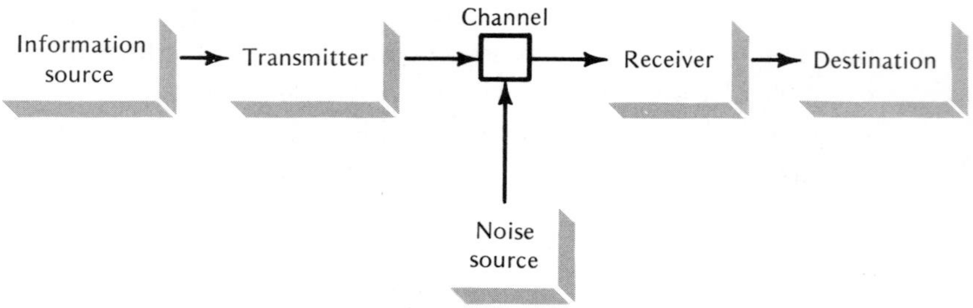

Source: Claude E. Shannon and Warren Weaver, *The Mathematical Theory of Communication*, University of Illinois Press, Urbana, IL, 1949, p. 98. Reprinted in Johnson, et al., *The Theory and Management of Systems*, p. 98.

This model can be used to depict any communication system. We could, for example, use it to represent two people holding a phone conversation. The information source is the person speaking into the telephone's mouthpiece. The phone then acts as a transmitter/encoder, transforming speech vibrations into electrical impulses that are transmitted along the channel—the phone lines. At the other end of the line, the receiver/decoder takes these electrical impulses and transforms (decodes) them into vibrations, which are transmitted through the earpiece to the other person on the line, the destination. Electrical storms, faulty cables, and the like are potential sources of noise that could filter and distort the message between transmitter and receiver.[3]

As you can see from this model, a communication system can be no stronger than its weakest link. For example, if there is too much "noise" between transmitter and receiver so that the message is distorted, or if the receiver does not properly understand or decode the message, an accurate message will not reach the destination, and to that extent effective communication will not take place. In practice there are many such barriers to organizational communication, not the least of which include distortions caused by intergroup conflict and breakdowns caused by time pressure and an overload of information.

Formal and Informal Communications

Most writers distinguish between *formal* and *informal* organizational communications. Formal communication involves messages that are explicitly recognized as official by the organization; these usually involve things like orders (from superiors to subordinates) and various formal, written reports on sales levels, status of work in progress, and so on. *Informal* communication is not officially recognized by the organization; it includes rumors (the "grapevine"), as well as the somewhat more functional day-to-day interdepartmental messages that are necessary for the organization to function, but that are not formally sanctioned and required by the organization.

Formal Organizational Communication. Formal organizational communication can take many forms, from oral instructions from a superior to a subordinate, to highly complex computerized management information systems. In between these extremes are a multitude of formal communication systems consisting, for example, of budget reports, production reports, and monthly sales forecasts.

An Example: An Operations/Manufacturing System.[4] The operations/manufacturing system illustrated in Exhibit 13.2 is a good example of a formal organizational communication system. It is aimed at communicating,

Exhibit 13.2 Formal Communication System Linking Production/Operations Sys-tem

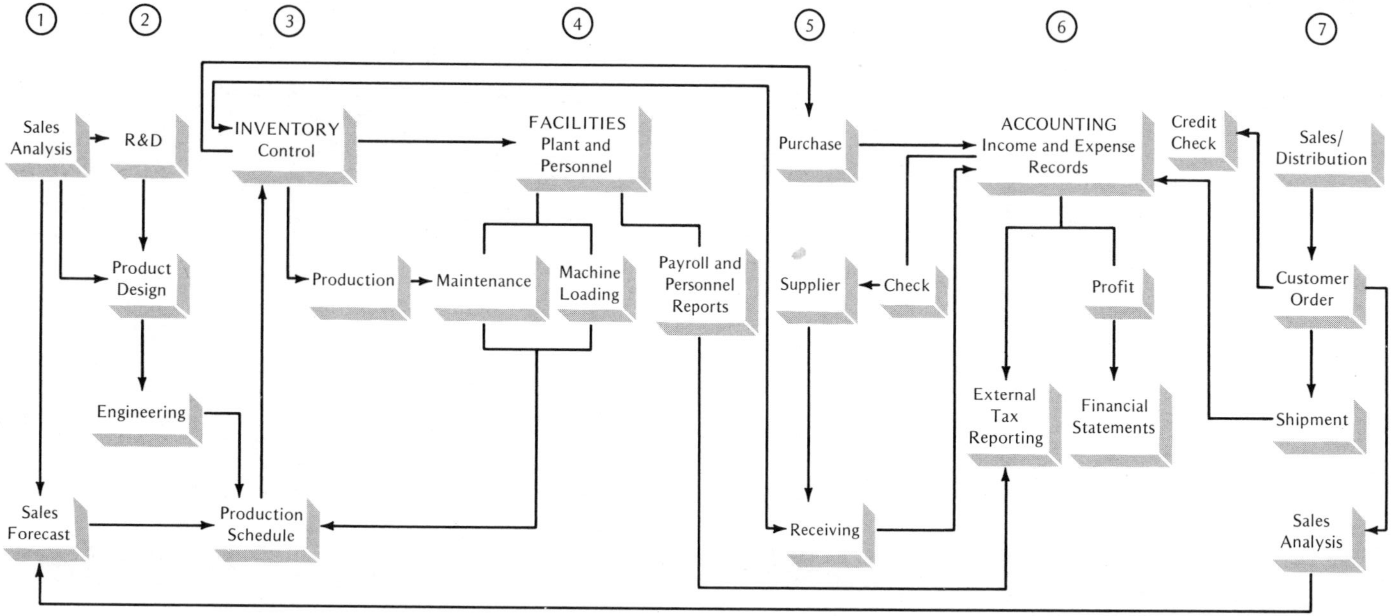

1   Sales Analysis
2   Engineering
3   Inventory Control and Production Scheduling
4   Production/Operations Facilities
5   Purchasing
6   Financial
7   Sales and Distribution

Source: Joel Ross, *Modern Management and Information Systems* (Reston: Reston), p. 130.

to all necessary parties, information concerning the physical flow of goods and services in the organization. As in most formal communication systems, the forms to be used and the required flow of information for this system would probably be specified in the organization's policies and procedures manual and job descriptions.

In this particular example, notice (on the right of the exhibit) that when an order comes in, this information is communicated by the sales department to departments such as product design and engineering. Then, information (on, for example, the specifications of the product and its required delivery date) is sent to the production scheduling department. Information on production schedules and related matters is then communicated to the inventory control department and to the production department for actual production. Information concerning the status of each order in process also has to be communicated to those in the production control and sales departments so they can monitor the order's progress and report back to the customer, as needed. Such a formal communication system might be entirely manual, and depend on the manual processing of forms like sales orders. Or, one or more steps in the system may be computerized. This is illustrated by the computerized "Work-in-process" status report shown in Exhibit 13.3. Information for a report like this is collected in the production shop, and then is inputted into the firm's computer system, which then generates a report like that in Exhibit 13.3.

Exhibit 13.3 A Production Control Report

WORK-IN-PROCESS STATUS

SHOP DATE 615

RAMAC ADDR.	SHOP ORDER		STOCK DATE	QUANTITY ORDERED	TOTAL STD. HRS.	TOT. ACT. HRS. TO DATE	STD. HRS. TO COMPL.	NO. OPS.	LAST OP.		DAYS		REASON CODE
	PART NO.	LOT NO.							DAY	NO.	EARLY	LATE	
20400	358006	020–0	632	68	1597	269	1414	13	612	50		3	1
20800	358006	030–0	649	69	1615	8D	1582	13	613	20	2		
21800	358117	040–0	617	100	976	815	161	16	614	180		1	4

The Organization Structure. Most organizations use formal communications systems like the one discussed above, but they *all* rely, first and foremost, on their organization structures for ensuring effective formal communication.

The organization structure (as depicted in an organization chart) *restricts communication to certain formally sanctioned routes.* In Exhibit 13.4, for example, the production manager is formally authorized to communicate with the production foreman and with the vice-president for production. On the other hand, the production manager would generally *not* be expected to communicate directly with the sales manager: instead, if, for example, the production manager thought an order was going to be delayed he should, strictly speaking, relay this information to the production vice-president who in turn would relay it to the sales vice-president, who would relay it to the sales manager. Thus, *organization structures restrict communications to a relatively few formally acceptable channels.* (This is especially true of the more "mechanistic" organization.)

Exhibit 13.4 Formal Communication Sanctioned by Organization Structure

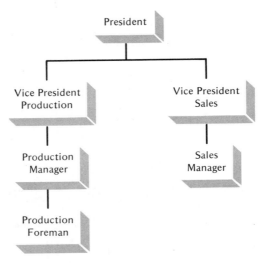

This restriction serves several purposes. Without it, everyone could potentially talk with everyone else whenever a problem arose, and the number of messages (most of them irrelevant) would soon become enormous. Furthermore, if communication was *not* more or less restricted to formal channels, interdepartmental coordination could possibly suffer. For example, suppose our foreman spoke with the salesmanager and obtained the latter's approval to delay a particular order for one month. Not knowing of this delay, however, the foreman's boss might have already scheduled other production jobs for the following month, jobs that would now have to be postponed.

Informal Organizational Communication. However, restricting organizational communication to formally "acceptable" channels also has a major drawback: it can lead to a lack of responsiveness. Thus (in the example above), it could take several days for the message from the production manager to make its way through the chain of command to the sales manager and for the latter's response to be returned, and in this time the customer might be lost. This is one reason why there is always some degree of "informal" communication in organizations—for example, between the sales and production managers.

Communicating Rumors: The "Grapevine." There is also a second kind of informal communication in organizations—*rumors.* Rumors are usually unconfirmed messages that may or may not be task related.

Rumors are spread by the organizational "grapevine," often with alarming speed:

> With the rapidity of a burning powder train, information flows like magic out of the woodwork, past the water fountain, past the manager's door and the janitor's mop closet. As elusive as a summer zephyr, it filters through steel walls, bulkheads or construction glass partitions, from office boy to executive.[5]

In one study of 100 operating employees, the researcher found that if management made an important change in the organization, most employees would hear the news *first* by "grapevine": "A supervisor" and "official memorandums" ran a poor second and third respectively.[6]

Why do rumors get started? According to Davis there are at least three reasons: lack of information, insecurity, and emotional conflict.[7] Lack of information is important because when employees do not know what is happening in their world they are likely to speculate about a situation—and thus a rumor is born. For example, employees who observe an unscheduled disassembly of a machine may speculate that machines are being transferred to another plant and that workers will be laid off. *Insecurity* is another basic cause of rumors. Davis says that insecure, anxious employees are more likely to perceive events negatively and to be more inclined to tell others of their worries. *Emotional conflicts* also foster rumors. For example, there are often emotional conflicts between union and management, or between two strong-willed executives, and rumors tend to develop as each side tries to interpret or distort the situation in a way most favorable to them.

Davis says that the best way to refute a rumor is to release the truth as quickly as possible, since the more a rumor is repeated the more it will be believed. On the other hand, remember that rumors often turn out to be reasonably accurate, if somewhat distorted. Most rumors usually are built around a kernel of truth, and it is this kernel that gives the rumor its believability.[8]

Patterns of Communication

Earlier we said that communications in organizations are restricted (or fairly well restricted) to a relatively few formal, official channels. As a result, the total number of messages is kept within reasonable bounds and coordination is facilitated.

There are, however, a *variety* of patterns to which communication can be restricted. In a five-person group, for example, we could, at one extreme, force four members to communicate only with the fifth and not with each other. At the other extreme we could eliminate all restrictions and allow each person to communicate with any or all of the other members. Various patterns are also possible between these two extremes.

Communication Network Experiments. Which pattern results in the fastest decision making? Which results in the strongest leader? Much of what we know about the relative efficiency of different communications patterns or networks derives from a series of studies carried out in the late 1950s.

In one study, the subjects were 100 undergraduate students. They were divided into 20 groups of five persons each, and each group was structured in one of the four types of networks shown in Exhibit 13.5.

Each subject was placed in a compartment at a table in such a way that his communication was restricted. For example, each subject in the "circle" network could communicate only with subjects to his left and to his right. Subjects in the "wheel" network could communicate only with the subject in the central position of the network, but this "central person" could communicate with the four remaining subjects in his network. (The lines in the networks show two-way linkages.) In the study, the overall structure of the network for any group was unknown to the subjects. All the person knew was to whom he could send messages and from whom he could receive them.

At first glance the networks may seem unrealistic, but they are representative of actual organization structures. For example, the wheel network is similar to the centralized structure shown in Exhibit 13.6, in which, for example, there is a president to whom four vice-presidents report. The vice-presidents can communicate only with their subordinates and the president, and the latter makes all interdepartmental decisions. On the other hand, the circle network is similar to the more decentralized structure also shown in

Exhibit 13.5 Four Communication Networks Used in Leavitt Experiments

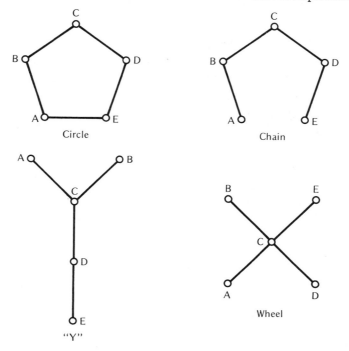

Note: Each person (A,B,C,D, and E) could communicate only with the person or persons he was linked to *directly*. Thus, in the "wheel" network, "C" could communicate with all 4 people, but "E" could communicate *only* with "C."

Exhibit 13.6.[9] In this case there is a president and two vice-presidents, one for production and one for marketing. Each vice-president in turn can communicate either with the president or with his or her own subordinates—the production manager and sales manager respectively. In addition, though, because the production manager and sales manager can also communicate *directly*, decision making in this organization is more *decentralized*: more decisions can be made lower in the hierarchy.

The early network studies involved having the groups solve simple, uncomplicated problems. In one study, for example, each network member held a card bearing five symbols, only one of which was common to the cards of all members. Their objective was to discover what symbol they had in common, and they could communicate only by passing notes through partitions. When a person thought he knew the common symbol, he could signal the researchers; when all five members had signaled, the trial was ended.

The wheel network usually solved this straightforward problem fastest. It minimized the number of communication links and so arrived at a

Exhibit 13.6 How Networks are Similar to Actual Organizations

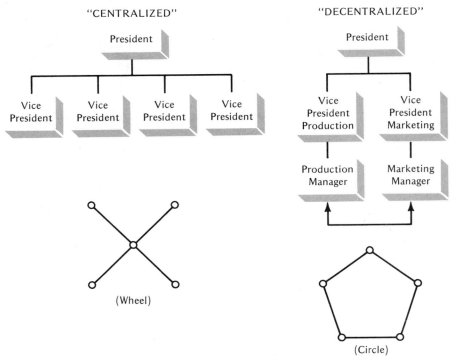

Note: Each organization chart shows how communications are restricted in the organization, and how these restrictions make organization on left similar to "wheel," and
that on right similar to "circle."

decision on the common symbol more quickly than did the other networks.
Furthermore, a leader—the person in the central position—arose immediately
and was generally the one who identified the common symbol. The circle and
chain groups were generally the slowest to solve the problem. However,
morale was usually higher in these groups than in the wheel groups.

A follow-up study in which groups had to solve a more complex problem resulted in different findings. In the early studies, the problem facing
each group member was clear: he had to identify the symbols he had and
impart this information to the members he could communicate with. In later
studies the problem was made more complex by giving the subjects marbles
that were difficult to describe. Two people looking at identical marbles could
describe them quite differently: for instance, what one might view as
"greenish-yellow," another might call "aqua."

In this case it was the more decentralized circle network that solved
the problems the fastest. One reason seemed to be the relatively free-flowing

communications in the circle networks, which were able to send many more messages than were the wheel networks. Once again, however, leaders emerged more quickly in the wheel networks, while group members continued to be more satisfied in the circle networks, possible because everyone had more opportunity to communicate.

In summary, the pattern to which communications are restricted has an important influence on things like the speed with which the unit solves its problem and the number of messages sent. For simple problems that do not involve much problem solving a centralized wheel-type network is best. Here the "coordinator" simply has to get individual inputs from each subordinate, identify commonalities, and make a decision. For complex problems, on the other hand, a more decentralized circle type network that permits interactions among all members solves the problem fastest: In a "real" organization this might mean letting lower level managers communicate directly, or having special liaison personnel coordinate the two (or more) departments. However, regardless of the type of problem, decentralized networks send more messages, and their members tend to be more satisfied, probably because they are all more actively involved in communicating. On the other hand, leaders emerge much more quickly in the more restricted, centralized network, since there is only one person with whom the rest of the members can communicate. These findings are summarized in Exhibit 13.7.

Exhibit 13.7 Relative Performance of Centralized (Wheel, Chain Y) and Decentralized (Circle) Networks for Simple and Complex Tasks

	Simple problems*	Complex problems†
Time		
Centralized faster	X	
Decentralized faster		X
Messages		
Centralized sent more		
Decentralized sent more	X	X
Errors		
Centralized made more		X
Decentralized made more		
Satisfaction		
Centralized higher		
Decentralized higher	X	X

*Simple problems: symbol-, letter-, number-, and color-identification tasks.

†Complex problems: arithmetic, word arrangement, sentence construction, and discussion problems.

Source: Reprinted with permission from M. E. Shaw, "Communication Networks." In L. Berkowitz (Ed), Advances in Experimental Social Psychology. Vol. 1. (New York: Academic Press, 1964) pp. 111–147. Reprinted in Shaw, Group Dynamics, p. 144.

IMPROVING
ORGANIZATIONAL COMMUNICATIONS

In this book we will explain how to improve three kinds of organizational communication. First, in this chapter, we focus on how to improve *lateral* communication (between 2 or more departments), and upward communication (from subordinate to superior). Then, in the next chapter we turn to interpersonal, "face to face" communication, and to an explanation of improving *downward* communication from manager to subordinate.

Improving Communication Between Departments

For an organization to function with any degree of effectiveness, there has to be adequate communication between its departments. If production refuses to provide essential scheduling data to sales, for example, the latter's effectiveness in dealing with its customers will suffer and with it the organization's performance. Similarly, if the employees of two (or more) departments consistently fail to communicate with each other and make their own joint decisions, they may continually have to refer their problems to the boss they both share, and he or she might soon become "overloaded" with requests and unable to function. Poor communication is often also a sign of (and a *cause* of) intergroup conflict, as we discussed in Chapter 11.

We have already discussed some methods for improving interdepartmental communications. One important way is by managing intergroup conflict, perhaps through "confrontation meetings" or rewarding units based on their joint performance. Now we turn to another method for improving interdepartmental communications, one that emphasizes *organizational design*.

Jay Galbraith says an organization can improve intergroup communication and coordination by "redesigning" its structure and instituting special "lateral relationships." These include *liaison roles, committees, matrix organizations,* and *integrators.*[10]

Liaison Roles. Galbraith suggests that "When the volume of contacts between any two departments grows, it becomes economical to set up a specialized job to handle this communication." For example, an engineering liaison person may be part of the engineering department but be physically located in the production plant. In that way, he or she can advise production personnel concerning what product decisions are feasible and also ensure that all items produced meet the engineering department's specifications.

Committees and Task Forces. Liaison personnel are effective when just two or three managers or functions are involved. But when problems arise that involve perhaps seven or eight departments, liaison roles often do not suffice. Increasingly, problems are referred upward for solution, and the more unpredictable the groups' tasks, the more this is liable to happen.

It is at this point that managers create interdepartmental committees, task forces, or teams. These are usually composed of representatives of the seven or eight interdependent departments, and they meet periodically to discuss and solve common problems and to ensure interdepartmental coordination.

Matrix Organizations. Many companies, such as those in the aerospace industry, find it necessary from time to time to organize around a series of one-time projects, and these projects often call for more full-time attention than can be provided by a task force or committee. In this case, the solution may be a matrix organization. In the example in Exhibit 13.8,

Exhibit 13.8 Matrix Departmentation

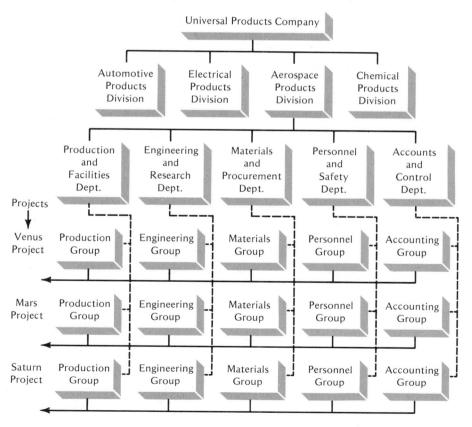

Source: Adapted from John Mee, "Matrix Organizations," *Business Horizons,* Vol. VII, No. 2 Summer (1964), 70–72; reprinted in David Hampton, *Modern Management Issues and Ideas* (Belmont: Dickerson, 1969), pp. 92–95.

the company's aerospace projects division is functionally (process) oriented —production, engineering, and so forth. Notice, though, that there is also a purpose-oriented departmentation superimposed over this functional organization. There are three purpose-oriented groupings—for the Venus project, Mars project, and Saturn project.

This is a typical matrix organization. A manager is put in charge of each project and given the authority and responsibility for completing the project. He is assigned a number of personnel from the various functional departments (production, engineering, and so on). He has the authority for relieving his personnel from their "regular" functional group assignments and for rewarding them with promotions, salary increases, and the like. This is a temporary kind of departmentation, and, on completion of the project, the personnel return to their functional departments for reassignment. While they exist, the matrix groupings ensure a self-contained department for each project, one that can devote its continuous and undivided attention to the needs of its own project and in which effective intergroup (production, engineering, etc.) communication is facilitated.

Independent Integrators. Lawrence and Lorsch have found that many organizations improve interdepartmental communication by creating special independent integrators which may be either individuals or departments. In either case, their entire role is to coordinate the activities of several departments. They differ from liaison personnel in that the integrators are independent of (not attached to) the departments they are coordinating. Instead, they might report to the same manager that the departments they must coordinate report to.

Improving Upward Communication

Benefits of Upward Communication. Many organizations establish special mechanisms through which subordinates can communicate their feelings and opinions upward, to their superiors.

Providing for such upward communication can be beneficial. For example, it provides superiors with feedback concerning whether or not subordinates understand orders and instructions. It contributes to an acceptance of top management's decisions by giving subordinates a chance to discuss the merits and effects of proposed actions. It gives subordinates a chance to "blow off steam," and to satisfy the basic human need to be heard and listened to. And, it encourages subordinates to offer ideas of value to themselves and the organization.

There are many matters that can, and probably should, be communicated upward. For example, managers should be interested in what subordinates are doing, including their work, achievements, and progress. Also of interest are unsolved work problems with which subordinates may need help and suggestions for improving the department and organization.

Many organizations also use upward communication to "take the pulse" of how subordinates feel about their jobs, superiors, subordinates, and organization. For example, we saw that some companies periodically administer attitude surveys: In this way, management can get answers to questions like, "Are working hours and shift rotations perceived as reasonable?" "Do employees feel that the boss has favorites?" and "Do employees consider cafeteria prices fair and the quality good?" Managers can then assess the need for change and correct any problems that need solving.

Methods for Encouraging Upward Communication. A variety of methods are available for encouraging upward communication. Usually, however, "by far the most effective way of tapping the ideas of subordinates is sympathetic listening in the many day-to-day, informal contacts within the department and outside the workplace."[11] Other methods include the following:

1. *Social gatherings* including departmental parties, outings, picnics, and recreational events provide good opportunities for informal, casual communications.

2. *Union publications* (in unionized organizations) can provide management with useful insights concerning employee attitudes.

3. *Scheduled meetings.* Particularly where the number of subordinates is large, it is often easy to neglect contacting or communicating with subordinates, especially the more introspective ones. For this reason, some experts suggest that supervisors keep a checklist of those subordinates they have spoken with during the month so that meetings can be scheduled with those that might have been missed. Some supervisors formally schedule a monthly meeting with each of their subordinates, in addition to the informal contacts that take place during the month.

4. *Performance appraisal meetings* usually provide good opportunities for seeking out an employee's opinions concerning his or her job and job attitudes.

5. *Grievance procedures* can be important. Grievances are often symptoms of misunderstandings, and provide top management with useful insights concerning problems at the operational level.

6. *Attitude surveys.* For example, attitude surveys can provide superiors with useful information concerning employee morale.

7. The formal *suggestion system*—even one as simple as a "suggestion box" in which employees can anonymously drop suggestions—is another good way to encourage upward communication.

8. An *"open door" policy*, which allows subordinates to transmit concerns through a channel outside the normal chain of command can act as a useful safety valve. Related to this, a formal appeals process (where no formal grievance process is in effect) can show subordinates that their requests and complaints will receive fair treatment, even if they are not satisfied with the response of their immediate superior.

9. Finally, *indirect measures* including absence and turnover rates, safety records, and so on can be a valuable indicator of unstated, uncommunicated problems that exist at the operational level.

Whichever of these mechanisms are used, there are at least three principles that can enhance their effectiveness. First, the system should be *formalized*—through scheduled meetings, suggestion plans, yearly surveys, and so on. Second, there has to be a climate of *trust* in the organization, since subordinates are unlikely to speak freely (even anonymously) if they mistrust management's motives.[12] Finally, it is important that management *react* to the opinions and problems expressed in upward communications, even if just to acknowledge that they have been received. If the problem cannot be solved it should be made clear why; if the problem can be eliminated, it should be.

DECISION MAKING IN ORGANIZATIONS

Managers hope that improved communications will result in better decisions in their organizations. Whether the information being communicated involves grievances, turnover, company policy, production schedules or some other subject, it is always intended to be used as the basis or premise of a decision, and it has to be communicated clearly and unambiguously for the decision to be valid.

But, while having valid, timely information is certainly a major element in good decisions, there are also many more factors involved. Even given the same information, for example, some people are simply better decision makers than others. And, a person's capacity for withstanding stress, his or her values, and the person's "perceptual set" and work group are some of the other factors that affect the ultimate decision. Therefore, to get a more complete picture of how effective decisions are made we have to turn from our discussion of communication to a closer look at decision making itself.

Rationality in Decision Making

There was a time not too long ago when most experts believed that decision makers were generally "rational" in that they carefully evaluated all the information at their disposal, considered all possible alternatives, and then arrived at the best or optimal choice. Are decision makers really all that "rational"? Let us begin our discussion of decision making by answering this question.

Economic Man. Prior to the Hawthorne studies most classical (management and economic) theorists assumed that the decision maker was operating in a very predictable environment in which all possible alternatives, and the outcome for each, were known with certainty. This decision maker, who has come to be known as *economic man*, has complete information on all matters pertaining to his consumption decisions. He knows the full range of goods and services available on the market, and the capacity of each good or service to satisfy his wants. He or she also knows the exact price of each good or service, and that these prices will not be changed by his actions in the market, since (it is assumed) he has an inconsequentially small part of the market. This person also knows precisely what his monthly income will be during the planning period and is able to order his preferences for different bundles (or budgets) of products or services. He can thus choose whatever combination best satisfies his needs (or "maximizes his utility"). Under this theory, businessmen were concerned only with profits, and employees only with maximizing their wages.

This "rational" approach to decision making was one of the pillars underlying management theory prior to the Hawthorne studies. Based on the assumptions we just outlined, management theorists could conveniently assume that workers were motivated not by "needs" or "group pressure" but by the desire to maximize their "utility," and in classical management theory "maximum utility" was always equated with maximum pay. As a result, we have seen that the early approach to "behavior" in organizations put an undue emphasis on monetary rewards and incentives.

Administrative Man. In contrast to this somewhat mechanical economic man, Simon and his associates proposed an alternate decision maker: *administrative man*. Administrative man, they say, does not have complete knowledge, and although his decisions may be "rational," they are only so giving the person's values, needs, and aspirations. Simon and his associates therefore substitute the concept of *subjective rationality* for that of objective rationality. The behavior of any single individual, they say, cannot reach any high degree of rationality because:

The number of alternatives he must explore is so great, the information he would need to evaluate them so vast, that even an approximation to objective rationality is hard to conceive.[13]

Because of these "cognitive limits on rationality," administrative man "satisfices" rather than maximizes. According to March and Simon, "Most human decision making, whether individual or organizational, is concerned with the discovery and selection of *satisfactory* alternatives; only in exceptional cases is it concerned with the discovery and selection of optimal alternatives."[14]

The Confirmer. A third type of decision maker has also been proposed. Soelberg has found that decision makers do seem to take a more rational, step-to-step approach than that implied by Simon's administrative man, although not nearly as completely rational as that exhibited by economic man. In one study, Soelberg's subjects were business school graduate students who were making their post-graduate job decisions. Soelberg and his colleagues carried out a series of open-ended interviews with the students, and a picture of how they made their decisions emerged. First, each student decided on "an ideal job," and then laid out a set of operational criteria for evaluating specific job alternatives. Second, the person began sifting through several alternatives, screening *each* against the operational criteria established. But, contrary to administrative man assumptions, the students did *not* necessarily halt their search once they had identified a satisfactory alternative. And when they did finally end their search for new alternatives, they usually had more than a single acceptable alternative in their "active rosters." Third, after actually ceasing the search, each person usually refused to admit that his or her choice had already been made. Instead, before recognizing this choice explicitly, the person often engaged in a two- or three-month "confirmation" process, in which, for the first time, all alternatives were compared to each other, criterion by criterion. These alternatives were generally reduced to two: the choice candidate and a "confirmation" candidate. This confirmation process apparently helped resolve any residual uncertainties or problems connected with the choice candidate and helped arrive at a decision that convinced the student that the choice candidate was best. In a follow-up study Soelberg found that almost 90 percent of the students had actually made up their minds 10 days or more before the date on which they reported having made their decisions.

Soelberg's findings suggest that decision makers do not "satisfice" in any easily discernible way. On the other hand, they also suggest that decision making is not quite as "rational" as envisioned by classical theorists.[15]

Summary. Although the research evidence on this point is not entirely consistent, there are at least two conclusions we can come to concerning the question, "Just how rational are decision makers?" First, the prevailing evidence argues for a view of decision making that is considerably less "rational" then that envisioned by classical theorists. It seems rather likely that decision makers do not (and cannot possibly) consider every scrap of relevant information before making their choice, nor do they review all alternatives and assign some sort of relative values to them. Instead, intuition, values, perception, and a multitude of relatively "irrational" factors seem to enter into a person's decision.[16]

Second, it appears that just how "rational" a person is depends on several things. For example, researchers have found that where the number of available alternatives is small, and where evaluating alternatives is not expensive, people tend to satisfice less, and to optimize more.[17]

The Decision-Making Process

Regardless of just how rational a decision maker is, just about all decision making involves four basic steps: identifying the central problem, developing alternatives, analyzing the alternatives, and making the final decision. We will examine each of these steps in turn.

Identifying the Central Problem. All decision making is usually sparked by the identification of a problem. Perhaps the fuel shortage is causing sales to drop, or you are faced with a problem of increased advertising by competitors. These, and a multitude like them, are the sorts of problems managers face daily.

At first glance it might seem that identifying the problem is a fairly straightforward matter, but this is not the case. A major fallacy in defining problems is emphasizing the obvious or being misled by symptoms. A good example of this is the "elevator consulting" case we discussed in Chapter 10. Recall they decided to define the problem as "the tenants are upset because they have to wait for an elevator" rather than "there are slow-moving elevators" and, as a result, they came up with a quick, inexpensive solution. The point is worth repeating: a decision maker has to be very careful about how he or she defines the problem. This means, first, that one has to peel away the obvious "problems" until he or she hits on the heart of the matter. And, it also means that the antecedents—the standards—by which the person is to be measured have to be crystal clear. For example, a sales manager who is simply told to "do your best" might well view an increase in competitors' advertising as a very different (and less serious) problem than would a sales manager who has been told to "double your product's market share in the next two years."

Developing Alternatives. To do any sort of meaningful decision making, the person has to have several alternatives to choose from. Whether one is choosing between alternative plans, job candidates, cars, or equipment, the existence of some *choice* is a prerequisite to effective decision making. In fact, when a person does not have a choice, he or she really doesn't have any decision to make—except perhaps to "take it or leave it."

Sometimes, developing many good alternatives is no problem. For example, you might advertise for a groundskeeper for your factory and be deluged with applications. But as often as not, developing good alternatives is no easy matter; it takes a good deal of creativity, thought, and discussion.

One important factor here is the creativity you "build into" your organization. First, of course, whether or not an organization is creative or not depends to a large extent on the people hired. Anyone who has ever seen a painting by a great artist, or heard a concert by a great composer, will agree that some individuals are clearly more creative than others.

However, just hiring creative people does not ensure that creativity will emerge. For one thing, creative people—artists, musicians, engineers, and so on—usually cannot be very creative when they feel closed in or under a lot of pressure. Therefore, providing an atmosphere or climate that facilitates creativity is important, and this atmosphere is usually characterized as follows. There is: (1) open communication between employees; (2) an enjoyment of experimenting with new ideas; (3) an enjoyment of work; (4) an acceptance for the need for change; (5) an emphasis on the value of creativity; and (6) a de-emphasis on control reports and "sticking to the rules."[18]

Group decision making (which we discussed in Chapter 10) can also be important. For example, we saw that given the proper leadership, groups can be a fruitful source of ideas and alternatives, especially when they are allowed to freely "brainstorm."

Analyzing Alternatives. Once the decision maker has his or her alternatives, the alternatives have to be evaluated. Should the person rent the house, or buy it? Should the store be opened on the north side of the street, or the south? Should we produce more of product "A," or of product "B"? Evaluating the pros and cons of such alternatives is the point of the "analyzing alternatives" step in decision making, and here there are a variety of tools the decision maker can bring to bear. For example, a *problem-solving group* can be useful not only for developing alternatives, but for analyzing these alternatives (and, eventually, for helping to make the decision). Various *mathematical and financial tools* including "operations research," "capital budgeting," and "break-even analysis" can also be useful, as can high-speed computers. For the organizations (and managers) that can afford them, special *staff* groups or individuals can also be useful in that they can take the time to fully research the pros and cons of each alternative and present their summarized recommendations to the manager.

Making the Decision. Once a person has compared the pros and cons of the alternatives, the next step is to make the actual decision, but, as Robert Heilbroner points out, "there is nothing in the world so common and ordinary and yet so agonizingly difficult as a tough decision."[19] Some of his guidelines for making the task easier are as follows:

Marshall the Facts: Effective decision-making is based on facts—facts concerning what the real problem is; what your alternatives are; and what are the pros and cons of each. Most good managers quickly learn that when a sticky problem cannot be solved, it is usually for lack of facts and they therefore send it back for more data. So the first guideline is: make sure you have all the facts.

But, do not misuse the idea of fact-collecting. Do not continue getting advice and facts so long that you never get around to making the decision!

Consult Your Feelings: Here is what Sigmund Freud had to say about making important decisions:

> When making a decision of minor importance I have always found it advantageous to consider all the pros and cons. In vital matters, however, such as the choice of a mate or a profession, the decision should come from the unconscious, from somewhere within ourselves. In the important decisions of our personal life, we should be governed, I think, by the deep inner needs of our nature.

Heilbroner says that usually you can tell when a decision accords with your inner nature, for it brings an enormous sense of relief. Good decisions, he says, are the best tranquilizers ever invented; bad ones often increase your anxiety.

Make Sure the Timing Is Right: Most people's behavior is affected by their passing moods. Researchers at Columbia University have found that when subjects felt "down," their actions tended to be aggressive and destructive. Yet when they felt good ,their behavior swung toward tolerance and balance. People tend to be lenient when they are in good spirits, and "tough" when they are grouchy. The third guideline, then, is to take account of your "emotional temperature" before making an important decision. If the "temperature" is not right, postpone the decision.

Do Not Overstress the "Finality" of the Decision: Remember that very few decisions are "forever"; there is much more "give" in most decisions than we realize.

Talk It Over: It usually helps to talk big decisions over with others. Part of the reason is that another's opinion may point up aspects of the problem of which you were not aware. But talking things over will also help you sort out and clarify your own thoughts and feelings.

Analyze the Problem With an Open Mind: Herbert Simon says that people make decisions based on their own *perceptions* of the world. Thus each of us is always looking at the world through a window tinted by our own personal values, personality, and abilities. Because of this, it's important to remember that as a manager your own values and personality influence the way you "see" the world. And you have to be constantly on guard against seeing only those things that you *want* to see. So: keep an open mind.

Know Yourself: Effective managers usually have a clear understanding of who they are.[18] Their actions are stable, consistent, and predictable. When making decisions they do not have to struggle with first deciding "who they are" that day. So the final guideline is: "know yourself."

Improving Decision Making in Organizations

The performance of any organization depends largely on the quality of the decisions that are made in that organization. This is true whether those decisions are major (as when deciding whether to sell products throughout the country, or just on the East coast) or minor (as when deciding whether to buy a machine or lease it). Ultimately, in fact, just about everything that happens in an organization is prompted by a decision, and so improving organizational decision making plays an important role in improving organizational performance.

In this book, we have already touched on three specific ways in which managers can improve decision making in their organizations. In Chapter 7 we explained the Vroom-Yetton model of participative decision making and described how it can be used by a manager who wants to determine the degree to which he or she wants subordinates involved in decision making. In Chapter 10 we discussed Maier's comments on the "assets and liabilities" of group decision making, and we went on to explain how you can use a group to more effectively analyze a problem and make a decision. Finally, in the present chapter we listed Heilbroner's guidelines for making better decisions. All three of these discussions can contribute to better decision making in organizations. Our purpose now is to supplement these guidelines with an additional perspective.

Improving Decision Making, and the "ABCs" of Performance. We can apply our "ABCs" of performance to develop some "decision-improvement" guidelines to supplement those discussed previously. How do the *antecedents* of behavior influence decision making? How does the person's *behavior* (ability to behave) influence the decision? How do the *consequences* of the decision influence it? These are the sorts of questions we address in this section. In other words, given the fact that a person has made a poor decision, how can we understanding that decision—and improve it in the future—by focusing on the antecedents, behavior, and consequences of that decision? Ask, for example:

ANTECEDENTS: Does the person know what is expected of him? The quality of a decision can often be improved just by ensuring that the person making the decision knows exactly what is expected of him, and what he or she is expected to accomplish. Often, in fact the main reason the person's decision is "no good" from the organization's point of view is not that it was not an intelligent decision, but, rather, that he did not understand what was expected of him. To repeat our earlier example, a sales manager who is simply told to "do your best" is likely to make rather different decisions (even given the same information) then is a sales manager who is told to "double your market share in the next two years." Therefore, the first question to ask when confronted with a poor decision is, "Does the person know what is expected of him or her?"

BEHAVIOR: Could the person make a good decision if he or she wanted to? In many cases, the person could not make a good decision even if he or she wanted to. For example, if organizational communications are inadequate and the person receives too much, too little, untimely, or garbled information, the decision he or she makes will suffer accordingly. Similarly, if there is intergroup conflict such that each group is "hiding" information from the other, decision making is going to suffer. In summary, when faced with a poor decision, ask, "Could the person make a good decision if he or she wanted to?" or "Are there factors like conflict or an inadequate organization structure or communications system that are inhibiting good decision making?

CONSEQUENCES: What are the consequences of making the decision? For example, in some organizations employees quickly learn that they are rarely rewarded for good decisions but are always "chew out" for bad ones. As a result, their decisions tend to get increasingly "bureaucratic," and instead of making decisions themselves they push the responsibility onto someone else. As another example, we saw that the decisions made by two departments can often be improved by rewarding both departments based on their joint performance rather than on the individual performance of each unit. Thus, in Chapter 11 we saw that the decisions made by Sears store managers improved (from the point of view of the corporation as a whole) when managers in an area began getting rewarded based on their joint performance, rather than on the performance of each individual store. Therefore, in analyzing ways to improve the decision, ask: "What are the consequences of making a good decision?" "Is the person rewarded or chastised for making a risky decision?" "Does the person gain by not making a good decision, or by shifting the responsibility for the decision to someone else?"

CHAPTER SUMMARY

1. Shannon and Weaver developed a basic model of communication that describes communication in terms of five steps: information source, transmitter, channel, receiver, and ultimate destination.

2. Most writers distinguish between formal and informal organizational communications. Formal communications are explicitly recognized as official by the organization. Informal communication is not and include rumors as well as the more functional day-to-day interdepartmental messages that are necessary for the organization to function but that are not formally sanctioned by it. We described two examples of a formal communication system, an operations/manufacturing system and the organization structure (which restricts communication to formally sanctioned routes).

3. Communications in organizations can be restricted (or forced to flow) in various patterns. The network experiments show that a more restrictive, centralized pattern is best for solving simple, straightforward problems where a lot of "give and take" is not required; a less restrictive, more decentralized pattern is best for solving ambiguous problems where more give and take is required.

4. One can improve communication between departments in several ways. One (discussed in Chapter 11) is by *resolving conflicts* between two or more departments. In this chapter we described another method for improving communications between departments, one that emphasizes organizational design. This involves instituting special integration or coordination mechanisms like liaison roles, committees, matrix organizations, or integraters, all of whose purpose it is to maintain open, freely flowing communications between two or more departments.

5. Upward communication is also important to an organization's performance since those higher in the organization have to be apprised of problems in a timely manner. Methods for encouraging upward communication include social gatherings, union publications, scheduled meetings, and attitude surveys.

6. Although the research evidence is not entirely consistent, there are at least two conclusions we can come to concerning the question "Just how rational are decision makers?" First, the prevailing evidence argues for a view of decision making that is considerably less "rational" than that envisioned by classical theorists. A person's perceptions and ability for absorbing information *do* seem to limit his or her capacity for making decisions as administrative man advocates claim. On the other hand, "confirmer" decision-making advocates have found that decision makers do make an attempt to find the "best" alternative—although not as thorough an attempt as assumed by classical theorists.

7. The decision-making process involves four basic steps: identifying the central problem, developing alternatives, analyzing the alternatives, and making the final decisions.

8. Focusing on the "ABCs" of performance can help one improve decision making in organizations. For example, in analyzing why a decision was inadequate, one can ask: "Did the person know what was expected of him or her?" "Could the person have made a good decision if he or she wanted to—or were there factors like conflict or an inadequate organization structure inhibiting good decision making?" and "What are the consequences of making the decision?"

ISCUSSION QUESTIONS AND PROJECTS

1. Have four or five students in the class form a group that will obtain all the documentation they can concerning the formal communication system in the academic affairs division of their college or university. For example, this might include copies of the organization chart, policies and procedures indicating who is to be contacted concerning various matters, forms used in making class schedule changes, and so on. Then, the class as a whole should try to map out the formal communication system of the academic affairs area, similar to the operation's/manufacturing system illustrated in Exhibit 13.2. Do you think the system is adequate? Did the group in its endeavors discover any shortcomings of the current communication system?

2. Discuss the shortcomings identified in question 1 by applying our "ABCs" of performance.

3. Based on the classes' answers to question 1 above, how would you compare the formal communication system with the different communication networks (wheel, circle, etc.) we discussed in this chapter? Why?

4. Explain how you would go about improving communication between departments in an organization. Do you think your prescriptions would work for the colleges' organization that you discussed in question 1?

5. Do you think it matters whether decision makers are "rational" or not? "Why? Why not?

6. Write two short incidents that illustrate the need to identify the central problem of a situation.

CASE EXERCISE

Locks versus Lives

On the first of May, the administrator of the state mental hospital learned that keys to security wards for dangerous criminals had been lost or stolen when he received an early morning telephone call from the night administrator of the hospital. Since duplicate keys were available in the hospital safe, the administrator, Mr. Jackson, knew that loss of the keys would not interfere with the routine functioning of the hospital, but he decided to call a general staff meeting the next morning to consider the problem.

At the meeting, Mr. Jackson explained the problem of the missing keys and asked for suggestions on what to do. The assistant administrator suggested that the matter be kept confidential among the staff since public knowledge could lead to damaging publicity and possibly to an investigation by higher officials in the department of health and rehabilitative services.

The head of security for the hospital reported that only two keys were missing, and although he could not yet determine if the keys had been stolen or lost, he thought they probably had been stolen. He emphasized that the missing keys were "master keys" that could open the doors to all the security wards where the most dangerous criminals were housed. In his opinion immediate replacement of the locks on those doors was required.

The director of accounting estimated the cost of replacing the locks at over $5,000. He reminded the meeting that the operating costs of the hospital already exceeded the operating budget by about 10 percent due to unexpected inflation and other unforeseen expenses, and that an emergency request for a supplemental budget appropriation to cover the deficit had been sent to the Department of Health and Rehabilitative Services the previous week. In sum, he concluded, no funds were available for replacing the locks, and an additional request for $5,000 might jeopardize the request for supplementary operating funds that had already been submitted. Besides, since it was early May, the hospital would begin operating under the budget for the next fiscal year in approximately 60 days. The locks could then be replaced, and the costs charged against the new budget. Another staff member reasoned aloud that if the keys had been lost, any person finding them would not likely know of their purpose and that if the keys had been stolen, they probably would never be used in any unauthorized way.

Mr. Jackson thanked the staff members for their contributions, ended the meeting, and faced the decision. He reflected upon the fact that behind the doors to the security wards were convicted first-degree murderers and sexual psychopaths, among others. He also remembered his impeccable 13-year record as an efficient and effective hospital administrator.

As Mr. Jackson continued his deliberations, the thought occurred to him that perhaps the most important action would be to find and place the blame upon the person who was responsible for the disappearance of the two keys. Moreover, security procedures might need reviewing. Mr. Jackson could not clearly see how best to proceed.

Questions

1. What is the central problem here? What are the symptoms?

2. Has the administrator followed our "guidelines" for effective decision making? How would you apply them to this case?

3. What decision would you make if you were the administrator?

4. How, in terms of our "ABCs" of behavior, would you go about getting performance back "on the track"?

NOTES FOR CHAPTER 13

1. Daniel Katz and Robert Kahn, *The Social Psychology of Organizations* (New York: John Wiley & Sons, 1966).

2. Claude Shannon and Warren Weaver, *The Mathematical Theory of Communication* (Urbana: University of Illinois Press, 1949).

3. Fremont Kast and James Rosenzweig, *The Theory of Management Systems* (New York: McGraw-Hill, 1973), p. 98.

4. This is based on Joel E. Ross, *Modern Management and Information Systems* (Reston, Va.: Reston Publishing Co., 1976), pp. 128–60.

5. Joseph K. Shepherd, *Indianapolis Star Magazine*, 1959, quoted in E. Rogers and R. Agarwala-Rogers, *Communication in Organizations* (New York: The Free Press, 1976), p. 82.

6. Eugene Walton, "How Efficient is the Grapevine?" *Personnel* (March–April 1961), pp. 45–49. Discussed by Keith Davis, "Grapevine Communication among Lower and Middle Managers," *Personnel Journal* (1969), pp. 269–72, in Keith Davis, *Organizational Behavior: A Book of Readings* (New York: McGraw-Hill, 1977).

7. Keith Davis, "Cut Those Rumors Down to Size," *Supervisory Management* (June 1975), p. 206.

8. Rogers and Rogers, *Communications in Organizations*, p. 83.

9. Harold Leavitt, "Some effects of certain communication patterns on group performance," *Journal of Abnormal and Social Psychology*, Vol. 46, 1951, pp. 38–50.

10. This is based on Gary Dessler, *Organization Theory* (Englewood Cliffs, N.J.: Prentice-Hall, 1980), pp. 98–100. And, Jay Galbraith, "Organizational Design: An Information Processing View," *Interfaces*, 4, No. 3 (May 1974), 28–36, reprinted in J. Richard Hackman, Edward Lawler III and Lyman Porter, *Perspective on Behavior in Organizations* (New York: McGraw-Hill, 1977), pp. 207–14. For a more extensive treatment see Jay Galbraith, Organizatioh Design (Reading, Mass.: Addison-Wesley, 1977).

11. Earl Plenty and William Machaner, "Stimulating upward communication," in Jerry Gray and Frederick Starke (eds.), *Readings in Organizational Behavior* (Columbus: Merrill, 1977), pp. 229–40.

12. For a discussion of this see Karlene Roberts and Charles O'Reilly III, "Failures in upward communication in Organizations: three possible culprits," *Academy of Management Journal*, 17, No. 2 (June 1974), pp. 205–15.

13. Herbert Simon, *Administrative Behavior* (New York: Free Press, 1976).

14. James March and Herbert Simon, *Organization* (New York: John Wiley & Sons, 1958), pp. 140–41.

15. Peer Soelberg, "Unprogrammed Deciison Making," *Papers and Proceedings, 26th Annual meeting, the Academy of Management* (December 1966), pp. 3–16.

16. For a little of the research evidence on this point see, for example: Robert Ludke, Fred Stauss, and David Gustafason, "Comparison of Five Methods for estimating subjective probability distributions," *Organizational Behavior and Human Performance*, 19, No. 1 (June 1977); Henry Mintzberg, Duru Raisinghani, and Audrey Theoreth, "The Structure of 'unstructured' decision processes," *Administrative Science Quarterly*, 21, No. 2 (June 1976); Robert Libby, "Man versus model of man: the need for a nonlinear model," *Organizational Behavior and Human Performance*, 16, No. 1 (June 1976); George Saunders, "Personality as an influencing factor in decision making," *Organizational Behavior and Human Performance*, 15, No. 2 (April 1976).

17. See, for example: William Glueck, "Decision making: organization choice," *Personnel Psychology*, Vol. 27 (1974), pp. 77–95. R. Taylor and M. Dunnette, "Influence of Dogmatism, Risk taking propensity, and Intelligence on Decision Making Strategies for a Sample of Industrial Managers," *Journal of Applied Psychology*, Vol. 59 (1974), pp. 420–23.

18. Carl E. Gregory, *The Management of Intelligence* (New York: McGraw-Hill, 1967), pp. 188–190; Larry Cummings, Bernard Hinton, and Bruce Gobdel, "Creative Behavior as a Function of Task Environment: Impact of objectives, procedures, and rules," *Academy of Management Journal*, 18, No. 3 (September 1975); Robert Fulmer, *The New Management* (New York: Macmillan, 1975).

19. Adapted from Robert Heilbroner, "How to make an intelligent decision," *Think* (December 1960), pp. 2–4, reproduced in Harold Lazarus, E. Kirby Warren and Jerome Schnee, *The Progress of Management* (Englewood Cliffs, N.J.: Prentice-Hall, 1972), pp. 197–201.

IV: ORGANIZATIONAL CHANGE AND PERFORMANCE

The main purpose of this part of the book is to explain how a manager can improve the performance of his or her employees and organization through organizational change and development.

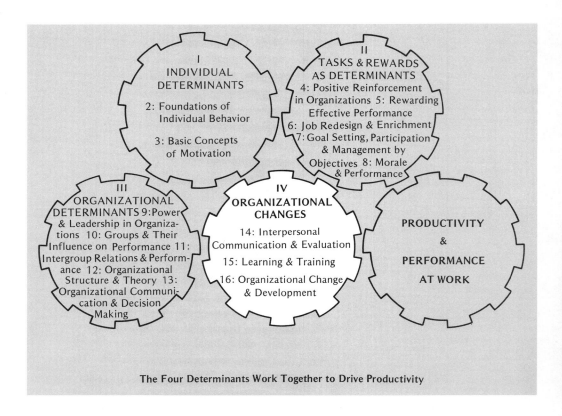

I INDIVIDUAL DETERMINANTS

2: Foundations of Individual Behavior

3: Basic Concepts of Motivation

II TASKS & REWARDS AS DETERMINANTS
4: Positive Reinforcement in Organizations 5: Rewarding Effective Performance 6: Job Redesign & Enrichment 7: Goal Setting, Participation & Management by Objectives 8: Morale & Performance

III ORGANIZATIONAL DETERMINANTS 9: Power & Leadership in Organizations 10: Groups & Their Influence on Performance 11: Intergroup Relations & Performance 12: Organizational Structure & Theory 13: Organizational Communication & Decision Making

IV ORGANIZATIONAL CHANGES

14: Interpersonal Communication & Evaluation

15: Learning & Training

16: Organizational Change & Development

PRODUCTIVITY & PERFORMANCE AT WORK

The Four Determinants Work Together to Drive Productivity

There is an ongoing need to evaluate organizational performance, identify performance problems, and change the organization or its employees. As employees are hired, for example, they often require training to adequately perform their new jobs. Similarly, many organizations find that they can improve the cohesiveness of their work groups, the cooperativeness with which different groups work together, and the organization's capacity for adjusting to unforeseen problems by "developing" its managers. Still other organizations find they have to implement other changes—reorganizing, redesigning jobs, installing a new reward system, and so on.

Therefore, in this final part of the book we explain how to evaluate employee performance, train new employees, and implement organizational changes. In Chapter 14, Interpersonal Communication and Evaluation: Developing Supervisory Skills, we focus on *improving interpersonal communication*, since this sort of "face-to-face communicating" is a vital skill that underlies almost all that a manager does—interviewing job applicants, setting goals, evaluating performance, and working out conflicts, for example. To perform a job effectively the employee needs the necessary skills—for example, a secretary should be able to type—and so in Chapter 15, Learning and Training, we explain how to determine what sort of training a particular job demands, and some techniques for training employees. Finally, in Chapter 16 we discuss two separate, but related topics: organizational change and organizational development. We first explain how to assess what sort of change is required, by describing how to diagnose a problem using some of the "problem analysis" concepts we developed in Chapter 4 (Positive Reinforcement in Organizations). Next, we explain how to minimize employee resistance to change. Finally, we explain Organizational Development—what it is, and why it is needed—pointing out that it is an approach aimed at increasing the level of trust and communication in an organization. In turn, this increase in trust and communication can make it easier for an organization to react to problems (like the introduction of a new product by a competitor) by enabling the organization's managers and groups to work together more cooperatively.

The topics we discuss in this part can all effect the "ABCs" of performance. For example, in analyzing a problem involving inadequate performance, ask:

> *Antecedents.* Does the person understand what is expected? In terms of *interpersonal communication*, have I made myself clear to this subordinate concerning what I expect of him?

> *Behavior.* Could the person do the job if he or she wanted to? Does he or she require *training*? Do the department's employees require *development* in order to get them to cooperate with one another?

> *Consequences.* Are the consequences for performing positive? Are rewards clearly tied to performance? Are *performance appraisals* viewed as fair and valid so that there is a clear link between performance and rewards?

14 *Interpersonal Communication and Evaluation: Developing Supervisory Skills*

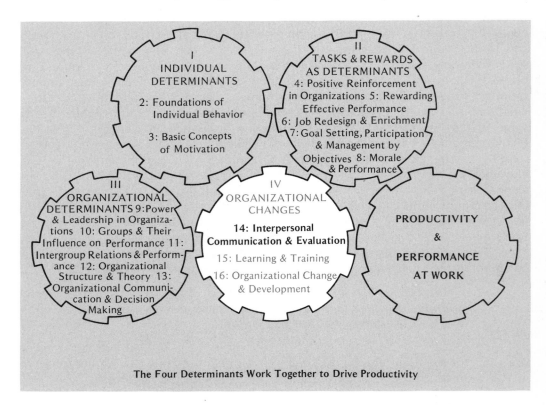

The Four Determinants Work Together to Drive Productivity

BY THE TIME YOU FINISH STUDYING THIS CHAPTER, YOU SHOULD BE ABLE TO:

1. *More effectively interview a job candidate.*
2. *Carry out an effective performance appraisal.*
3. *"Actively" listen to what someone is telling you.*
4. *Explain the prerequisites to disciplining.*
5. *Discipline a subordinate more effectively.*

OVERVIEW

The main purpose of this chapter is to explain how to improve four interpersonal communication and evaluation skills—interviewing, evaluating, coaching, and disciplining employees. We discuss interviewing and the factors that affect the usefulness of interviews, such as premature decisions and pressure to hire. An effective performance appraisal system is the cornerstone of an organization's reward system, and we explain how to use several tools (like "graphic rating scales") that are used to appraise performance. Interpersonal communication and coaching underlies interviewing, evaluating, and disciplining, and we therefore discuss some important guidelines for effective communication and coaching and the technique of transactional analysis, which can be used to improve interpersonal communications. Finally we discuss disciplining, which is important because when a rule is broken, it has to be made clear that such behavior will elicit a negative consequence when it occurs.

INTRODUCTION: WHY INTERPERSONAL COMMUNICATION IS IMPORTANT

Effective interpersonal communication contributes to better performance at work in two ways. First, almost everything a manager does—giving orders, getting advice, meeting with peers, and so on—involves face-to-face communicating, and unless he or she can communicate effectively—make himself understood and understand his subordinates—the manager's performance (and that of his subordinates) is bound to suffer. Second, and, related to this, communicating is vital to our "ABCs" of performance. For example, when goals are set and expectations clarified between boss and subordinate, it is often during interpersonal, face-to-face meetings. Similarly, when the boss evaluates subordinates and provides them with feedback (be it praise, rewards, or discipline), it is again very often in face-to-face meetings. Being able to communicate effectively is therefore an important supervisory skill; so in this chapter we focus on four topics that all rely on interpersonal communication: *interviewing* job candidates, *evaluating* employees, and then *coaching* and *disciplining* them.

IMPROVING INTERVIEWING SKILLS

Almost every manager makes extensive use of interviews. They provide a good way for you to size up a candidate directly rather than through application blanks, tests, or references. And the interview also gives you a good opportunity to provide the candidate with information and a realistic preview of the available job and the company.

Basics of Interviewing

Interviews can be either directed or nondirected. In the directed interview, you use a form such as shown in Exhibit 14.1 to guide the conversation. It asks "standard" questions like "are you employed now?"

The basic idea behind the *nondirected* interview is to get the candidate to talk freely. One good way to do this is by restating or repeating his or her key phrases. For example, if the candidate says "I really enjoyed that job," you might say "you really enjoyed that job?" This will probably get the person to elaborate on why he or she liked the job, and is usually more effective than asking a direct question like "why did you like that job?"

Remember, though, that whether you are using a directed or nondirected approach, the important thing is to get the *interviewee* to talk, perhaps by using some of the interpersonal communication techniques we discuss below.

How to Hold Better Interviews

While interviews are widely used, there is much debate about just how useful they are. We know, for example, that several interviewers who examine the same applicant often come away with different opinions concerning his or her abilities.

As summarized in Exhibit 14.2, there are certain problems that typically undermine an interviewer's effectiveness. For example, interviewers tend to form *stereotypes* of the "perfect" candidate, and to compare all candidates to this stereotype whether it is accurate or not. *Unfavorable information* from (or about) the candidate tends to weigh more heavily in the interviewer's decision than does favorable information. And *biases* for (or against) a candidate are often formed early in the interview—often just based on the person's application blank or appearance.

What can you do to avoid these problems? First, make sure you know the job, and what sorts of skills and abilities it actually entails. Make sure you consider *all* relevant information from the candidate, and try to form a balanced impression of the person. Also, try to go into the interview with an open mind—some suggest not looking at the person's application blank before the interview, but instead using the interview to form an independent judgment.

Exhibit 14.1 Structured or Patterned Form for Directed Interviews

PATTERNED INTERVIEW FORM — EXECUTIVE POSITION

Date_____19____

SUMMARY

Rating: [1] [2] [3] [4] Comments:_____

In making final rating, be sure to consider not only what the applicant can do but also his stability, industry, perseverance, loyalty, ability to get along with others, self-reliance, leadership, maturity, motivation, and domestic situation and health.

_____

_____

_____

Interviewer:_____ Job considered for:_____

Name_____ Date of birth_____ Age_____; Phone No. _____

Present address_____City_____State_____How long there?_____
Is this a desirable neighborhood? Too high class? Too cheap?

Previous address_____City_____State_____How long there?_____
Is this a desirable neighborhood? Why did he move?

What kind of a car do you own?_____ Age_____Condition of car_____
Will he be able to use his car if necessary?

Were you in the Armed Forces of the U. S.? Yes, branch_____ Dates_____19____to_____19____

_____19____to_____19____

If not, why not?_____

Are you employed now? Yes ☐ No ☐. (If yes) How soon available?_____
What are his relationships with present employer?

Why are you applying for this position?_____
Is his underlying reason a desire for prestige, security, or earnings?

WORK EXPERIENCE. Cover all positions. This information is very important. Interviewer should record last position first. Every month since leaving school should be accounted for. Experience in Armed Forces should be covered as a job.

LAST OR PRESENT POSITION

Company_____City_____From_____19____to_____19____
Do these dates check with his application?

How was job obtained?_____Whom did you know there?_____
Has he shown self-reliance in getting his jobs?

Nature of work at start_____Starting salary_____
Will his previous experience be helpful on this job?

In what way did the job change?_____
Has he made good work progress?

Nature of work at leaving_____Salary at leaving_____
How much responsibility has he had?   *Any indication of ambition?*

Superior_____Title_____What is he like?_____
Did he get along with superior?

How closely does (or did) he supervise you?_____What authority do (or did) you have?_____

Number of people you supervised_____What did they do?_____
Is he a leader?

Responsibility for policy formulation_____
Has he had management responsibility?

To what extent could you use initiative and judgment?_____
Did he actively seek responsibility?

Form No. EP-302-R   Copyright, 1973, The Dartnell Corporation, Chicago, Ill. 60640. Printed in U.S.A.
                                     Developed by The McMurry Company

Source: Published by the Dartnell Corporation, Chicago, by permission.

Exhibit 14.2 Avoiding Interviewing Problems

What Two Researchers Found Out About Interviewing Problems:		*And Some Hints for Avoiding These Problems*
First Researcher	*Second Researcher*	
1. Interviewers seem to develop stereotypes about a good applicant and seek to match interviewees with their stereotype.	1. Interviewers agree on which facts they say they consider in making decisions, and can agree on the goodness or badness of an interviewee's record, but they do not agree on whether they should *hire* the person.	1. Provide interviewers an *accurate picture* of the "good" employee so that all interviewers can work with the same stereotype. Put the stereotype in behavioral terms and require the interviewer to make a prediction about job behavior.
2. Unfavorable information about an interviewee is more influential on the interviewer's decision than favorable information.	2. The impact of favorability of information is a function of the characteristics of the people *already* interviewed and/or the others with whom the interviewee is presented; an average applicant after or among poor applicants is rated above average. Further, when "bodies" are needed (when the interviewer has a quota to fill) an average applicant receives a higher rating. Interviewers agree more on unfavorable applicants.	2. Require interviewers to *consider all relevant information* in making decisions.

3. Do not give interviewers *quotas* for bodies. |
3. Interviewer decisions are affected by whether the information is provided a little piece at a time or all at once.	3. The impact of factual information on the interviewer's judgment is a function of (1) whether the interviewer follows a structured interview schedule and (2) whether the interviewer takes notes. Those who do neither seem to make decisions based on a global impression ("halo").	
4. Biases for or against an interviewee are established early in the interview.	4. Only highly structured interviews generate information that enables interviewers to agree with each other; experience is not the important element *unless interviewers receive feedback on their interviews.* Then more experienced interviewers are more reliable. Experience also makes the interviewer less susceptible to external pressure such as quotas (see number 2 above).	4. Require interviewers to use a standardized, highly *structured interview schedule* and to take extensive notes to be used *later* in making their decisions. The guidelines should concentrate on assessment of factual material, not on evaluations.
5. Experienced interviewers can agree on the rankings (from best to worst) to be given a group of interviewees.		5. Make sure the information to be sought *in* the interview *and* the interviewer have been validated. *Provide feedback to interviewers* on their performance so they can engage in self-correction behavior. Some people seem to be better users of information than others.

Source: Developed by Schneider, *Staffing Organizations*, p. 196.

APPRAISING PERFORMANCE

Once a candidate has been interviewed and hired, his or her *performance* often has to be appraised, and so this is the next interpersonal activity we focus on.

As we explained in Chapter 5 (Rewards), Performance Appraisal is a cornerstone of an effective reward system. Ideally, a person's rewards should be tied to his performance, and to do this, you have to appraise that person's performance fairly, and effectively. If, for example, employees come to believe that appraisals are biased, unfair, or misleading, the performance → appraisal → reward link will be broken, and performance will deteriorate. Consequences, in other words, will no longer be seen as stemming from performance, and as a result performance will suffer.

Methods For Appraising Performance

Graphic Rating Scales. Graphic rating scales are probably the most widely used performance appraisal tools, because they are relatively easy to develop and use. A typical rating chart is presented in Exhibit 14.3. Notice that the chart lists a number of traits (job knowledge, versatility, etc.) as well as a range of performance (from Unsatisfactory to Exceptional) for each.[1] You rate your subordinates by circling or checking the score that best describes his level of performance for each trait. The circled values for each trait are then added up and totaled.

The Alternation Ranking Method. Another popular, simple method for evaluating employees is to rank them from best to worst on one or more job related traits like quality of work. Since you will usually find it is easier to distinguish between your worst and best employees than to simply rank them, an alternation ranking method is most popular. First, you list all subordinates to be rated and then cross out the names of any you do not know well enough to rank. Then, on a form such as that in Exhibit 14.4, you indicate the employee who is the highest on the characteristic being measured and also the one who is the lowest. Then you choose the next highest and the next lowest, *alternating* between highest and lowest until you have all the employees to be rated.

Paired Comparison Method. The paired comparison method is aimed at making the ranking method more effective. For every trait (quantity of work, quality of work, and so forth) every subordinate is compared to every other subordinate in pairs.

Suppose, as in Exhibit 14.5 (p. 378), five employees are to be rated. In the paired comparison method you would make a chart of all possible pairs

Exhibit 14.3 Example of a Graphic Rating Scale

Employee: _____ Job title: _____ Date: _____

Department: _____ Job number: _____ Rater: _____

FACTOR	SCORE – RATING				
	UNSATISFACTORY So definitely inadequate that it justifies release	FAIR Minimal; barely adequate to justify retention	GOOD Meets basic require-ment for retention	SUPERIOR Definitely above norm and basic requirements	EXCEPTIONAL Distinctly and consistently outstanding
QUALITY Accuracy, thoroughness, appearance and acceptance of output					
QUANTITY Volume of output and contribution					
REQUIRED SUPERVISION Need for advice, direction or correction					
ATTENDANCE Regularity, dependability and promptness					
CONSERVATION Prevention of waste, spoilage; protection of equipment					

Reviewed by: _____ (Reviewer comments on reverse)

Employee comment: _____

Date: _____ Signature or initial: _____

Note: In this form, the supervisor checks the appropriate box.

Source: Dale Yoder, *Personnel Management and Industrial Relations* (Englewood Cliffs, N. J.: Prentice-Hall, 1970) p. 240

Exhibit 14.4 Rating-Ranking Scale Using Alternation-Ranking Technique

---

RATING-RANKING SCALE

Consider all those on your list in terms of their (quality). Cross out the names of any you cannot rate on this quality. Then select the one you would regard as having most of the quality. Put his name in Column I, below, on the first line, numbered 1. Cross out his name on your list. Consult the list again and pick out the person having least of this quality. Put his name at the bottom of Column II, on the line numbered 20. Cross out his name. Now, from the remaining names on your list, select the one having most of the quality. Put his name in the first column on line 2. Keep up this process until all names have been placed in the scale.

COLUMN I (MOST)	COLUMN II (LEAST)
1.	11. ....
2.	12. ....
3.	13. ....
4.	14. ....
5.	15. ....
6.	16. ....
7.	17. ....
8.	18. ....
9.	19. ....
10.	20. ....

Source: Dale Yoder, Personnel Management, p. 237.

of employees (A and B; A and C; B and D, etc.). Then for each trait you would indicate who is the better employee of the pair. Next, the number of times an employee is rated "high" is computed. In Exhibit 14.5, employee "B" was ranked highest for quality of work, while "A" was ranked highest for creativity.

Forced Distribution Method. The forced distribution method is similar to "grading on a curve." With this method, predetermined percentages of ratees are placed in various performance categories. For example, you may decide to distribute your employees as follows:

15% High Performers

20% High-Average Performers

30% Average Performers

20% Low-Average Performers

15% Low Performers

Exhibit 14.5 Ranking Employees by the Paired Comparison Method

FOR THE TRAIT "QUALITY OF WORK"						FOR THE TRAIT "CREATIVITY"					
Men Rated:						Men Rated:					
As Compared to:	A	B	C	D	E	As Compared to:	A	B	C	D	E
A		+	+	−	−	A		−	−	−	−
B	−		−	−	−	B	+		−	+	+
C	−	+		+	−	C	+	+		−	+
D	+	+	−		+	D	+	−	+		−
E	+	+	+	−		E	+	−	−	+	

              ↑   ↑

    B Ranks Highest Here   A Ranks Highest Here

Note: + means "better than"; − means "worse than." For each chart, add up the number of +'s in each column to get the highest ranked employee.

One practical way of doing this is to write each employee's name on a separate index card. Then, for each trait being appraised (quality of work, creativity, etc.) you place the employee's card in one of the appropriate categories.

    Critical Incident Method. One of the problems with the appraisal tools we have discussed is that they are usually filled in only once or twice a year. Because of this, they may only reflect the employee's performance over the two- or three-week period immediately preceding the appraisal. And when you sit down with your subordinate to review his appraisal, you could find yourself with very few "hard facts" for explaining his good or poor performance.

    Because of these kinds of problems many more companies are using the critical incident appraisal technique. Here you keep, for each subordinate, a running record of uncommonly good or undesirable incidents (like those in Exhibit 14.6). Then every six months or so, you and your subordinate sit down and discuss his or her performance based on these specific incidents.

Exhibit 14.6 Examples of Critical Incidents for an Assistant Plant Manager

Continuing Duties	Targets	Critical Incidents
Schedule Production for Plant	Full utilization of personnel and machinery in plant; orders delivered on time	Instituted new production scheduling system; he decreased late orders by 10% last month; he increased machine utilization in plant by 20% last month
Supervise procurement of raw materials and inventory control	Minimize inventory costs while keeping adequate supplies on hand	He let inventory storage costs rise 15% last month; over-ordered parts "A" and "B" by 20%, underordered part "C" by 30%
Supervise machinery maintenance	No shutdowns due to faulty machinery	Instituted new preventive maintenance system for plant; he prevented a machine breakdown by discovering faulty part

Problems to Avoid When Appraising Performance

Most of us are quite familiar with the types of inequities that can undermine appraisal systems. For example, you have probably noticed that some instructors are "easy" graders and tend to give higher grades on the average than others. And some students (or subordinates) become "teacher's pets" and tend to get rated high regardless of their performance.

Problems like these can destroy the usefulness of your performance appraisal system. They not only result in inaccurate, invalid appraisals, but in unfair ones as well. And once your subordinates find out that the appraisal system is unfair, the performance → appraisal → reward link will be broken, and performance will likely suffer. It would be helpful, therefore, to discuss some of the specific problems one can encounter when appraising performance.

The Clarity of Standards Problem. One problem concerns the clarity of the performance standards. For example, look at the graphic rating chart in Exhibit 14.7. While the chart seems objective enough, actually it might result in very unfair ratings. This is because the traits and degrees of merit are open to various interpretations. For example, different supervisors would probably define "good" performance, "fair" performance, and so on, differently. The same is true of traits such as "quality of work" or "creativity."

Exhibit 14.7 A Graphic Rating Scale—With Unclear Standards

	EXCELLENT	GOOD	FAIR	POOR
Quality of Work				
Quantity of Work				
Creativity				
Integrity				

For example, What is meant by "good"; quantity of work; and so forth.

Some traits, such as "integrity," may be almost impossible to rate objectively.

Therefore, it is important that you obtain consensus among your supervisors regarding the meanings of the traits and degrees in the rating form. One way to do this is by including descriptive phrases which define each trait—as was the case in Exhibit 14.3. Training the raters can also help alleviate this problem.

The Halo Effect Problem. There is a halo effect in the appraisal when the appraiser assigns the same rating to *all* traits regardless of an employee's actual performance on these traits. The problem often occurs with employees who are especially friendly (or unfriendly) toward the supervisor. For example, the "unfriendly" employee will often be rated as unsatisfactory for all traits rather than simply for the trait "gets along well with others." A five- or ten-minute training program, showing supervisors what to avoid, can help alleviate this problem.[2]

The Central Tendency Problem. Most people have a central tendency when filling in questionnaires or rating scales. For example, if the scale ranges from one through seven, many people will tend to avoid the highs (six and seven) and lows (one and two) and put most of their checkmarks between three and five.

On a graphic rating chart, such as shown previously in Exhibit 14.3, this central tendency could mean that all employees are simply rated "average." Needless to say, this restriction can seriously distort the evaluations. It can make them almost useless for promotion, salary, or counseling purposes. The *ranking* tools we discussed are aimed at avoiding this central tendency problem, since ranking your people prevents you from rating them all "average."

The Leniency or Strictness Problem. Some supervisors (or instructors) tend to rate all their subordinates consistently high (or low). For example, some instructors are notoriously high graders, and others are not. This strictness/leniency problem is much more acute with graphic rating scales, since the supervisor can conceivably rate *all* his or her subordinates either high or low. When using some form of ranking system, on the other hand, the supervisor is forced to distinguish between high and low performers. Thus, strictness/leniency is not as much of a problem with ranking systems.

  The Problem of Bias. There is another problem in performance appraisal which in many ways is much more difficult to deal with than the other problems we have discussed. This is the problem of how the employee's sex or race affects the rating he or she obtains.

  One reason this problem is more difficult to deal with is that the bias is sometimes for and sometimes against the person being rated. For example, we know that some people are prejudiced against blacks, or against females, or against some other minorities. They tend to rate them low, regardless of their actual performance. Yet we also know that even when objective performance measures (such as graphic rating scales) are used, high-performing females are often rated significantly higher than high-performing males. Similarly low-performing blacks are often rated significantly higher than low-performing whites.[3]

  At present there is no easy way to predict just what effect this "bias" problem may have on an appraisal. About the best one can do is be on guard against being a "biased" appraiser.

  Avoiding the Appraisal Problems. The performance appraisal problems we just discussed are very real. Yet virtually all organizations still use some type of appraisal system, since the information such systems provide is crucial.[4] Your main concern should be to effectively implement your system, so as to keep the problems to a minimum. There are at least two things you can do in this regard.

  First, we know that *providing clear instructions, and training* can help to minimize or elimniate problems like the halo effect. In fact (to repeat), even where the training is just for five or ten minutes, managers who are trained to minimize rating errors do far better than those who are not trained:[5]

  You can also minimize many of the problems by choosing *the right appraisal tool.* Each of the tools, such as the graphic rating scale or forced distribution method, has a number of advantages and disadvantages that you should consider before implementing your own system. These are summarized in Exhibit 14.8. Graphic rating scales, for example, are the easiest to use, but ranking methods help you avoid many of the problems that plague rating scales.

Exhibit 14.8 Important Advantages and Disadvantages of Appraisal Tools

	Advantages	*Disadvantages*
Graphic Rating Scales	Simple to use: provides a quantitative rating for each employee.	Standards may be unclear; halo effect, central tendency, leniency, bias can also be problems here.
Alteration Ranking	Simple to use (but not as simple as graphic rating scales). Avoids central tendency and other problems of rating scales.	Ranking may still not be precise.
Paired Comparison Method	Results in more precise rankings than does alternation ranking.	More difficult than ranking.
Forced Distribution Method	Here you end up with a predetermined number of people in each group.	But your appraisal results depend on the adequacy of your original choice of cut-off points.
Critical Incident Method	Helps specify what is "right" and "wrong" about the employee's performance; forces manager to evaluate subordinates on an ongoing basis.	Difficult to rate or rank employees relative to one another.

INTERPERSONAL COMMUNICATION AND COACHING

Interpersonal Communication Problems

Once the performance appraisal is completed, you will probably want to feed back the results to your subordinates. In most cases this involves getting together with them once or twice a year to review their performance ratings. Well-developed interpersonal communication and coaching skills, which we discuss next, are essential for these kinds of reviews, as well as for interviews, disciplining, and, for that matter, virtually all the activities one is involved in as a manager.

Unfortunately, most people are not as effective at interpersonal communication as they could be and they make a number of common mistakes. For example, while most people *hear* what the person they are speaking to is saying, much of it doesn't "register," because the listener is busy trying to formulate an answer, or because his mind is wandering, or because he simply is not working hard enough to figure out the actual meaning and feelings behind the speaker's words. Other people make the mistake of trying to make their point through *arguing,* or by *cajoling* or *prodding.* This kind of behavior is rarely effective at getting another person to change his or her position, and has the added disadvantage of distracting the listener himself: he may become so preoccupied with "making his point" that he misses the meaning behind the speaker's words. *Criticizing* is another barrier to effective interpersonal communication, one that is almost guaranteed to have an adverse effect on the speaker.[6] Another common mistake is to attack the other person's *defenses*, for example, by saying that "you are just denying fault because you are insecure." While it may be true that the person's denial is just a "defense mechanism" used to protect his or her self-image, attacking that defense could well demolish the person. Being able to avoid problems like these can help ensure effective interpersonal communication, and this, in turn, can improve your own performance and that of your subordinates.

Guidelines For Improving Interpersonal Communication and Coaching

Avoid Making Your Subordinates Defensive. Defenses help protect our self-images. When you attack subordinates (through criticizing, arguing, or giving advice), it is natural for them to try to defend themselves: they might do this by *denying* they are at fault, by getting *angry*, or by *retreating* into a "shell." Therefore, Feinberg suggests the following:

1. *Recognize that defensive behavior is normal.*
2. *Never attack a man's defenses.* Do not try to "explain a man to himself" by saying things like "you know the reason you're using that excuse is because you can't bear to be blamed for anything." Instead, try to concentrate on the act itself (inadequate sales, decreasing profits, etc.) rather than on the man.
3. *Postpone action.* Sometimes the best thing to do is nothing at all. People often react to sudden threats by instinctively hiding behind their "masks." But, given sufficient time, a more rational reaction takes over.

Be an Active Listener. There are several things to keep in mind here.

First, *listen for total meaning.* Most messages have two components: the *content* and the *feeling.* Make sure you understand not only the content, but more importantly the feeling or attitude underlying it.

Second, *reflect feelings.* Respond to the speaker's statements by restating or reflecting the underlying attitudes or feelings. Incidents, justifications, details of arguments and reasons, and so forth, are relatively unimportant. But how the person feels about any of these things is important. Thus you should reflect these feelings back to your subordinate. In other words, try to help your subordinate get a more objective view of his or her feelings by restating them or reflecting them. (Thus, if an obviously annoyed subordinate says "What? We have to work overtime again?" You might respond to the feelings underlying his question by saying "Having to work overtime again *is* pretty annoying, isn't it.")

Third, *note all cues.* Remember that not all communication is verbal. Make sure you're aware of all cues—including facial expressions, the inflection of his or her voice, etc.

Fourth, don't act as a "judge." Remember that the important thing is not selling your own ideas, but bringing about a constructive change. Passing judgments and giving advice usually just result in defensive behavior.

Do Not Criticize. Experts have found that employees who are criticized—rather than coached to do better—subsequently perform less well than those who are coached. Criticism is a negative consequence—a form of punishment—and while it may help diminish unwanted behavior, it is of little use in eliciting the desired behavior.

Counsel on a Day-to-Day Basis. It is important to avoid "critical broadsides" and to give reinforcement immediately. Therefore try to counsel often, on a day-to-day basis, rather than just once or twice a year.

Use Critical Incidents. No one likes being told with vague generalities that his or her performance is not up to par. Go into the appraisal conference with concrete critical incidents—specific examples of effective and ineffective behavior. Try to be especially specific about the behavior you consider unsatisfactory: Was a report not finished on time? Are customers complaining? Are too many machines breaking down? And so forth.

Agree on Standards for Improvement. We have seen that the best results are usually achieved when the boss and subordinate set specific high goals to be achieved. Therefore, emphasize goal-setting. Facilitate improvement by jointly setting specific targets that your subordinate can shoot for. Related to this, jointly set up a timetable with some intermediate goals. This gives you the opportunity to provide reinforcement more often (say weekly) and ensures that the goals (or intermediate goals) are more attainable from the subordinate's point of view.

Get the Appraisee to Talk. To get your subordinates to analyze their own attitudes, and change, it's important that they—rather than you—do most of the talking. One way to do this is with reflective summaries, as in the "active listening" example above. Here you reflect back to the person his attitudes and feelings; this will usually encourage the person to elaborate on his ideas. Another technique is to repeat the person's key words or phrases, perhaps as questions. Thus if he says, "I don't think we can get that order out," you restate this as a question: "You don't think you can get that order out?" This will usually get the person to elaborate on his or her thoughts. It is also important to avoid "turning off" the appraisee. For example, do not ask too many direct questions (especially those that can be answered with just a "yes" or "no").

Do Not Try to be an Expert. Finally do not try to psychoanalyze your subordinates or to "explain" them to themselves—leave that to a trained psychologist. Concentrate on actively listening, mutually setting goals, and reviewing achievements.

Using Transactional Analysis

What is Transactional Analysis (TA)?[7] Transactional analysis is a relatively new analytical tool that can help a manager analyze the interpersonal transactions and communications between himself and his subordinates. It can enable a manager to better analyze any interpersonal situation he or she is in, by helping answer questions like: "Why am I saying what I am saying to this subordinate?" and "Why is he saying what he is saying to me?"

The Three Ego States. To use TA a person has to be able to analyze the particular *ego state* that he or she is in, as well as that of the person he is talking to: in TA theory there are three such ego states, *parent, adult,* and *child.*

When a person is in a particular ego state, he or she *behaves in characteristic ways.* For example, characteristics of a person acting in the *parent* state include being overprotective, distant, dogmatic, indispensable, and upright. A person in this state tends to argue not on the basis of logical facts, but on the basis of rules, or ways that were successful in the past. The person, in other words, argues and explains much like his or her parent might have, all the while wagging a finger to show displeasure.

On the other hand, a person in the *adult* state takes a rational, logical approach. He or she functions much like a computer, processing new data, carefully seeking out new information, thoughtfully considering this data, and then basing the argument on the facts.

Finally, a person in the *child* ego state reflects all those behaviors that we normally attribute to "childishness." For example, a person in the child state tends to take illogical, precipitous actions that provide him or her with immediate satisfaction. In an argument or discussion this person's actions may include temper tantrums, silent compliance, coyness, and giggling.

Each person probably has one predominant state but all healthy people are in fact able to move from ego state to ego state.

Analysis of Transactions. Transactional analysis involves identifying and analyzing the ego states of two people involved in a transaction, with the aim of helping each person communicate and interact more effectively. For example, being able to identify your own (and the other person's) ego state can be useful, since it can help you to understand what is prompting the other person's behavior and, therefore, how you should frame your argument or respond to the other person's statements.

In TA jargon, three types of transactions are possible: complementary, noncomplementary (or "crossed"), and ulterior. With *complementary* transactions (as in Exhibit 14.9) the lines of communication are parallel in that the employee's state complements that of the manager; each gets an *expected* response (a "positive stroke") to what he or she says. Thus, if the manager is in the parent state and says "All Miamians work slower than New Yorkers because of the heat," the employee in the child state might simply say "Yes sir," instead of arguing with the manager as he or she might if in the adult state. Some other complementary transactions would be as follows:

> *Adult (manager)—adult (employee)*. If both the manager and employee are in the adult state, the manager might say, "Sales increased ten per cent last year because of our improved sales incentive program." To this, the employee might replay, "Yes, and our studies show that the incentive plan works especially well for those salesmen in the urban areas."
>
> *Child—child*. Here the manager might say, "I'll show them we won't work with those people. Stop the machines." And, the employee might respond, "Great! Let's take a long coffee break."
>
> *Child—parent*. Here the manager might say, "I'll show them I won't work with those people. Stop the machines." To which the employee might respond. "It's against the rules to stop the machines. The plant manager will be mad at you if you stop the machines."

Notice again that the distinguishing aspect of a complementary transaction is that each party is getting a "positive stroke"—a response of the sort that they want and expect.

On the other hand, in a noncomplementary or crossed transaction this is not the case. Here instead, because the person is interacting with someone who is *not* in a complementary state, each person gets a response that they neither want nor expect (a "negative stroke"). This is also illustrated in Exhibit 14.10). For example, a manager in the adult state might say that by increasing sales by 10 percent the salesman could boost his commissions correspondingly, to which the salesman might respond, "Quit picking on me." In this case, the manager was in the adult state and expected the subordinate to be, too. Instead, though, the salesman was in the child state, and the result was a crossed transaction. Notice again that the thing that distinguishes a crossed transaction from a complementary one is that in the crossed transaction each person does not get the *hoped for* response. Thus, as another example, the boss in the child state might say to the employee, "Please help me, I don't know what to do," hoping for a "parent" response

Exhibit 14.9 Examples of Complementary (*top*) and Crossed (*bottom*) Transactions

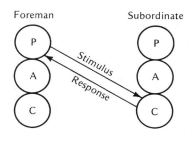

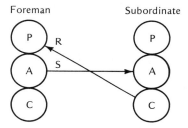

Source: U. P. Luchsinger, and L. L. Luchsinger, "Transactional Analysis for Managers, or How to be more O.K. with O.K. organizations, *MSU Business Topics*, Spring, 1914, pp. 5–12. Reproduced in Keith Davis, *Organizational Behavior: A Book of Readings*, (New York: McGraw-Hill, 1977), p. 111.

Exhibit 14.10 Ulterior Transaction

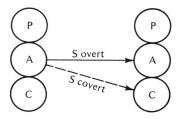

Source: H. Randolph Bobbitt, Jr., Robert Brienholt, Robert Doktor, and James McNaul, *Organizational Behavior* (Englewood Cliffs: Prentice-Hall, 1978), p. 315.

from his employee. Instead, the employee responds from the adult state, saying, "If we don't do our jobs we'll lose our bonus."

Finally, there are *ulterior* transactions. Here, as in Exhibit 14.10, the overt stimulus *seems* aimed at, say, the adult state, but in fact the person has an ulterior motive and is actually trying to elicit a response from, say, the child state. For example, a manager in an adult state might say to a subordinate "I've just been to a training program that shows how effective participative management can be, and I therefore want you to help me solve this problem." In this case the manager *seems* to be appealing to the employee's adult state, hoping for some response like "Good: let's begin by analyzing the data for the problem." In fact, however this manager may be engaging in an ulterior transaction since he has already decided that only his own solution will do. In this case, an adult response from an unsuspecting employee might result in an ineffective transaction, while a child response like "Please tell me what to do" (from an employee who is used to the manager's manipulative tendencies) would result in a more satisfactory transaction (at least for the manager).

Summary. In summary, TA can improve your effectiveness in interpersonal communication and coaching by enabling you to analyze and better understand *why* you and the person you are interacting with are each saying what you are saying. An employee who is obviously in a child state will not react well to adult arguments that are based on fact and logic. Instead, a more parental argument like "That's the way its always been," or "You may get fired if you don't" would probably be more effective. Similarly, it behooves you as a manager to try to determine what state you are in when you are interacting with someone, both to avoid a crossed transaction and to ensure that you are not being parental ("Those are the rules"), or a child ("They can't do this to us, let's take a long lunch break"), when what you *really* want is to be an adult ("Here are the facts and figures I am going to present to the boss to show him why I think we should do it this way").

DISCIPLINING EMPLOYEES

Disciplining also leans heavily on the manager's interpersonal skills. Its purpose, according to Bittel, is to encourage employees to behave sensibly at work, and in this case sensible behavior means adhering to the rules and regulations. In an organization, rules and regulations serve about the same purpose that laws do in society, and discipline is called for when one of these rules or regulations is violated.[8] While *positive* reinforcement may be the preferable way to change behavior, there inevitably comes a time when a rule is broken, and it has to be made clear to all concerned that such behavior will elicit a negative consequence—discipline—when it occurs.

Prerequisites to Discipline

There are three prerequisites for effective disciplining: communicated rules and regulations, progressive penalties, and an appeals process.

Communicated Rules and Regulations. The purpose of rules and regulations is to inform employees *ahead of time* as to what is and is not acceptable behavior. Rules and regulations therefore have to be *communicated.* Employees have to be told (usually in writing) what is not permitted. This is typically done during the employee's orientation, and the rules and regulations are also usually listed in the employee's orientation handbook.

A System of Progressive Penalties. A system of progressive penalties is a second prerequisite to effective disciplining. In most organizations penalties range from simple oral warnings, to written warnings, to suspension from the job, to discharge.[9] The severity of the penalty is usually a function of the type of offense and the number of times the offense has occurred.

An Appeals Process. Finally, it is important to have an appeals process built into your disciplinary procedures: this helps to ensure that discipline is meted out fairly and equitably. Remember that in civil life, if a person appears to have broken a law, the policeman only arrests him. The person is then tried before a jury of his or her peers and sentenced by an impartial judge. You normally do not have this separation of functions in organizations. Instead, the manager is often the policeman, jury, and judge. Most managers are fair, and in most instances this "nonseparation of powers" therefore works fairly well. But there is always a chance of a bad decision on the part of a manager, and therefore it is important for everyone to know ahead of time that there is a formal appeals process.

Guidelines For Effective Disciplining[10]

Disciplining is one of the only forms of punishment most organizational experts would sanction. But, since it *is* a form of punishment, it is important to have safeguards against its misuse. These safeguards include, first, rules, progressive penalties, and an appeals process. Beyond these, the following guidelines are important as well:

Do Not Rob Your Subordinate of His or Her Dignity. Specifically, discipline your subordinate in *private,* and do not attack his *personal worth* for specific offenses. *Attack the act, not the man,* and do not base comments about the person's overall worth on one or two specific offenses.

The Burden of Proof is on You. In our society, a person is always considered innocent until proven guilty. This is also the case with disciplinary matters: the burden of proof is always on the manager to prove that a rule or regulation was violated and that the penalty was necessary. You therefore have to make sure you have "your ducks lined up" before disciplining a subordinate. Make sure you can prove there was a clear-cut breach of a rule or regulation and that you can back this up with positive evidence. Similarly, make sure you keep adequate records of offenses and warnings. This is not only good management practice: it is also crucial when defending your decision to superiors, union arbitrators, and others—like the EEOC.

Get the Facts. Any good law enforcement officer will tell you it is important to "get all the facts." Do not base your decision on hearsay evidence, or on your "general impression." Instead get the facts.

Do Not Act While Angry. Very few people can be objective and sensible when they are angry. It is therefore a good idea to "cool off" a bit before disciplining subordinates.

Provide Adequate Warning. There are few offenses that require immediate suspension or discharge. In most cases (particularly for a first or second offense) an oral or written warning is adequate. If your decision is appealed—to your own superior, to the union, etc.—you will often be asked to show proof that you did in fact warn your subordinate. And when matters like these are brought before union arbitrators or the EEOC, there are few more convincing arguments you can make than those provided by your record or prior warnings.

Do Not Make the Punishment Too Severe. The saying "let the punishment fit the crime" is appropriate when disciplining. Chances are that penalities that are too severe are going to be viewed as unfair and unjust by your subordinates. And that means the rules may not have the desired effect—that of encouraging compliance. Furthermore, an overly severe penalty will more likely be overturned if your decision is appealed.

Make Sure the Discipline Is Equitable. No one likes to be treated in a manner they think is not just. That is why overly severe penalties, inconsistently applied rules, favoritism, and other discriminatory actions breed dissatisfaction. Make sure that rules and penalties are applied equitably—the same to everyone.

Get the Other Side of the Story. You should, remember, "get all the facts." Therefore, it is a good idea to always let your subordinate fully explain what happened and why it happened. You may find that there were mitigating circumstances, or that he was not aware of the rule. Or, you may find that the person had conflicting orders or even permission to break the rule for some reason.

Do not Back Down When You Are Right. When you know you are right—that the rule was broken, that adequate warning was given, that the penalty is not too severe, etc.—it would probably do more harm than good to back down or compromise on the penalty—especially once the decision is announced. In most cases "being soft" is not viewed as a virtue. Instead, employees either assume that the rule itself is frivolous, or that the rules and penalties are being applied inconsistently. In either case backing down is not advised—at least when you know you are right.

Do Not Let Disciplining Become Personal. One sure way to destroy your effectiveness as a manager is to make your subordinates mistrust your motives. Yet this is exactly what happens when they see you "playing favorites" or exhibiting prejudices when meting out discipline. Similarly, once you have disciplined your subordinate, assume that you are then starting with a clean slate: do not harbor a grudge that makes others assume you are prone to engaging in vendettas.

Summary. In summary, effective disciplining can be analyzed in terms of our "ABC s" of performance: For example, assume a person has broken a rule, and that you want to determine if disciplining is appropriate. Ask: Did the employee know the rules, and what was expected of him? Could he have behaved properly—had he the necessary training, for example—and was he to blame, rather than, say, inadequate machine maintenance? and, Were the consequences of violating the rules made clear ahead of time, and is disciplining viewed as a direct consequence of such a violation?

CHAPTER SUMMARY

1. To improve interviewing: use a structured guide; know the requirements of the job; do not give interviewers a quota; let the interviewee do most of the talking; taking notes; and delay your decision. (See exhibit 14.1).

2. *Performance appraisal* is important because it is a cornerstone of an effective reward system, and because it provides an opportunity to discuss solutions to subordinate performance problems. Tools for appraising performance include: graphic rating scales; the alternation-making method; paired comparison method; forced distribution method; and the critical incident method.

3. Problems to avoid when appraising performance include: unclear standards, central tendencies, leniency or strictly, and bias.

4. Guidelines for effective communication and coaching include: avoid making your subordinates defensive; be an active listener; do not criticize; counsel day to day; use critical incidents; agree on standards for improvements; get the appraisee to talk; and do not try to be an expert.

5. Transactional analysis (TA) can help a manager analyze the interpersonal transactions and communications between himself and his subordinates. It involves determining which ego state (parent, adult, and child) the manager and subordinate are each in, and determining if the transactions between the two are complementary or crossed.

6. Disciplining employees is important because when a rule is broken it has to be made clear that such behavior will elicit a negative consequence. Prerequisites in disciplining include: communicated rules and regulations, a system of progressive penalties, and an appeals process.

7.   Guidelines for effective disciplining include: do not rob your subordinate of his or her dignity; the burden of proof is on you; get the facts; do not act while angry; provide adequate warning; do not make the punishment too severe; make sure the discipline is equitable; get the other side of the story; do not back down when you are right; and do not let disciplining become personal.

DISCUSSION QUESTIONS AND PROJECTS

1. Discuss the pros and cons of at least four performance appraisal tools.

2.   Develop a graphic rating scale for the following jobs: secretary, engineer, directory assistance operator, and college instructor.

3.   Explain how you would use: the alternation-ranking method, the paired comparison method, and the forced distribution method.

4.   Write a short presentation entitled "How to be Effective as an Interview*ee*."

5.   What is transactional analysis? How can a manager make use of it?

6.   Explain why disciplining might not be recommended for bringing about some desired change in behavior.

CASE EXERCISE

Get Off My Back

Joe Toby, director of management services, schedules a counseling session with Herman Sutherland, a management consultant on his staff:

Joe: As you know, Herman, I've scheduled this meeting with you because I want to talk about certain aspects of your work. And my comments are not all that favorable.

Herman: Since you have formal authority over me, I guess I'll have to go along with the session. Go ahead.

Joe: I'm not a judge reading a verdict to you. This is supposed to be a two-way interchange.

Herman: But you called the meeting, so go ahead with your complaints. Particularly any with foundation. I remember once when we were having lunch you told me that you didn't like the fact that I wore a brown knitted suit with a blue shirt. I would put that in the category of unfounded.

Joe: I'm glad you brought appearance up. I think you create a substandard impression to clients because of your appearance. A consultant is supposed to look sharp, particularly at the rates we charge clients. You often create the impression that you cannot afford good clothing. Your pants are baggy. Your ties are unstylish and often food stained.

Herman: The firm may charge those high rates. But as a junior the money I receive does not allow me to purchase fancy clothing. Besides, I have very little interest in trying to dazzle clients with my clothing. I have heard no complaints from them.

Joe: Nevertheless, I think that your appearance should be more business-like. Let's talk about something else I have on my list of things in which I would like to see some improvements. A routine audit of your expense account shows a practice that I think is improper. You charged one client for a Thursday night dinner for three consecutive weeks. Yet your airline ticket receipt shows that you returned home at three in the afternoon. That kind of behavior is unprofessional. How do you explain your charges for these phantom dinners?

Herman: The flight ticket may say three P.M. but with our unpredictable weather, the flight could very well be delayed. If I eat at the airport, then my wife won't have to run the risk of preparing a dinner for me that goes to waste. Food is very expensive.

Joe: But how can you eat dinner at three P.M. at the airport?

Herman: I consider any meal after one in the afternoon to be dinner.

Joe: Okay for now. I want to comment on your reports to clients. They are much more careless than they should be. I know that you are capable of more meticulous work. I saw an article you prepared for publication that was first rate and professional. Yet on one report you misspelled the name of the client company. That's atrocious.

Herman: A good secretary should have caught that mistake. Besides, I never claimed that I was able to write perfect reports. There are only so many hours in the working day to spend on writing up reports.

Joe: Another thing that requires immediate improvement is the appearance of your office. It's a mess. You have the worst-looking office in our branch. In fact, you have the worst-looking office I have ever seen in a C.P.A. or management-consulting office. Why can't you have a well-organized, good-looking office?

Herman: What's the difference? Clients never visit me in this office. It's just a work place. Incidentally Joe, could you do me one favor?

Joe: What's that?

Herman: Get off my back.

Questions

1. What "communications" mistakes has Joe Toby made?
2. Has Joe been an "active listener"?
3. How would you describe Herman's reactions?
4. If you were Joe, how would you have handled this situation?
5. What questions would you have asked if you had been interested in analyzing the "ABCs" of Herman's behavior?

EXPERIENTIAL EXERCISE 1

Purpose: The purpose of this exercise is to give you some experience in counseling and active listening.

Required Understanding: You should be familiar with our discussions of face-to-face communicating.

How to Set Up the Exercise/Instructions:

1. Divide the class into groups of three students. In each group one person will act as observer, a second will play the role of Bob, the interviewee, and the third person will play the role of Mike, the interviewer. (Extra students can join groups as observers.) Their "roles" are presented below, but *please make sure you only read the role of the person whose part you are taking.*

2. ROLES

Role of Bob (the interviewee) (only "Bob" should read this role): Today, as the saying goes, has not been your day. You overslept this morning and in your rush to get to work you got a ticket for not stopping at a stop sign. You got to sleep late because you spent most of the night trying to fix a leaking pipe in the bathroom, which your wife has just informed you will cost $95 to have a plumber fix. You got into work late this morning and in your rush to catch up machined (you're a machinist) about 50 metal parts down to the wrong diameter: you'll now have to remachine all of them, and you know your supervisor, Mike, is probably steaming. He just told you to be in his office at 4:30 P.M. sharp, a fact which upsets you both because you're afraid you're being "called on the carpet," and because you'd wanted to leave work a few minutes early to keep an eye on the plumber.

Role for Mike, the interviewer (only Mike should read this role): The performance report for your department for last month was not as good as it should have been, and your boss has told you to get costs back in line with what they should be. You were therefore startled to be told that Bob has to remachine 50 parts, a process that will probably kill half a day. To make matters worse remachining the parts will probably require overtime (an added expense) since the parts were for a rush job that has to be finished by the end of the week. You're not quite sure what you're going to say to Bob when he comes in, but your first inclination is to "read him the riot act."

Role for the observer (only observers should read this): The observer should not enter into the conversation at all, and should simply take notes of what he or she hears: How well is Mike following the guidelines we set down in this chapter? What could he have improved on? Was he an active listener?

3. Once you have read your respective roles, "Bob" and "Mike" should meet for their "4:30 meeting." Their conversation should last about 15 to 20 minutes.

After the "meeting" the three group members should discuss the following questions (please don't read this until after the "meeting"): Was Mike an active listener? (Be specific.) What could he have done to improve his effectiveness as a communicator? Was Bob an active listener? Why? Why not?

EXPERIENTIAL EXERCISE 2

Purpose: The purpose of this exercise is to give you practice in developing and using a performance appraisal form.

Required Understanding: You are going to develop a performance appraisal form for an instructor and should therefore be thoroughly familiar with the discussion of performance appraisal in this chapter, and Exhibit 14.11.

How to Set Up the Exercise: Divide the class into groups of four or five students.

Instructions

1. First, based upon what you now know about performance appraisal, do you think the Exhibit is an effective scale for appraising instructors? Why? Why not?

2. Next, your group should develop its own tool for appraising the performance of an instructor. Decide which of the appraisal tools (graphic rating scales, alternation ranking, etc.) you are going to use, and then design the instrument itself.

3. Next, have a spokesman from each group put his or her group's appraisal tool on the board. How similar are the tools? Do they all measure about the same factors? Which factor appears most often? Which do you think is the most effective tool on the board? Can you think of any way of combining the best points of several of the tools into a resulting performance appraisal tool?

Exhibit 14.11 A Scale for Appraising Instructors

INSTRUCTOR

DEPARTMENT

COURSE NUMBER OR TITLE

I. The following items reflect some of the ways teachers can be described in and out of the classroom. For the instructor named above, please circle the number which indicates the degree to which you feel each item is descriptive of him or her. In some cases, the statement may not apply to this individual. In these cases, check *Does not apply or don't know* for that item.

	Not at all Descriptive	*Very Descriptive*	*Doesn't apply or don't know*
1. Has command of the subject, presents material in an analytic way, contrasts various points of view discusses current developments, and relates topics to other areas of knowledge	1 2 3 4 5 6 7		( )
2. Makes himself clear, states objectives, summarizes major points, presents material in an organized manner, and provides emphasis.			
3. Is sensitive to the response of the class, encourages student participation, and welcomes questions and discussion.			
4. Is available to and friendly towards students, is interested in students as individuals, is himself respected as a person, and is valued for advice not directly related to the course.			
5. Enjoys teaching, is enthusiastic about his subject, makes the course exciting, and has self-confidence			

Note: (Additional items may be presented by instructor and/or department.)

Source: Richard Miller, *Developing Programs for Faculty Evaluation* (San Francisco: Jossey-Bass Publishers, 1974), p. 43.

NOTES FOR CHAPTER 14

1. Dale Yoder, *Personnel Management and Industrial Relations* (Englewood Cliffs, N.J.: Prentice-Hall, 1970).

2. Gary Latham, Kenneth Wexley, and Elliot Pursell, "Training Managers to Minimize Rating Errors in the Observation of Behavior," *Journal of Applied Psychology*, Vol. 60, No. 5 (October 1975).

3. William Bigoness, "Effect of Applicants Sex, Race, and Performance on Employees Performance Ratings: Some additional findings," *Journal of Applied Psychology*, Vol. 61, No. 1 (February 1976).

4. Allen Patz, "Performance Appraisal: Useful but still resisted," *Harvard Business Review* (May–June, 1975).

5. G. Latham, K. Wexley, and E. Pursell, "Training Managers . . ."; Walter Borman, "Effect of Instructions to Avoid Halo Error on Reliability and Validity of Performance Evaluation Ratings," *Journal of Applied Psychology*, Vol. 61, No. 2 (April 1976).

6. Herbert Meyer, Emmanuel Kay, and John French, Jr., "Split Roles in Performance Appraisal," *Harvard Business Review*, 43 (January–February 1965), pp. 123–29, reprinted in Dale Beach, *Managing People at Work* (New York: Macmillan, 1977), pp. 148–56.

7. Except where noted this section is based on V. P. Luchsinger and L. L. Luchsinger, "Transactional Analysis for Managers, or How to Be More OK with OK Organizations," *MSU Business Topics* (Spring 1974), pp. 5–12, reprinted in Keith Davis, *Organizational Behavior: A Book of Readings* (New York: McGraw-Hill, 1977), pp. 108–20.

8. This section is based on Lester R. Bittel, *What Every Supervisor Should Know* (New York: McGraw-Hill, 1974), pp. 285–98. See also Dale Beach, *Personnel* (New York: Macmillan, 1970), pp. 608–12.

9. Dale Beach, *Personnel* (New York: Macmillan, 1970), pp. 608–12.

10. These are based on George Odiorne, *How Managers Make Things Happen* (Englewood Cliffs, N.J.: Prentice-Hall, 1961), pp. 132–43; Bittel, *What Every Supervisor Should Know*, pp. 285–98. Beach, *Personnel*, pp. 605–10; Robert Mathis and John Jackson, *Personnel* (St. Paul: West, 1976), p. 349.

15 *Learning and Training*

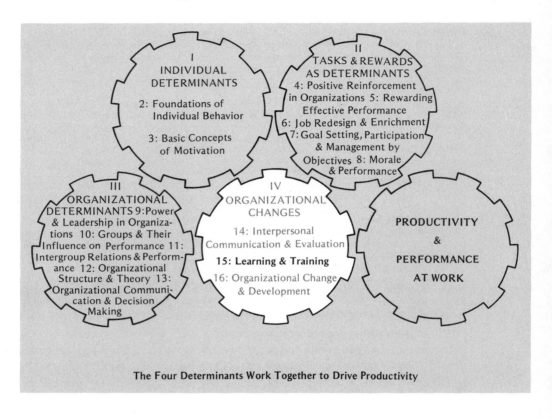

I
INDIVIDUAL DETERMINANTS

2: Foundations of Individual Behavior

3: Basic Concepts of Motivation

II
TASKS & REWARDS AS DETERMINANTS
4: Positive Reinforcement in Organizations 5: Rewarding Effective Performance 6: Job Redesign & Enrichment 7: Goal Setting, Participation & Management by Objectives 8: Morale & Performance

III
ORGANIZATIONAL DETERMINANTS 9:Power & Leadership in Organizations 10: Groups & Their Influence on Performance 11: Intergroup Relations & Performance 12: Organizational Structure & Theory 13: Organizational Communication & Decision Making

IV
ORGANIZATIONAL CHANGES
14: Interpersonal Communication & Evaluation
15: Learning & Training
16: Organizational Change & Development

PRODUCTIVITY & PERFORMANCE AT WORK

The Four Determinants Work Together to Drive Productivity

BY THE TIME YOU FINISH STUDYING THIS CHAPTER, YOU SHOULD BE ABLE TO:

1. *Develop and implement a more useful training program.*
2. *Discuss five training techniques.*
3. *Explain how you would go about identifying training requirements.*
4. *List seven principles of learning.*
5. *Prepare a job instruction training chart for a job.*

OVERVIEW

The main purpose of this chapter is to increase your effectiveness as a trainer. We discuss how to assess training requirements, how to apply "principles of learning," and how to use training techniques like job instruction training. In terms of our "ABCs" of performance, training is important because it is largely through training that employees (1) find out what you expect of them; (2) develop the necessary skills that enable them to do their jobs; and (3) learn something about the consequences of performing effectively or ineffectively.

INTRODUCTION: TRAINING AND THE "ABCs" OF PERFORMANCE

Training—improving an employee's job related skills—is an important prerequisite for performance. In analyzing performance problems, for example, we usually ask, "Could the person do this job if he or she wanted to?" And, often, without training, the answer is "no." Often, in other words, when a person is performing poorly, it is not because he or she does not *want* to do better, but, rather, because he hasn't the skills to do the job well: training can often rectify such a problem.

Keep in mind, however, that when a person is not performing well, it is often *not* for lack of training. Instead, the antecedents—standards—may not be clear, or the consequences of performance may be negative. For example, a training program aimed at getting workers to wear safety hats might *appear* to have failed because workers are not wearing their hats. In fact, though, the training might have been fine. But once the workers were on the job with their hats, perhaps they found they were too hot, and that their coworkers laughed at them, and that there hadn't been an accident in the last two years. The problem, in other words, was in the *consequences*, not in the training.

HOW TO DETERMINE WHAT TRAINING IS REQUIRED

In determining what sort of training is required, it is useful to distinguish between the training needs of *new* employees, and of *present* employees.

Assessing the training needs of new employees is perhaps the easier task. Here, particularly with lower echelon workers, it is common to hire inexperienced personnel and train them—give them the necessary skills to perform the task. For such people the training needs are fairly obvious.[1] Here your aim is to develop the skills and knowledge required for effective performance, and so the training is usually based on a detailed study of the job itself to determine what specific skills and knowledge are required.

Job description and analysis is helpful in this regard. *Job analysis* is aimed at determining what constitutes the job, the methods that are used on the job, and the human skills required to perform the job adequately. This analysis leads to a *job description* (which lists the actual duties to be performed), and a *job specification* (which lists the human skills and knowledge required). This list of duties and required skills then becomes the basic point of reference in developing the training program for the job.

Determining the training needs of *present* employees is often more complex. Here the need for training is usually prompted by problems (like excess scrap) or by foremen's requests, and so those in charge of training have the added task of determining if "training" is in fact the solution. Often, for example, performance is down because standards are not clear, or because rewards are inadequate.

Analyzing Problems: Is Training Required?

Analyzing performance problems in order to assess the need for training basically involves the procedure we discussed in Chapter 4:

1. Identify a performance improvement area (like quality control), and determine acceptable standards;
2. Measure actual performance, and identify deficiencies (or problems);
3. Analyze the cause of the problem: does it lie in the antecedents, behavior, or consequences?
4. Take remedial action.

A typical analysis might be as follows:

First, it comes to the attention of those in charge of training that there is some sort of problem. For example, there may be *obvious problems* like: work standards not being met; accidents; excessive scrap; high turnover; too many low ratings on performance evaluation reports; fatigue; or deadlines not being met.[2] In most cases first-line supervisors are the first to notice such problems, and so *management requests* for training begin making their way to the training department, on the (often erroneous) assumption that "better training" is the solution. Then:

1. Having determined that a problem may exist, those in charge of training begin to analyze the problem. First, they list the duties and tasks of the job under consideration (using the job description as a guide), as well as the acceptable standards of work performance.[3]
2. Next, they interview and closely observe the employees involved, and determine their *actual* present performance. If actual performance is significantly below the acceptable standards for the job, a *performance deficiency* or problem does in fact exist.
3. The next step is to analyze the *cause* of the problem, using the "ABC s" of performance. For example, ask: are the standards clear to the employee? Does he or she know what is *expected*, in terms of good performance? Could the person do the job if he or she *wanted* to? What parts of the job are giving the person trouble? What are the *consequences* of good performance? Does he or she get rewarded anyway?
4. Next, having identified the cause of the problem, one can plan and implement the necessary change.

As often as not, the solution *does* turn out to be training, and so in the rest of this chapter we will discuss how to train employees. Remember, however, that the problem often lies not in the employees' skills, but in the fact that he or she doesn't know what is expected, or that material doesn't arrive at the person's station on time, or that the consequences for performing are negative or inadequate. In other words, there may in fact be a need for training—the person hasn't the *skills* to do the job. But on the other hand, the solution may lie in setting clearer standards, removing organizational impediments to performance, or providing positive consequences. With that in mind, we can turn to a discussion of training, beginning with an explanation of how people learn.

PRINCIPLES OF LEARNING

Training is essentially a learning process and so to train subordinates, you should understand something about how people learn. Research into why people learn (and how to get them to learn) has been going on for years and there are still no sure-fire answers. But we do have some findings that are useful, and we discuss these "principles" of learning in this section.

Make the Method Meaningful

First, we know it's easier for trainees to understand and remember material that is *meaningful*. And, Wexley and Yukl say there are at least six ways in which you can make your training materials more meaningful:[4]

1. At the start of training, provide the trainees with a *bird's eye view* of the material to be presented. Knowing the overall picture and understanding how each part of the program fits into it helps make the entire program more meaningful.
2. Make sure you use a variety of *familiar examples* when presenting material to the trainees.
3. *Organize the material* so that it is presented in a logical manner and has meaningful units.
4. Split the material up into *meaningful chunks* rather than presenting it all at once.
5. Try to use terms and concepts that are already *familiar* to the trainees.
6. Use as many *visual* aids as possible to augment "theoretical" materials.

Make Provision for Transfer of Learning

You may sometimes have to train employees away from the jobsite (perhaps in a classroom) and if you do, you obviously want to make sure that what is learned is transferred back to the job. Here are some hints for accomplishing this.[5]

1. *Maximize the Similarity between the Training Situation and the Work Situation.* For example, if your employee will have to work in a noisy environment make sure he gets some practice during training producing under noisy conditions.
2. *Provide Adequate Experience with the Tasks during Training.* As a rule, the more your employee can practice the task, the better will be his or her transfer of learning back to the job.
3. *Provide for a Variety of Examples when Teaching Concepts or Skills.* For example, if you're trying to "get across" a concept, present examples of instances which represent and do not represent the concepts—like the right and wrong way of doing some task.
4. *Label or Identify Important Features of the Task.* For example, if you're training a machine operator, it's useful to give each important part of the machine a label (e.g., starter switch). And it's also useful to label each step of the procedure (e.g., start machine; place tube in press; etc.).
5. *Make Sure that the Trainee Understands General Principles.* This is really a variation on the idea that you should make the material as meaningful as possible. Thus, if your trainee understands the general principles underlying what is being taught he'll probably

understand it better than if he were just asked to memorize a series of isolated steps.

Provide Feedback

As you might imagine, based on our discussions of positive reinforcement, trainees who are given feedback on their progress usually learn faster and perform better than those who aren't. As a rule, feedback should be fast and frequent. This is especially so for lower-level jobs which are often routine and quickly completed.

Motivate Your Trainee

Educational psychologists know that to get students (or trainees) to learn, you have to first get them to *want* to learn. And if you think about classes in which you have done especially well (or badly), you will probably agree that this is so.

How do you go about motivating trainees? Make sure your trainee understands how his training can be *instrumental* in his success. Clarify the *goals* of the training. Explain how job performance is related to *rewards* like incentives. And explain how the training can *improve his performance* and thereby boost his *rewards*.

Some of the other learning guidelines we just discussed are also relevant here. For example, making the material *meaningful* and providing *quick feedback* and *reinforcement* will help motivate your trainee. The reinforcement aspect is especially important: provide quick, positive reinforcement (this might just take the form of a "reward" like a compliment for "a job well done").

Provide for Practice and Repetition

Practice and repetition are important for learning new skills. Skills that are practiced often are better learned and less easily forgotten.

Seven Principles of Learning for Trainers

Based upon our previous discussion and the work of a number of psychologists, here are some important principles of learning to keep in mind:[6]

1. *Trainees learn best by doing.* Try to give them as much "real life" practice as possible.
2. Trainees learn best when correct responses on their part are immediately *reinforced*.

3. *Provide reinforcement as quickly and frequently as possible.* Don't wait until the end of the day to tell trainees they've "done well." Instead, reinforce frequently, whenever they do something right.

4. *Provide for practice in a variety of settings.* This helps ensure that your trainees become familiar with performing the task in a setting similar to the one they'll find "on the job." It also helps them apply their learning in a variety of settings.

5. *Motivate your trainees.* Trainees who are motivated are more likely to learn and apply their new knowledge and skills than those who are unmotivated. Make sure they see how the training will be to their success and rewards.

6. *Make the learning meanful* by using familiar examples and summaries and by intelligently organizing the material.

7. Finally, we know that trainees learn better when they *learn at their own pace.* Think about how you would feel with someone looking over your shoulder and prodding you as you try to learn a new subject. Most people don't learn well under these conditions. Instead, they learn best when they are allowed to proceed at their own pace.

TRAINING TECHNIQUES

Job Instruction Training

Many jobs consist of a logical sequence of steps and are best taught in this manner—step-by-step. This step-by-step learning has been called job instruction training (JIT).[7] It involves listing all necessary steps in the job, each in its proper sequence. Alongside each step you also list a corresponding *key point* (if any). The steps show *what* is to be done, while the key points show *how* it is to be done—and *why.* The following is an example of a job instruction training sheet for teaching a trainee how to operate a large motorized paper cutter (these are used in printing factories):

Steps	*Key Points*
1. Start motor	None
2. Set cutting distance	Carefully read scale—to prevent wrong-sized cut
3. Place paper on cutting table	Make sure paper is even—to prevent uneven cut
4. Push paper up to cutter	Make sure paper is tight—to prevent uneven cut

Steps	*Key Points*
5. Grasp safety release with left hand	Do not release left hand—to prevent hand from being caught in cutter
6. Grasp cutter release with right hand	Do not release right hand—to prevent hand from being caught in cutter
7. Pull cutter release with right hand	Keep both hands on corresponding releases —to avoid hands being on cutting table
8. Wait for cutter to retract	Keep both hands on releases—to avoid having hands on cutting table
9. Retract paper	Make sure cutter is retracted; keep both hands away from releases
10. Shut off motor	None

Lectures

Lectures are one of the most simple ways of imparting knowledge to trainees. Here the training instructor presents a series of facts, concepts, or principles, and explains relationships.[8] As most students are painfully aware, lectures are usually a means of "telling" trainees something. The students (or trainees) participate mainly as listeners. In training, the most important uses of lectures include:

1. Reducing anxiety about upcoming training programs or organizational changes by explaining their purposes.
2. Introducing a subject and presenting an overview of its scope.
3. Presenting basic material that will provide a common background for subsequent activities.
4. Illustrating the application of rules, concepts, or principles; reviewing, clarifying, or summarizing.[9]

The main advantage of the lecture method is that it is simple and efficient. The trainer can present more material in a given amount of time than he or she can by almost any other method,[10] and can do so with very large groups.

But as most students know, lectures have some important drawbacks. They usually don't provide for student participation, and unless the material is very interesting, little learning may take place. People learn skills by doing, and therefore lectures are inadequate by themselves for teaching new skills or for changing attitudes. We also know that the necessary stress on verbal communication can prove very frustrating to some students.[11] And while a skillful lecturer can adapt his material to the specific group, usually it is almost impossible to adjust it for individual differences *within* a group.

Programmed Learning

Whether the programmed learning device itself is a textbook or a machine, programmed learning always consists of three functions:

1. Presenting questions, facts, or problems to the learner.
2. Allowing the person to respond.
3. Providing feedback on the accuracy of his or her answers.

A page from a programmed textbook is presented in Exhibit 15.1. The main advantage of programmed learning is that usually it reduces training time by about one-third.[12] And since it lets people learn at their own rate, provides immediate feedback and reduces the risk of error, it should also facilitate learning.

We know, however, that trainees usually do *not* learn much more with programmed learning than they would with a conventional textbook approach.[13] Yet the costs of developing the manuals, books, and machinery for programmed learning can be quite high. Therefore you have to carefully weigh the cost of developing such programs against the accelerated (but not better) learning which should occur.

Conferences

Conferences can be used in various ways.[14] Sometimes the trainer guides the discussion and presents information in such a way that the facts, principles, or concepts are explained. At other times the purpose of a conference is to find an answer to a question or a solution to a problem. Here the group is used to develop the best solution. The instructor's job is to define the problem and encourage full participation in the discussion.

The main advantage of conferences is that they permit your people to actively engage in discussions. This is important because, for most people, the opportunity to express one's own views can be very stimulating.

The main limitation to using conferences is probably the lack of good conference leaders.[15] A good conference leader can:

1. Clearly identify the central problem.
2. See to it that all participants are encouraged to present points of view and develop alternatives.
3. See to it that there is a clear agenda to follow.
4. Minimize debate over unimportant details.
5. Prevent domination by one or two individuals.
6. Provide clear summaries on each point.

Exhibit 15.1 A Page from a Programmed Textbook

Sec. 2   Graphs

---

17   The most direct way to plot the graph of a function $y = f(x)$ is to make a table of reasonably spaced values of x and of the corresponding values of $y = f(x)$. Then each pair of values (x,y) can be represented by a point as in the previous frame. A graph of the function is obtained by connecting the points with a smooth curve. Of course, the points on the curve may be only approximate. If we want an accurate plot we just have to be very careful and use many points. (On the other hand, crude plots are pretty good for most purposes.)

Go to 18.

---

18   As an example, here is a plot of the function $y = 3x^2$. A table of values of x and y is shown and these points are indicated on the graph.

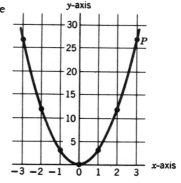

x	y
−3	27
−2	12
−1	3
0	0
1	3
2	12
3	27

To test yourself, encircle below the pair of coordinates that corresponds to the point P indicated in the figure.

$\lceil$(3,27) | (27,3) | none of these$\rceil$

Check your answer. If correct, go on to 19. If incorrect study frame 16 once again and then go to 19.

Source: Daniel Kleppner and Norman Ramsey, *Quick Calculus,* copyright © 1965 by John Wiley & Sons, Inc. Reprinted by permission of John Wiley & Sons, Inc.

On-the-Job Training (OJT)

Virtually every employee, from mail-room clerk to company president, gets some "on-the-job training" when he or she joins a firm. This is why Tracey calls it "the most common, the most widely accepted, and the most necessary method of training employees in the skills essential for acceptable job performance."[16] In many companies, OJT is the *only* type of training available to employees.

There is a variety of OJT methods. Probably the most familiar is the *"coaching"* or *"understudy"* method. Here the employee is trained on the job by his or her immediate superior. At lower levels, the coaching may simply involve having the trainee observe his supervisor so as to develop the skills necessary for running a machine. But this technique is also widely used at top management levels. Here the positions of "assistant" and "assistant to" are often used for the purpose of training and developing the company's future top executives.[17] Some hints for using OJT, such as "put the learner at ease," are presented in Exhibit 15.2.

Job rotation, in which the employee (usually a management trainee) moves from job to job at planned intervals, is another OJT technique. The jobs usually vary in content, and you will often find the trainee being moved periodically from production, to finance, to sales, and so on.

Special assignments and *committees* are OJT techniques used to provide lower level executives with first-hand experience in working on actual problems. Executives from various functional areas serve on "boards" and are required to analyze problems and recommend solutions to top management.[18]

Management Games

People learn best by getting actively involved in the activity itself, and management games can be very useful for gaining such involvement. In the typical game, trainees are divided into five- or six-man "companies." They are given a goal, such as "maximize sales," and are told that they can make several specific decisions. For example, they may be allowed to decide 1) how much to spend on advertising; 2) how much to produce; 3) how much inventory to maintain; 4) and how many of which product to produce. Usually the game itself compresses a two- or three-year period into hours, days, or months.

As in the real world, each company usually doesn't get to see what decisions the other companies have made, although these decisions obviously affect their own sales. For example, if a competitor decides to increase his advertising expenditures, he may end up increasing his sales at the expense of yours.

Exhibit 15.2 The Four Step Method of On-the-Job Training: Some Hints

STEP 1: *Preparation of the Learner*

1. Put the learner at ease—relieve the tension.
2. Explain why he is being taught.
3. Create interest, encourage questions, find out what the learner already knows about his job or other jobs.
4. Explain the why of the whole job, and relate it to some job the worker already knows.
5. Place the learner as close to his normal working position as possible.
6. Familiarize him with the equipment, materials, tools, and trade terms.

STEP 2: *Presentation of the Operation*

1. Explain quantity and quality requirements.
2. Go through the job at the normal work pace.
3. Go through the job at a slow pace several times, explaining each step. Between operations, explain the difficult parts, or those in which errors are likely to be made.
4. Go through the job at a slow pace several times, explain the key points.
5. Have the learner explain the steps as you go through the job at a slow pace.
6. Have the learner explain the key points as you go through the job at a slow pace.

STEP 3: *Performance Tryout*

1. Have the learner go through the job several times, slowly, explaining to you each step. Correct his mistakes, and, if necessary, do some of the complicated steps for him the first few times.
2. You, the trainer, run the job at the normal pace.
3. Have the learner do the job, gradually building up skill and speed.
4. As soon as he demonstrates that he can do the job put him on his own, but don't abandon him.

STEP 4: *Follow Up*

1. Designate to whom the learner should go for help if he needs it, or if he needs to ask questions.
2. Gradually decrease supervision, checking his work from time to time against quality and quantity standards.
3. Correct faulty work patterns that begin to creep into his work, and do it before they become a habit. Show him why the learned method is superior.
4. Compliment good work; encourage him and keep him encouraged until he is able to meet the quality/quantity standards.

Source: William Berliner and William McLarney, *Management Practice and Training* (Homewood, Ill.: Richard D. Irwin, 1974), pp. 442–43. Reproduced by permission of the publisher.

There is usually a great sense of excitement and enjoyment in playing the game. And in addition to being an enjoyable way to develop problem-solving skills, games also help focus attention on the need for planning rather than on "putting out fires." The companies are apt to elect their own officers and develop their own division of work. They can therefore be useful for developing leadership skills, and for fostering cooperation and teamwork.

A major problem with games is that they can be very expensive to develop and implement, particularly when the game itself is computerized. Also, management games usually force the decision maker to choose alternatives from a "closed" list; in real life managers are more often rewarded for creating new, innovative, alternatives.[19] On the whole, though, trainees almost always react favorably to a well-run game, and it is a good technique for developing problem-solving and leadership skills.

Behavior Modeling

Behavior Modeling is a relatively new training method that has proved quite successful.[20] It has been used, for example to:

1. Train hard-core employees (and their supervisors) to take and give criticism, ask and give help, and establish mutual trust and respect.
2. Train first-line supervisors to better handle "eight common supervisor-employee interactions," including giving recognition, disciplining, introducing changes and improving poor performance.
3. Train middle managers to better handle interpersonal situations involving, for example, giving directions, discussing a performance problem, discussing undesirable work habits, reviewing performance, and discussing salary problems.

To date, behavior modeling has been used primarily to improve employees' interpersonal skills. However, the basic technique, described below, could conceivably be used for other types of skill building, such as teaching employees how to set up a piece of machinery.

The basic behavior modeling procedure can be outlined as follows:

1. *Modeling.* First, trainees watch films or video tapes that show model persons behaving effectively in a problem situation. In other words, trainees are shown the "right" way to behave in a simulated but realistic situation. The film might show, for example, a supervisor disciplining a subordinate, if teaching "how to discipline" is one objective of the training program.
2. *Role Playing.* Next, the trainees are given "roles" to play in a simulated situation; here they practice and rehearse the effective behaviors demonstrated by the models.
3. *Social Reinforcement.* The trainer provides reinforcement in the form of praise and constructive feedback, based on how the trainee performs in the role playing situation.
4. *Transfer of Training.* Finally, trainees are encouraged to apply their new skills when they are back on their jobs.

Behavior modeling has been quite successful as a training method. In the case of the hard-core employees and the supervisors, for example, three fourths of the hard-core employees trained to handle job related problems stayed on their jobs after six months, as compared with only about one fourth of those not trained. In another case, supervisors who were training to handle work-related problems (like disciplining employees) subsequently performed significantly better than those who were not.

Part of the method's success stems from the fact that it applies many of the principles of learning we discussed at the start of this chapter. For example, it gets trainees actively involved, the material is meaningful, and actual examples are used. Similarly, in terms of our "ABC s" of performance, the technique ensures: that trainees know what is *expected* of them (by showing a model of the desirable behavior); that they can practice *actually performing* and perfecting the desirable behavior (in the role playing); and that the *consequences* of performing are positive (via the praise they receive).

EVALUATING THE TRAINING EFFORTS

It is unfortunate (but true) that most managers don't spend much time appraising the effects of their training programs. For example, are your trainees learning *as much* as they can? Are they learning *as fast* as they can? Is there a *better method* for training them? These are some of the questions you can answer by properly evaluating your training efforts.

The Relative Effectiveness of Different Training Methods

How do training directors rate the different training methods we have discussed? Three researchers surveyed 200 training directors from large companies (on *Fortune's* list of 500 corporations) to find out. They asked the training directors to fill out a questionnaire and to rank various training methods from "highly effective" to "not effective". The directors were asked to rate each method for how effective it was for each of the following training objectives:

1. Acquisition of knowledge
2. Changing trainees' attitudes
3. Increasing trainees' problem-solving skills
4. Increasing trainees' interpersonal skills
5. Increasing trainees' acceptance of the training method
6. Trainees' retention of knowledge

Findings. The researchers' findings are presented in Exhibit 15.3.[21] This table shows each training method's ranking—from best (1) to worst (9) —for each training objective. For example, the training directors believe that *programmed instruction* is the best method for getting trainees to acquire knowledge. *Lectures* (with questions) are the worst methods. For improving problem-solving skills, case study was the best method, while lectures were again the worst.

Exhibit 15.3 Ratings by Training Directors of Alternative Training Methods

Training Method *	Knowledge Acquisition Mean Rank	Changing Attitudes Mean Rank	Problem Solving Skills Mean Rank	Inter- personal Skills Mean Rank	Participant Acceptance Mean Rank	Knowledge Retention Mean Rank
Case Study	2	4	1	4	2	2
Conference (Discussion)	3	3	4	3	1	5
Lecture (with questions)	9	8	9	8	8	8
Business Games	6	5	2	5	3	6
Movie Films	4	6	7	6	5	7
Programmed Instruction	1	7	6	7	7	1
Role Playing	7	2	3	2	4	4
Sensitivity Training (t group)	8	1	5	1	6	3
Television Lecture	5	9	8	9	9	9

*1 is high, 9 is low

Source: Stephen Carroll, Jr., Frank Paine, and John Ivancevich, "The Relative Effectiveness of Training Methods," *Personnel Psychology*, Vol. 25 (1972), pp. 495–99; reprinted in Clay Hamner and Frank Schmidt, *Contemporary Problems in Personnel* (Chicago: St. Clair Press, 1974), p. 219.

One thing apparent from this table is that you have to fit the training method to the objective. Thus a method like programmed instruction, while excellent for knowledge acquisition, seems poor for building problem-solving skills.

You will also notice that (for most of the training objectives) about half the training methods listed were seen as not very effective. For example, lectures seem fairly ineffective for both knowledge acquisition and retention.

These findings might be a bit misleading. For example, the researchers thought that the training directors may have underestimated the usefulness of lectures. Similarly, they may have overestimated the usefulness of programmed learning.

In any case, it is apparent that some training methods are more effective than others. And it is also apparent that some training methods are more appropriate for some training objectives than others. Because of this it is important to constantly review your own training efforts to see that you are accomplishing the desired results.

One of the first things for you to consider in this regard is the outcomes you are to evaluate. Two writers say there are four basic categories of outcomes you can measure.[22]

1. *Reaction.* First, evaluate your trainees' reactions to the program. Did they like the program? Did they think it worthwhile? etc.

2. *Learning.* Did your trainees learn the principles, skills, and facts that you wanted them to learn?

3. *Behavior.* Next, ask whether your trainees' behavior on the job changed because of the training program.

4. *Results.* Last (but probably most important) ask: What final results were achieved? Did the trainee learn how to work the machine? Did scrappage costs decrease? Was turnover reduced? Are production quotas now being met? and so forth. This last outcome is especially important. Your training program may succeed in terms of the reactions you get from trainees, increased learning, and changes in behavior. But if you don't get the *results* you were seeking, then, in the final analysis, the training has probably failed.

Perhaps the training was not effective. Remember, however, that the results may also be inadequate because it was not a "training" problem in the first place, or because when your employees returned to their jobs they found that the consequences of performing—for example, of wearing their safety hats—were negative.

Conclusion: Training in Industry.[23] Which training techniques are used most often in industry? Results of one survey indicate that in manufacturing firms, job instruction training, training conferences or discussions, apprenticeship training, and job rotation were most prevalent. In non-manufacturing firms the top techniques were job instruction training, conferences or discussions, and job rotation.

CHAPTER SUMMARY

1. In this chapter we focused on skills training for new employees and for present employees whose performance is deficient. For either, uncovering training requirements involves analyzing the cause of the problem and determining what (if any) training is needed. Remember to ask "Is it a training problem"? Make sure your "problem" is not being caused by some more deep rooted problem like poor selection or low wages.

2. We discussed some principles of learning that should be understood by all trainers. The guidelines include: make the material meaningful (by providing a

bird's eye view, familiar examples, organizing the material, splitting it into meaningful chunks, and using familiar terms and visual aids); make provision for transfer of training; provide feedback; try to motivate your trainee; provide for practice and repetition; and follow our seven principles (such as "trainees learn best by doing").

3. We discussed five training techniques. *Job instruction training* is useful for training on jobs that consist of a logical sequence of steps. *Lectures* are perhaps the simplest way of imparting knowledge, but do not provide for trainee participation. *Programmed learning* cuts training time by about one third, but is usually expensive to implement. *Management* games are useful since they allow your people to actively engage in problem solving.

4. On-the-job training is another training technique. It might involve the "understudy" method, job rotation, or special assignments and committees. In any case it should involve four steps: preparing the learner; presenting the operation (or nature of the job); performance tryouts; and a follow-up.

5. Most managers don't spend time evaluating the effects of their training program although this should be an important consideration. We also know that some training techniques are more appropriate for accomplishing certain objectives than others. In measuring the effectiveness of your training program there are four categories of outcomes you can measure: reaction, learning, behavior, and results. In some cases where training seems to have failed, it may be because "Training" was not the appropriate solution, or because the consequences of performing are negative.

DISCUSSION QUESTIONS AND PROJECTS

1. You are the foreman of a group of employees whose task it is to assemble tuning devices that go into radios. You find that quality is not what it should be and that many of your group's tuning devices have to be brought back and reworked: your boss says that you had "better start doing a better job of training your workers."

> a. What are some of the other factors that could be contributing to this problem?
> b. Explain how you would go about assessing whether it is in fact a training program.

2. Explain how you would apply our principles of learning in developing a lecture, for example, on how to train employees.

3. Divide the class into groups of four to five students. Then each group should pick out some task with which they are familiar—mowing the lawn, tuning a car, etc.—and develop a job instruction training sheet for it.

CASE EXERCISE

Charlie, The Railroad Agent

Charlie Bagley was employed by a railroad in Farlin, Kansas, a city of about 30,000 people. As the railroad agent, Charlie was in charge of all the company's operations in the community. Before becoming agent in Farlin, Charlie had been an agent in a small one-man agency for approximately forty years. When the one-man agency was closed, Charlie asserted his seniority rights and became agent in Farlin.

At the present location, Charlie had approximately thirty-five men for whom he was either directly or indirectly responsible. At age seventy-two, Charlie was still working full time since the company had no mandatory retirement age for agents. Because of Charlie's age, though, the company preferred that he retire; but he had maintained his present position for twelve years with no major difficulties.

One September evening, an unidentified automobile driver crossing the railroad tracks ran off the crossing, into a switch stand, back onto the road, and drove off. The accident was witnessed and reported by an employee of the company. The telegrapher on duty called the section foreman directly responsible for the condition of the tracks.

The foreman inspected the tracks and the switch stand and called Charlie. He told Charlie there was no damage to the tracks but there was about $5 damage to the switch stand. He also said that he could repair the stand the following day and that no report was necessary. Charlie did not make a report as was technically required by the rules and regulations and forgot about the incident. This was not an abnormal practice when everyone agreed to cover up an accident and save several hours required in filling out the long accident reports used by the company.

At the end of the month the section foreman turned in a claim for overtime for making the inspection, thereby bringing to the attention of the division headquarters that an accident had not been reported. The section foreman absolved himself of any responsibility by denying he had told Charlie that a report was unnecessary. Giving due consideration to the fact that Charlie had more than fifty years of service to the company and the fact that Charlie had two sons employed as agents, the superintendent asked Charlie to retire and take his pension. Charlie refused and replied that, after fifty years of service, working from eight to ten hours a day, six days a week, he had no other interests and that he was also financially committed to purchase a home, which would be impossible with only the income from a pension.

The incident prompted a formal investigation by the superintendent with union officials present; they decided that Charlie should be fired. Charlie was fired and signed up for his pension. Since Charlie had always maintained his membership in the telegraphers' union, the local chairman for the union instigated a claim for Charlie's reinstatement. After two years, the full process of labor-management grievance procedures had been exhausted, and the case went to arbitration. The arbitrator's decision stated that an accident so trivial as this was insufficient cause to dismiss an employee of fifty years' service. The arbitrator ordered that Charlie be reinstated in his job as agent, that he receive full back pay from the date of his dismissal two years ago, and that a comparable place be found for the man who had been working Charlie's job.

Questions

1. Analyze the problem in terms of our "ABCs" of performance.

2. Is there a need for training in this company? If so, who needs training? If needed, what should the nature of the training be?

3. Do you think the facts of this case support the need for a mandatory retirement age?

4. How would you go about convincing employees of the need to follow rules and regulations.

EXPERIENTIAL EXERCISE

Purpose: The purpose of this exercise is to give you practice in developing a training program.

Required Understanding: You should be thoroughly familiar with the training methods we discussed in this chapter: job instruction training; lectures; programmed learning; conferences; on-the-job training; management games; and behavioral modeling. Since you'll be developing a training program for directory assistance operators you should read the following description of a directory assistance operator's duties:

> Customers contact directory assistance operators to obtain the telephone numbers of persons whose numbers are not yet listed, whose listings have changed, or whose numbers are unknown to the customer. These operators look up the requested number in telephone books issued daily and transmit numbers to the customers. A number must be found quickly so that the customer is not kept waiting. It is often necessary to look under various spellings of the same name since customers frequently give incorrect spellings.

Next, read this: imagine that you are the supervisor of about ten directory assistance operators in a small regional phone company that has no formal training program for new operators. Since you get one or two new operators every few months you think it would raise efficiency for you to develop a "new directory assistance operator's training program" for your own use in your department. Consider what such a program would consist of before proceeding to your assigned group.

How to Set Up the Exercise: Divide the class into groups of four or five students.

Instructions

In keeping with the procedure we discussed for setting up a training program, your group should, at a minimum, go through the following steps:

1. List the duties and responsibilities of the job (of directory assistance operator) using the description provided above.

2. List some assumed standards of work performance for the job.

3. Within your group, develop some assumptions about what parts of the job give new employees the most trouble (you'd normally be able to do this based on your experience as the operators' supervisor).

4. Determine what kind of training is needed to overcome these difficulties.

5. Develop a "new directory assistance operator's training package." In this you'll provide two things. First you will provide a one-page outline showing the type(s) of training each new operator in your unit will go through. (For example, you might indicate that the first two hours on the job will involve the new operator observing existing operators; then four hours of lectures, etc.) Second, in this package, you'll also expand on exactly what each training technique will involve. For example if you are going to use job instruction training, show the steps to be included; if you're going to use lectures, provide an outline of what you'll discuss; etc.

If time permits, a spokesman from each group can put his or her group's training program outline on the board, and the class can discuss the relative merits of each group's proposal.

NOTES FOR CHAPTER 15

1. E. J. McCormick and J. Tiffin, *Industrial Psychology* (Englewood Cliffs, N.J.: Prentice-Hall, 1974), p. 245.

2. William Berliner and William McLarney, *Management Practice and Training: Cases and Principles* (Homewood, Ill.: Richard D. Irwin, 1974), p. 438.

3. W. Berliner and W. McLarney, *Management*, pp. 438–39.

4. Based on Kenneth Wexley and Gary Yukl, *Organizational Behavior and Personnel Psychology* (Homewood, Ill.: Richard D. Irwin, 1977), pp. 289–95; McCormick and Tiffin, *Industrial Psychology*, pp. 232–40.

5. Adapted by Wexley and Yukl, *Organizational Behavior*, from H. C. Ellis, *The Transfer of Learning* (New York: Macmillan, 1965).

6. R. E. Silverman, *Learning Theory Applied to Training* (Reading, Mass.: Addison-Wesley, 1970), ch. 8, in McCormick and Tiffin, *Industrial Psychology*, pp. 239–40.

7. Berliner and McLarney, *Management Practices*, pp. 441–42.

8. William R. Tracey, *Designing Training and Developing Systems* (New York: American Management Association, 1971), p. 192.

9. Tracey, *Designing*, p. 192; G. H. Proctor and W. M. Thornton, *Training: A Handbook for Line Managers* (New York: American Management Association, 1971).

10. Tracey, *Designing*, p. 192.

11. F. Reissman, "The Culturally Deprived Child: A New View," in eds., E. P. Torrence and R. D. Strom, *Mental Health and Achievement* (New York: John Wiley & Sons, 1965), pp. 312–19; McCormick and Tiffin, *Industrial Psychology*.

12. G. N. Nash, J. P. Muczyk, and F. L. Vettori, "The Role and Practical Effectiveness of Programmed Instruction," *Personnel Psychology*, 24 (1971), 397–418; McCormick and Tiffin, *Industrial Psychology*.

13. R. Hedberg, H. Steffen, and D. Baxter, "Insurance Fundamentals—A Programmed Text vs. A Conventional Text," *Personnel Psychology*, 9 (1964), 165–71; McCormick and Tiffin, *Industrial Psychology*, p. 264.

14. Tracey, *Designing*, p. 191.

15. Tracey, *Designing*, p. 191.

16. Tracey, *Designing*, p. 30.

17. Robert J. House, *Management Development* (Ann Arbor: University of Michigan), p. 74.

18. House, *Management Development*, p. 75.

19. B. Taylor and G. Lippitt, *Management Development and Training Handbook* (London: McGraw-Hill, 1975), p. 223.

20. This section based on: Allen Kraut, "Developing Managerial Skills via modeling techniques: some positive research findings—a symposium; Robert Burnaska, "The Effects of Behavior Modeling training upon Manager's Behavior and Employees' perceptions"; Joseph Mases and Richard Ritchie, "Supervisory relationship training: a behavioral evaluation of a behavior modeling program"; Preston Smith, "Management modeling training to improve morale and customer satisfaction"; all in *Personnel Psychology*, Vol. 29, No. 3 (Autumn 1976), pp. 325–61.

21. Steven J. Caroll, Jr., Frank T. Paine, and John J. Ivancevich, "The relative effectiveness of training methods—expert opinion and research," *Personnel Psychology*, 25 (1972), pp. 495–509, reprinted in W. Clay Hamner and Frank Schmidt, *Contemporary Problems in Personnel* (Chicago: St. Claire, 1977), pp. 199–209.

22. R. E. Catalanello and B. I. Kirkpatrick, "Evaluating Training Programs—the state of the yard," *Training and Developing Journal*, 22 (May 1968), pp. 2–9; McCormick and Tiffin, *Industrial Psychology*, pp. 269–70.

23. Robert Wenig and William Wolansky, *Review and Synthesis of Literature on Job Training in Industry* (Columbus: ERIC Clearinghouse, 1972), p. 23.

16 *Organizational Change and Development*

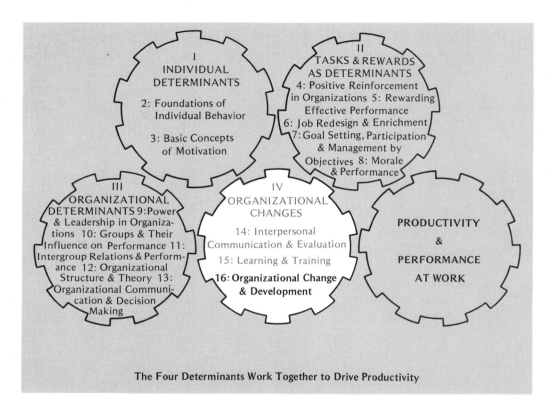

I INDIVIDUAL DETERMINANTS

2: Foundations of Individual Behavior

3: Basic Concepts of Motivation

II TASKS & REWARDS AS DETERMINANTS
4: Positive Reinforcement in Organizations 5: Rewarding Effective Performance 6: Job Redesign & Enrichment 7: Goal Setting, Participation & Management by Objectives 8: Morale & Performance

III ORGANIZATIONAL DETERMINANTS 9: Power & Leadership in Organizations 10: Groups & Their Influence on Performance 11: Intergroup Relations & Performance 12: Organizational Structure & Theory 13: Organizational Communication & Decision Making

IV ORGANIZATIONAL CHANGES
14: Interpersonal Communication & Evaluation
15: Learning & Training
16: Organizational Change & Development

PRODUCTIVITY & PERFORMANCE AT WORK

The Four Determinants Work Together to Drive Productivity

BY THE TIME YOU FINISH STUDYING THIS CHAPTER, YOU SHOULD BE ABLE TO:

1. *Explain the steps in the change process.*
2. *Define "unfreezing," "changing," and "refreezing."*
3. *Answer the question: "Why do people resist change?"*
4. *Minimize employee resistance to change.*
5. *Discuss three approaches to bringing about change.*
6. *Define organizational development and discuss how it can be used.*

OVERVIEW

The main purpose of this chapter is to explain how to implement organiza-tional changes—changes in the structure, technology, or people in the or-ganization. We discuss the steps in the change process, how to deal with resistance to change, and how to diagnose the problem. We also discuss "organizational development" techniques, techniques that are aimed at increasing the level of support and trust among employees and open confron-tation of organizational problems. These organizational development tech-niques (and, for that matter the training we discussed in the last chapter) are aimed at changing behavior, as is behavior modification. However, or-ganizational development and training are different from behavior modifi-cation in that they are aimed at changing employees' skills, attitudes, and values and thereby their behavior, rather than at modifying behavior through the use of reinforcement.

INTRODUCTION: THE NEED FOR CHANGE AND DEVELOPMENT

The main purpose of this chapter is to discuss two separate but related topics: *organizational change,* and *organizational development.*

Virtually every topic we've discussed to this point implies the need for *change.* Every organization sooner or later finds, for example, that new pay plans are needed, a reorganization or job redesign is required, or an MBO program is called for, and being able to make these kinds of changes is a mark of effective management. It is therefore fitting that we explain how to implement change in this last chapter.

We also explain *organization development,* an approach that is basi-cally aimed at increasing the level of trust and open communication in the organization. In turn, this increase in trust and communication can make it easier for an organization to react to problems (like the introduction of a new product by a competitor) and to change, by enabling the organization's managers and groups to work together more cooperatively.

THE CHANGE PROCESS

Over 400 years ago Machiavelli, a shrewd observer of management behavior, made the following statement in regard to change, and it is as applicable today as it was then:

It must be considered that there is nothing more difficult to carry out, nor more doubtful of success, nor more dangerous to handle, than to initiate a new order of things. For the reformer has enemies in all those who would profit by the old order, and only lukewarm defenders in all those who would profit by the new order, this lukewarmness arising partly from fear of their adversaries, who have the laws in their favor; and partly from the incredulity of mankind, who do not truly believe in anything new until they have had actual experience of it. Thus it arises that on every opportunity for attacking the reformer, his opponents do so with the zeal of partisans, the others only defend him halfheartedly, so that between them, he runs great danger.[1]

Why is it so difficult to implement a change? What is the best way to implement a change? What are some important techniques you can use to make the change? These are some of the questions we answer in this chapter.

Stages in the Change Process[2]

Experts agree that most organizational changes do not take place overnight, instead, they proceed in stages. One way to think of these stages was proposed by Lewin years ago. He identified three stages of change and called these: unfreezing, changing, and refreezing. The first, *unfreezing stage* is necessary for prodding people into seeing the need for change. Here some provocative problem or event is usually necessary to get people to recognize the need for a change and to search for new solutions.

In the second, *change stage* the new change is introduced and implemented. In the last, *refreezing stage* you provide the necessary reinforcement to ensure that the new behavior patterns are adopted on a more permanent basis. Lewin's three stage process is important because it underscores the need to "unfreeze" the parties and then "refreeze" them once the changes are made.

In general, however, one can use the same "problem analysis" procedure that we discussed in chapters 4 and 15 to diagnose what change is needed, and implement it. In other words, assuming that some problem has been brought to management's attention:

1. Identify a "performance improvement area," and set standards. (Note, here, that the "area" you focus on depends on the problem. If only one employee is having problems—say, with excess scrap—you might focus on that person as the "area" to improve. If quality is a chronic problem throughout the plant, you might make "quality control" the area for improvement, and thus analyze the entire raw materials inspection/manufacturing/quality monitoring process. Or, the problems may be so widespread and pervasive that the

organization *as a whole* must be analyzed—including its goals, plans, competitors, and structure, for example. This is sometimes termed *organizational analysis.*)
2. Next, analyze the present performance, and determine if there is a performance deficiency;
3. Analyze the cause—the ABC s—of the problem; and finally,
4. Plan and implement the change.

HOW TO DEAL WITH RESISTANCE TO CHANGE

Why Do People "Resist" Change?[3]

Whether you are trying to implement small changes in work procedures or major changes (like reorganizing your firm), overcoming or minimizing employees' resistance to the change will often be your major hurdle. This is because such resistance can quickly undermine and destroy your change efforts and can manifest itself in many ways including decreased output, absenteeism, strikes, and hostility.

Why do people resist change? Lawrence says that resistance is not a necessary concomitant of change and that a change—if handled correctly—may evoke little or no resistance. He says this is because it is not the "technical" aspects of the change that employees resist, but rather the social consequences of the change—"the change in their human relationships that generally accompany the technical change." (For example, they may see in the change diminished responsibilities for themselves and therefore lower status in the organization and less job security.) Thus the important thing to remember is that it is not the technical change itself most employees object to, but rather the social consequences of these changes.

Three Approaches to Organizational Change

Assuming it is useful to minimize employee resistance, what is the best way to bring about an organizational change? If you think about it for a moment you will see there are two extreme approaches you can take to implement that change. On the one hand you could *unilaterally decree* that the change will take place, and hope for the best. At the other extreme you could *delegate the problem*—tell your employees what the problem is and let them come up with solutions and proposed changes.

Larry Greiner says you needn't just deal in these two extremes, and that a third, "middle ground" approach (which he calls "shared power") is possible. Here is how he categorizes his three approaches to making a change, and some examples:[4]

A. Unilateral Power

1. *The decree approach.* A "one-way" announcement originating with a person with high formal authority and passed on to those in lower positions.

2. *The replacement approach.* Individuals in one or more key organizational positions are replaced by other individuals. The basic assumption is that they will in turn change the organization's practices.

3. *The structural approach.* Instead of decreeing or injecting new blood into work relationships, management changes the required relationships of subordinates working in the situation. By changing the structure of organizational relationships, organizational behavior is also presumably affected.

B. Shared Power (participation)

4. *The group decision approach.* Here there is participation by group members in selecting from several alternative solutions specified in advance by superiors. This approach involves neither problem identification nor problem-solving, but emphasizes the obtaining of group agreement to a particular course of action.

5. *The group problem-solving approach.* This takes "participation" one step further, and there is problem identification and problem solving through group discussion. Here the group has wide latitude, not only over choosing the problems to be discussed, but in developing solutions to these problems.

C. Delegated Power

6. *The data discussion approach.* Presentation and feedback of relevant data (for example, concerning decreasing product quality) to the "client" usually by a consultant. Organizational members are encouraged to develop their own analyses of the data, which are presented in the form of survey findings, data reports, etc.

7. *The sensitivity training approach.* Here managers are trained in small discussion groups to be more sensitive to the underlying processes of individual and group behavior. Changes in work patterns and relationships are assumed to follow from changes in interpersonal relationships. Sensitivity approaches focus on interpersonal relationships first, then hope for, or work toward, improvements in work performance. "Data discussion" and "sensitivity training" both give the employee much more latitude to analyze the data, identify problems, and develop solutions.

Using "Participation"

Each of these approaches to organizational change can be useful. For example, in some chaotic situations a unilateral approach to change (in which you simply issue your decree and ram through the change) may be appropriate. Yet, in other situations, a "delegated power" approach is called for; here you will use techniques like "organizational development" to get your people themselves to work out the necessary changes.

But as often as not it is going to be Greiner's middle-of-the-road "shared power" approach that you will find useful. It involves gaining the employees' commitment to the change, by letting them *actively participate* in selecting from several alternative solutions. However, remember that there is more to "participation" than just calling a meeting and asking some carefully calculated questions. Participation, according to Lawrence, is a *feeling* on the part of people, not just the mechanical act of being called in to take part in the discussions. "Participation" works because employees feel that you are honestly interested in their opinions, and that they are actually involved in the change. If they don't get this feeling, your attempts at "participation" will probably backfire.[5]

ORGANIZATION DEVELOPMENT

Methods for Changing Organizations

Your analysis of the performance problem should enable you to determine what sort of change is needed, and here there are a multitude of changes to choose from: providing clearer goals, job redesign, reorganization, conflict management, training, and implementing a new positive reinforcement program are just some of these. (In fact, implementing virtually any of the techniques we discussed in this book involves *change*).

Many of these changes (as Greiner points out) will involve either "unilateral" or "shared" power. In other words, some change (like a new MBO program, or reward system) may either be *unilaterally* imposed on the parties involved, or may be brought about with their participation and advice (*shared power*). On the other hand, many believe that some situations call for a *delegated power* approach to change. *Here the idea is to change the attitudes and values of the parties involved, on the assumption that the parties involved will in turn develop and implement the necessary changes.* For example, some would suggest dealing with intergroup conflict by first making the members of each group more "sensitive" to others. Then, supposedly, the members of each group will be able to work out the problem themselves—by setting superordinate goals, for instance. The technique used to bring about such changes in attitudes and values are collectively called *Organization Development* or "OD."[6]

Why Use OD?

Today, new forms of organizations are emerging—ones that are more organic and adaptable to change. They are characterized by less adherence to the chain of command, more enlarged jobs, and "Theory Y" values, which emphasize openness, trust, and participative leadership.

Managers sometimes find it necessary to make their own organizations more organic. Perhaps your organization suddenly has to adapt to a competitor's new and unique product. Or perhaps you're faced with emerging conflict between several of your department heads, conflict that is undermining your unit's creativity and flexibility. These are the kinds of situations that lead managers to turn to OD.[7]

Objectives of Organizational Development

While there are many different OD techniques, they are all aimed at accomplishing the following objectives:

1. Increasing the level of support and trust among participants.
2. Increasing open confrontation of organizational problems.
3. Increasing the openness and authenticity of organizational communications.
4. Increasing personal enthusiasm and self-control.[8]

This emphasis on the "people" aspects of organizations does not mean that OD practitioners don't try to bring about changes in organization structure, policies, or practices; they often do. But *the typical OD program is aimed at changing the attitudes, values, and beliefs of employees so that the employees themselves can identify and implement such organizational changes.*

Characteristics of OD

We can get a better feel for what OD is by looking at some of its distinguishing characteristics. These include:[9]

1. OD is an *educational experience* intended to bring about some planned or organizational change.

2. The organizational changes sought are usually the result of some *"exigency"* or outside problem. This often results in intergroup conflict or questions of organizational identity.
3. OD almost always relies on a technique that involves *direct experience.*
4. OD programs utilize *change agents,* who are almost always outside consultants.
5. A change agent usually has a social philosophy or set of values concerning people in organizations that are like those of McGregor's *Theory Y.*
6. The goals that the change agent seeks to accomplish through OD tend to reflect this Theory Y orientation. For example, he aims for better conflict resolution, increased understanding, more considerate leadership, and better conflict resolution.

No two OD programs are exactly alike but they all tend to follow a basic three-step process:

1. *Gathering data* about the organization and its operations and attitudes.
2. *Feedback* of data about the organization and its problems to the parties involved.
3. *Team Planning* of the solution to these problems.

An Actual OD Change Program: An Example

Here is a brief summary of an actual OD program that was carried out recently:[10]

1. *Initial diagnosis:* The diagnosis consisted of three steps. First, a series of *interviews* was held with a sample of 15 supervisory and managerial personnel (including the plant manager and his immediate staff). Second, *group meetings* were held with those interviewed to examine the results and to identify problem areas and priorities. Finally, the plant manager, his immediate staff, and the external consultants met to finalize the *design* of the OD program, which consisted of steps 2 through 7 below.
2. *Team skills training:* Foremen, general foremen, assistant superintendents, and superintendents participated with their peers (in groups of approximately 25 individuals) in a series of "team building" exercises during a two-and-a-half-day workshop. This was aimed at developing closer, more open communications in each work group, and might include, for example, lectures on "how to communicate more effectively."

3. *Data collection:* Immediately following the team skills training, all foremen completed two questionnaires. The first concentrated on the plant's performance. The second asked them to describe the behavior of their immediate supervisor—general foremen or assistant superintendents. This information became the basis for the ensuing "data confrontation" and problem solving discussions amongst the work groups.

4. *Data confrontation:* In this phase various work groups were asked to review the data collected above and determine problem areas, establish priorities in these areas, and develop some preliminary recommendations for change.

5. *Action planning:* Based on the data and conversations during the data confrontation, each group developed some recommendations for change and plans for how the changes should be implemented. The plans included what should be changed, who should be responsible, and when the action should be completed.

6. *Team building:* Each work group in the plant (including the plant manager and his immediate staff of superintendents), then met for two days. The agenda consisted of identifying blocks to effectiveness for the specific group and developing change goals and plans to accomplish the desired changes.

7. *Intergroup building:* This phase consisted of two-day meetings between groups that were interdependent in the plant. The groups met for the purpose of establishing mutual understanding and cooperation between the groups and to enhance collaboration on shared goals or problems.

The sequence in which the interventions occurred is outlined below in Exhibit 16.1.

Exhibit 16.1 Actual Timetable for O.D. Program Described in Text

Intervention	Initiated	Completed
Initial diagnosis	12-1-69	12-31-69
Team skills training	1-9-70	2-28-70
Data collection	1-10-70	3-1-70
Data confrontation	5-9-70	8-19-70
Action planning	9-1-70	12-31-70
Team building	1-1-71	2-1-71
Intergroup building	2-2-71	2-28-71
Data Collection	3-15-71	3-15-71

Source: Kimberly and Warren, *"Organization Development and Change in Organizational Performance"* p. 193.

Specific OD Techniques

As you can see in Exhibit 16.2 there are many different OD techniques. In the next few sections we will concentrate on four representative ones: sensitivity training, the managerial grid, survey feedback, and role playing.

Exhibit 16.2 Different Types of O.D. "Interventions," and Their Target Groups

Target Group	Types of Techniques or "Interventions"
Interventions designed to improve the effectiveness of INDIVIDUALS	Life- and career-planning activities Role analysis technique Coaching and counseling T-group (sensitivity training) Education and training to increase skills, knowledge in the areas of technical task needs, relationship skills, process skills, decision making, problem solving, planning, goal setting skills Grid OD phase 1
Interventions designed to improve the effectiveness of DYADS/TRIADS	Process consultation Third-party peacemaking Grid OD phases 1, 2
Interventions designed to improve the effectiveness of TEAMS & GROUPS	Team building—Task directed —Process directed Family T-group Survey feedback Process consultation Role analysis technique "Start-up" team-building activities Education in decision making, problem solving, planning, goal setting in group settings
Interventions designed to improve the effectiveness of INTERGROUP RELATIONS	Intergroup activities —Process directed —Task Directed Organizational mirroring (three or more groups) Technostructural interventions Process consultation Third-party peacemaking at group level Grid OD phase 3 Survey feedback
Interventions designed to improve the effectiveness of the TOTAL ORGANIZATION	Technostructural activities Confrontation meetings Strategic planning activities Grid OD phases 4, 5, 6 Survey feedback

Source: Wendell French and Cecil Bell, Jr., *Organization Development* (Englewood Cliffs, N. J., Prentice-Hall, Inc., 1973) p. 107.

Sensitivity Training

Sensitivity, Laboratory, or *T-group* training (the T is for Training) is a very controversial development method. According to Chris Argyris, it is:

A group experience designed to provide maximum possible opportunity for the individuals to expose their behavior, give and receive feedback, experiment with new behavior, and develop . . . awareness of self and of others.[11]

As an example, here is an outline of a typical T-group program:[12]

1. A group of 10 to 15 meets away from the job without a planned agenda.
2. The discussion focuses on the "here and now." In other words, the participants are encouraged to let each other know how "they're coming across" to each other *in the group* rather than in terms of their past behavior.
3. Some trainees usually try to impose some "structure" on the discussion, for example, by developing agendas. The trainer usually heads off such attempts.
4. The feedback process is all important. The trainees have to feel secure enough to inform each other truthfully about how their behavior is being seen and to interpret the kind of feelings it produces.
5. The success of the T-group, therefore, depends on the level of "psychological safety" the trainees perceive. In other words, the trainees have to feel safe to reveal themselves, to expose their feelings, and to drop their defenses.

Does sensitivity training work? We know that trainees usually do become more sensitive to others and more open after going through T-group training.[13] Furthermore, researchers have found that sensitivity training can also result in increased organizational performance and profits.[14]

Criticisms of T-Group Training: However, sensitivity training is also a very controversial technique, because of the depth of emotional involvement required of trainees. Since they literally have to bare their souls in the training session, the training is very personal in nature. Sensitivity training has therefore been widely criticized. Writers point out, for example, that:

1. Sensitivity training is based on creating *stress situations* for their own sake.
2. The participants (and trainers) are often unaware of what the *outcome* of a session will be.
3. Its stress on collaboration and openness is often *inconsistent* with the business and economic world in which we live.
4. *"Anybody"* with a registration fee can attend.
5. When you suggest that a subordinate participate in a T-group program, his or her attendance cannot be considered strictly *voluntary*.

6. T-group training has been known to result in nervous *breakdowns* of trainees.[15]

T-Group Hints. In light of these criticisms T-group training should be used with caution, and the following guidelines are useful in this regard.

1. *T-group training is more appropriate for developing "organic" organizations.* When this type of openness and flexible organization is not appropriate—such as on an assembly line—sensitivity training is not appropriate.[16]
2. Programs should be strictly *voluntary.*
3. Careful *screening* of participants should take place.
4. The training consultant should be an *experienced* T-group professional.
5. Make sure that you give a great deal of attention to building in mechanisms for *transferring the learning* back to your organization.
6. Make sure that all trainees know *ahead of time* what sort of "training" they are getting into.[17]

Grid Training

The *managerial grid* is another OD technique. The grid itself is presented in Exhibit 16.3, and represents several possible leadership styles. Each style represents a different combination of two basic orientations—*concern for people* and *concern for production.* For example, the 9.1 leader emphasizes production but deemphasizes the needs of his people. On the other hand, the 1.9 leader is very concerned about people and not too concerned about production.

There is an extensive development program built around the managerial grid. The program is aimed at developing open confrontation of organizational problems and 9.9 (high people-high production) leaders.

The following is an outline of the program, which usually lasts three to five years.[18]

Phase 1. This usually involves a one-week conference. Here trainees are taught the fundamentals of grid training, such as how to develop better communications.

Phase 2. Here you and your subordinates discuss, analyze, and solve your unit's practices and problems: *teamwork* is stressed.

Phase 3. Here you use the techniques developed in Phase 2 to discuss, analyze, and jointly solve problems between your unit and others in the organization.

Phase 4. Next, top management meets with various groups. Here the aims are to work out company-wide problems and to set some development targets for the company as a whole.

Phase 5. In this step, specific procedures are outlined for accomplishing the company's development targets.

Phase 6. Here you evaluate your unit's and your company's accomplishments and begin work on any remaining (or new) problems.

Exhibit 16.3 The Managerial Grid©

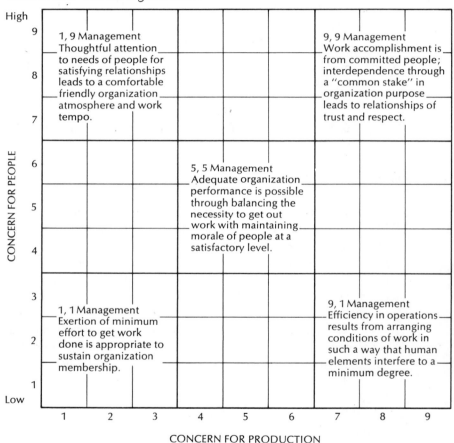

Note: The Managerial Grid Illustrates Different Combinations of People and Production Orientation.

Source: Robert Blake and Jane Morton, *Corporate Excellence Through Grid Organization Development,* "The Managerial Grid" © 1968 (Houston, Texas: Gulf, 1968).

Survey Feedback

Attitude surveys can be very useful as an organizational development technique. They can be used to dramatically underscore the existence of some

problem (like low morale), thereby "unfreezing" the system. And they can be used as a basis for discussion among employees and for developing alternative solutions. Finally, they can also be used to "follow up" on the change to see if it's been successful ("refreezing").

As we discussed in Chapter 8, Myers has proposed what he calls an *involvement approach* to using attitude surveys.[19] At the Texas Instruments Company, where this approach was developed, a questionnaire is administered to a 10 to 20 percent sample of employees throughout the company. Results are then compiled for all departments and fed back to department managers. Then, the manager and his or her subordinates themselves develop solutions to problems, thus getting them *involved* in the solutions.

Role Playing

Role playing involves the spontaneous acting out of a situation by two or more persons under the direction of the trainer. (Several of our end-of-chapter exercises—including the one for this chapter—depend on role playing.) A dialogue usually ensues and—often before anyone realizes it—the participants are enthusiastically playing out their roles.

We have reproduced the roles from a famous role-playing exercise in the exercise at the end of this chapter. The exercise is called "The Change of Work Procedure."

Role-playing exercises like this one can develop conference-leader skills, as well as the decision-making skills of the entire group. With "The Change of Work Procedure" participants attitudes can also change, for example as they learn the importance of participation in bringing about *acceptance* of decisions. The role players can also drop their inhibitions and experiment with new ways of acting. For example, a foreman could experiment with being both considerate (people oriented) and autocratic (production oriented). In the real world he or she might not have this opportunity to experiment with different styles. Role playing can be very time-consuming, and without competent leadership it can be a waste of time. But, on the whole, we do know that role playing is an effective technique for developing leadership skills and changing attitudes.[20]

CHAPTER SUMMARY

1. There are several stages in the change process. Kurt Lewin called these "unfreezing," "change," and "refreezing." Generally, however, our procedure for analyzing performance problems can be used.

2. A major requirement is implementing a change is to minimize employee's resistance to change, and the first step in doing so is to remember that it's not

the technical aspects of the change that employees resist, but rather the social consequences of that change (ensuring that the *consequences* are positive is therefore advisable).

3. We discussed three broad approaches you can take to implement an organizational change: unilateral power, shared (participative) power, and delegated power. Each has its uses, but we especially know that the "middle of the road" participation approach has been useful for gaining commitment and minimizing resistance to change.

4. Organizational development is aimed at changing participants' attitudes, values, and interpersonal skills on the assumption that the participants themselves will then be able to accomplish the necessary organizational changes. The Managerial Grid program is a good example of this. Team building and problem solving are stressed first, and then participants themselves unearth, analyze, and solve important organizational problems. As is often the case with OD, the aim is to get the participants to work together more effectively, on the assumption that they will then be able to make the necessary changes.

5. Survey feedback and particularly the "involvement" approach can be useful for "unfreezing" employees and getting them to recognize the existence of problems. Role playing (in which participants become actively involved in playing out their roles) can teach new skills, attitudes, and understanding.

6. Sensitivity (or "T-group") training can be effective. It can result in managers who are more sensitive to their subordinates and a climate that is more open and less hostile. But remember that it is also widely criticized. So before embarking on such a program, you should be sure that your aim is to develop an open, organic organization; that the program is strictly voluntary; that participants are carefully screened; and that the consultant is an experienced professional.

DISCUSSION QUESTIONS AND PROJECTS

1. You recommend to your boss that he hire someone to be in charge of training and development of your company, and he replies, "training and development is useless. No one has ever shown that it is effective, and you know darn well you just can't change people." How would you respond to his remarks?

2. Write an essay on "Organizational Development: Concepts and Methods." Make sure to discuss its objectives, characteristics, and an outline of a typical OD program.

3. What are the criticisms of T-group training? In light of these criticisms, discuss some hints for setting up a T-group training program.

4. Explain the managerial grid development program.

5. Explain why people resist change.

6. What are Greiner's three approaches to organizational change? Give some examples of conditions under which each would probably be more appropriate.

7. Your conpany's consultant have just suggested to you that you put all your subordinates through sensitivity training. What are some of the questions you would ask of your consultants at this point?

8. Your boss has just suggested that you attend a sensitivity training laboratory. What are some of the questions you would ask of him or her?

9. Working in groups of four or five, interview a local organization's training manager. How does this person identify training or development needs? Which training and/or development techniques does the person use? What does he or she think are their advantages and disadvantages?

CASE EXERCISE

What We Need Around Here Is Better Human Relations

Hank called his three highest-ranking managers together for a surprise luncheon meeting. "Have a drink on United Mutual," said Hank, "you may need it to loosen up your thinking about an important topic I want to bring to your attention."

After Madeline, Raymond, and Allen ordered their drinks, Hank launched into the agenda:

"As office manager, I think we have to move into a rigorous human relations training program for our front-line supervisors. It's no longer a question of whether we should have a program; it's now a question of what kind and when."

Allen spoke out, "Okay, Hank, don't keep us in suspense any longer. What makes you think we need a human relations training program?"

"Look at the problems we are facing. Twenty-five percent turnover among the clerical and secretarial staffs; productivity lower than the casualty insurance industry national standards. What better reasons could anybody have for properly training our supervisory staffs?"

Madeline commented, "Hold on Hank. Training may not be the answer. I think our high turnover and low productivity are caused by reasons beyond the control of supervision. Our wages are low and we expect our people to work in cramped, rather dismal office space."

Hank retorted, "Nonsense. A good supervisor can get workers to accept almost any working conditions. Training will fix that."

"Hank, I see another problem," said Allen. "Our supervisors are so overworked already that they will balk at training. If you hold the training on company time, they will say that they are falling behind in their work. If the training takes place after hours or on weekends, our supervisors will say that they are being taken advantage of."

"Nonsense," replied Hank. "Every supervisor realizes the importance of good human relations. Besides that, they will see it as a form of job enrichment."

"So long as we're having an open meeting, let me have my input," volunteered Raymond. "We are starting from the wrong end by having our first-line supervisors go through human relations training. It's our top management who needs the training the most. Unless they practice better human relations, you can't expect such behavior from our supervisors. How can you have a top management that is insensitive to people and a bottom management that is sensitive. The system just won't work."

"What you say makes some sense," said Hank, "but I wouldn't go so far as to say top management is insensitive to people. Maybe we can talk some more about the human relations program after lunch."

Questions

1. Should Hank go ahead with his plans for the human relations training program? Why, or why not? How would you analyze the situation in terms of the "ABCs" of performance?

2. What do you think of Raymond's comment that top management should participate in human relations training first?

3. What is your opinion of Hank's statement that good leadership can compensate for poor working conditions?

4. If you were in Hank's situation, would you try to get top management to participate in a human relations training program?

5. What type of human relations training program would you recommend for first-line supervision at United Mutual?

EXPERIENTIAL EXERCISE [21]

Purpose: The purpose of this exercise is to give you some experience in dealing with some problems encountered in implementing a change.

Required Understanding: You should be familiar with the contents of this chapter although this exercise can precede a reading of the chapter.

How to Set Up the Exercise: Divide the class into groups of four persons. The instructor can assign extra persons to various groups as observers.

Once the class is divided into groups, all students should read the "general instructions" and should assign roles to each group member. *Each person should read his or her instructions only.* (Roles are presented at the end of this exercise.)

It would help if roleplayers Jack, Walt, and Steve wore name tags so that Gus, the foreman, can call them by name. (It also helps to have all Guses stand up when they have finished reading their roles.) They may also continue to refer as needed to the data supplied with their instructions.

Instructions

1. When all the Guses are standing, the instructor can remind the Jacks, Walts, and Steves that they are waiting for Gus in his office. When he sits down and greets them, this will indicate that he has entered his office, and each person should adopt his role.

2. At the instructor's signal, all Guses are seated. All groups should begin the role-play simultaneously.

3. About 25 minutes should be required for the groups to reach a decision. If certain groups have trouble, the instructor may ask Gus, the foreman, to do the best he can in the next minute or two.

4. While groups are role playing the instructor will write a table on the chalk board with the following column headings: (1) Group Number, (2) Solution, (3) Problem Employees, (4) Expected Production, (5) Method Used by Foreman, and (6) Sharing of Data.

5. Collecting results.

    a. Each group should report in turn, while remaining seated as a group. The instructor will enter in Column I the number of the group called on to report.

    b. Each Gus reports the solution he intends to follow. The solutions may be of four types: (a) continuation of old method (i.e., rotation through all positions); (b) adoption of new method with each person working his best position; (c) a compromise (new method in the morning, old in the afternoon); or (d) integrative solution containing features of old and new solutions (e.g., each man spends more time on best position; two men exchange positions and third works on his best position; all three exchange but confine changes to work their two best positions). The instructor will enter type of solution in Column 2 and add notes to indicate whether a trial period is involved, a rest pause is added, etc.

    c. Each Gus reports whether he had any special trouble with a particular employee. If so, the initial of the problem individual is entered in Column 3.

    d. Jack, Walt, and Steve report whether production will stay the same, go up, or down, as a result of the conference. The estimates of Jack, Walt, and Steve should be recorded as "0," "+," and "−" signs in Column 4.

    e. Group observers report on the way Gus handled the group and how the group responded. Enter a descriptive term in Column 5 for Gus's method (e.g., tried to sell his plan, used group decision, blamed group, was participative, was arbitrary and somewhat abusive, etc.). If no observers were present in a group, data should be supplied by the group itself. For leading questions about method, see "Instructions for Observer."

6. Class discussion. Discuss differences obtained and see if they can be related to the attitude and the method of Gus. What kinds of resistance were encountered? Classify them into fear, hostility, etc. What are the proper methods of dealing with each of these kinds of resistance? To which study that we discussed is this situation similar to?

The instructions and roles following. Please be sure to read only the general instructions and the roles which you have been assigned.

1. General Instructions

You work in a plant that does a large number of subassembly jobs. such as assembling fuel pumps, carburetors, and starters. Gus Thompson is foreman of several groups, including the one with which we are concerned today. Jack, Walt, and Steve make up your particular group, which assembles fuel pumps. The assembly operation is divided into three positions or jobs. Since the three jobs are rather simple and each of you is familiar with all of the operations, you find it desirable to exchange jobs or positions. You have worked together this way for a long time. Pay is based on a team piece rate and has been satisfactory to all of you. Presently each of you will be asked to be one of the following: Gus Thompson, Jack, Walt, or Steve. In some instances an observer will be present in your group. Today, Gus, the foreman, has asked Jack, Walt, and Steve to meet with him in his office. He said he wanted to talk about something.

2. Instructions for Observers (Read only if you are an observer)

Your job is to observe the method used by Gus in handling a problem with his men. Pay especial attention to the following:

a. Method of presenting problem. Does he criticize, suggest a remedy, request their help on a problem, or use some other approach?

b. Initial reaction of members. Do group members feel criticized or do they try to help Gus?

c. Handling of discussion by Gus. Does he listen or argue? Does he try to persuade? Does he use threats? Or does he let the men decide?

d. Forms of resistance expressed by the group. Did members express fear, hostility, satisfaction with present method, etc.?

e. What does Gus do with the time-study data- (1) Lets men examine the table; (2) mentions some of the results; or (3) makes little or no reference to the data.

Best results are obtained if Gus uses the data to pose the problem of how they might be used to increase production.

3. Roles for Participants (please read only your own role)

Role for Gus Thompson, foreman

You are the foreman in a shop and supervise the work of about 20 men. Most of the jobs are piece-rate jobs, and some of the men work in teams and are paid on a team piece-rate basis. In one of the teams, Jack, Walt, and Steve work together. Each one of them does one of the operations for an hour and then they exchange, so that all men perform each of the operations at different times. The men themselves decided to operate that way and you have never given the plan any thought.

Lately, Jim Clark, the methods man, has been around, and studied conditions in your shop. He timed Jack, Walt, and Steve on each of the operations and came up with the following facts:

	Time per operation			
	Position 1	*Position 2*	*Position 3*	*Total*
Jack	3 min.	4 min.	4½ min.	11½ min.
Walt	3½ min.	3½ min.	3 min.	10 min.
Steve	5 min.	3½ min.	4½ min.	13 min.
				34½ min.

He observed that with the men rotating, the average time for all three operations would be one-third of the total time or 11½ minutes per complete unit. If, however, Jack worked in the No. 1 spot, Steve in the No. 2 spot, and

Walt in the No. 3 spot, the time would be 9½ minutes, a reduction of over 17 per cent. Such a reduction in time would amount to saving of more than 80 minutes. In other words the lost production would be about the same as that which would occur if the men loafed for 80 minutes in an eight-hour day. If the time were used for productive effort, production would be increased more than 20 per cent.

This made pretty good sense to you so you have decided to take up the problem with the men. You feel that they should go along with any change in operation that is made.

Role for Jack

You are one of three men on an assembly operation. Walt and Steve are your team mates and you enjoy working with them. You get paid on a team basis, and you are making wages that are entirely satisfactory. Steve isn't quite as fast as Walt and you, but when you feel he is holding things up too much each of you can help out.

The work is very monotonous. The saving thing about it is that every hour you all change positions. In this way you get to do all three operations. You are best on the No. 1 position so when you get in that spot you turn out some extra work and so make the job easier for Steve who follows you in that position.

You have been on this job for two years, and you have never run out of work. Apparently your group can make pretty good pay without running yourselves out of a job. Lately, however, the company has had some of its experts hanging around. It looks like the company is trying to work out some speedup methods. If they make these jobs any more simple you won't be able to stand the monotony. Gus Thompson, your foreman, is a decent guy and has never criticized your team's work.

Role for Steve

You work with Jack and Walt on an assembly job and get paid on a team piece rate. The three of you work very well together and make a pretty good wage. Jack and Walt like to make a little more than you think is necessary, but you go along with them and work as hard as you can so as to keep the production up where they want it. They are good fellows; often help you out if you fall behind; and so you feel it is only fair to try and go along with the pace they set.

The three of you exchange positions every hour. In this way you get to work all positions. You like the No. 2 position the best because it is easiest. When you get in the No. 3 position, you can't keep up and then you feel Gus Thompson, the foreman, watching you. Sometimes Walt and Jack slow down when you are on the No. 3 spot and then the foreman seems satisfied.

Lately the methods man has been hanging around watching the job. You wonder what he is up to. Can't they leave guys alone who are doing all right?

Role for Walt

You work with Jack and Steve on a job that requires three separate operations. Each of you works on each of the three operations by rotating positions once every hour. This makes the work more interesting and you can always help out the other fellow by running the job ahead in case one of you doesn't feel so good. It's all right to help out because you get paid on a team piece-rate basis. You could actually earn more if Steve were a faster worker, but he is a swell guy and you would rather have him in the group than someone else who might do a little bit more.

You find all three positions about equally desirable. They are all simple and purely routine. The monotony doesn't bother you much because you can talk, daydream, and change your pace. By working slow for a while and then fast, you can sort of set your pace to music you hum to yourself. Jack and Steve like the idea of changing jobs, and even though Steve is slow on some positions, the changing around has its good points. You feel you get to a stopping place every time you change positions and this kind of takes the place of a rest pause.

Lately some kind of efficiency expert has been hanging around. He stands some distance away with a stop watch in his hand. The company could get more for its money if it put some of those guys to work. You say to yourself, "I'd like to see one of these guys try and tell me how to do this job. I'd sure give him an earful."

If Guy Thompson, your foreman, doesn't get him out of the shop pretty soon, you're going to tell him what you think of his dragging in company spies.

NOTES FOR CHAPTER 16

1. From *The Prince*, written in approximately 1513. Translation by Luigi Ricci, revised by E. R. P. Vincent (New York: New American Library of World Literature, Inc., 1962), p. 55, quoted in Keith Davis, *Organizational Behavior* (New York: McGraw-Hill, 1977), pp. 245.

2. See Larry Greiner and Lewis Barnes, "Organizational Change and Development," in Paul Lawrence, Lewis Barnes, and Jay W. Lorsch, *Organizational Behavior and Administration* (Homewood, Ill.: Irwin, 1976), pp. 621–33.

3. Paul Lawrence, "How to Deal with Resistance to Change," *Harvard Business Review* (May–June 1954; For a fascinating description of the effects of resistance to change see Nicole Woolsey Biggart, "The Creative-destructive Process of Organizational Change: The Case of the Post Office," *Administrative Science Quarterly*, Vol. 22, No. 3 (September 1977), pp. 410–26.

4. Quoted from Larry Greiner, "Patterns of Organization Change," *Harvard Business Review* (May–June 1967, quoted in Greiner and Barnes, "Organizational Change," pp. 623–24.

5. Paul Lawrence, "How to Deal with Resistance to Change," *Harvard Business Review* (May–June 1954).

6. Note that with its stress on changing organizations by first changing attitudes and values *Organizational Development* is a fundamentally different approach than Behavior Modification, which aims to change behavior directly, through reinforcement. See, Kenneth N. Wexley and Wayne Nemeroff. "Effectiveness of Positive Reinforcement and Goal Setting as Methods of Management Development," *Journal of Applied Psychology*, Vol. 60 (August 1975).

7. See Gary Dessler, *Organization and Management* (Englewood Cliffs, N.J.: Prentice-Hall, 1976), pp. 293–304.

8. NTL Institute, "What Is OD?" News and Reports from NTL Institute for Applied Behavioral Science, Vol. 2 (June 1968), 1–2. See also Dessler, *Organization and Management*, p. 294; Wendell French, *The Personnel Management Process* (Boston: Houghton Mifflin, 1974), p. 665.

9. Based on Warren G. Bennis, *Organizational Development: Its Nature, Origins, and Prospects* (Reading, Mass.: Addison-Wesley, 1969), p. 10.

10. John Kimberly and Warren Neilsen, "Organization Development and Change in Organizational Performance," *Administrative Science Quarterly* (June 1975), pp. 191–206.

11. Chris Argyris, "A Brief Description of Laboratory Education," *Training Directors Journal* (October 1963), reprinted in Harold Lazarus, E. Kirby Warren, and Jerome Schnee, *The Progress of Management* (Englewood Cliffs, N.J.: Prentice-Hall, 1972), pp. 384–86.

12. J. P. Campbell and M. Dunnette, "Effectiveness of T-group Experiences in Managerial Training and Development," *Psychological Bulletin*, Vol. 70 (1968), pp. 73–104; in W. Scott and L. Cummings, *Readings in Organizational Behavior and Human Performance* (Homewood, Ill.: Irwin, 1973), pp. 568–95; Dessler, *Organization and Management*, p. 300.

13. Campbell and Dunnette, "Effectiveness of T-group Experiences in Managerial Training and Development," pp. 73–104.

14. Kimberly and Neilsen, "Organizational Development," p. 203; see also Peter B. Smith, "Controlled Studies of the Outcome of Sensitivity Training," *Psychological Bulletin*, Vol. 82 (1976), pp. 597–622.

15. George Odiorne, "The Trouble with Sensitivity Training," *Training Directors Journal* (October 1963); George Odiorne, *Training By Objectives* (New York: Macmillan, 1970), Ch. 4; House, *Management Development*, p. 71; Andre Delbecq, "Sensitivity Training," *Training and Development Journal* (January 1970), pp. 32–35; reprinted in Fred Luthans, *Contemporary Readings in Organizational Behavior* (New York: McGraw-Hill, 1972), pp. 409–17.

16. Bennis, *Organization Development*, p. 10.

17. Delbecq, "Sensitivity Training," pp. 32–35.

18. Robert Blake and Jane Mouton, *Buiding a Dynamic Corporation Through Grid Organization Development* (Reading, Mass.: Addison-Wesley, 1969), pp. 76–109. Some researchers have suggested that the grid approach is flawed, a position that has been attacked by Blake and Mouton. See H. John Bernardin and Kenneth Alvarez, "The Managerial Grid as a Predictor of Conflict Resolution Method and Managerial Effectiveness," *Administrative Science Quarterly*, Vol. 21, No. 1 (March 1976): Robert Blake and Jane Mouton, "When Scholarship Fails, Research Falters: A Reply to Bernardin and Alvarez," *Administrative Science Quarterly*, Vol. 21, No. 1 (March 1976).

19. M. Scott Meyers, "How Attitude Surveys Help you Manage," *Training and Development Journal*, Vol. 21 (October 1967), pp. 34–41. See also Robert Solomon, "An Examination of the Relationship Between a Survey Feedback O.D. Technique and the Work Environment," *Personnel Psychology*, Vol. 29, No. 4 (Winter 1976). For another description of the use of survey feedback see Thomas Harrell, "An Organizational Change Triggered by a Survey: The Army Air Forces in World War II," *Academy of Management Review*, Vol. 2, No. 4 (October 1977), pp. 684–87.

20. See, for example, Wayne Cascio and Bernard Bass, "The Effects of Role Playing in a Program to Modify Attitudes Toward Black Employees," *The Journal of Psychology*, Vol. 92 (1976), pp. 261–66.

21. Norman Maier, Psychology in Industrial Organizations (Boston: Houghton Mifflin, 1973), pp. 295–99.

INDEX

443